Methods of
Teaching Accounting

Methods of Teaching Accounting

Second Edition

Vernon A. Musselman

Professor Emeritus, Business Education
University of Kentucky
Lexington, Kentucky

J Marshall Hanna

Professor Emeritus, Department of Business Education
The Ohio State University
Columbus, Ohio

David H. Weaver

Director of Research
McGraw-Hill Book Company
New York, New York

Henry J. Kaluza

Professor, Department of Business and Computer Studies
University of Western Ontario
London, Ontario, Canada

Gregg Division/McGraw-Hill Book Company

NEW YORK   ST. LOUIS   DALLAS   SAN FRANCISCO   AUCKLAND
BOGOTÁ   DÜSSELDORF   JOHANNESBURG   LONDON   MADRID
MEXICO   MONTREAL   NEW DELHI   PANAMA   PARIS
SÃO PAULO   SINGAPORE   SYDNEY   TOKYO   TORONTO

Associate Editor: Larry Wexler
Senior Editing Supervisor: Linda Stern
Editor: Elisa Adams
Art Director: Frank Medina
Designer: Carol Basen
Production Supervisor: Robert Sánchez

Library of Congress Cataloging in Publication Data

Main entry under title:
Methods of teaching accounting.

First ed., by V. A. Musselman and J Marshall Hanna,
published in 1960 under title: Teaching bookkeeping and
accounting.
Includes index.
1. Accounting—Study and teaching. I. Musselman,
Vernon A. II. Musselman, Vernon A. Teaching bookkeeping
and accounting.
HF5630.M87   1979   657'.07'1273   77-16171
ISBN 0-07-044132-4

Methods of Teaching Accounting, Second Edition

Previously published under the title **Teaching Bookkeeping and Accounting,** by Vernon A.
Musselman and J Marshall Hanna.

2 3 4 5 6 7 8 9 0 DODO 7 8 7 6 5 4 3 2 1 0 9

Preface

Important changes have taken place in the fields of accounting and education since the previous edition of *Methods of Teaching Accounting* was published. This second edition reflects these changes and explores their impact on teaching accounting at various educational levels—secondary, community college, and university. By presenting different aspects of teaching methodology as well as accounting concepts and principles, this book closes the gap that has existed in accounting methods materials available to teachers at the high school and college levels.

Readers will actually enjoy their work in accounting methods because the authors help them to understand the "why" of the teaching methods and of the accounting principles involved. Little or nothing is taken for granted. If a teacher needs background information to grasp a new point or topic, this information is thoroughly explained before the method of teaching the point or topic is presented.

Methods of Teaching Accounting contains many excellent illustrations and examples. These illustrations will give the new teacher confidence, and using the illustrations in class will help drive the lesson home with maximum impact. Because the text contains so many precise answers and workable ideas, the new teacher will use it as a handbook long after graduation.

Changes in the Fields of Accounting and Education

Some of the important changes that are covered in this book include the following.

New Insights in Methodology. Many new insights have been gained in the area of methodology. There has been growth in the use of the equation approach to teaching accounting, starting with the early topics of the beginning accounting cycle. Few educators today use the formal balance sheet approach; instead, they have adopted the equation approach.

Different Teaching Plans. Research has been conducted in order to better serve the varied learning styles and learning abilities of students today. Much of this experimentation deals with breaking out of the traditional lock-step approach to teaching. Thus we have seen an increased use of teaching plans such as team teaching, modular scheduling, and program instruction.

Teacher Accountability. The growth in the use of accountability in the educational field has involved the identification, writing, and communication of performance goals (instructional objectives).

Data Processing. The dependence of business upon all methods of data processing, especially computer methods, has caused a shift in emphasis from teaching bookkeeping to teaching accounting concepts and systems and data processing procedures. Emphasis is placed on teaching data processing within the accounting cycle.

Flowcharting. The use of flowcharting in the business world and in teaching situations has been adapted to the accounting classroom. Flowcharting facilitates the study of systems work in accounting.

Refinement of Financial Accounting. The presentation of financial accounting in the classroom has been refined so that greater emphasis is given to the presentation of generally accepted accounting principles and to the correct use of accounting terms.

Managerial Accounting. Managerial accounting has been introduced and accepted into the classroom. No longer is the entire accounting course based on financial accounting.

New Topics and Special Features

This edition of *Methods of Teaching Accounting* covers many new topics and contains numerous special features that are important to the teaching of accounting. Among these are the following.

Accounting Proofs. The broad concept of accounting proofs is covered, including the traditional trial balance, as well as new topics such as the zero-proof, the journal voucher proof, and the cash proof, which includes the method of teaching bank reconciliation.

Basic Concepts in Accounting. The basic concepts in accounting are discussed as they appear in the accounting cycle. Such items as journals, ledgers, adjustments, and financial statements are presented in their broadest forms—from the simplest to the most complex.

Accounting Systems. Complete work flow procedures are covered, with emphasis on the methods of introducing internal control systems and the use of systems flowcharts.

Generally Accepted Accounting Principles. The introduction of generally accepted accounting principles begins in first-year accounting courses. These principles are presented and explained.

Periodic and Perpetual Inventory Procedures. Methods for teaching a comparison between the periodic and perpetual inventory procedures are given. A basic understanding of the perpetual method is essential in applying computer methods to the processing of inventory records.

Teaching Problems. The full range of teaching problems is covered on a very practical, "down-to-cases" level. For the beginning teacher, the authors single out typical teaching difficulties and present specific remedies that really work. For the more experienced teacher, the authors offer new ideas for course improvement and enrichment. Each chapter ends with cases dealing with these areas.

Accounting Fundamentals. The basic accounting fundamentals for each topic are reviewed *before* the suggested methods are examined. For example, the generally accepted principle of depreciation is covered before the updated methods for teaching depreciation are presented.

Performance Goals. Examples of performance goals (instructional objectives) are given for most accounting topics.

Lesson Plans. Examples of lesson plans for launching the course and for subsequent lessons are given.

Vocabulary. The latest accounting vocabulary appears in the text. Emphasis is placed on the correct use of accounting terminology (*revenue* is used instead of *income;* depreciation is described as a process of *allocation,* not *valuation*).

Activities. At the end of each chapter there are Problems, Questions, and Projects that explore the material presented in the chapter. In addition, Case Problems provide an opportunity for the reader to apply what has been learned to actual teaching situations.

Canadian and United States Laws. Although accounting techniques are similar in Canada and the United States, important differences do exist in areas such as payroll accounting. In treating the methods of teaching payroll accounting, therefore, we have acknowledged the laws of both countries with regard to payroll deductions and practices.

Acknowledgments

The authors are greatly indebted to those teachers who contributed suggestions and to those who read and criticized portions of the manuscript. We are also deeply indebted to the accountants from business, government, and educational institutions who provided us with invaluable assistance in preparing this book.

VERNON A. MUSSELMAN
J MARSHALL HANNA
DAVID H. WEAVER
HENRY J. KALUZA

Contents

Methods of
Teaching Accounting

CHAPTER 1

Accounting: Its Objectives and Place in the Curriculum

Over three quarters of a million secondary school students enroll each year in courses in accounting, bookkeeping, and recordkeeping. An even larger number enroll in accounting courses in evening schools, technical institutes, business colleges, community colleges, universities, and correspondence schools. Among business subjects, only typewriting has a comparable total enrollment.

As a subject area, accounting is clearly a well-established part of the curriculum; but despite its popularity, there is little agreement as to what the objectives of the course should be and, indeed, what type of a program should be offered. Even in a relatively small sampling of schools, one could find these different points of view:

- In some schools the major objective of the course is to provide vocational or vocationally related preparation. In others, the subject is taught primarily for its personal-use values.
- Some schools adapt the subject matter to emphasize recordkeeping activities, thereby hoping to meet the needs of students with limited abilities. Other schools stress accounting concepts and only admit students of above average ability to the course.
- Some schools use a competency-based approach and structure their programs around an individual student's ability to master one or more accounting tasks. Others follow a traditional approach and require students to demonstrate understanding of all or most of the course content.
- Some schools offer only a one-year course. Others offer as many as three years.

Why do these wide variations exist? Historically, no group of business education students comes to the classroom with as great a range of abilities and career interests as does the typical accounting class. Intelligence, listening ability, writing skill, and quantitative ability vary greatly from one student to another. A typical class may include disinterested students and highly motivated ones, slow learners and fast learners, students who take the course to prepare for entry-level jobs in accounting and those who take it to prepare for college.

Clearly, no one inflexibly structured course can fully prepare some students to assume the responsibilities of a full-time accounting position and, at the same time, prepare others to perform competently the recording duties related to a specific clerical or merchandising position. Nor can this same inflexibly structured course provide still other students with all the accounting preparation they need as potential managers, business owners, and investors. Even if all these types of preparation could be incorporated into one standard class, it would not be possible to predict which students should receive which training.

Accounting in Business

In order to develop a first-year accounting course that is broad enough to reconcile the differences in student abilities and interests, one should first look to end-use of the skills and knowledge acquired in the course. While the accounting course has many personal-use values, many teachers question whether the course can be justified primarily by its nonvocational objectives; they believe that all one needs to know about the keeping of personal records may be learned in a course in general business, consumer economics, or business mathematics. Because the vocational or vocationally related uses of an accounting course should be primary determinants in shaping the course, it is appropriate to examine briefly how business uses accounting and what kind of worker business wants to perform its accounting functions.

The Accounting Process

Over the years, there have been a number of changes in the methods used by business to process financial data. New systems and procedures have been developed to cope with these changes. In consequence, traditional accounting jobs have been transformed or phased out, and new ones have been created. An overall view of the accounting process in a typical business firm is shown in Figure 1.1. Note that the process begins with the recording of the dollar results of an economic event that affects the business enterprise. The second stage of the accounting process is to classify the transactions under meaningful headings in order to develop useful information. The classified dollar figures are then totaled and summarized to produce a variety of accounting reports and statements. Observe that two distinct groups of reports are produced by the accounting process. One group consists of special-purpose reports which are intended for managerial decision making inside the firm. Among these would be reports for periodic sales, a variety of costs, a variety of budgets, and monthly financial statements. Since these special-purpose reports are intended for management

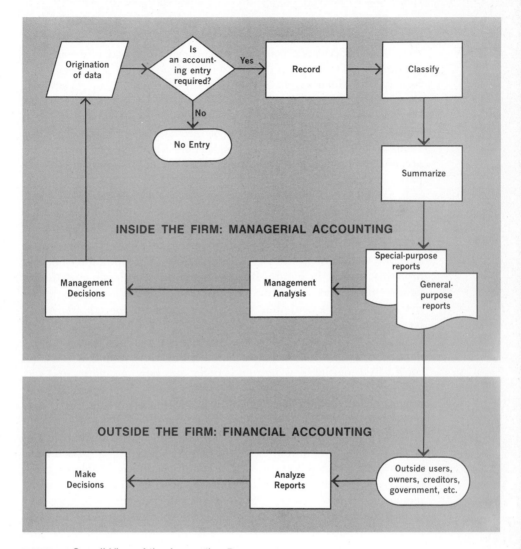

FIGURE 1.1 Overall View of the Accounting Process

only, this branch of the accounting process is often called *managerial accounting.*

The other branch of the accounting process shows the production of general-purpose reports for interested persons outside the firm. For the outsiders—owners (stockholders), potential investors, banks and other lending institutions, government agencies, labor unions, etc.—the general-purpose reports consist of the traditional year-end financial statements. Since these general-purpose financial statements are intended for the use of outsiders, this branch of the accounting process is often called *financial accounting.*

THE ROLE OF BOOKKEEPING IN ACCOUNTING. Now, what part of the accounting process is bookkeeping? Specifically, bookkeeping is only the record-making part of accounting. In the beginning stages of the accounting process, bookkeeping is organized to do three things: (1) to record, day by day, the dollar results of business transactions; (2) to classify and summarize the recorded dollar figures under meaningful headings; and (3) to prove the arithmetical accuracy of the book records. The recording of transactions in any business tends to be mechanical and highly repetitive. From an overall point of view, bookkeeping is only a small part of the accounting process and is probably the simplest and most straightforward part.

In a small firm, a bookkeeper may record all of the business transactions, post the debits and credits to the ledgers, prepare trial balances and other summaries, and even prepare the financial statements. But in a large business enterprise, a bookkeeper usually spends the day recording only one kind of transaction, for instance, sales on account. The work is routine and primarily clerical in nature. Because of the highly repetitive nature of bookkeeping, many large firms have installed computer systems to process the recording function, thus eliminating the need for the traditional bookkeeper.

ACCOUNTING AND DATA PROCESSING. As applied to the accounting process, data processing may be described as the *how*. How transactions are recorded in a journal, how posting is done, and how summaries and special-purpose reports are prepared—whether by manual, mechanical, punched-card, or computer methods—falls within the broad field of data processing.

Traditionally, the processing of accounting information by manual and mechanical methods has been organized under accounting departments. Where these methods prevail today, accounting still has complete responsibility over the data processing. However, with the introduction of the punched-card method in the 1950s and especially with the use of computers in the 1960s, the trend has been, and continues to be, toward an ever-increasing degree of specialization. It is not uncommon today to find accounting and data processing in separate but complementary departments. For example, look at the organization chart of a finance department for a large auto assembly plant as shown in Figure 1.2.

Observe that the traditional accounting activities, such as general accounting, payroll, accounts receivable, and accounts payable, are organized in separate departments and are very much distinct from the data processing area. What is, then, the relationship between the two areas? While both the accounting and data processing departments are vital to the total financial information system of a company, they in fact have different roles to play. It is widely held in many firms that accounting is the *functional responsibility* of the financial system. For example, the general accounting department's main function is to provide accurate information to update the general ledger file. Similarly, payroll accounting is responsible for

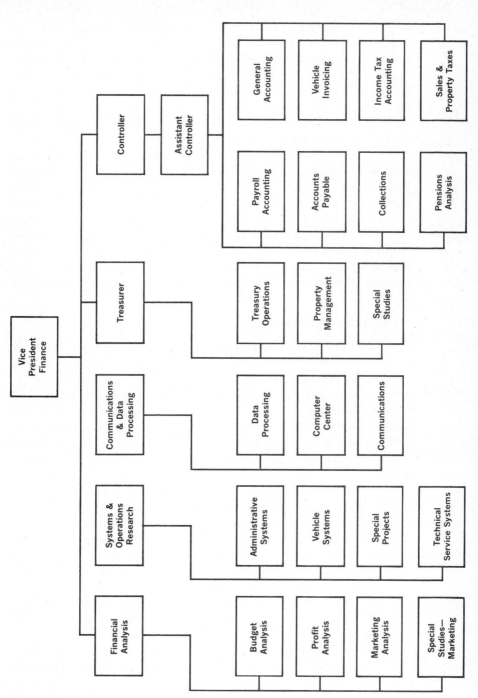

FIGURE 1.2 Organization Chart of a Finance Department

providing accurate information to process the regular payroll. On the other hand, the perspective taken on computer systems is that they are essentially *methods* rather than functional responsibilities. In simple terms, the computer system is the method through which the general ledger may be updated, the payroll may be processed, and other special-purpose reports for management produced. In modern business, it should also be recognized that computing services are used for other functional areas, such as marketing, production, and financial analysis.

If accounting is held as a functional responsibility, then it seems clear that those working in accounting departments must have a working knowledge of the data processing method used to process financial information. For instance, the personnel in the general accounting department would need to have exposure to the computer system in order to provide the necessary input data to update the general ledger file. In addition, they would require a working knowledge of the computer in order to control that input data and also interpret the output. A knowledge of data processing methods, therefore, is very much a part of modern accounting.

Employment Opportunities

It would be ideal if one could pinpoint with complete accuracy exactly the number and type of accounting or accounting-related jobs that would be available in any given year and then match training to meet these job openings. Unfortunately, unexpected upturns and downturns in the economy, new technologies, changes in national policy, and a myriad of other factors combine to prevent such preciseness; however, fairly reliable projections are provided by federal, state, and local agencies. Careful consideration should be given to these projections when planning the accounting course.

ACCOUNTING WORKERS. Estimates based on United States Department of Labor data indicate that over three million workers were employed as accountants, bookkeepers, cashiers, and computer personnel in the late 1970s. This represents the second largest employment group in the clerical occupations. The number is expected to increase by the addition of over 135,000 new jobs each year for the next few years. Thousands of new workers will be needed each year to maintain this work force—to fill new jobs and as replacements. Thus, the accounting area offers beginning employment opportunities to a large number of qualified people each year.

OTHER CLERICAL WORKERS. Over three million stenographic and secretarial workers were employed in the late 1970s, and another two million or more were employed as typists, office machine operators, shipping and receiving clerks, and receptionists. For most of these jobs, a knowledge of accounting is highly desirable.

MERCHANDISING WORKERS. In the late 1970s, well over five million people were engaged in sales and distribution. While not all merchandising employees perform work directly related to the accounting process, a knowledge of accounting provides them with a better understanding of business and of their work in relation to the other functions of business. Moreover, many merchandise workers go on to become owners or managers of small retail establishments. A lack of adequate records and the inability to properly use whatever information their records do provide are major causes of business failure.

BUSINESS MANAGEMENT.   The value of accounting knowledge to business executives and managers is generally recognized. Not only are business firms required by federal, state, and local laws to maintain certain records, but they have also discovered how essential a management tool good records can be. Modern methods of processing data have not only made accounting data available but have also made it possible to have the data in time for use in making management decisions.

THE IMPACT OF AUTOMATION ON EMPLOYMENT OPPORTUNITIES.   So far, the effect that automation has on employment opportunities in accounting is far from clear. Experience to date indicates the following:

1.   Automation does not decrease employment opportunities; rather, it develops new jobs and alters existing jobs faster than they can be filled.
2.   Automation does not decrease the volume of data to be processed; on the contrary, it makes more data available at a faster rate of speed and increases the importance of understanding how to use the data in decision making.
3.   Automation reduces the amount of routine clerical work involved in processing data.

Although the use of computers to process data is increasing daily, it is unrealistic to predict the early exit of manual recording. Even in a computerized system, some accounting records may be kept manually, and input data for much of the computer applications is prepared manually.

There are several million businesses in the United States and Canada, and most of them are relatively small concerns. Furthermore, many business firms do not have the need for either the speed or the sophisticated treatment of data that the computer provides. It seems reasonable to conclude, therefore, that the shift to electronic data processing will be a continuing but gradual process and that thousands of people will continue to be employed in some aspects of manual data processing for many years to come. There is no question, however, that an increasing number of graduates will find employment in businesses using some form of automated data processing.

Developing a Comprehensive Course

The adoption by business of new technology, particularly automation, to process financial data dictates that the emphasis in the accounting course be shifted from performing repetitive manual work to understanding accounting concepts and principles so that the students can readily adapt to a variety of systems and procedures. Moreover, in keeping with the concept of career education that stresses that students be ready when they leave school either to perform a job with competence or to pursue further education, an accounting course must provide students with a foundation of skills and knowledge with which to confidently and competently enter the world of work or, if they prefer, go on to advanced study.

Course Objectives

The following objectives provide broad, general direction for the first-year accounting course.

1. To develop an understanding of basic accounting concepts and principles. By concentrating on accounting concepts and principles, students develop the theoretical basis for understanding all accounting systems.
2. To develop an understanding of basic accounting procedures so that students see the interrelationship of various parts of the total system. The emphasis should not be on the procedures themselves—that is, as something to be memorized, mastered, and followed—but on procedures as a means of applying the relevant concepts and principles.
3. To make students aware of the basic methods of processing data.
4. To develop an understanding of how financial data is used to make business decisions and policies.
5. To provide the skills and knowledge necessary to enable students to perform competently on entry-level jobs.
6. To provide additional skills and knowledge for career advancement.
7. To provide the necessary background for further study in accounting or an accounting-related field.
8. To develop an economic understanding of business.
9. To develop good work habits and a business vocabulary.

PERFORMANCE OBJECTIVES. The nine objectives that have been identified give general direction to the accounting course. They are, however, intended to serve more as a description of the course than as specific objectives designed to guide the day-to-day classroom activities. Much more clearly defined objectives are needed to determine what procedures are to be followed, what content is relevant and what is not, what instructional methods or devices should be utilized, what specifically should be measured, what standards should be achieved, and when the student has demonstrated satisfactory achievement. Many educators believe that to be functional an objective must be stated in performance terms; that is, the objective must identify and name the overall behavior, act, or performance the learner will be able to demonstrate when he or she has achieved the objective, the conditions under which the behavior or act is to occur, and what is acceptable performance. Thus, the objective "to be able to make adjusting entries" lacks specificity. It begs these questions: What adjusting entries (prepaid, accruals, deferred)? Where are they to be made (worksheet, journal, ledger)? What is given to the student to work with (list of accounts, accounts to be adjusted, list of amounts, trial balance)?

The objective becomes specific when it is stated as follows: "Given a correct trial balance, the unused amounts in prepaid expense accounts, expenses incurred but not journalized, and the final merchandise inventory, the student should be able to enter the trial balance on a worksheet form, and make the required adjustment entries in the adjustments columns of the worksheet with 100 percent accuracy."

Objectives are constructed to give direction to the learning activities. These activities involve the student; therefore, the objective must be communicated to the learner. This communication cannot take place unless the objectives are stated in clearly defined measurable terms; that is, the learner must know exactly what he or she is to learn or be able to do. Unless this is done, the teacher will not be able to measure whether or not the objectives have been achieved, and furthermore the student will not be able to measure his or her own progress.

Behavioral objectives are given in those chapters in this book where the methodology of teaching specific topics in the accounting course is presented.

Course Title

Traditionally the secondary school's accounting course was called *Bookkeeping,* and the term *accounting* was reserved for the college-level introductory course. The high school course once emphasized procedures—the recording activities. Students were taught *how* to journalize, *how* to post, *how* to rule and balance, etc. As the objective of the course was to prepare journal and ledger clerks, the course title seemed appropriate; however, the emphasis today has shifted from *how* to *why,* from routinized recording procedures to the development of concepts and an understanding of the accounting process as a whole. More time is spent on report preparation; the use and interpretation of accounting data are emphasized; and the study of various accounting systems and automated data processing has been introduced into the course.

In keeping with trends toward automating the recordkeeping function of accounting, there has also been a gradual change in the job titles used in modern business. The former title *bookkeeper* has limited job appeal today. It is difficult to get competent young people in a space-conscious age excited about becoming a bookkeeper. Consequently, many businesses have revised their job classifications to the more challenging titles of *junior accountant, accounting assistant, accounting clerk, off-line accounts payable clerk, senior clerk,* etc., so as to give more status to the positions. Job titles have also become more specific, as accounts receivable clerk and payroll clerk.

These changes in job title correspond to a shift in business usage away from the terms *recordkeeping* and *bookkeeping* to the newer terms *data processing* and *financial records handling* (accounting). Bookkeeping has come to be identified in the office with pen-and-ink journals, pen-and-ink ledgers, and pen-and-ink trial balances. Accounting and data processing, however, are much broader terms and encompass the total accounting process from input (originating of data) to output (reports) and the use of accounting information in making management decisions.

As a result of these developments, many business educators have thought that the title of the secondary school course should be changed from *Bookkeeping* to *Accounting* and thus give the course a new image. They believe the dichotomy between titles in the high school and college courses has been detrimental, for it has downgraded the high school course. Furthermore, they contend that the objectives of the secondary school course are not to prepare bookkeepers. The emphasis is on an understanding of accounting principles that underlie all data processing methods, whether financial data is processed by hand, machine, or computer. Thus, the course should be more closely identified with the data processing concept of input, processing, and output than with the pen-and-ink bookkeeping concept. They further contend that the use of the two different course titles has led to artificial distinctions in terminology. For example, the equation is commonly called the *bookkeeping equation* in high school and the *accounting equation* in college—yet it is the same equation. Similarly, the *bookkeeping cycle* becomes the *accounting cycle* when taught in college.

The change in course title in the secondary school from *Bookkeeping* to *Accounting* is in transition. Many schools and teachers will doubtless continue for some time to use the older title *Bookkeeping,* while other schools and teachers will have adopted the newer title, *Accounting.* Throughout this book the title *Accounting* has been used to identify the course.

Grade Placement

A number of factors must be considered in determining the grade placement of the high school accounting course.

PROVISIONS FOR GUIDANCE. For most students, accounting is primarily a vocational or vocationally related course. Two widely accepted principles of vocational education are that vocational guidance should precede the student selection of any vocational program or course, and that courses which have vocational implications should be delayed as far as practical in the educational program of the student. The guidance role of the general business course has been widely accepted. Since general business is most commonly taught in the ninth and tenth years, the accounting course would need to be placed later in the curriculum. Furthermore, it is highly questionable whether any vocational course should be placed earlier than the eleventh year in the secondary school.

NUMBER OF YEARS. When two years of accounting are taught, the courses are generally placed in the eleventh and twelfth years. When only one year is taught, the question arises as to whether the course should be placed in the eleventh or twelfth year. As a vocational course, it should be placed as close as possible to the time the students are ready to enter employment, which would be the twelfth year. However, other factors may make this plan impractical or even undesirable. The twelfth year may already be crowded with other courses. An office practice, office machines, or data processing course for which accounting is a valuable prequisite may be offered in the twelfth year. In this case, the accounting course should be offered in the eleventh year.

Advanced Acounting

Should more than one year of accounting instruction be offered in the high school? This question must be answered primarily in terms of the number of students in a given school who could profit from a second-year course. A one-year course in accounting is sufficient for many students who are planning to enter office or merchandising work. However, as a result of their experiences in the first-year accounting course, some students definitely plan to make accounting work their career. They hope to enter positions requiring a knowledge of advanced work in the area. Some students, because of their learning rates, would benefit from moving more slowly through a program, taking two years to cover the needed content. Others may be planning to study accounting in college. These groups of students would benefit from a second-year course. We have as much responsibility to provide these students with the second-year, or advanced, course in their potential field of work as we have to provide advanced shorthand for the stenographic student, advanced foreign language for the language student, or advanced science for the science student.

Some schools have worked out an arrangement with colleges and universities whereby students in science, mathematics, and foreign language take an advanced standing examination upon entering the university. If they do well on the examination, they are permitted to enroll in an advanced course in college. Such a practice should be as feasible in accounting as in other subjects and would add considerable status and importance to the second-year accounting course in high school.

SMALL SCHOOL. In small schools, the number of students is too few to justify the offering of an advanced course each year. There are ways, however, that these schools can meet this need, if the school administration and the accounting teacher use imagination and initiative.

One plan is to alternate the offering of the first-year and the second-year courses. Such a plan doubles the number of potential students who may be eligible to take the advanced course. Another plan is to arrange for those few advanced accounting students to take the course through a supervised correspondence program. All students taking correspondence courses (often in various fields) are brought together in one class under the supervision of a teacher. The accounting teacher may be consulted when needed. A third plan is to have the advanced accounting students meet with the beginning accounting class, but to assign to the former special projects and practice-set materials. Only those students who have an interest in accounting and who have a good background in the first-year course would be permitted to register for the advanced work. Such students, with a minimum of assistance, will be able to make satisfactory progress.

Problems, Questions, and Projects

1. Do you think the high school course should be called *Bookkeeping* or *Accounting?* Give the arguments for your conclusion.

2. Interview a person employed in one of the following types of work: **(a)** stenographic or secretarial, **(b)** clerical, or **(c)** sales. Determine how knowledge of accounting is of assistance.

3. Prepare a bulletin board display designed to interest secondary school students in accounting as an occupational field.

4. Community occupational surveys are frequently used as the basis for determining the need for a vocational program in a given secondary school. What are some of the limitations of the community survey as a basis for curriculum determination?

5. What changes in the high school accounting course have technological developments in data processing made necessary?

6. What is meant by the term *accounting process?* What is one method of presenting this concept to students?

7. Explain the relationship of the accounting function to data processing in a firm that uses a computer to process financial information.

8. Do you agree with this statement? "It does not seem a wise use of educational time to guide high school students into a full-year or semester course in bookkeeping for the sole purpose of acquiring the personal-use bookkeeping knowledge and skills that can be taught within several months." Support your reaction.

9. There is a difference of opinion as to whether the high school accounting course should attempt to prepare for specific jobs in business or should emphasize primarily basic concepts and principles. What is your opinion on this issue?

10. What factors should determine whether a second-year (advanced) accounting course should be offered in the secondary school? What should be the nature of the second-year course if it is offered?

Case Problems

1. The first-year course in accounting has been required of all business students in Central High School. The teachers have recommended to the business department head that accounting be eliminated from the stenographic and clerical program. They have presented the following arguments in support of their recommendation:

a. Businesses are rapidly converting to electronic data processing, and the need for workers trained for manual accounting work is rapidly being eliminated.

b. Offices are becoming highly specialized, and the majority of stenographic, secretarial, and general clerical workers do not keep any records.

c. The time the students now spend in accounting could be more profitably spent in an automated data processing course to be offered in the senior year.

d. The accounting course has proved very difficult for many students. Because of the difficulty they had with the course, some students who did well in shorthand and typing have become discouraged in continuing their business program.

Assume you are the business department head. What is your reaction to the recommendation? Give the reasons to support your point of view.

2. Tom Julson's parents come to your office to discuss whether Tom should enroll in the elementary accounting course. Tom is now in the eleventh grade and has had no business subjects. School records show that this student is superior, ranking in the upper one-fourth of the class. Tom's father is the president and major owner of a firm manufacturing filing equipment and employs approximately three hundred workers. Most of the records of the firm are processed on a computer by a data processing service bureau. The future of the company appears to be good, and Tom plans to enter the business after completing his college work. Tom is currently thinking of enrolling in the business administration program in college, but may eventually decide to take engineering, as it is not certain whether an engineering or business administration background would be more helpful when it is time to take over the company.

Would you recommend that Tom enroll in the accounting course in high school? Give the reasons for your recommendations.

CHAPTER 2

Coping With Student Differences

The typical accounting class is composed of students who differ from each other in many ways—ability, economic and social background, interests, work experience, reading and arithmetic skills, and study habits. They also have different reasons for enrolling in the course. The successful teacher recognizes these differences, understands how they affect learning, and tailors instructional patterns to fit the needs of the class.

This chapter presents ways of coping with the wide differences that exist in every classroom in two basic skills—reading and arithmetic. It also examines the extent to which various instructional plans meet the challenge of individual differences.

Reading Problems

Teachers in all disciplines encounter students with major reading problems. Because accounting, unlike such subject areas as English and history, is a course with which students have had no previous acquaintance, the accounting teacher frequently has an unusually large number of such students. This reading problem is generally a result of one or more of three factors: (1) the relatively heavy vocabulary load, (2) the reading difficulty of the instructional materials, (3) the relatively low reading level of many students in the class.

Vocabulary Load

Accounting students have always been required to learn, quite early in the course, a relatively long list of new terms, and the introduction of data processing into the course has added new terminology to the list. The vocabulary problem is further complicated by the number of terms used interchangeably; for example, the terms *accounting period, fiscal period,* and *financial period* are often used to express the same time span. Although these and other terms may have different precise meanings and preferred usages, some teachers are unaware of the differences and may interchange the terms freely.

Additional confusion stems from the tendency of some teachers to state transactions in different ways at different times; for example, a teacher may use the phrases *enter the transaction, journalize the transaction,* and *record the transaction* to express the same desired action from class members. Also, the language used by the teacher may differ from that used in the textbook; for example, what the textbook refers to as *revenue* may be called *income* by the teacher.

Reading Difficulty of Text Materials

The most commonly used formulas for determining readability measure sentence length, syllable intensity, and vocabulary. The longer the sentence, the greater the syllable intensity, and the higher the vocabulary level, the more difficult the reading.

Although an accounting textbook may meet the criteria for a low reading level according to the formula, it does not mean that the book is easy to read. The reading formulas do not take into consideration three important aspects of readability—syntax, use of visuals, and density of concepts. Thus the selection of learning materials must be based on several aspects of readability: the flow of concepts, the way the words are put together, the use of illustrations in the textual material, and the rapidity with which concepts and procedures are presented.

Low Reading Level

The reading level of members of a typical beginning accounting class often encompasses a wide range. Some students may read at the college level, but more often than not a sizable number of students may have difficulty reading at the seventh- or eighth-grade level. Whatever factors caused this low reading level can be only of academic interest to the teacher who has to deal with the deficiency in a manner that is not prejudicial to the more advanced class members.

Meeting the Reading Problem

Several methods for coping with the reading problem have been proven useful by many experienced accounting teachers.

APPLY SOUND PRINCIPLES OF LEARNING TO VOCABULARY BUILDING. Memorization of word lists and definitions as a means of developing vocabulary has been generally discredited. Words become a permanent part of one's vocabulary only when they are given meaning through experiences or association with experiences.

For example, the word *assets* has little meaning to the student until it is associated with things that are real and meaningful, such as a car, a radio, or clothing. Similarly, the term *merchandise inventory* takes on added meaning if the class can make a field trip to a store at inventory time and observe store employees counting and recording the merchandise on hand.

PREPARE VOCABULARY LISTS.   Analyze each topic or chapter and prepare a list of accounting terms that are introduced for the first time. (Frequently, a list of this kind appears in the textbook along with other end-of-chapter activities.) Also prepare a list of common words or phrases appearing in the assigned reading that have a special accounting connotation.

In planning the lesson, study each term to determine what associations can be made between the term and the students' experiences. This is made easier if early in the course a questionnaire has been prepared that provides data on the students' backgrounds.

BE CONSISTENT IN USING TERMINOLOGY.   Much confusion can be eliminated in the early weeks of the course if terms describing the same procedures or documents are not used interchangeably. Later on in the course, it may be preferable to vary the terms to enrich the students' vocabulary. Remember also to use the terminology employed in the textbook.

TAKE TIME TO SHOW STUDENTS HOW TO READ THE TEXT.   Accounting requires a different reading pattern from that with which most students are accustomed. Most accounting texts are well illustrated. The illustrations are keyed to the reading and must be included as part of the reading pattern. Help the students study an illustration so that they see in it what is there. For example, students may be directed to observe that the heading of an illustrated balance sheet contains three parts, that the balance sheet is divided into two sides, that the assets are listed on the left side and the liabilities and owner's equity on the right, and that the totals of the two sides are the same and are written on the same line. One way to direct the students' attention during home study is to provide a series of questions to be answered about an illustration: On what date was the balance sheet prepared? Where did you find that date? On which side are the assets listed? Is the total of the assets the same as the total of the liabilities and owner's equity? If the textbook does not provide such questions, they may be readily constructed and duplicated. Daily oral reading demonstrations are an essential part of the lesson plans for the first few days of the accounting course.

USE STUDY GUIDES AS A LEARNING AID AND NOT AS CHAPTER TESTS.   The workbooks that accompany most accounting textbooks provide learning or study guides for each topic. When these study guides are misused as chapter tests—and this is frequently done—the student is being denied a valuable learning aid.

Correctly used, the study guide is completed by the student as the text is read. The guide focuses the student's attention on the text material, and aids the student in reading.

Arithmetic Problems

Many students enter an accounting course with an arithmetic deficiency. High school and college accounting students lack skill in basic arithmetic and problem solving, and it is toward the latter—problem solving—that the major focus should be directed. With the availability of inexpensive calculators, many students are spared the tedium of mentally computing the basic arithmetic processes. Unfortunately, students frequently fail to realize that even the most sophisticated calculator is only the *instrument* with which to solve a problem; it cannot solve the problem by itself.

Business Mathematics as a Prerequisite

Some schools have attempted to solve the arithmetic problem by having a business mathematics course as a prerequisite for admission to accounting. There is no evidence, however, that such a prerequisite is justified. Studies show that students who have had business mathematics rate only slightly higher in accounting than those who have not. Research further shows that the study of business mathematics has only a slight bearing on the mastery of the arithmetic of accounting.

Certain aspects of arithmetic can be more effectively taught in the accounting course than in a separate business mathematics course, for it is in accounting that arithmetic becomes the means to an end and not the end itself. The student sees the need for arithmetic knowledge, and establishing a need is the first step toward achieving understanding.

Meeting the Arithmetic Problem

Many teachers have found that a number of suggestions have helped them cope with the arithmetic problem in their classes.

DRILL IN THE ART OF PROBLEM SOLVING. Many students have never been taught—and still fewer consistently pursue—a disciplined attack on an arithmetic problem. More often than not, they tend to approach each problem by the trial and error method. The following steps in solving a problem, therefore, need to be illustrated, explained, and drilled: (1) Read the problem to determine what is sought and what is given. (2) Identify the steps to be followed. (3) Estimate the answer. (4) Make the computations. (5) Check the solution.

A person who is said to have "number sense" simply has the ability to assess the reasonableness of answers. The reasonableness test avoids exaggerated answers that come from a misplaced decimal point or from the failure to conduct one or more steps in the process. Even the worker who performs all calculations by machine must apply the reasonableness test to each answer. Skill in estimating answers can be developed through drill. Problems of computing extensions (quantity, price), discount, interest, depreciation, and gross earnings in which the student is asked to record an estimated answer before computing the problem can be highly challenging even to the more able students.

SEPARATE THE ARITHMETIC PROBLEM FROM THE ACCOUNTING PROBLEM. Accounting principles and procedures, when being presented, should be "demathematized." This may be done by the use of round numbers in the initial presentation. Round numbers permit the students to concentrate on the procedure or principle without being distracted by the arithmetic involved. Another suggestion is to give the students the arithmetical solutions related to the transaction so that they will not need to make the calculations—for example, the amount of discount, the amount of interest, the balance due, the account balance, the total of the column, the sum received from a customer. After the students have recorded a number of entries in which the arithmetic has been done for them in advance, they may be given transactions in which they are required to do the necessary arithmetical calculations.

USE ONLY REALISTIC ARITHMETIC PROBLEMS IN ACCOUNTING. Unfortunately, arithmetic problems which are unrealistic in business are sometimes introduced in the classroom. An example of this type of problem is a transaction where the student is asked to record a check. The check is for a net figure after a cash discount has been deducted. The student is required to determine the amount of discount and the gross amount, working from the net-cash figure only. Or the student is told that the company receives a check in payment of an invoice less discount, without being given a copy of the check or being told the amount for which it is drawn. Such problems are unrealistic and consume time that might be used more profitably.

While some of the more able students may be capable of completing complicated interest and bank-discount problems, many will experience difficulty. The business way is to use interest and discount tables. The use of such tables in the classroom not only simplifies the arithmetic problem and saves time, but it also provides experience in accordance with business practice.

TEACH HORIZONTAL ADDITION AND SUBTRACTION. Across-the-page addition and subtraction on payrolls, in multicolumn journals, on worksheets, and when determining account balances are examples of opportunities to use horizontal addition and subtraction in accounting. Most students have been taught and conditioned to add and subtract only vertical columns of figures, and frequently recopy figures in vertical columns before making additions and subtractions.

WRITE LEGIBLE NUMBERS. Many arithmetical errors in accounting may be traced to the failure of students to write numbers legibly and properly aligned in columns. Additions are certain to be incorrect when 7s are mistaken for 9s; 4s for 7s; 2s for 3s; and 8s for 0s.

TEST ARITHMETIC SEPARATELY. An accounting examination may be more a test of arithmetic than of accounting. For example, a test provides a list of accounts and account balances, and the student is requested to prepare a worksheet, adjust entries, and prepare financial statements. For the completion of each part of the test, accurate additions are required. Unsatisfactory results on the test may be caused by a lack of understanding of the accounting elements (identification of account balances, classification of accounts, adjusting of entries) or by incorrect addition. Thus the result of the test is not very helpful to either the student or the teacher in determining what the student knows and does not know about accounting. The arithmetic element can be largely eliminated from such a test by using round numbers for account balances and by keeping the number of accounts to the necessary minimum, thus greatly simplifying the addition process. Another illustration is the test that requires the student to compute interest or trade and cash discounts before recording the transactions. The arithmetic element in such a test can be eliminated by giving the student the amounts of the interest or discounts.

Instructional Patterns

Accounting teachers and school systems have sought to take care of individual differences among students through a variety of different instructional plans and course organizational patterns. Most of these plans fall into one of four broad classifications: (1) ability grouping, (2) class or group instructional plans, (3) individualized study methods, and (4) experimental programs.

Ability Grouping

A few schools have attempted to cope with the range of individual differences in students by ability grouping—scheduling students for accounting classes according to their expected achievement potential. Scholastic average, intelligence quotient, and reading and arithmetic test scores have been used as the basis for dividing students into homogeneous class groups. Research indicates that there is a positive and significant correlation between these factors and achievement in accounting. Classes based on homogeneous grouping, however, are complicated to schedule, and the practice is feasible only in a relatively large school. Thus only a very few secondary schools and a smaller number of colleges attempt homogeneous grouping.

RECORDKEEPING FOR SLOW LEARNERS. Some schools vary the group ability plan by dividing the students into two ability groups and offering courses at two levels: recordkeeping for the less able students and accounting for the average or above average students. The recordkeeping course emphasizes the mechanical aspects of the recording process—the *how*. Its objective is to give the student job competency in the performance of routine recording activities. No effort is made to relate the recording activities to principles or concepts.

Since the recordkeeping course is confined largely to teaching routinized recording activities, questions arise as to what activities should be taught in the course, how these activities should be performed, and how valuable such training is. Three facts stand out in answering these questions: (1) Recording procedures vary widely from business to business; thus training in specific procedures has limited application. (2) Automation is taking over the performance of more and more of the routine data processing activities. (3) Employers express the need for workers who are adaptable, who can understand principles and not just routines. Many educators question the efficacy of the recordkeeping course. They point out that such a course may be a means of keeping slow students occupied and impeding the progress of the more able students, but that it has little vocational value.

Group Instructional Plan

The most commonly used instructional plan in accounting is the one in which all members of the class proceed through the course in a lockstep pattern. The teacher gives a common presentation and assignment to the class, and the class proceeds as a unit from one topic to the next. Within this basic plan, however, two fundamentally different methods are used.

ASSIGNMENT–CLASS-DISCUSSION METHOD. In the assignment–class-discussion method, the teacher generally begins a new topic by assigning the topic or chapter to be read and studied from the text. Problem material is assigned to be done by all students upon completion of the reading. The succeeding class periods are devoted to answering questions the students raise, examining the students' understanding of the assigned reading, checking problem work, and testing and completing additional problems. Several class periods may be spent on one topic; the emphasis, however, is always on answering questions, completing problems, and testing. Some teachers question the effectiveness of this method for these reasons:

1. It assumes that all students can read, study, and understand the textbook.
2. It promotes memorization, not understanding, since the criterion of understanding is being able to submit completed problems and respond to an objective-type test. Some students tend to memorize the entries and procedures but fail to understand the basic principles involved.
3. It encourages copying. If students are unable to read and understand the textbook, they cannot complete their assigned problems. Many resort to copying to avoid failing the course.
4. It fails to create and hold the interest of many students.
5. It results in a high dropout and failure rate. Many students enter the course with enthusiasm and anticipation. After struggling with the text material, with a vocabulary load that seems formidable, and with a teaching plan which places the burden of learning upon the student with a minimum of teacher help, students often lose interest and drop out or accept failure in the course.

TEACHER-EXPLANATION–DEMONSTRATION METHOD. Under the teacher-explanation–demonstration method, all new content is presented and explained by the teacher before it is studied from the textbook by the class members. Following the explanation of a principle (or along with it), one or more problems may be worked out on the overhead projector or the chalkboard to show the application of the principles to problem situations. The students are not assigned textbook reading or problems until the teacher is certain that the students have the necessary background to read the text and do the problems with success and satisfaction. This instructional method has several advantages.

1. It gives the students confidence. They turn to their textbook reading and problem work with a feeling of assurance.
2. It uses the textbook as a teaching aid, not as the major instructional medium. The textbook becomes a reference source and supplements the class presentation.
3. It centers upon the teacher the responsibility for teaching.
4. It permits the use of sound teaching principles. Accounting words and terms can be related to student experiences, new meaningful experiences provided, concepts dramatized, and principles visualized to aid students.
5. It places a premium on understanding as opposed to memorization. Copying is discouraged because students have confidence in their ability to do the work on their own.

A major disadvantage of the method is that it may not provide for differences in learning rate. The speed with which the course moves from topic to topic must be geared to a particular student level. If the rate is geared to the more able student, it is too rapid for the slow student. If it is geared to the slower student, the course may lose its challenge for other students. A time schedule that is appropriate for all students in a class is difficult, if not impossible, to establish.

Some teachers gear the course progress to the average-to-slow student but assign additional problems to those students who are capable of achieving more. The problems are generally selected from the supplementary problems that accompany the textbook. If these supplementary problems were provided to give extra drill on the topic, they obviously serve no useful purpose for the more capable student. They become primarily busywork. If, however, the supplementary problems are of the enriching type, designed specifically to challenge, then they do serve a very useful purpose and are a means of providing for individual differences.

Another method used by some teachers is to assign to the more capable students class responsibilities, extra projects, and, where possible, work experience.

Assigning of Class Responsibilities. Such responsibilities as helping the slower students, auditing (checking) problems, preparing classroom demonstrations, planning test questions, and preparing bulletin-board and other display materials are assigned to the faster students. These responsibilities, when properly controlled to avoid student exploitation, have educational values for the more able students and are of great assistance to the slower students as well as to the teacher.

21

Organizing Extra Projects. These projects are related to the accounting course and are planned and developed by individuals or committees composed of the faster students. Examples of projects are a community survey to determine the employment opportunities, a survey of graduates to learn their data processing responsibilities and duties, an analysis of the duties performed by accounting clerks, a study of the accounting systems used by various types of businesses in the community, and preparation of reports indicating the various methods of presenting financial statements. Such projects greatly enrich the course and provide valuable activities for those students who complete their work before the slower members of the class.

Promoting Work-Experience Opportunities. Some of the more able students are placed in jobs where their knowledge of accounting is used for a portion of each school day. The work experiences may be either out of school or in school. When it is not practical to place students in business, arrangements are made for them to keep the cafeteria records and records of clubs and school organizations, and to assist with the records in the administrative office.

The Contract Plan. Some teachers attempt to take care of individual differences by use of a contract assignment plan. Under this plan, the assignment provides two or more options. To receive a minimum passing grade, the student completes a designated minimum assignment. To obtain a higher grade, additional work is required, usually additional problems. Thus the student contracts to do a certain amount of work. The student has the option of varying input into the course according to the desired grade.

The success of this plan is contingent, in part, upon the organization and the quality of the problem material provided. If the additional problems the student does to receive a higher grade merely provide more of the same drill, the student is being rewarded for busywork. If the problems introduce new content, the teacher has the difficulty of determining where to draw the line between the minimum level and the bonus level. Critics of the plan say it tends to widen the gaps between students. As the course progresses, gaps grow between the student who does minimum contract work and the one who does beyond-minimum work.

Individualized Study Plan

Awareness of the limitations of the class-group plan which forces all students in a class to move through the accounting course at the same speed has caused some teachers to experiment with an individualized study or instructional plan.

The structure of the accounting course is such that its content would appear to be readily adaptable to individual study. Few subjects have as orderly a content structure: Each topic is built on the preceding topic. Readiness to move from topic to topic does not come at the same time for all students. The amount of time and practice required for a student to achieve sufficient competency on a topic so as to move to the next topic will not be the same for all students. Therefore, a plan which would permit each student to move through the course at his or her own speed would appear to be practical and desirable.

Many individualized study plans used in the past have been primarily teacher-prepared assignment or job sheets to accompany the conventional textbook and workbook. Teachers who have used these plans have reported a number of difficulties. The above-average student is able to read and follow the assignment sheets, study the text, complete the problems, and evidence satisfactory achievement on the tests with a minimum of teacher personal direction. The slower student, however, is unable to make satisfactory progress without a great deal of assistance from the teacher. In general, the good students progress, while the poorer students soon become discouraged.

A good individual study plan should have incorporated in it these four essential features:

1. The materials should be self-instructive and self-corrective.
2. The students should be able to test their understanding of the topic as they work through it.
3. The students should be able to have immediate feedback from the self-tests through a self-checking device.
4. Recycling material should be provided at the end of each segment so that students can move on to the next topic only after demonstrating mastery of the work up to that point.

Experience has shown that when this type of instructional material is supported by a resourceful teacher, a learning situation can be provided in which the needs of both the slower as well as the more able students can be met.

Experimental Programs

In addition to those instructional plans already discussed, there are a number of plans that are in the tryout or experimental stages. All of the plans are directed to meeting the basic problems of providing for variable learning rates within a program. Although some of the plans—such as programmed instruction—have been around for some time, they are classified here as experimental because they have yet to gain wide acceptance.

PROGRAMMED INSTRUCTION. Essentially, programmed instruction is a self-instruction method in which a program leads the student through a highly structured sequence of activities in such an organized manner that the learner will master the subject matter. The information to be learned is broken down into a series of ideas, which are revealed to the student in a sequence of frames. The student must respond to each frame and then immediately check the accuracy of the response before proceeding to the next frame. The student cannot go on until the correct response has been made. Students work at their own speed, adjusting learning time to their own pace.

The learner may use a programmed textbook or some form of teaching machine. Some teaching machines are rather simple devices designed primarily as a means of manipulating and displaying the program. Other teaching machines, however, are much more sophisticated. One of the newer developments is known as computer-assisted instruction (CAI). The student interacts with a computer through a terminal. The program is stored in the computer. The student responds on the terminal to a series of questions or directions presented by the computer. As the student enters on the terminal a response to each question or direction, he or she receives immediate feedback from the computer as to the accuracy of the response and directions as to the next step the student is to take.

Programmed textbooks and computer-assisted instructional units for use on the college and adult level have been produced. Some research has been done on similar materials for the high school level. The development, however, has not been as extensive and widespread as predicted for a number of reasons:

1. Programmed instructional material is expensive to write and to produce; and computer terminals and computer time are still too costly for wide use.
2. Not all students react favorably to programmed material. Its challenge appears to wane for some students after the novelty wears away.
3. There is disagreement among educators and psychologists as to its effectiveness.

Programmed and computer-assisted instruction will probably make its greatest contribution as a teaching aid to reinforce a basic text presentation as opposed to becoming the primary means for teaching the accounting course. Certainly, such material and facilities could give the accounting teacher an additional valuable instructional tool. It would free the teacher from conducting routine drills on certain phases of the course. It would provide a ready source of material for individualized remedial instruction. It would assist but not replace the teacher.

COMPUTER-AUGMENTED INSTRUCTION. In computer-augmented instruction, the computer is used to perform the recording activities involved in completing a problem or project and not as a programmed instructional device as is the case with computer-assisted instruction. A pattern similar to the following may be used. Each student is to complete an accounting project or application. The student analyzes the source documents and/or transactions and codes the input information for each transaction on an input sheet. The student or someone else punches these data on a keypunch into punched cards from the input sheet. When the cards have been punched for all transactions, they are fed into a computer along with program cards. The computer does the recording and prints out the trial balance for the student. If the trial balance is not correct, the student must find the error, correct the input data, and repeat the process until a correct trial balance is obtained. The student may next code the adjusting and closing entries, which in turn are punched into cards and fed into the computer. The computer prints out the financial statements.

Under this plan, the computer is being used to do the recording activities—the manipulative aspects of the process. The student has to make the decisions, determine what accounts are affected, adjusted, closed, etc.

MODULAR SCHEDULING.   Analysis of the varied instructional activities of the accounting course indicates that some are appropriate for large-group instruction—perhaps one hundred or more students at one time. Other activities, however, are practical for only relatively small groups where the teacher can give attention to individuals. Still other activities are designed for independent self-study time. The chart shown in Figure 2.1 illustrates possible classification of activities according to group size.

Examination of the activities shown in Figure 2.1 indicates that some of them should be planned for relatively long uninterrupted class periods. For example, the development of the worksheet and the steps in locating errors in a trial balance or closing the books usually require a block of time

LARGE GROUP ACTIVITIES	SMALL GROUP ACTIVITIES	INDIVIDUAL STUDY
Introduction to course—motivation.	Review of topic presented in large-group sessions.	Reading text and reference material.
Presentation of new topics through explanation, lecture, demonstration, visualization.	Question and answer sessions.	Working problems, projects, practice sets assignments.
	Discussion sessions.	Completing study guides.
Showing of films and film strips.	Group remedial work.	Preparing reports and demonstrations.
	Development of charts and displays.	Taking makeup tests.
Presentations by resource persons from school and community.	Committee or small-group work.	Engaging in work experience.
Explanation of assignments.	Review of problems, projects, accounting applications, study guides, tests.	Using business machines in completion of assignments.
		Completing makeup assignments.
Testing.	Presentation of student reports and demonstrations.	Completing programmed instructional materials.
		Reshowing films and filmstrips.

FIGURE 2.1

25

equivalent to two or more class periods. Other activities, such as viewing a film, class discussion, questions and answers, drills, and tests, are better suited for short instructional periods.

The typical secondary school time schedule provides one period per day, five days per week, thirty-six weeks per year for each subject. Double periods may be provided for laboratories. This schedule is inflexible and forces the instructional methods and content to be adjusted to the time schedule as opposed to the schedule being adjusted to the instructional needs of the subject.

To give flexibility, a few schools are experimenting with a modular scheduling pattern, which provides a short instructional work period on some days and a longer period on others. Two or more groups are combined into one group for a presentation on some days, yet meet separately on others for discussion or review. Long or short self-study sessions are provided as needed.

The strength of modular scheduling lies in the opportunity it provides for the teacher to work with individual students and with small groups. It also requires the student to assume more responsibility for directing his or her own learning. Both of these elements are important in adjusting instruction to meet individual needs.

TEAM TEACHING. Although modular scheduling and team teaching complement each other, they are not necessarily interdependent. Under a team teaching plan, two or more teachers, usually assisted by a teaching aid, are assigned a block of students. The teachers cooperatively plan the program so as to meet the instructional needs of *all* the students in the group.

All students taking accounting (several class sections) may be assembled for one teacher to make a presentation and/or demonstration on one topic. For example, one teacher might explain to the total group the punched-card code and use an overhead projector and a movie film in the presentation. Following the large-group session, the students may be subdivided into smaller groups. The teacher in charge of each group will review the card code, answer questions, and help the students to get started on the assigned problem material. The students may then proceed to individual study in a learning laboratory where each student completes the assigned problems. In the laboratory, the student may consult references, reshow the film (which was shown to the large group) to clarify some point, and if needed, seek assistance from the instructor in the laboratory.

A teaching assistant helps. For example, the assistant might set up the film for the showing to the large group, keep class records, check problems, and assist students in locating material in the learning laboratory. In short, the teaching assistant takes over duties in order to free the teachers so that the teachers may have more time to plan and to work with individual students.

The adoption by schools of modular scheduling and team teaching has not been as extensive as predicted. These concepts are new, experimentation has been scattered, and much research remains to be done. Furthermore, their development is closely linked to the development and acceptance of new instructional media, such as individualized instructional materials, audiovisual packets for small-group or individual instruction, and computer-assisted instruction, all of which are designed to revolutionize the role of the teacher and the structure of the classroom.

Selecting a Plan

The advantages and disadvantages of several instructional plans have been discussed. A method appropriate for one group of students may not be effective for another. A class plan that will work at the end of the elementary course may not necessarily be appropriate for the beginning of the course. Some topics adapt themselves more readily to one type of presentation than to another type. An instructional pattern effective for advanced accounting may not work well in the elementary course. Thus a teacher should not use any one method to the exclusion of the others. Variety adds interest to classroom procedure. The wise teacher will be flexible in adapting teaching methods to the background and abilities of the students.

Problems, Questions, and Projects

1. Two accounting sections are scheduled for the same class period with different instructors to permit the dividing of the students into two groups—a faster group and a slower group. The basic difference between the instruction for the two groups is that one group will cover more material and, hopefully, will have time to deal with some advanced topics. Assume that you are given the responsibility of dividing the students. What selective factors would you use? Explain why these factors were selected.

2. Examine an accounting textbook and list the accounting words and terms that are introduced in each of the first four chapters.

3. Do you agree with the statement that "certain aspects of arithmetic can be more effectively taught in the accounting course than in a separate business arithmetic course"? Explain your answer.

4. Examine an accounting textbook to determine the arithmetic skills and knowledge that a student would need in order to do the work satisfactorily. Classify the skills and knowledge by chapters, thus showing what new skill and/or knowledge is required in each chapter.

5. When students are to work together in small groups (three to five students), what is the best plan for determining how to group them? Give reasons for your suggestions.

6. Assume that you follow a teaching pattern whereby all members of the class are kept together. If you were asked to explain why you use this plan, what reasons would you give?

7. "Learning is an individual process, but it takes place best in a social setting." What are the implications of this principle for accounting instruction?

8. The criticism is made that today's schools promote mediocrity. What does this mean to you? How can it be avoided in the teaching of accounting methods and principles?

9. Select one topic in first-year high school accounting, and indicate how this topic could be developed through a team-teaching approach. Identify the composition of the team and the contribution each team member would make.

Case Problems

1. Enrollment in elementary accounting necessitated the scheduling of six classes. One teacher recommended that an effort be made to group students in the classes according to their ability. The head of the business department opposed the plan and presented the following arguments:

    a. Homogeneous grouping of students is undemocratic. It constitutes a reflection on the slow students and gives the fast learners a feeling of superiority.

    b. Aptitude for accounting cannot be measured. No prognostic test has been established as sufficiently valid to justify its use. Whatever factors might be used to divide the students would not be much better than a guess.

    c. One teacher would have only the slow learners (if they could be identified), which is not fair to this teacher.

    d. Even if the classes were divided, the school has a uniform time schedule and uniform tests. All classes would still have to proceed at the established rate in keeping with the time and test schedules.

What is your reaction to the recommendation and to the arguments of the department head?

2. Mr. Carney is a novice high school accounting teacher. To avoid discipline problems, the first day of class he established a set of rules which were to govern the conduct of the class. He advised the students that any violation of the rules would result in the violator's receiving extra assignments. A few days later, a student violated one of the rules. To make an example of him, even though the violation was rather minor, Mr. Carney assigned him a long series of extra assignments. When the student did not do the assignments, Mr. Carney asked that he stay after school and work them under his direction. The student reported that he was employed after school and therefore could not stay. Mr. Carney then advised the student that he had until the end of the term to submit the extra assignments, and if the work was not completed, he would fail the course. The student did not turn in the penalty assignments but did all other assigned work, made high scores on tests, and caused Mr. Carney no further discipline problem. At grading time, Mr. Carney was faced with a choice of making good on his ruling or of passing the student and running the risk of losing face and possible disciplinary control of future classes. The entire incident had been so publicized that students were fully aware of the situation, as the ruling had been made in the presence of the whole class. Mr. Carney gave the student a passing grade but a lower one than his record otherwise justified.

Did Mr. Carney make the right decision? What would you suggest as an alternative solution?

3. There were three business education teachers in the Bedford High School. One teacher taught all the accounting courses; another, the shorthand courses; and the third, the typewriting and office practice courses. The faculty of the high school voted to institute a team-teaching pattern for all courses for the next school year. The business teachers were not enthusiastic about the plan but were willing to give it a try. They designed the following plan for the accounting program. The three teachers constituted one team. The teacher who had been in charge of the accounting courses was designated master teacher for accounting. The master teacher planned the program for the year. All 120 students in accounting were combined in one section on Monday and Wednesday for a 40-minute lecture-demonstration period. The master teacher introduced, demonstrated, explained all new topics, and made assignments in this lecture-demonstration period. On Tuesday, Thursday, and Friday the students were divided into six sections of 20 students each and met for an 80-minute block of time. Each of the three teachers was placed in charge of two of these 80-minute sections. At this time, the students were to mainly work on problems; however, the teacher in charge was to answer questions, help individual students, and supervise the problem material. The teacher was also responsible for checking the problems of the students in her sections.

A comparable plan was set up for shorthand and typewriting. The former teacher of the subject was designated the master teacher and the others assisted.

At the end of the year, the business teachers were very dissatisfied with the team-teaching plan and voted to return to their previous teaching plan where each teacher worked in her or his area of specialization only.

What errors were made in organizing the team-teaching plan which may have resulted in the negative reactions of the teachers?

CHAPTER 3

Planning for Instruction and Using Community Resources

Once an instructional pattern that accommodates differences in student ability has been chosen, the teacher must develop detailed lesson plans to implement that pattern. In this chapter, the major elements of an effective lesson plan are discussed, and since teachers should not work in a vacuum, suggestions are provided for making use of community resources.

Planning for Instruction

Most worthwhile accomplishments are the results of planning—architects plan new buildings, politicians plan election campaigns, speakers plan their presentations. Teaching is no exception to this general principle—in fact, nothing that a teacher does is more important than planning, for planning helps to ensure successful action.

Some of the basic questions that must be answered when developing a lesson plan are these:

1. What are the objectives to be achieved?
2. How is interest to be stimulated and maintained?
3. What materials are needed?
4. What techniques, procedures, and illustrations are most suitable?
5. How can the degree of success be measured?

The problem of lesson planning becomes one of thinking through a series of logically organized steps to be followed in developing the lesson. One form of outline that has proved effective in accounting classes is this:

1. Topic Title.
2. Objectives or Basic Principles to Be Taught.
3. Materials to Be Used.
4. How the Topic Is to Be Launched.
5. Teaching Procedure to Be Used—Developing the Topic.
6. Illustrations to Be Used.

7.   Posters or Other Visual Aids.

8.   Evaluation.

Each of these items in the list, except Topic Title, is discussed in the following paragraphs.

Objectives

Objectives serve as directional guides and are therefore essential to teaching. They not only determine what is to be done but also limit teaching activities by ruling out discussion that in no way aids in reaching those objectives. The choice of objectives greatly influences the selection of teaching techniques to be employed, teaching materials to be utilized, and evaluation items to be used.

We hit more targets when we aim for them, and we can aim more accurately when targets are specific and are in full view. Broad general objectives, such as "to develop good personality traits," "to improve penmanship," "to increase arithmetical skill," "to show the effect of transactions on accounts," and "to give an appreciation of the value of records" are objectives which may apply to every lesson in accounting. Certainly, every class period should contribute to the attainment of these objectives. However, they are not very helpful as specific targets for any particular lesson topic. To be most useful, objectives must be specific, for example, "to learn the similarity between the balance sheet and the accounting equation," "to understand why closing entries are needed to bring the capital account up to date," and "to know how to use the straight-line method of computing depreciation."

Objectives must be realistic in the sense that they are attainable within the time provided. A major pitfall of inexperienced teachers is to attempt to cover too much in any one lesson. This practice results in too rapid coverage, confusion by the students, and wasting of time by the teacher. There are many days in a school term, and only a small amount of work need be covered each day. If definite and realizable objectives are selected and the teaching procedure is carefully planned and executed, the day-to-day program will progress smoothly and effectively.

Materials

The teacher must decide which materials will be needed in the presentation or development of the lesson. Even the most experienced teachers take time to itemize the materials they will need. Nothing detracts more from a class presentation than the teacher's interrupting the class to obtain or look for materials which should have been ready for immediate use. Although the teacher's ability to improvise grows with experience, the best illustrations, the best demonstrations, and the best overall presentations result from careful preclass planning. Textbooks and other instructional media are discussed in detail in Chapter 4.

Launching the Topic

Three principles should be observed in introducing any new unit of subject matter.

INTRODUCE NEW MATERIAL IN TERMS OF PREVIOUS KNOWLEDGE AND EXPE-RIENCES OF STUDENTS. This necessitates building upon knowledge gained earlier in the course. Accounting is unusually rich in this regard because it continually uses those principles and concepts previously studied. The teacher's role is one of showing how the principle or concept to be intro-duced on a given day is related to that which the student already knows. In addition to building upon the students' knowledge of accounting, the teacher may capitalize on their experiences outside the classroom.

For example, when computing the balance in the Cash account, the student needs to relate this figure to the meaning of assets learned earlier. Sales returns for a business enterprise may be related to students' experi-ences of returning merchandise after Christmas because certain gifts received were the incorrect size, wrong color, etc. Later in the year, when studying the topic of bad debts, the teacher may draw upon certain class members' earlier experiences when as newspaper carriers they were unable to collect from some of their customers.

SHOW A NEED FOR THE NEW INFORMATION. Although unit topics vary considerably one from another, most new topics can be justified on the basis of need. Often, the new procedure represents a better, quicker, or shorter technique than the one previously employed. A good example here is the special journal. Only total of the sales journal is posted to the credit of the sales account, for example. If there are 30 transactions recorded in the journal, this represents a saving of 29 posting actions. Similarly, before bad debts can be recorded, one must learn some method of estimating the amount anticipated from bad debt losses. The following devices have been used by successful teachers for creating interest in new topics.

1. Use case studies. Student interest is always high when the teacher is describing an actual business situation or relating a true experience of a friend or neighbor.
2. Use charts and other visual aids. A thought-provoking chart or bulletin board or transparency may stimulate interest. Films and filmstrips may also be used for this purpose.
3. Use guest speakers. A talk by a credit manager may spark enthusi-asm for a discussion of procedures in handling sales on credit. An explanation of purchasing procedures by a purchasing agent may develop interest in the unit on handling purchases.
4. Use committee field trips and reports. When an entire class cannot be taken on a field trip, a committee of students may serve as a substitute.
5. Use classroom problems. Problems encountered by students in one topic may kindle interest for other topics. For example, inability to

get a trial balance "in balance" may be all that is necessary to launch a lesson or unit on steps to be followed in discovering errors on a trial balance.

MAINTAIN A PROPER BALANCE BETWEEN MOTIVATION AND PRESENTATION. Some teachers go to great lengths to motivate student interest in a new topic. For example, an entire day or two might be devoted to a study of credit as the background and setting for studying sales on credit or bad debts. A credit manager may be asked to speak to the class. Other teachers plunge right in with a discussion of new accounting theory without preparing their students for the new topic. Neither extreme can be justified. We need motivation and an understanding of the background or setting for new theory. But we must remember that the purpose of motivation is to set the stage for learning. We should not spend so much time launching a new topic that there is insufficient time left for needed explanations, discussion, and practice.

Teaching Procedures—Developing the Topic

Detailed and specific teaching procedures that are helpful in developing the various principles of accounting are explained in Chapters 7 through 16, but there are certain common characteristics which identify good lesson planning whether the lesson topic is opening entries, preparing a trial balance, or completing a tax report.

OBJECTIVES OF THE LESSON ARE DEFINITE. A well-developed plan includes provisions for ensuring that all students are fully aware of the objectives of the lesson. If objectives are to be realized, students must know and accept them. Some teachers write the objectives of the lesson on the board at the beginning of the period. With the aims of the lesson constantly before the students, there is greater probability of a direct flow of work toward the goal.

EMPHASIS IS PLACED ON UNDERSTANDING, NOT ON MEMORIZING. Many facts in accounting can be memorized profitably. However, memorized facts are of little value to students unless they understand the applications. Effective teaching in accounting results in the ability to understand and use what is learned.

Students who merely learn how to record transactions might be able to apply their debit and credit knowledge with sufficient proficiency to earn good marks in school but will have difficulty in making the transition from the records used in the classroom to those found in business. Consideration of the why of every activity will develop a true understanding of the accounting equation and the principles of debit and credit; the purposes of special columns and special journals; the need for proofs and controls; and the relationship of inventory, purchases, sales, credit and collection, and production procedures. And it will enable students to apply their knowledge intelligently in any situation.

PROPER BALANCE IS PROVIDED BETWEEN PRESENTATION AND APPLICATION. In planning, provisions should be made for a proper balance in time and emphasis between subject-matter presentation and application.

REALISTIC MATERIALS AND PROCEDURES ARE USED. Learning is most effective when the subject matter is presented as nearly as possible in the setting in which it will eventually be used. Applied to lesson planning for accounting, this means that materials used, teacher presentation, and student practice must be as realistic as conditions permit.

STUDENT PARTICIPATION IS PLANNED. Action, not only by the teacher but also by the students, should be planned. If the teacher does all the talking, explaining, and demonstrating and if the students are largely passive—giving perfunctory answers to questions—very little learning is taking place. To learn, students must be actively engaged in solving problems, raising questions, criticizing suggestions offered, and evaluating practices.

STUDENT TIME IS CONSERVED. Five minutes of lost time each day accumulated over a year adds to several weeks of instructional time. Time is lost when class time is used to place on the chalkboard needed materials and forms which could have been prepared before class; when transactions and problems that could have been duplicated are dictated to students; when time-consuming methods are used in class to check problems and tests; when assignments and instructions are customarily repeated because some students were not attentive; and when students do not have proper tools, materials, and supplies.

PROCEDURAL FUNCTIONS OF THE CLASSROOM ARE ROUTINIZED. Such daily routine tasks as checking attendance, distributing and collecting materials, placing work on the chalkboard, and other classroom chores are routinized so that they take up a minimum of teacher and student time.

MONOTONY IS AVOIDED. While routinized procedures should be established for the handling of many aspects of the daily lesson, the general teaching procedure and class pattern should vary from day to day. If each day is only a repetition of the preceding day, sooner or later boredom is certain to set in. Variety in teaching procedure should be planned.

DIFFICULTIES ARE ANTICIPATED. In planning for a lesson, the teacher should anticipate difficulties which may interfere with the smooth development of the lesson during the class period as well as difficulties that the students may encounter in completing the assigned homework. The difficulties may include troublesome arithmetic computations, vocabulary problems, unfamiliar wording of instructions and transactions, errors in the textbook, and misleading figures. If these difficulties are anticipated in the teacher planning, both class time and student study time may be conserved.

LABORATORY PRACTICE IS USED. A lesson plan must include activities that follow class presentations of new topics. Learning of accounting requires more than an understanding of the theory; it also requires practice in applying the theory. Part of this application can and should be completed as part of the class period, when the teacher will have an opportunity to supervise the work of the students. In fact, some teachers find that their students can complete nearly all of their assignments in class. The remaining application must be done outside the class period in study hall or as homework.

ASSIGNMENTS ARE WELL EXPLAINED. Assignments are far too important to be shouted at the pupils after the bell rings at the end of the period. They should be explained well before the end of the class period. In many instances, it is useful to make the first two or three entries of an assignment on the chalkboard as the students do the same at their seats. Difficult entries should be explained and potential stumbling blocks should be clarified.

When students are given generous amounts of class time to work on their assignments, they are better able to carry them through to completion without special help when they must continue working on assignments outside of class.

Illustrations

Illustrative problems are solved on the chalkboard or by using transparencies similar to the problems which are to be assigned. The illustrations in the textbook are referred to and explained. In addition, examples and illustrations from students' previous experience are extremely valuable.

VISUAL MATERIALS. Some form of visual material may be effectively used with almost every accounting lesson. The use of such materials, however, requires considerable prelesson planning. It will not suffice merely to list in the lesson plan the suggestion to "show a film" or "illustrate a balance sheet." The plan must be more specific: It should list the specific film to be shown, provide the specific balance sheet to be illustrated, or identify the specific chart to be used. Some visual materials require special preparation. Reservations must be made for films and projection equipment; bulletin boards must be planned and prepared several days before the date of intended use. One must keep in mind the objectives of the lesson, and the material must be chosen to aid in the accomplishment of these objectives.

When audiovisual materials are mentioned, many teachers immediately think of films and filmstrips. These constitute a small part of audiovisual materials; in the teaching of accounting they play a minor role. Posters, charts, diagrams, bulletin boards, chalkboard demonstrations, and transparencies are used more frequently than are filmstrips. In fact, most up-to-date accounting teachers rely heavily on transparencies—those they have purchased or prepared themselves.

Evaluation

A well-prepared lesson plan indicates how the lesson is to be evaluated. This evaluation is to be done by both the students and the teacher.

STUDENTS EVALUATE THEIR OWN WORK. Students must be encouraged to evaluate their own work, and their evaluation should correspond rather closely with that of the teacher. To obtain this harmony of evaluation, either permit the students to work with you in establishing the evaluative criteria or explain to the students in detail the basis for judging their work. One suggestion is that the students' assignments should be prepared on varying levels of difficulty. Each student's choice of an assignment is one indication of the degree of confidence the student has in being able to prepare the solution. How well the student performs on the assignment chosen is another criterion.

Students may grade themselves on such abilities as willingness to work with others, courtesy, neatness, and promptness. Some teachers follow the practice of using a checklist with many of these qualities. Each student is asked to rate himself at the end of each grading period. A comparison of a later checklist with one completed earlier should reveal progress. In many instances, the students and the teacher prepare this checklist cooperatively at the beginning of the course.

TEACHERS EVALUATE THE STUDENTS' WORK. Several factors must be considered in evaluating and grading students' work. Evaluation, to be most effective, must be in terms of the objectives to be achieved. These factors are discussed in Chapter 5.

TEACHERS EVALUATE THEIR TEACHING. Teachers who prepare good lesson plans are very likely to attain success in teaching. Teachers who fail to prepare their work thoroughly are quite likely to wander from the immediate task and fail to accomplish the lesson objectives.

Teachers who have more than one class of accounting may not remember exactly what has been discussed in each class. In some instances, they may find that a few points were never adequately explained to one or more groups.

Teachers seeking to improve their teaching skill will be eager to use every means available. In some schools teachers are rated by their students by the use of checklists. In this way, a teacher discovers points of strength and weakness.

Making Use of Community Resources

Graduates frequently report that they do not keep records in business as they were taught to do in school. This, of course, is true. Records in business are, to a certain degree, tailor-made in terms of the needs of the particular business. An accounting system appropriate for one type of business may not be adequate for another. Underlying all double-entry records, however, are the same basic principles, but the application of these principles may vary from one business to another. To attempt to cover in an instructional program the various applications of the principles to the hundreds of different types of businesses would be impractical.

The relationship between the principles and the procedures as taught in the classroom and their application in business can be shown (1) by taking students to business offices to observe how records are processed, (2) by bringing people from business into the classroom as resource persons, and (3) by using records drawn from businesses in the community in the instructional process. Thus, utilizing community resources is essential if the accounting course is to be practical.

A wide variety of different types of records can be observed in the business areas close to most schools. There are usually chain stores, service-type businesses, small specialty shops, restaurants, and offices of professional people. There may be a public utility, a manufacturing concern, a small department store, an accounting firm, and a bank—and do not overlook the records kept in the school office. Some of the businesses may be large; others may be small. Some may be single proprietorships; some, partnerships; and others, corporations.

The proximity of businesses to the classroom makes possible the arrangement of group field trips to business firms without disrupting the students' school program. Many trips may be made within the regular class period. Others may be arranged for free periods and after school.

Field Trips

The following listings suggest the types of activities that students can observe on local field trips.

1. At the local bank.
   a. Procedures for making a deposit in a checking and savings account—types of deposit slips.
   b. Procedures for making withdrawals—writing of checks.
   c. How a loan is processed.
   d. Use of safe-deposit boxes and night depositories.
   e. How the bank keeps its records with depositors.
   f. How checks are cleared.
   g. Data processing equipment.
2. At offices of local doctors, dentists, and lawyers.
   a. How appointments are recorded.
   b. How patient and client records are kept.
   c. How cash payments are made.
   d. Use of petty cash records.
   e. Use of cash basis or accrual basis of accounting.
3. At a local chain store.
   a. How the cash register is used to control cash.
   b. Method of balancing and proving cash.
   c. How incoming merchandise and invoices are checked.
   d. How inventory records are maintained.
4. At the office of a manufacturing company.
   a. Payroll records and procedures.
   b. Procedures for controlling cash.
   c. Fixed assets records and method of recording depreciation.

      d. Procedures for determining costs.
      e. Billing procedures.
      f. System of inventory control.
      g. The organization of the accounting function.
      h. The system of data processing.
5. At the office of the electric or gas company.
      a. How utility bills are computed and recorded.
      b. How cash receipts are controlled.
      c. Data processing equipment.
6. At a department store, service station, or specialty shop.
      a. Use of charge plates.
      b. Procedures for charging and billing customers.
      c. Procedures for controlling inventory.
      d. Purchasing procedures.
      e. Procedures for controlling cash.

The field trip gives students an opportunity to see accounting in action. It makes the classroom instruction more meaningful and can be a tremendous motivating factor. Teachers and students report that the visits to businesses are the most interesting and enriching projects of the year.

Student Committees

When class field trips are not possible or desirable, student committees may be used. Instead of taking the entire class to one business, the teacher may divide the class into committees of four or five students each. Each committee is assigned the responsibility for obtaining certain information from a designated business. For example, in a discussion of the various ways that accounts receivable are kept by businesses, different committees may be responsible for obtaining the information from a doctor's or a dentist's office, from a lawyer's office, from a department store, from a grocery store, and from a manufacturing firm. Each committee plans its visit, obtains the information, and reports its findings to the class.

Similar committee assignments may be made when the class is studying systems for the control of cash receipts and cash payments, credit purchases, credit sales, inventory procedures, property records and depreciation, payroll records, automated data processing, and employment opportunities in the field of accounting.

Work Experience

The opportunity for providing some students with actual work experience in businesses in the community should never be overlooked. No better learning situation can be provided than that of having students employed in part-time accounting work and, at the same time, studying accounting in the classroom with the instructor coordinating the two activities.

Work-experience programs can be highly organized and may involve all class members, as is done in certain schools; or they may be less formalized and involve only a few members of the class. These students may be selected from the more capable students, thus providing opportunities to meet individual differences. A few students working in business will greatly enrich the classroom experiences of all the students through the reports and comments they bring to the classroom.

Many students are employed in some form of part-time work. Because of this work connection, these students are in a position to obtain information about the accounting procedures followed by businesses. As the students' ability in accounting grows, perhaps the teacher can be influential in obtaining assignments to duties requiring a greater use of recording skills.

The Junior Achievement program provides an opportunity for a limited number of students to obtain practical and valuable work experience. In those communities where Junior Achievement programs are in operation, the accounting teacher may wish to encourage students to participate in the program.

Experience Through School Organizations

One does not need to go outside the school itself to provide practical accounting experiences for some students. The school bank, the school cafeteria, and the school clubs and organizations require records. In addition, benefits or drives, such as those held by the Red Cross and the Community Chest, must keep records. Some of this work can be brought into the classroom and used as the basis for class discussion, to illustrate certain procedures, and to provide practical experience for some students. In assuming work of this nature, however, the teacher must make certain that all the work done by students is carefully guided and checked. Otherwise, student inaccuracies may subject the teacher and the class to justifiable criticism. The possibility that a student may be expected to spend more time on such an assignment than its educational values justify needs to be examined.

Business Forms

Students respond favorably to live material. The use of source documents and financial statements bearing the names of local firms with which students are acquainted brings an atmosphere of reality into the classroom. For this reason, many business teachers maintain an extensive file of documents and reports that have been obtained from the local community. This file contains sales slips, invoices, checks, deposit slips, monthly statements, purchase orders and requisitions, inventory sheets, payroll forms, journal and ledger forms, petty cash receipts, financial statements, and other similar forms from a variety of businesses in the community.

So that the forms may be protected for use year after year, they may be mounted on cardboard or some other firm surface and covered with clear plastic film. Transparencies may also be made from the forms for classroom discussion.

Guest Speakers From Business

Local business people, accountants, former graduates, and government officials are usually very cooperative in coming to the school to discuss with classes problems concerning accounting, personnel, and other business matters.

BUSINESS PEOPLE. Business people may discuss their records, business procedures, employment opportunities, personal and educational requirements for employees, and other similar topics.

GRADUATES. Former graduates can be invited to report and discuss their experiences. They can explain the forms and records used by their firms, specify the skills and knowledges required in their work, and give valuable suggestions to the students preparing to work in business.

PUBLIC ACCOUNTANTS. Because of their wide experience with many types of records and with both large and small businesses, public accountants can discuss many aspects of business records with students. There is probably no one better able to emphasize the importance of accuracy and neatness in accounting work. They can also give valuable guidance to those students who may be interested in preparing for the accounting profession.

GOVERNMENT OFFICIALS. Officials from the Internal Revenue Service, if an office is located in your community, will be glad to discuss the preparation and filing of individual tax returns. Representatives of the state employment service welcome the opportunity to discuss employment possibilities with classes.

CLASS PLANNING. Planning for and with the guest speaker is necessary. A few days before the appearance of a guest speaker, the students prepare questions that they would like to have answered. Plans are also made for the question-and-answer period with the speaker. As many business people are not accustomed to talking to student groups, the speaker is usually provided with a list of questions and topics that the class would like to have discussed. The time schedule also may be indicated so that adequate time will be provided for class questions following the talk. The following nine points should be included in the invitation to the speaker: (1) subject and grade of class, (2) age range, (3) topic under study, (4) size of class, (5) time and length of period, (6) suggested topic of talk, (7) why the invitation has been extended, (8) questions students will expect to have answered, and (9) suggested illustrative materials or demonstrations which the class and teacher believe would be helpful.

The appearance of business people as guest speakers is more than an opportunity to enrich the course; it also constitutes a medium of public relations for the business department and the school. Therefore, the plans for guest speakers should be carefully made so that the speakers will leave with a feeling of having done a good job, that the class appreciated their efforts, and that their time was well spent.

If a tape recorder is available, the guest's talk might be recorded. Excerpts from the recording may then be used in the class discussion which should always follow the appearance of a guest speaker. These discussions are necessary to clarify questionable points and misinterpretations on the part of students and to evaluate what the students gained from the presentation.

Advisory Committees

A group of local business representatives may be selected by the department to advise the teachers in regard to new developments and needs of businesses in the community. This is an excellent opportunity for a teacher to keep in touch with changes in local accounting jobs. The teacher can get many valuable ideas on how to make accounting instruction more realistic by referring to examples that exist in the immediate community.

Teacher-Community Involvement

The experienced teacher has learned early to get out into the community in order to improve accounting instruction. Without community involvement, few field trips would materialize, individual student projects would lack direction, work experience programs would not be possible, and guest speakers would be infrequent. But how does a business educator get involved in the community?

One of the best ways to get involved is to take membership in a business community organization. Of interest to the accounting teacher would be membership in a local chapter of organizations such as AMS (Administrative Management Society), DPMA (Data Processing Management Association), and the Chamber of Commerce. In participating actively in one or more of these organizations, the teacher not only keeps up to date with trends in accounting, data processing, and business management, but also has a good source for contacts. In addition, these organizations will generally assist with work-experience programs and community surveys of office occupations and office equipment.

Opportunities may also be present in a teacher's community to keep well informed about accounting. For example, a teacher should request that the school be placed on the mailing list of professional accounting and management bodies for information on updating seminars, lectures, and workshops. Among the numerous ones in the United States are the local, state, or national chapters of the Society of Certified Public Accountants, American Accounting Association, Federal Government Accountants' Association, National Association of Accountants, American Management Association, National Society of Public Accountants, and American Society of Women Accountants. In Canada, teachers can write to their provincial

41

chapter of Chartered Accountants, Certified General Accountants' Association of Canada, and Society of Industrial and Cost Accountants of Canada. Along the same lines, every accounting teacher should support the local business teachers' association by attending annual conventions and special workshops. Attendance at these functions provides an excellent forum for obtaining updated information, valuable contacts, and an exchange of teaching methods.

Other Suggestions

The following additional suggestions may be helpful in the use of community resources.

1. Make a survey of the businesses located close to your school. See how many different types of records may be found within a radius of a few blocks from your school.
2. Plot the businesses on a large poster. Make this poster a permanent exhibit in your accounting classroom. Make these businesses your accounting laboratory.
3. Help your students to see the practical values of your accounting course by showing through class, committee, and individual field trips the application of the course to the businesses in your community whenever possible.
4. Take the "excursion" out of the field trip (a) by using the resources near your school, (b) by planning each trip so that it can be completed within one or two class periods, and (c) by designing each trip to provide observation of a specific recording activity, not an overall tour of an office or of a complete accounting system.
5. Experiment with class, committee, and individual field-trip plans and determine which is the most effective for you, your students, the observation point, and your community.
6. In planning and executing field trips, give your students an opportunity to assume responsibility, to develop initiative, and to exercise self-expression.
7. Keep a file on local businesses for your use in planning class, committee, or individual field trips. The file should contain such information as name of person to consult, description of records, special recording features that should be observed, summary of previous field trips, and common questions students ask on their return.

Problems, Questions, and Projects

1. Select a topic normally taught in first-year accounting. Describe ways of introducing the topic so as to accomplish the following:

a. Relate the topic to the everyday experiences of the students.

   b. Relate the new knowledge to previous learning in accounting.

   c. Show how the new knowledge is needed.

   2. What are some important features of assigning homework problems effectively?

   3. Frequently, students ask questions in class that relate to some phase of a future lesson. When should the teacher depart from the day's objectives to answer such questions?

   4. Select a topic normally taught in first-year accounting. Prepare a list of what you consider to be the minimum essentials that must be covered when teaching the topic.

   5. Select a topic normally taught in first-year accounting. Describe an illustration that might be used to help clarify this principle as a part of a lesson plan to be used when teaching the topic.

   6. Some teachers who do not use community resources contend that business people do not wish to be bothered by students. They argue that business people are busy and should not be asked to take time to answer student questions, gather materials, provide information, or give talks to classes. Do you agree with the statement? What safeguards can you suggest to ensure that students do not become nuisances in gathering materials and information for your accounting classes?

   7. Your school principal objects to field trips on the grounds that they disrupt the entire school program, they require absences from other classes, and they are more excursions than educational experiences. How would you justify the use of field trips?

   8. Select a school with which you are familiar and make a survey of the various types of businesses located within a one-mile radius of the school. Prepare a chart or a bulletin-board display showing the findings of your survey.

   9. Assume that you wish to arrange a field trip for the accounting class to a local bank. Indicate the specific steps you would follow in planning the trip.

   10. Indicate the specific steps you would take in planning for, consulting with, and following up a guest speaker for your accounting class.

Case Problem

Through the cooperation of their local chapter of the American Management Society, the business teachers of Hamilton High School had arranged for a Business-Office Education Day to be held early in the school year. The plans for the day were that each student in the accounting and shorthand classes would spend one day at an office. Each student was to be assigned to a specific office worker and was to spend the day observing the kind of work done by this person. The day of observation was to be followed by a dinner at which time a panel of business people would discuss what they looked for in hiring office employees.

   When the plan was submitted to the high school principal for approval, he objected on the grounds that a full day was too much to spend in observation and that the same objectives could be accomplished by having the students visit the offices in the afternoon only. He further objected to having both junior and senior students participate. He expressed the opinion that while such an activity might be appropriate for seniors, especially if it were held late in the school year and just before they went into employment, he could see little value in it for juniors. The juniors, he stated, could participate next year when they were seniors.

To what extent do you agree or disagree with the principal?

CHAPTER 4

Learning Resources

A major influence on the structure and effectiveness of any course of instruction is the learning material selected to implement the course objectives, and perhaps nowhere is the judicious selection of learning resources more vital than in beginning accounting courses. Fortunately, publishers of business education material traditionally have been responsive to the needs of both students and teachers. They offer a wide variety of complete programs that include such resources as textbooks, workbooks, individual learning guides, practice sets, accounting applications, simulations, visual aids, tests, and teacher's manuals and keys.

In addition, many teachers find it useful—indeed, in some localities are strongly encouraged—to develop learning activity packages tailored to specific individual needs. And finally, state and local departments of education, as well as the professional business organizations, not only provide a valuable forum for the exchange of information about learning resources and methodology, but also develop and supply highly original material.

Textbooks

The primary resource of any beginning accounting course is the textbook, and to a large degree the learning approach taken in it governs how and when individual topics are introduced and developed. In most instances, the beginning teacher has little or no voice in textbook selection: The textbook has already been selected by an adoption committee—often for a period of four or five years—and the teacher must adapt his or her teaching philosophy to accommodate the adopted text. Later, however, as one adoption cycle ends and another begins, teachers have a greater opportunity to participate in the decision-making process; therefore, some insight into the various approaches taken by textbook writers is useful.

Over the years, textbook authors have generally agreed that the best method to introduce the beginner to the study of accounting is to take the student through these essential steps of the accounting cycle:

1. Preparing source documents.
2. Journalizing.
3. Posting.

4. Proving the ledger.
5. Preparing financial statements.
6. Adjusting and closing the books.
7. Balancing and ruling the ledger.
8. Preparing a postclosing trial balance.
9. Interpreting financial information.

Some authors have preferred a different version of the accounting cycle and have included or excluded certain steps, such as the preparation of a worksheet. While the majority of writers have agreed that the beginner learns accounting best through a study of an accounting cycle, not all have agreed on the specific order of presenting the steps in that cycle. For example, many authors in the past began their cycle in the traditional order, commencing with the study of the journal; hence, this order of presentation was given the label *the journal approach.* On the other hand, other writers believed that the analysis of transactions in ledger accounts should be introduced first; hence the label *account,* or *ledger, approach.* Very few, if any, texts today begin with either approach. In recent times, more and more authors have supported one of two newer approaches: either the *balance sheet approach,* that is to say, one commencing with the study of a balance sheet; or the *equation approach,* that is, one beginning accounting with the development of a basic equation. Regardless of the approach taken, it is important to recognize that the steps in the accounting cycle are eventually covered. The chief difference among writers today is a matter of identifying the order of covering those steps.

An examination of textbooks today also reveals that many writers prefer to give some general business and economic background to the study of accounting prior to the introduction of the balance sheet approach or the accounting equation approach.

Presenting the Economic Setting in Accounting

Students who register in a beginning accounting course come from varied school backgrounds. Some will have had an exposure to basic business and economic subject matter; others will have had no background simply because not all schools offer a complete business education program. Moreover, in schools with complete business programs, an introduction to business may not be required prior to registration in accounting. To offer flexibility to curriculum planning, therefore, many teachers support a textbook that provides a preliminary section on the economic setting in accounting. These instructional objectives may be considered in the development of such a setting.

Students should be able to:

1. Identify the main characteristics of a free enterprise system—private ownership of property, operation of businesses by private individuals, competition among businesses, and profit seeking.

2. Define the four major types of business ownership—the single proprietorship, the partnership, the corporation, and the cooperative (a special form of corporation).
3. Compare the three major types of business ownership.
4. Present the relationship of a successful business to the good management of that enterprise.
5. Underscore the importance of an accounting system for good business management.
6. Distinguish between a bookkeeper and an accountant.
7. Explain in simple terms the importance of accounting to a country's economic system.

In presenting this topic, teachers may use a variety of techniques. Some teachers may assign the topic in the form of a textbook reading assignment, to be followed by a class discussion on the following day. Other teachers, however, may prefer to initiate a class discussion through a series of well-developed questions. For example, some or all of the following questions may be discussed briefly:

1. What is the free enterprise system?
2. Who owns the nation's businesses?
3. Why do businesses need financial data on their operations?
4. Why do other persons outside the firm (creditors, shareholders, governments, labor unions) require financial information?
5. What is the role of the accountant?

Following this discussion, teachers may then assign the first reading of the topic in the text together with a series of problems and questions.

The number of lessons required to achieve the planned objectives of the topic will, of course, vary with the needs of each class. Teachers generally agree that presenting an economic setting to the study of accounting does offer several advantages, and a textbook that provides this setting is preferable to one that does not. Some of these advantages are as follows:

1. The students can be made aware that they will be studying an area that is exceedingly important to the economic life of the country.
2. A discussion of the three forms of business ownership provides the necessary background for the later introduction of the balance sheet concepts for owner's equity, partners' equity, and shareholders' equity.
3. A discussion of the role of accounting in business and the entire economic system will bring out the basic purpose of accounting, that is, to provide useful information for effective decision making by both insiders and outsiders.
4. And if not previously considered, the added topic of careers and opportunities in accounting can easily be introduced to complete the economic setting.

Comparing the Balance Sheet and Accounting Equation Approaches

Is there any difference between the balance sheet approach and the accounting equation approach? After all, is it not true that the balance sheet does contain the accounting equation? Consider closely the steps in the two approaches outlined below. Are there any marked differences between them?

The steps in the first accounting cycle under the balance sheet order of presentation are the following (keep in mind that variations do exist among some textbooks):

1. Presenting a student's statement of personal "net worth." (This concept of net worth is misleading from the balance sheet perspective.)
2. Introducing the formal balance sheet, generally for a service firm and owned by a single proprietor. At this stage, the balance sheet is usually unclassified and is in the account form. (Textbooks for college courses often use the corporate form of business enterprise.)
3. Analyzing transactions affecting the balance sheet either with a journal (two-column or multicolumn) or with the aid of T accounts only.
4. Analyzing revenue and expense transactions with a journal (two-column or multicolumn) or with the aid of T accounts only.
5. Introducing the journal to record both balance sheet and revenue and expense transactions. (College texts generally show the use of special journals immediately.)
6. Posting to accounts in one ledger only. (The standard or balance ledger form is usually introduced at this stage.)
7. Preparing a trial balance. (The worksheet may or may not be used at this point.)
8. Preparing financial statements. The income statement and the report form of the balance sheet are usually introduced at this stage. Some teachers also introduce the classified balance sheet.
9. Closing the accounts in the ledger. (The adjusting entries will precede this stage if adjustments are introduced on the worksheet.)
10. Preparing a postclosing trial balance.

The steps under the accounting equation approach are presented as follows. (Again, some variations will exist among different authors.)

1. Establishing a business by acknowledging a basic equation: Economic resources (assets) on the left side of the equation are equal in dollar amounts to the claims against those assets on the right side.
2. Identifying the three fundamental elements of the accounting equation: Assets = Liabilities + Owner's Equity. (College courses generally use the corporate form of Shareholders' or Stockholders' Equity.)
3. Introducing the account form of balance sheet as a detailed

summary of the accounting equation. (The service firm of a single proprietorship is widely used at the high school level, while college accounting courses use the corporate form.)

4. Analyzing balance sheet transactions within the equation. (Note that no journal and no accounts are used at this stage.)

5. Expanding the equation to analyze revenue and expense transactions and to introduce the concept of net income within the equation. (Again, note that no journal and no accounts are used.)

6. Introducing the income statement as a detailed summary of the revenue and expense transactions analyzed previously in the expanded accounting equation.

7. Introducing the net income within the balance sheet to show the relationship between the two financial statements.

8. Introducing the T account to record the opening entries and to record changes in asset, liability, owner's equity, revenue, and expense accounts.

9. Introducing the journal, usually in the two-column form. (College courses will often use special journals immediately.)

10. Posting the accounts to a formal ledger (to either a standard or balance ledger form).

11. Taking a trial balance.

12. Preparing financial statements. The report form of the balance sheet is usually introduced at this stage. Some teachers will also prefer to introduce the classified balance sheet. (The worksheet may or may not be used prior to this point.)

13. Closing the accounts in the ledger. (Adjusting entries will precede this stage if adjustments are introduced on the worksheet.)

14. Taking a postclosing trial balance.

In comparing the two approaches, notice the marked differences between the steps in the early stages. In the first place, the equation approach establishes only the basic equation in the first step; the details of the balance sheet then follow. On the other hand, the balance sheet approach places the emphasis on acquiring the details of the complete financial statement immediately from the beginning. The equation is introduced only after a detailed balance sheet has been developed. In the second place, notice that in the balance sheet approach the transactions affecting the statement are analyzed in T accounts or in a journal; the other approach returns to the equation to show how any one or more of the three elements may change. In the third place, notice that in the balance sheet approach the concept of net income is *not* introduced until the end of the accounting cycle, with the worksheet and the income statement. In the equation approach, however, the analysis of revenue and expense transactions are introduced in an expanded equation. From this expanded equation, the concept of net income is presented without the details of the worksheet. It is only after the net income concept is established within the equation that the formal income statement is presented. One final comment is worth emphasizing. Observe once again that the revenue and expense transactions in the balance sheet approach are analyzed in T accounts or in a journal. The equation approach, on the other hand, analyzes these transactions first within an expanded equation. The need for an account is introduced only after the concept of changing the three elements in the equation is firmly established.

Of course, similarities do exist between the two approaches. Both tend to delay the introduction of ledger accounts for transaction analysis, and both eventually cover a first, or elementary, accounting cycle. Which of the two approaches to select is a matter of individual teacher decision. Obviously, a textbook that reflects this decision is a more comfortable working aid than one that does not.

Students' attitudes toward the accounting textbook are important. The textbook represents a source of information and a valuable reference tool. The kind of attitude that students have toward the textbook is shaped to a certain extent by how the textbook is presented and used. When first introducing the textbook to the students, present it as something that the students should be proud of and will find helpful. Direct student attention to the preface, the table of contents, the glossary, and the index. A few fast drills on how to locate topics by means of the index may be appropriate.

Workbooks

A good accounting textbook contains a variety of exercises and problems, often with varying degrees of difficulty to accommodate differences in student abilities. Most publishers supplement their textbooks with correlated workbooks which consist of the business forms, journals, ledgers, financial statements, and other working papers that the student requires to complete the textbook problems.

Workbooks offer many advantages to both the teacher and the student. They save time: accounting paper does not have to be identified and distributed in class. They help the teacher in checking assignments: the answers always appear in the same location. Students do not waste paper; the right form and the right amount of space are provided. And since all the papers are the same size and bound together, they are more convenient than loose accounting paper.

Learning Guides

Some workbooks also contain learning or study guides, again closely correlated to a textbook. These guides—usually one or two pages per topic—are designed to help students gauge their understanding of the material presented in the topic. Moreover, the guides provide a convenient aid to students as they review the topic prior to testing.

Recently, some publishers have begun to offer individualized learning guides. These guides enable students to proceed at their own pace on a step-by-step basis, or they can be used to help a student make up missed classroom instruction. The learning guides usually include the following:

1. Performance objectives.
2. Text reading assignments and reading checks.
3. Answers, to permit students to verify their work.
4. Working papers necessary for the problems in the guide.
5. Additional problems to accomplish special objectives.

Practice Sets or Accounting Applications

A practice set is, in essence, a problem much longer than those found at the end of topics or chapters, and it is usually provided by the publisher as a separate component of an accounting program. Practice sets usually cover more than one accounting period and contain source documents that serve as the basis for most of the transactions.

Generally, a practice set integrates all the principles and procedures covered up to a given point in the textbook into one learning situation. For example, a practice set for a service business might include procedures for payroll, banking, and petty cash; therefore, it could be used any time after these topics have been covered. On the other hand, a practice set for a merchandise business might include subsystems for cash receipts, cash payments, purchases, sales, and payroll; thus it would be presented much later in the course.

Interacting Simulations

As realistic as publishers try to make their practice sets, two important features of a real working situation are missing: the interaction of individual students and a continuous flow of work. An interacting simulation provides these missing elements: Each student's work affects another's, and the work flow is uninterrupted.

In an interacting simulation, each student is assigned a specific task; for example, one student may be designated purchases clerk, while another is given responsibility for accounts payable. As in the real world of work, a mistake made by one accounting worker has a direct bearing on the work of a colleague. Participants in an interacting simulation are evaluated on such factors as attendance, cooperation, and mastery of job skills.

Tests and Teacher's Manuals

Most publishers provide teachers with tests correlated to the textbooks and with teacher's manual and keys. In some instances, the testing material consists simply of test banks from which the teacher can devise an examination. In other instances, printed test booklets or test masters are available from the publisher on request or are given in the teacher's manual.

The teacher's manual and keys run the gamut from those that simply provide solutions to textbook, workbook, and practice set problems to those that provide detailed teaching suggestions for each topic, solutions for all problems, lesson plans, and transparency and test masters.

Audiovisual Materials

Student understanding of concepts is greatly facilitated when ideas and relationships are presented visually. When used correctly, such visual and audiovisual materials as transparencies, chalkboards, bulletin boards, films, and filmstrips can add immeasurably to the teaching-learning situation. But because accounting is so rich in opportunities for using visual materials and the choice of possible materials is so wide, particular care should be taken to ensure that the material selected is appropriate to the situation and, more important, that it enhances and does not detract from student understanding.

There are several factors to consider when determining the appropriateness of one media over another. Is the learning situation one that requires a step-by-step presentation? If so, perhaps transparencies or chalkboards would be most effective. Should the material to be displayed be in view over a long period of time? If so, perhaps infrequently used chalkboards or bulletin boards are the best media.

Transparencies

The primary visual aid for teaching accounting is the transparency. Excellent transparencies are available from publishers, or they can be easily made by the teacher.

Some ready-made transparencies are simply blank accounting forms. While these may be useful for certain procedures, the same effect can be more economically achieved by running transparency masters provided in many teacher's manuals through a copying machine that makes transparencies. Other ready-made transparencies are designed to correlate with specific accounting textbooks. A set of these transparencies usually includes visuals that make use of color, overlays, and masks to provide a step-by-step presentation of the topic. Because of their direct tie-in with the textbook, they serve equally well to preview a topic, to reinforce instruction, or to review material that has been previously taught. Moreover, these transparencies are generally accompanied by guide notes that identify what should be emphasized with each transparency, provide points for discussion, and offer other teaching suggestions.

Chalkboards

With the possible exception of transparencies, accounting teachers use the chalkboard for demonstrations more frequently than they use any other type of visual aid. The following suggestions are proven methods of improving the effectiveness of chalkboard demonstrations.

ARRANGE FOR ALL TO SEE. An elementary principle of good teaching is that all board work should be so arranged and presented that every student can see and hear.

The direction of the lighting, the location and amount of chalkboard space, and the physical arrangement of the rooms vary so widely as to make specific suggestions impractical. Every teacher, however, should observe these precautions and checks:

1. Check all parts of the room to make certain that light glare does not obscure the view of the board from any part of the room. The light glare should be checked several times, as it varies with the time of day.
2. Make certain that the board is washed frequently so that the contrast between the board and the chalk is at a maximum.
3. Use yellow chalk to improve visibility.
4. Make certain that all board writing is high enough so that students in rear rows can see it.

PLAN FOR COMPLETION WITHIN PERIOD. The request "Do Not Erase" plagues many a teacher who shares classrooms with other teachers. It is a great temptation to retain on the board materials that have been carefully developed and that will be needed in a subsequent period. To tie up board space needed by other teachers, however, indicates a lack of consideration of others.

In planning a board demonstration, therefore, organize the material so that the demonstration can be completed within the class period. By limiting each illustration to the development of one key point, by stripping each illustration of all but the essentials, by preparing the preliminary work before the start of the class period, and by so planning the demonstration as to avoid any unnecessary delays, most accounting procedures can be demonstrated in one period.

Bulletin Boards

The bulletin board is especially useful for introducing a new topic, summarizing a unit of work, displaying student work, keeping abreast of current happenings in business, and exhibiting samples of business forms and records. As a motivational device, it sustains interest and serves as a source of challenge, pride, and aesthetic appeal. It helps to set the tone of a classroom and serves as a standard for neatness. A glance at the classroom bulletin board frequently gives an index to the personality of the teacher, the teacher's professional awareness, and the class achievement.

The following basic rules should be observed when using the bulletin board:

1. A bulletin board exhibit should have a purpose. Start with an idea rather than with material.

2. An exhibit should relate to the topic being studied.
3. The materials used should be accurate and up to date.
4. Bulletin boards should be changed frequently.

Films and Filmstrips

Where available, films and filmstrips are effective teaching aids for an accounting course. Films are particularly useful in the first session of the class to capture student interest in the course. Students respond especially well to those films that realistically present accounting workers in situations with which they can readily identify.

Filmstrips can serve many of the same functions that transparencies serve. Among these are the following:

1. To preview, summarize, or review topics.
2. To provide remedial instruction.
3. To help students make up missed classroom instruction.

Professional Organizations

A valuable and all too often neglected source of learning material is that provided by such professional organizations as the National Business Education Association (NBEA), American Vocational Association (AVA), and Delta Pi Epsilon. In general sessions, seminars, and workshops offered at local, state, regional, and national meetings, each of these organizations makes available to its members—and in many instances, to nonmembers as well—a wide variety of useful material.

Problems, Questions, and Projects

1. Examine two accounting texts that compete for the same level of instruction. Prepare a report in answer to the following questions.
   a. What approach is taken by the authors to cover the early accounting topics?
   b. How many steps are presented in the first accounting cycle? Name these steps.
   c. How are assets and liabilities presented in the first balance sheet?
   d. How is the word *capital* defined?
   e. What type of business is used to serve as the model throughout the presentation of the accounting cycle?
   f. In your opinion, what are the salient features of each of the approaches you studied?
2. Some teachers use one, others two, and still others use three practice sets during the first-year accounting course. What factors should be considered in determining the number of practice sets that should be used in such a course?

3. Demonstrate how you would teach one of the following by using transparencies.

    a. Punched-card or magnetic code.

    b. Computing net pay.

    c. System for controlling purchases.

4. Prepare a bulletin board display for use in motivating interest in some accounting topic.

Case Problems

1. Mrs. Morgan, an accounting teacher, disagrees with the balance sheet or equation approach to accounting. She prefers the journal approach. She starts by teaching the journal, and the students learn how to journalize transactions. Next, they learn the form of an account and how to post and to use the ledger, then how to prepare a trial balance, how to prepare financial statements, and so on, to complete the steps in the accounting cycle in sequence. Mrs. Morgan supports her approach with the following points:

    a. It teaches accounting in the same sequence as it is performed.

    b. It avoids relearning. The journals, accounts, and procedures are consistent from the beginning.

    c. It is faster, as the student begins the use of the ledger within the first few days of the course, and the presentation of the entire accounting cycle is speeded up.

What do you think of this approach?

2. To aid in checking of assignments, Mr. Trevino has the previous night's homework assignment placed on the chalkboard at the beginning of the class period. The students exchange papers and check the work against the board. Mr. Trevino reported having difficulty getting students to place their homework on the board until he announced that he would add 10 points to the grade of the paper of any student who volunteered to arrive at class early and place the work on the board. The daily rush of students arriving before class to earn the 10 points became so great that he had to set a maximum quota of 10s to be earned by any one student.

What do you think of this plan?

CHAPTER 5

Measuring and Evaluating Student Progress

Two of the primary responsibilities of any teacher are measuring and evaluating student progress; however, it is in the discharge of these responsibilities that the most marked differences in teaching philosophy, policy, and practice frequently occur.

This chapter examines methods of measuring student performance, with particular emphasis on testing, and presents suggestions for making value judgments based on the measurements. In this examination, as throughout this survey of the methods of teaching accounting, the importance of competency-based education models is stressed.

Measuring Student Performance

The essential aim of any evaluation method is to assess a student's progress toward specific goals, and it is on these goals that the two major types of student measurement are based. One type of measurement, *norm-referenced measure,* provides data about a student's progress only as it relates to the progress of other students. The other type of measure, *criterion-referenced measure,* provides data about a student's progress in relation to an established standard of performance.

Norm-Referenced Measures

Except in certain instances, the use of norm-referenced measures for determining student progress has been generally discredited. Clearly the major weakness of this type of measure is that it reveals almost nothing about a student's ability to perform a given task. At best, it might indicate that—when ranked together—Marie performs a specific accounting task better than Sam does; it does not indicate whether either Marie or Sam can or cannot successfully perform the task. In accounting, as in any competency-based discipline, the successful accomplishment of an assigned task is the essential criterion.

An evaluation based on norm-referenced measures thus has little or no merit in the accounting class. Indeed, many accounting teachers believe that the only appropriate application of norm-referenced measures is the use of standardized tests to determine students' reading levels and their understanding of basic mathematics.

Criterion-Referenced Measures

Precise data on a student's ability to perform a given task can be collected, however, through criterion-referenced measures, and such measures are a necessary element in any competency-based program. If, for example, the criterion for reconciling a bank statement is that the statement is to be reconciled with zero errors, all students who meet that standard have demonstrated their mastery of the task. One student's ability to accomplish the task is not measured against another's. As it should be in the world of work, individual accomplishment is the essential factor.

A competency-based program using criterion-referenced measures does, of course, imply that expected behavioral objectives have been clearly stated. The expected standard of performance must be both unambiguous and realistic; otherwise, there is no reliable yardstick with which to measure the outcome.

Testing

Tests are the most commonly used measuring device, and they should be used to help both the teacher and the student assess the quality of learning. Tests measure the success of the teacher in making the subject clear to the students and help students acquire a sense of confidence in tackling new topics. A testing program can achieve none of these outcomes with any degree of satisfaction, however, unless a proper psychological attitude toward testing is developed by both the teacher and the students. The following suggestions should help foster this attitude:

1. Make the testing program an integral part of the total teaching program. Tests provide both the means of continual diagnosis of individual needs of students and the basis for remedial instruction. Testing for remedial teaching is a fundamental part of an instructional program; if tests are used for grading purposes only, their full potential is not being utilized.
2. Promote a positive attitude toward tests. Negative attitudes are developed when students feel that unless they make a certain score on a test they will fail, when too much emphasis is given to grades, and when students who make low scores are criticized or embarrassed because of them.
3. Avoid associating tests with punishment. Never use a test as a punishment device. Indeed, tests should be scheduled only for positive instructional gain, not as time-fillers or as instruments of retribution.

4. Return tests promptly. Because tests are given to assess student understanding and to determine whatever individual or class diagnostic assistance is required, papers should be marked and returned as soon as possible—during the next class meeting.
5. Reteach on the basis of what has been learned through the tests. When tests are used as the diagnostic tool that they should be, the students begin to acknowledge tests as a means of detecting and overcoming individual learning problems.

Types of Tests

An effective testing program should include both performance tests and objective tests. While it is true that the best evidence of a student's mastery of a specific accounting competency is demonstrated in performance tests, they should not be used exclusively. Well-constructed objective tests are highly useful means of drilling for understanding of intricate principles and procedures and of pinpointing possible student confusion.

OBJECTIVE TESTS. Items in objective tests can be divided into two basic categories: supply-type items and selection-type items. A supply-type item asks the student to provide a response to either an incomplete statement or to a direct question; the response may be as short as a single word in a completion-type test or as long as one or more paragraphs in an essay-type test. Selection-type items require that the student choose a response from a list of two or more alternative answers. The most common forms of selection-type items are true-false questions, matching questions, and multiple-choice questions.

Many teachers have found the following suggestions helpful in preparing objective tests. Some of the suggestions apply to all forms of objective tests, while others apply mainly to specific forms.

1. General Suggestions
   a. State each item in simple terms so that its meaning is clear.
   b. Limit each item to one idea or point.
   c. Word items positively.
   d. Make every item independent of every other item.
   e. State an item in such a way that it does not provide clues to another item.
2. Suggestions for True-False Items
   a. Each item should contain only one factor.
   b. Avoid using such words as *all, always, never, often, only, seldom,* and *usually.*
   c. Do not alternate true questions and false questions in such a way as to create a discernible pattern.
   d. Ensure that each item is approximately the same length as other items.
3. Suggestions for Completion Items

    a.   Put the blank in each statement at or near the end of the sentence if possible.

    b.   Use only one blank in each item.

    c.   Word the sentence in such a way that its meaning is clear even with the answer omitted.

    d.   Use blanks of equal length.

    e.   Avoid using sentences exactly as they are worded in the textbook.

4.   Suggestions for Multiple-Choice Items

    a.   Use the same number or alternative answers for each item—four choices are usually preferred.

    b.   All choices should be plausible.

    c.   The main stem should be complete in meaning. The answer choices should not have to be read to understand the item.

    d.   All choices should be as equal in length as possible.

5.   Suggestions for Matching Items

    a.   Have the answer list contain more items than the statement list.

    b.   Arrange the answer list alphabetically or numerically.

    c.   Indicate whether an answer may be used more than once.

    d.   Make sure that the answer list is complete on a single page. Do not divide it on two pages.

PERFORMANCE TESTS.   Tests used to check both theory and procedure are called *performance tests.* They can be *product performance tests,* which require that the student produce a tangible item, such as a completed worksheet; or they can be *process performance tests,* in which a series of continuous student actions—such as those involved in operating a punched-card machine—are observed.

Performance tests are particularly well suited for measuring the ability of accounting students. The student's understanding of the theory and procedure involved in journalizing, posting, balancing and ruling an account, and preparing a financial statement is best gauged when the student is thrust into a situation that requires the performance of those tasks. A test evoking that situation may be organized around a problem similar to those provided in the textbook, around supplemental problems, or around an accounting simulation. If regular textbook problems are used, they may require some adaptation along the following lines:

1.   The test should be planned so that most students can complete it within the time established for the test—usually less than one period. Some teachers who argue that speed as well as ability is important in evaluation use time performance tests and include the speed factor when evaluating the test.

2.   Insofar as is possible, sections of the test should be independent so that the accuracy of one item or entry is not dependent upon the accuracy of a previous entry. Such a division makes it easier to determine student difficulties and also lessens student frustration.

Frequency of Tests

Accounting teachers disagree on how often tests should be given. Some rely heavily on tests and offer daily quizzes, while others keep testing to the minimum required by school policies. It should be pointed out that some students do well on short daily quizzes but have limited retention and do poorly on end-of-chapter and term tests. On the other hand, some students require several days to absorb new knowledge and skills and thus may do better on end-of-chapter and term tests than they do on daily quizzes.

DAILY QUIZZES.   In order to check on the degree of mastery of each lesson, many teachers give short daily quizzes. Some teachers give these short tests at the beginning of each period. Test questions designed to cover the topic covered in the preceding lesson are duplicated or written on the chalkboard, and the students begin work on the test as soon as they enter the classroom. Other teachers prefer to give these short tests at the end of the lesson to determine which points need further clarification before assignments are given for the next meeting.

These short quizzes are constructed by the teacher and vary in structure depending on the topic being tested. The students may be asked to complete a short problem, answer a series of four or five objective questions, or analyze one or more transactions. Generally, the tests are sufficiently short to be completed in less than ten minutes. Since the purpose of such tests is to determine what reteaching may be necessary, the tests are generally corrected immediately, often by simply having the students exchange papers and check answers. A show of hands gives the teacher an immediate error analysis to establish which points require reteaching. Usually, no records are kept of the scores made on these quizzes.

END-OF-CHAPTER TESTS.   A test at the end of each chapter is highly recomended. These tests focus attention on student difficulties in time for effective remedial instruction; they give the students the opportunity to evaluate their progress at regular intervals; and they provide the teacher with the information needed to determine necessary changes in teaching plans.

TERM TESTS.   End-of-term tests, unlike tests given throughout the term, can serve no real remedial purpose; rather, they can only serve as a device to measure what and how much the student has learned as a result of instruction.

Some teachers place great emphasis on these tests, pointing out that accounting is a pyramiding subject and that students should master all aspects of it. Others believe more in a cluster concept. They see accounting, like other competency-based subjects, as a cluster of individual competencies, each with a series of specific tasks. These teachers argue that if a student can master one or more of these separate competencies—for example, payroll or accounts receivable—full recognition should be made of that skill. They believe further that this concept is much more compatible with business practices, pointing out that many accounting workers in business function extremely well in limited-task jobs.

There is greater agreement, however, on usefulness of midterm tests. Like end-of-chapter tests, they serve as a valuable diagnostic tool and can assist a teacher in identifying areas of student confusion and the need for revising the lesson plan.

Evaluating Student Performance

Teachers who adhere to a strict interpretation of a competency-based educational model generally see no value in assigning specific grades. In their view, a student either demonstrates mastery of a given competency (or cluster of competencies) or does not. These teachers prefer to acknowledge this mastery by awarding the student a simple certificate. Teachers can easily prepare certificates that say, "This is to certify that _____ has successfully completed the training program for accounts receivable clerk. Signed _____." These can be duplicated for use.

Even the more traditional accounting teachers are divided on the subject of grading policy. Some believe in a strict numerical pattern: all work submitted by a student is graded and recorded; and the final grade is a numeric average of all the grades given to the students' assignments, tests, and other work. Other teachers primarily consider examination results. They feel that the important thing is what the student knows at the end of the term and that the test is the best index of what a student knows.

Still others believe that the best measure of student achievement is day-to-day homework and accordingly give extra weight to homework when assigning grades. While these teachers acknowledge that homework can be copied, they discount the possibility of continued copying going undetected. To some teachers, attitudes and growth in work habits are of paramount importance, while others contend that these intangibles are too subjective and too difficult to measure to be considered in grading.

Grades Based on General Criteria

Teachers who do not follow the philosophy of competency-based education models have a particular responsibility to be able to explain each student's grade. Because the inability to do so may lead to student resentment, the teacher must compile sufficient data—available in a form that is easily understood by the student—to justify an assigned grade.

For example, students' grades for a specific period might be based on several identifiable factors, as in this model:

Class contributions	25 percent
Homework assignments	25 percent
Test results	25 percent
Practice set	25 percent

This elementary model includes a variety of grading criteria, and it gives equal weight to all factors. Naturally, a teacher who feels that more weight should be given to some factors and less to others would adjust the percentages to reflect that philosophy. Others would add to or subtract from the list of factors to accommodate their grading policy.

Because teachers—even those within the same school system—do have different grading criteria, it is important that they tell their classes as early as possible in the term what factors will be included in the final grade and what weight is given to each factor. Once the grading model for a specific period of time has been established and announced to the class, the teacher should adhere to it.

The Individual File Folder

To accumulate data for grading, some teachers keep a file folder for each student. The following materials are placed in the folder:

1. Selected assignments. After assignments have been submitted, checked, and returned to the student for whatever correction, review, or discussion is needed, selected papers are filed in the student's folder. As an aid both in checking homework assignments and in reviewing them at the end of the marking term, some teachers duplicate a report sheet, which is attached to the assignments. This report sheet provides space for identifying the assignment and a place for recording with a check mark such information as whether the assignment was submitted on time or late and evaluation of neatness, handwriting, arithmetic calculations, form, and other points that the teacher wishes to emphasize. Space is provided for comments by the teacher.
2. All test results.
3. Other data that the teacher considers important in evaluating: special reports, committee work, evidences of attitude, leadership, and similar qualities.

At the end of the term, the teacher has in the folder a comprehensive picture of each student's work during the term. With this material and in conference with the student, the teacher is able to evaluate such points as the following:

1. The general quality of the student's homework.
2. Evidence of improvement or lack of improvement during the term.
3. Evidence of growth or lack of growth in neatness, handwriting, accuracy, promptness in submitting work, quality of work, attention to details, and ability to follow instructions.
4. Evidence of growth of knowledge as indicated by test scores and whether or not the student appears to be working up to capacity.

With these data at hand, the teacher is able, through conference, to point out to the student persistent weaknesses in his or her work, give suggestions for improvement, and thus explain and justify the student's grade.

Grading Based on Assignments at Different Levels

In almost any class, the abilities of the class members vary widely. To take care of individual differences, some teachers give assignments at different levels of difficulty. This is possible when the first problem for each new topic is a relatively easy one that gives practice in mastering the basic principles of the lesson and is to be worked by all students. The succeeding problems are of varying degrees of difficulty, and students may choose which ones they wish to attempt. The difficulty of the problem and the degree of success with which it is solved determine the grade. In most cases, the student may earn at least two different letter grades for each problem worked. An acceptable solution would earn the lower of the two grades, whereas an excellent solution would receive the higher of the two.

Problems, Questions, and Projects

1. Explain the difference between norm-referenced measures and criterion-referenced measures. Which do you think is more appropriate for assessing the abilities of accounting students?
2. Explain the purpose of a good testing program.
3. Choose some topic normally taught in the first-year accounting course. Prepare 15 true-false, 15 completion, and 15 multiple-choice test items based on this topic.
4. Choose a topic normally taught in first-year accounting, and prepare a product performance test covering that topic.
5. What are the advantages of daily quizzes?

Case Problem

Mr. Kahn finds himself facing a problem concerning one of his favorite students, Karen Hall, who has these qualities:

1. She regularly comes to class well prepared.
2. She is an aid to the teacher during discussion periods by asking meaningful questions and responding positively to Mr. Kahn's questions.
3. She does neat and accurate work on her daily lessons and always hands them in on time.
4. She consistently makes low scores on all tests taken—both performance and written tests.
5. She has a pleasant attitude toward school, is very interested in learning accounting, and enjoys the accounting class.

Mr. Kahn considers Karen the best student in his class. He has checked with her other teachers, and they report that she performs the same way in their classes—excellent on daily work but poorly on tests.

Mr. Kahn wants to give Karen the highest mark used by the school—an A—but he realizes that the other students in the class know that her test scores are low. He thinks he would be accused of favoritism by the other students.

What would be your advice to Mr. Kahn? Do you feel he should award a grade of A? If so, how would you justify this grade in view of her low test scores?

CHAPTER 6

Introducing the Course

Getting the accounting course off to the right start determines to a large degree the ultimate success of the course. Experienced teachers generally point to a number of considerations as contributing to much of their success. Among these are the preliminary preparations prior to the school's opening, the opening session, and the approach taken to develop the initial topics in the accounting course.

Preliminary Preparations

Arrive at the school a day or two before classes begin. (Many schools require this so that the teacher can attend the first faculty meeting.) In general, one should check to see that school-provided materials and supplies are available, that the classroom and chalkboards are clean, that the overhead projector and screen are in place, that the furniture and any calculators are arranged properly, and that all equipment is in working order.

In addition to these preliminaries, one should prepare an adequate supply of blank seating chart forms. Preparing a seating chart for each class offers a number of advantages.

1. A seating plan will prove valuable in learning the students' names rapidly and calling them by name after the second class period. Knowing students' names early is especially important when using the Socratic (question and answer) technique.
2. A seating chart will enable the teacher or a student proctor to check the roll in a few seconds.
3. If students are seated according to alphabetic or numeric plans, papers can be collected in proper order for recording. In a numeric plan, for instance, each student may be assigned a two-digit code. The first digit can represent the row; the second digit, the seat. Under this plan, students place assigned numbers next to their names on all papers.
4. A seating chart of each class allows the teacher to maintain reasonable control over valuable equipment and furniture. In this regard, up-to-date seating charts are especially important when two or more teachers share the same classroom.

5. And finally, a class seating chart gives the students the impression that the teacher is organized, and they assume that this same efficiency will be expected of them.

Perhaps the most important preliminary is the preparation of a teacher's curriculum guide. As the name suggests, a teacher's curriculum guide includes materials that assist the teacher to attain planned objectives. In general, this would include the broad aims of the course; a flexible time schedule of lessons based on a selected textbook and the amount of allotted teaching time; a list of supplementary materials, professional references, and other teaching aids; and an outline of specific performance goals by topic. As noted earlier, these performance goals or instructional objectives must be stated so that the teacher can communicate his or her instructional intent to the learner. It is important that these performance goals be stated in the teacher's own words. Failure to identify these instructional objectives, especially during the first few lessons to start the course, simply means that the teacher will not know what to expect of the students at the end of each instructional period. Furthermore, a total absence of carefully prepared instructional objectives will negate the usefulness of tests and examinations that may be used later. If students are to evaluate their own progress at any place along the learning route, then clearly defined performance goals must be included in a teacher's curriculum guide *before* the start of the course.

The Opening Session

The opening session will vary from school to school. In some school systems, teachers may be required to distribute books and supplies to each class; in other systems, this distribution may be done by the homeroom teacher; while in other schools, students may be required to obtain texts and supplies from a central bookstore or some other distribution center. In addition to distributing texts and other materials, many schools require the formal registration of students on the opening day. Where such procedures are required, they are bound to affect the amount of actual teaching time on the opening day. Consequently, some schools provide for an abbreviated teaching day to allow students to meet their teachers and to check their timetables; in other schools, students may be dismissed immediately after registration, thus deferring the opening session until the next day. Regardless of the system, the majority of experienced teachers support the view that formal instruction in accounting should begin only after administrative procedures are cleared and an opportunity has been given to organize the class and to motivate the students in the subject.

If formal instruction in accounting is to be deferred until after the first session, some of the following objectives may be included in the first teaching session.

Getting Acquainted

Successful teachers help students get acquainted with the teacher and with one another. Write your name on the board (or overhead projector) and pronounce it. Tell the class something about yourself and some of the things you enjoy doing in your spare time, or relate a humorous story or anecdote. In a large school or in a consolidated school where the students are not likely to know one another, it would be well to have students stand and introduce themselves, tell why they chose to study accounting, and how they plan to use it.

Class Organization

In the main, class organization involves the distribution of blank forms and other materials, the checking of the timetable and initial class roll, and the preparation of the class seating chart. As indicated earlier, the use of a seating chart is recommended for every class. The policy as to whether seats are assigned or whether students are to be allowed to select their own seats can be announced during this session. Students may be asked to select the seats they want the next day and thereafter keep those seats.

In addition, some teachers will assign classroom responsibilities such as erasing the chalkboard, taking the roll, and setting up audiovisual equipment. Before the teacher turns to the next part of the opening session's plan, it is recommended that a list of the essential supplies needed by each student for the course be placed either on a transparency for overhead projection, on the chalkboard, or on the bulletin board.

Survey of Students' Backgrounds

In order to become acquainted with the students, request each student to complete a form that provides autobiographical information or have them each write a brief autobiography.

Some teachers place information gained from the student biographies, such as previous courses, work experience, vocational objective, and occupations in the home, in code on the seating chart. This method assists in associating the information with the student for ready recall so as to involve the student in the class discussion.

Motivating the Students

Probably one of the most important objectives of the first session is to impart to the students a feeling that they are going to like both accounting and the teacher. Above all else, the opening day's session should be conducted in such a way that the students will leave their room at the end of the period feeling glad that they have been present.

How a teacher motivates the students in accounting during this first

67

session largely depends on the initiative and enthusiasm of the teacher for the subject, the availability of motivating aids, and the amount of class time. Clearly, what may work well for one teacher may not work at all for another; however, certain motivating aids have been tried by many teachers with a reasonable amount of success.

CLASS DISCUSSION. Some teachers can gain the interest of the students by discussing the values of studying accounting. This topic can be introduced as the students are introducing themselves, or it can be approached with the questions, "Why study accounting?" and "Of what value will the course be to you?"

Naturally, the type of answers will vary with the different objectives of the students. As the students volunteer answers, list each value on a transparency or on the chalkboard. A checklist should be prepared beforehand to make sure that the student answers do not exclude course values that can initiate a good class discussion. Such a list may include the following course values.

1. Provides an orientation to business operations and procedures.
2. Increases understanding of the economic aspects of business.
3. Gives preparation in recording financial activities, which one may be asked to assume in any office position.
4. Assists business owners and managers in making a decision; thus, the study of accounting is an important area of a management course.
5. Provides a background for the study of business data processing.
6. Provides a foundation for the continued study of accounting at post–high school institutions and with professional accounting bodies.
7. Provides competence in the management of personal business affairs.
8. Provides an opportunity to broaden one's general education through the study of a business language.

FILM ON ACCOUNTING. Where an appropriate film is available and class time permits, the showing of the film can generate enthusiasm for the study of accounting. In general, teachers agree that the film should be shown after the students have had an opportunity to present their reasons for registering in the course.

The film should be ordered well in advance of the viewing date, and the teacher should plan for some alternative should the film not arrive on the scheduled date or the order not be filled. When a film does arrive late, its showing will still be appropriate for any day during the first week.

CAREER BOOKLETS. Student interest can also be created through career booklets on accounting, which may be obtained from the different accounting bodies in the United States and Canada. Articles on accounting, culled from newspapers and magazines, provide another useful device through which student motivation can be gained.

SURVEY OF ADVERTISEMENTS.   The use of the overhead projector is especially recommended for a discussion of the varied positions available in accounting and related fields. Newspaper and magazine advertisements can easily be prepared on transparencies for presentation to a class.

The beginning students in accounting are often surprised to learn that accounting is often a springboard from which many top-level executive positions are filled. The teacher can enhance the appeal of the subject by including advertisements of positions like president, vice president of finance, treasurer, and controller, especially where a background in accounting is required. To keep up the enthusiasm for the subject, many teachers will assign class members the responsibility for maintaining a bulletin board display of current advertisements in accounting and related fields.

GUEST SPEAKER.   Guest speakers, particularly those with whom the students can identify, are an excellent means of opening students' minds to the potential of accounting and accounting-related jobs. Consider an accountant either in public, private, or government practice, or a former graduate who is using accounting in a business position.

Class Assignment

A fifth objective of the opening session's plan may include some form of motivating assignment. For example, some teachers may require the students to prepare a written report on the topic "Accounting and Me." Other teachers may ask students to talk to one or two adults to learn in what way accounting has been important to them. Several teachers may organize their classes to begin a bulletin board display of current advertised positions in accounting and other related fields. And still other teachers may prefer to exclude any form of assignment on this day. It is important to reemphasize the point that the objectives and instructions of any assignment must be communicated effectively. The successful teacher learns early that adequate class time must be provided to spell out the assignment details on the chalkboard, overhead projector, or on a duplicated handout, and also to give students the opportunity to ask questions.

In order to be at ease and have confidence when the class assembles, have a detailed plan for that first session—in fact, for each session. The plan should include a statement of the objectives to be accomplished and at least an outline of the day's procedure. One such lesson-plan outline that has proved successful is given in Figure 6.1.

Developing the Initial Topics

Once the necessary administrative procedures have been handled and the class has been organized and motivated, formal instruction can begin. Naturally, the methods used to develop the initial topics will be determined largely by the approach taken in the textbook selected for the course. Here

A First Day's Lesson Plan

PREPARATION BEFORE SCHOOL STARTS

1. Check equipment—desks and chairs, bulletin boards, chalkboards, calculating machines, projection equipment, projection screen, stapling machine, etc.
2. Check room arrangement—desks, lighting, window blinds, overhead projector, overhead screen.
3. Check supplies—chalk, erasers, board ruler, transparencies, projector lamp, adding machine tapes, wastepaper baskets, calendar.
4. Check textbook and workbook information.
   a. If materials are provided by school, note procedure for distribution and supply.
   b. If materials are purchased by students, note where they may be obtained.
5. Prepare required blank forms—seating charts, personal-data inventory sheets.
6. Prepare teacher's course of study.
7. Consider use of film or guest speaker.
   a. Arrange for obtaining film.
   b. Arrange for projection of film.
   c. Arrange for guest speaker.

OBJECTIVES

1. To get acquainted with the students.
2. To help students get acquainted with the teacher.
3. To help students get acquainted with one another.
4. To organize the class.
5. To get students interested in studying accounting—to sell the accounting course.
6. To maintain interest in accounting through an assignment.

PROCEDURES

1. Write name on chalkboard (overhead transparency), and call attention to spelling and pronunciation. (College teachers should give office location and hours.)
2. Write on the chalkboard (overhead transparency) the title, author, and publisher of the textbook and supplementary materials, and indicate where or how they are obtained.
3. List on the chalkboard (overhead transparency) supplies needed—pen, pencil, ruler.
4. Pass out personal-data sheets to be completed.
5. Pass out seating chart.
6. Have students introduce themselves.
7. Where applicable:
   a. Show film.
   b. Introduce speaker.
   c. Initiate discussion on course values.

(continued)

A First Day's Lesson Plan (*continued*)

    d. Distribute and review career booklets.

    e. Show survey of advertisements.

8. Where applicable, write assignment instructions on board or overhead transparency, and provide explanation.

MATERIALS

1. Copy of textbook, workbook, and all recommended supplies.
2. Blanks of personal-data sheets and seating chart.
3. Where applicable, film, prepared transparencies of advertised positions, career booklets.

Figure 6.1

the assumption is made that the textbook follows the equation approach, and lesson plans based on this approach are given for the first and second teaching sessions.

First Session

A lesson plan introducing the accounting equation is shown in Figure 6.2. In following this plan, note how quickly one can establish the first part of the equation by simply asking the question "What must a person have in order to begin a business?" Student responses will most likely include such items as cash, furniture, buildings, equipment. List these answers on the chalkboard, acknowledging that these are the economic resources of the business. Then explain that in the language of accounting these economic resources are called *assets*.

The next question, "How did the business acquire these assets?" will prompt the answer that the owner of the business must have contributed some money and possibly some of the other items. Emphasize that this contribution represents the investment of the owner in the business. If the other method of acquiring assets has not already been mentioned, point out that the remainder of the business assets must be obtained by borrowing. The relationship of debtor to creditor can be brought out at this point of the discussion.

From a teaching standpoint, notice that the accounting terms for liabilities and owner's equity have been avoided so far. These can be acknowledged later. At this point, it is important to establish the relationship of assets and the claims against the assets by presenting two basic equations as follows:

1.   Assets = Claims Against Assets
2.   Assets = Claims of Creditors + Claim of Owner

The stage is now set to present the basic accounting equation, using the **71**

A Lesson Plan to Introduce the Accounting Equation

OBJECTIVES

1. To identify at least three economic resources that a business person needs to begin a business.
2. To identify the two sources through which these economic resources are acquired: by borrowing and by the owner's investment.
3. To present the relationship of the economic resources (assets) and the claims against those assets in the form of a basic equation.
4. To present the accounting equation of a service firm owned by a sole proprietor.
5. To classify items under one of the three elements of the accounting equation.
6. Given the amounts of any two of the elements in the equation, to compute the amount of the third element.
7. To present an assignment on the accounting equation.

PROCEDURES

1. Ask the question, "What must a person have in order to begin a business?"
2. List on chalkboard (overhead transparency) suggested answers to the question.
3. Acknowledge these items as the economic resources of the business, and then explain that, in the language of accounting, these resources are known as *assets*.
4. Ask the question, "How did the business acquire these assets?"
5. List to the right of the assets previously suggested the two claims against the assets: borrowing (claims of creditors) and owner's investment (claim of owner).
6. Arrange the relationship of the assets and the claims against those assets in the form of a basic equation: Assets = Claims of Creditors + Claim of Owner.
7. Introduce the accounting equation with the three basic elements defined in accounting language: Assets = Liabilities + Owner's Equity.
8. Classify items under each element in the equation. (The word *capital* is to be avoided at this time; it will be introduced in the next lesson.)
9. Test the students' knowledge of computing one missing amount in the equation.
10. Write assignment details on the chalkboard or overhead transparency; then preview some of the problems.

MATERIALS

1. Clean chalkboard, white and colored chalk (or overhead projector plus transparencies and felt-tipped pens).
2. Textbook.
3. Workbook.

Figure 6.2

72

language of accounting. This equation could be illustrated as shown in Figure 6.3.

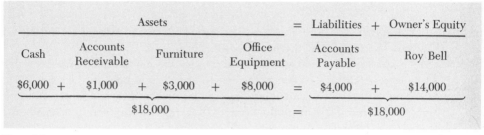

Assets				=	Liabilities	+	Owner's Equity
Cash	Accounts Receivable	Furniture	Office Equipment		Accounts Payable		Roy Bell
$6,000 +	$1,000 +	$3,000 +	$8,000	=	$4,000	+	$14,000
		$18,000		=		$18,000	

Figure 6.3

The critical teaching points in the above equation are these:

1.   The formal accounting term *liabilities* is used to relate to the earlier term *claims of creditors.*
2.   The term *owner's equity* becomes the formal accounting translation of the claim of the owner. Equity, therefore, is very quickly associated with the claim of the owner.
3.   Notice that both Accounts Receivable and Accounts Payable appear in the illustration. Discuss both terms without reference to the account records. There should be little difficulty since both terms are in common usage.
4.   Observe also that only round dollar amounts have been used to allow the student to compute easily and correctly the amount for owner's equity and to show that both sides of the equation have equality.
5.   And finally, notice that the term *capital* has been avoided; the owner's name is merely acknowledged under Owner's Equity. Many experienced teachers will agree that the term *capital* is much misunderstood by beginning accounting students; therefore, the term should be deferred until the next lesson. At this early stage, it is an advantage to get the students to learn and use the term *equity.*

Once the accounting equation has been presented, it is a simple matter to get the students to solve one unknown element in the equation. It is important, however, that the students recognize the placement of the three elements; that is, assets appear on the left and are equal to the liabilities and owner's equity, which are on the right. With this association, one unknown for either liabilities or owner's equity should easily be mastered.

Time should be planned to provide for a basic review and to introduce the class to an assignment that reinforces the understanding of the three elements of the accounting equation. This assignment should include basic problems (1) to test the students' knowledge to classify the fundamental elements of accounting and (2) to solve one unknown in a series of different equations.

Second Session

A lesson plan to follow the first lesson just described may be considered along the lines of the one illustrated in Figure 6.4.

As a general rule, teachers will use the first ten to fifteen minutes of the second teaching session of the accounting class to take up the solutions to the assigned problems. The actual procedures for reviewing these solutions will most likely be influenced by the type of problems assigned, the availability of equipment and teaching aids, and the objectives of the teacher. Some teachers will review assignment problems orally; that is, they will have different students read answers from their prepared solutions. Other teachers will prefer to take up the problems by assigning several students to the task of placing their solutions on the chalkboard. Where overhead equipment is available, however, many teachers now prepare transparency solutions for all assigned problems. Taking up assigned problems from prepared transparencies offers a number of advantages.

1. Valuable class time is saved. With prepared transparency solutions, the assignment review can be started immediately. No time is lost by requiring the solutions to be written on the chalkboard.
2. Students can view a model solution. A carefully prepared transparency will allow the students to check their answers against a model solution. This model becomes especially important when details in accounting forms and financial statements have to be learned.
3. The teacher is free to check students' work. Once a problem has been reviewed, the solution can remain projected to give the students an opportunity to make the necessary corrections. In the meantime, the teacher is free to walk around the room to inspect the work and to provide help to individuals where necessary.
4. Solutions can be stored for future use. After a permanent transparency solution is made, it can then be stored and used later as the need arises. This measure is particularly time-saving when publishers provide transparency masters from which teachers can make transparencies for the solutions to textbook problems.

The next part of the lesson plan calls for the reintroduction of the fundamental accounting equation used in the first session. After a quick review of the three fundamental elements, the teacher should establish the need for a more detailed summary of the equation in an accounting report known as the balance sheet. The teaching of the balance sheet in relationship to the accounting equation previously learned can be made effective through the teacher-explanation-demonstration technique. This teaching usually involves the following seven-step development.

A Lesson Plan to Continue the Discussion of the Accounting Equation

OBJECTIVES

1. To take up the solutions to the assigned problems.
2. To review the fundamental accounting equation presented in the first session.
3. To present the balance sheet in relationship to the accounting equation.
4. To introduce the balance sheet meaning for capital.
5. To review the balance sheet as to meaning, form, and details of writing dollar amounts and ruling.
6. To emphasize the meaning of the word *balance* in the balance sheet.
7. To provide assignment details on problems related to the equation and balance sheet.

PROCEDURES

1. Prepare transparency solutions to the assigned problems. Review the solutions from the overhead projector.
2. Review the fundamental accounting equation of the first session from a prepared transparency.
3. Using the teacher-explanation-demonstration technique, introduce the balance sheet in relationship to the fundamental accounting equation.
4. Teach the accounting concept for the term *capital.*
5. Review from the working model on the transparency the entire balance sheet. Stress meanings, form, and other specific details as to headings, writing dollar amounts in columns and outside money columns, ruling, balancing, and completing the financial statement.
6. Write assignment details on the chalkboard (or overhead projector) and preview the problems assigned.

MATERIALS

1. Prepared transparency of solutions to first session's assignment.
2. Prepared transparency of fundamental accounting equation.
3. Prepared transparency of working model of balance sheet in the account form.
4. Workbook (or blank balance sheet forms where working papers are not available).
5. Textbook.
6. Overhead projection pens.
7. White and colored chalk, chalkboard ruler.

Figure 6.4

STEP 1. Place on the overhead (or chalkboard) the model equation and the blank outline of the account form of the balance sheet shown in Figure 6.5. Be sure that the balance sheet form is aligned directly below the equation.

Distribute blank balance sheet forms to the class so that each student can

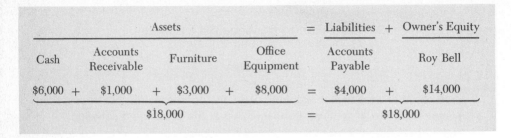

	Assets			=	Liabilities	+	Owner's Equity
Cash	Accounts Receivable	Furniture	Office Equipment		Accounts Payable		Roy Bell
$6,000 +	$1,000 +	$3,000 +	$8,000	=	$4,000	+	$14,000
		$18,000		=		$18,000	

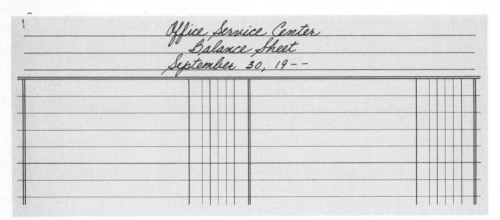

Office Service Center
Balance Sheet
September 30, 19--

Figure 6.5

make a copy of the financial statement as it is being taught for the first time. Present the need for a more formal presentation of the fundamental elements of the accounting equation.

STEP 2. Present a broad overview of the balance sheet form. Emphasize that there are two sections: (1) the heading to identify the statement and (2) the body in which the detailed summary of the accounting equation is entered.

STEP 3. Teach the heading section in answer to three basic questions: Who? (the name of the company); What? (the name of the statement); and When? (the date). The teacher-explanation-demonstration technique suggests a definite responsibility of the teacher to teach. Care must be taken to explain the three-line heading and how the heading is to be written. If the heading is to be centered over the body section, explain and demonstrate the procedure correctly; the students can translate this teaching to their working model. Of course, if the demonstration is poorly presented (either through weak chalkboard writing or through a weak transparency), students cannot be expected to attain the standards of the instructional objectives. It is important, therefore, that all teachers take time to improve both their chalkboard and overhead projection presentations.

STEP 4. Introduce the body section of the balance sheet in relation to the three elements of the fundamental accounting equation; therefore, the first element, assets, is presented on the left side of the balance sheet. This section can be illustrated on the overhead or the chalkboard as in Figure 6.6.

Assets				=	Liabilities	+	Owner's Equity
Cash	Accounts Receivable	Furniture	Office Equipment		Accounts Payable		Roy Bell
$6,000 +	$1,000 +	$3,000 +	$8,000	=	$4,000	+	$14,000
		$18,000		=		$18,000	

Figure 6.6

Once again, it is important to explain and demonstrate carefully each detail of the Assets section. The main teaching points to consider in presenting this section are the following:

a. The heading "Assets" is centered on the first line between the left margin and the left-hand money column.

b. The first asset is Cash. Explain and demonstrate the correct writing of both the asset item and the dollar amount in a money column. Explain the reason for the absence of the dollar sign in a ruled money column.

c. The second asset to be presented is Accounts Receivable. Notice that this item is summarized by indenting the name of the customer. If there are two or more customers, each name is indented and the separate amounts are written outside the money column. Explain the use of the dollar sign at the head of the column when a ruled money column is not used. Also explain and demonstrate how the single

77

line is ruled in order to extend the total of Accounts Receivable into the ruled money column.

Showing the term *Accounts Receivable* and the listing of the customers below it at this stage of teaching offers these advantages: First, students can relate customer names to the collective accounting term. Second, the breakdown of names supports the need for a detailed summary outside the accounting equation. And finally, the use of the term facilitates the later introduction of the need for a subsidiary ledger and the controlling account.

d.   After the last asset item, Office Equipment, is listed, stress the point that the total for the money column will be computed only after the other two elements in the equation are entered on the balance sheet.

Teachers often question the preferred order of listing the assets on the balance sheet at this stage of the accounting instruction. Some teachers avoid the issue by accepting any order listing at this time. Many high school teachers will teach the *liquidity order,* that is, in the order of converting each asset into cash, followed by nonconvertible assets. Formal classification of assets, they contend, can easily be introduced at a later point in the course. On the other hand, many college teachers insist on classifying the assets immediately into at least current assets and fixed assets in order to resolve the question. In the final analysis, the majority of teachers agree that it is important to present a specific order before the end of the first accounting cycle.

One other teaching point is worth considering before attention is directed to the right side of the balance sheet. Too many beginning students incorrectly believe that all of the asset "amounts" listed on the balance sheet represent actual market dollars. In general, this misconception stems from their common appreciation of assigning a dollar value to cash and accounts receivable. Now, while both cash and accounts receivable do show amounts that can be used to pay the debts and other expenditures of the business, it is also correct to say that other assets such as furniture and equipment are not acquired for the purpose of converting them into cash. In financial accounting, these assets represent economic resources that will be used to produce revenue through the sale of services (or goods as the case may be). To avoid any misunderstanding as to the dollar value in recording these assets, the accounting profession urges the teaching of the following generally accepted principle: A balance sheet does not purport to show either present values of assets to the enterprise or values that might be realized in liquidation. The accepted accounting basis for assets is the cost at the date of their acquisition.

In simple terms, explain that accountants prefer to record assets on the basis of the dollars that have been used to acquire these economic resources; the dollar amounts listed do not indicate the prices at which the assets could be sold. In the language of accounting, therefore, the "value" of an asset simply means the cost of that asset, and not the present value or worth of that asset.

STEP 5. The liabilities in the equation can now be presented in the balance sheet. Students should easily respond to a question for positioning the second element correctly in the balance sheet. A separate overlay may be used to illustrate this section, as in Figure 6.7. If the chalkboard must be used, then the Liabilities section can be illustrated in a different color.

Assets				=	Liabilities	+	Owner's Equity
Cash	Accounts Receivable	Furniture	Office Equipment		Accounts Payable		Roy Bell
$6,000 +	$1,000 +	$3,000 +	$8,000	=	$4,000	+	$14,000
	$18,000			=		$18,000	

Office Service Center
Balance Sheet
September 30, 19 - -

Assets		Liabilities	
Cash	6000 00	Accounts Payable:	
Accounts Receivable:		Modern Products	4000 00
King Stores	1000 00		
Furniture	3000 00		
Office Equipment	8000 00		

Figure 6.7

At this point, teachers who support the teaching of a specific order listing for assets introduce an order listing for liabilities. In general, this order could simply acknowledge that liabilities are listed in the order in which they must be paid. Two or three examples (bank loan, mortgage payable) could be used to illustrate the order. Of course, college instructors would probably insist on a more formal classification at this time.

STEP 6. In presenting the final element, the teacher can emphasize the importance of explaining owner's equity on the balance sheet. In review, the term *owner's equity* should be acknowledged as the general term that is used to indicate the total financial interest of the owner. It is at this point that the accounting concept for the term *capital* can be introduced. Just as the headings "Assets" and "Liabilities" have been expanded on the balance sheet to provide more explanation, so must the heading "Owner's Equity" be expanded. Explain carefully that to acknowledge the owner's investment on the balance sheet, use the term *Capital,* with a capital letter, after the owner's name. The concept of capital can be reinforced by showing the term both in the equation and in the balance sheet as in Figure 6.8.

	Assets			=	Liabilities	+	Owner's Equity
Cash	Accounts Receivable	Furniture	Office Equipment		Accounts Payable		Roy Bell Capital
$6,000 +	$1,000 +	$3,000 +	$8,000	=	$4,000	+	$14,000
		$18,000		=		$18,000	

Office Service Center
Balance Sheet
September 30, 19 - -

Assets			Liabilities		
Cash	6000 00		Accounts Payable:		
Accounts Receivable:			Modern Products	400 0 00	
King Stores	100 0 00				
Furniture	300 0 00		Owner's Equity		
Office Equipment	800 0 00		Roy Bell, Capital	1 400 0 00	

Figure 6.8

Why the delay in the introduction of the term *capital?* By introducing the word capital only at this stage, the correct meaning of the term in modern accounting practice is emphasized. In common usage, the word *capital* is often used to refer to money or wealth. Other traditional definitions, such as net worth, have also added to the confusion of beginning accounting students. To avoid any possible misconception, many accounting teachers favor the use of the general term *equity* in the equation first, and then introduce the more restrictive word *capital* in the balance sheet. The use of both terms can also serve to introduce a brief comparison of the equity section of the other two forms of business organization—the partnership and the corporation—as shown in Figure 6.9.

Single Proprietorship	Partnership
OWNER'S EQUITY	**PARTNERS' EQUITY**
Carl Case, Capital $7,400.00	Carl Case, Capital $7,400.00
	Ted James, Capital 7,400.00

Corporation

SHAREHOLDERS' EQUITY

Capital Stock $60,000.00

Figure 6.9

STEP 7. The final step in this first balance sheet is to present the concept of balancing. When explaining and demonstrating this concept, direct attention to the following details.

a. Place a single rule immediately below the final asset or the capital figure, depending on which one is farther down the money column.
b. Enter a similar single rule on the same line but on the opposite side.
c. Add each column and enter the total on the same line.
d. Place a double rule below each total to show that the balance sheet is now complete.

It is important again to emphasize the responsibility of the teacher to explain and demonstrate procedures. For example, students will learn how to rule a double line only when a teacher explains and demonstrates the ruling. The completed model would be similar to the one in Figure 6.10.

The remaining parts of the lesson plan call for a review of the entire balance sheet and the presentation of assignment details. At this point in the teaching, many teachers support the view that adequate time must be provided to allow students to complete the assignment in class. In this way, each student's working model could be checked and individual help offered where necessary.

Advantages of the Equation Approach

The salient features of the equation approach are these:

1. The use of the fundamental equation avoids the difficulty in teaching the details of the formal balance sheet. Teachers are able to concentrate on the three elements of the equation rather than on such details as asset and liability listing, use of money columns, and single and double rules.
2. The use of the term *capital* can be delayed until the balance sheet is presented.
3. The balance sheet is introduced as the formal presentation of the equation.

81

Assets				= Liabilities	+ Owner's Equity
Cash	Accounts Receivable	Furniture	Office Equipment	Accounts Payable	Roy Bell Capital
$6,000 +	$1,000 +	$3,000 +	$8,000 =	$4,000 +	$14,000
		$18,000		=	$18,000

Office Service Center
Balance Sheet
September 30, 19- -

Assets			Liabilities		
Cash		6000 00	Accounts Payable:		
Accounts Receivable:			Modern Products		400 0 00
King Stores		100 0 00			
Furniture		300 0 00	Owner's Equity		
Office Equipment		800 0 00	Roy Bell, Capital		1400 0 00
Total		1800 0 00	Total		1800 0 00

Figure 6.10

4. And finally, the teacher can now consider a return to the equation in order to analyze balance sheet transactions. In this way, a proper foundation can be laid to analyze the increases and decreases to the three elements without the use of accounts, journals, and the often troublesome accounting jargon of debits and credits.

Problems, Questions, and Projects

1. A prominent authority on the teaching of accounting says, "Tell your students the first day that the course will be easy, convince them that it will not be difficult, and then make good on your statement by teaching it in such a way that it is easy to learn." What is your reaction to this statement?

2. A class in methods of teaching accounting suggested the following activities as suitable for the first week of the course. Select those which you think are most worthwhile and indicate why.
   a. Invite one of last year's graduates to speak to the class.
   b. Have students tell why they are taking accounting.
   c. Give a brief history of accounting.
   d. Have each student visit someone she or he knows personally who is

employed in an office or doing some form of accounting work and discuss the employee's duties and activities.

e. Have students bring to class the classified section of the local newspaper and discuss the ads for people to work in the accounting area.

f. Distribute a complete outline of the course and discuss briefly each topic in the outline.

3. Assume that you have a beginning accounting class. In what order will you teach the listing of assets and liabilities on the first balance sheet? Give reasons for your answer.

4. Name the specific sections that you would include in a teacher's course of study.

5. The accounting equation may be stated in either of two forms: $A = L + OE$ or $A - L = OE$. Which form would you use to introduce the course? Give reasons for your answer.

Case Problems

1. Mr. Rutledge teaches in a high school serving primarily low-income families. Most of the students in his accounting class are underprivileged educationally, economically, and socially. The majority of the students in the accounting course are there because they "had to take something." They do not perceive themselves in the role of an office worker, as this type of work is outside their experiences. They have no contact with people who work in offices. The adults in their general circle work at non-office jobs. The students are not interested in school. Their major objective seems to be to "get out and make some dough." However, in the class there are a small number of sincere students, who, if properly trained, would be capable of obtaining jobs and working at the office-clerical level.

Mr. Rutledge is puzzled as to how he should proceed in order to (a) capture the interests of as many students as possible, (b) encourage more students to think of themselves in the role of an office worker, and (c) be sure that those who have the ability and interest can receive from the course the background needed. What suggestions would you make to him?

2. One teacher suggests that the last day of the first week in high school accounting be devoted to a discussion of good work habits. The teacher writes these words on the chalkboard, then discusses with the students the importance of these habits: neatness, care of equipment and supplies, promptness, regularity of attendance.

a. What do you think of this idea?

b. If you like it, how much time would you spend on it?

c. How could this point be presented more forcefully than by just telling students?

CHAPTER 7

Analyzing and Recording Business Transactions

When the teacher is certain that the students can identify the three basic elements (assets, liabilities, and owner's equity) and the relationship of these three elements in the formation of the basic accounting equation (Assets = Liabilities + Owner's Equity), the class is then ready to proceed to the next topic, analysis of business transactions. The introduction of the new topic, however, should not be rushed. The adage "make haste slowly" is especially applicable to accounting. Unless students thoroughly understand the basic principles presented in the beginning of the course, they may never understand accounting. Before examining the method of presentation, let us briefly review the accounting principles and procedures that are related to the analysis and recording of business transactions.

ACCOUNTING FUNDAMENTALS

1. Financial events that affect assets, liabilities, and owner's equity are called *transactions*.
2. A device called an *account* is used to record changes in assets, liabilities, and owner's equity resulting from transactions.
3. Each transaction affects at least two accounts, it must be expressed in terms of money, and the effect must leave the accounting equation in balance.
4. The left side of an account is the *debit* side; the right side, the *credit* side.
5. The *account balance* is the difference between the total debits and the total credits.
6. Asset accounts appear on the left side of the accounting equation. Thus they have *debit* balances. They are increased by entries on the debit side and are decreased by entries on the credit side.
7. Liability and owner's equity accounts appear on the right side of the accounting equation. Thus they have *credit* balances. They

(continued)

are increased by entries on the credit side and decreased by entries on the debit side.

8. A revenue increases assets and owner's equity; an expense decreases assets and owner's equity, or increases liabilities and decreases owner's equity.

9. Revenue and expense accounts are temporary owner's equity accounts.

Performance Goals

As mentioned in an earlier chapter, one way to state objectives for a lesson or unit is to present them as performance goals, also called *behavioral objectives*. As you will recall, a performance goal describes exactly what the student is to be able to do at the completion of the lesson or unit. The performance goals for the lessons on analyzing and recording business transactions are suggested below. The levels of performance that the student is expected to achieve are not included in the goal statement, since a number of factors, such as the ability levels of the students, the overall purpose of the course, and the measuring instrument to be used, must be considered when establishing performance levels.

1. Given the accounting equation showing the assets, liabilities, and owner's equity and their amounts, and given a list of transactions involving increases and decreases in assets, liabilities, and owner's equity, the student should be able to:
   a. Identify the basic elements changed by each transaction and determine whether the element is increased or decreased.
   b. Enter the amount of increase or decrease in the equation items changed by the transaction.
   c. Prove the equality of the equation after the transaction has been entered.
2. Given a series of incomplete statements involving the rules for recording in accounts the (*a*) balances and (*b*) increases and decreases in assets, liabilities, and owner's equity accounts, the student should be able to complete the sentences.
3. Given an accounting equation, the student should be able to prepare a T account for each item in the equation and enter the account balance on the correct side of the T account.
4. Given a series of transactions, the student should be able to:
   a. Analyze each transaction by identifying the accounts to be debited and the accounts to be credited.
   b. Record each transaction correctly in T accounts.
5. Given a list of definitions, the student should be able to identify the definition of each of the following terms:

85

net income	expenses	account title
net loss	account	debit balance
income	debit side	credit balance
revenue	credit side	

Method of Presentation

The importance of presenting new subject matter in terms of what the student already understands is emphasized in the preceding chapter. For this and other reasons, the accounting equation with which the students are now familiar is used as the point of departure in teaching the analysis of transactions. The equation for the service business is placed on the board or overhead transparency in the form illustrated in Figure 7.1.

	Assets		= Liabilities	+ Owner's Equity
Cash	Accounts Receivable	Furniture	Accounts Payable	Carl Case Capital
$6,000 +	$500 +	$1,500 =	$600 +	$7,400

Figure 7.1

The teacher may begin by saying, "Suppose the business takes $1,000 of the cash and purchases additional furniture with it. What changes will this make in the assets, liabilities, and owner's equity? What happens to the asset Cash? What happens to the asset Furniture? Are any of the other items affected?"

From the student responses, the teacher then shows on the board or transparency (see Figure 7.2) the changes that occur by adding and subtracting to the initial equation (already on the board or transparency).

The equation is then totaled to show that the total assets equal the total

	Assets		= Liabilities	+ Owner's Equity
Cash	Accounts Receivable	Furniture	Accounts Payable	Carl Case Capital
$6,000 +	$500 +	$1,500 =	$600 +	$7,400
−1,000		+1,000		
$5,000 +	$500 +	$2,500 =	$600 +	$7,400

Figure 7.2

liabilities and owner's equity; thus the equality of the equation has not been disturbed by the purchase of this asset.

The teacher then points out that financial events that affect one or more of the basic elements are called *transactions*. The purchase of the furniture was a business transaction because it affected the element assets. Each transaction must be analyzed to determine which basic elements are affected and how each element is changed. The transaction analysis shown in Figure 7.3 is then written on the board or transparency.

TRANSACTION	ANALYSIS
Paid $1,000 cash for furniture.	1. The asset *Furniture* increases by $1,000 because the business now owns more furniture. 2. The asset *Cash* decreases by $1,000 because the business now has less money.

Figure 7.3

Following the same procedure, these types of transactions are presented:

- Collecting an account receivable.
- Buying an asset on credit.
- Returning an asset bought on credit.
- Paying a liability.
- Increasing owner's investment.
- Decreasing owner's investment.

For these transactions, however, it is suggested that the sequence of presentation be changed by first analyzing the transaction and then showing its effect on the items in the equation. Thus, after each transaction has been presented, the class is asked to analyze it. The equation on the board or transparency then should be changed by adding or subtracting to show both the effect on the elements and the status of the equation after the transaction.

Each type of transaction should be repeated and reviewed until the students are able to analyze the transactions and record the changes on the basic equation. Homework, followed by testing, would be used to make certain that students are ready to move to transactions involving revenue and expenses. When the students are ready, revenue and expense transactions can be presented by adding to or subtracting from the equation.

Revenue and Expense Transactions

The equation is also used to explain revenue and expense transactions by pointing out that when a business sells services it obtains an asset—cash or an account receivable. Thus the left side of the equation increases. The right side of the equation consequently increases by the same amount because the total claim against the assets must always equal the total of the assets. Since liabilities are not affected by revenue transactions, the owner's equity must be increased.

In a like manner, the teacher may explain that when an expense is incurred, either the assets side of the equation decreases (expense is paid in cash) or the liabilities increase (an account payable is incurred), thus causing the owner's equity to decrease.

The revenue may be added to, or the expense subtracted from, the owner's capital amount in the equation. The preferred plan, however, is to list a new item called *net income* in the owner's equity section of the equation. Revenue is added and expenses are subtracted in this column, the balance of the column being the net income.

At this point, it will be necessary to explain (1) the meanings of *net income* and *net loss* and their relationship to owner's equity and (2) why it is preferred to identify this amount in a separate column instead of adding it to or subtracting it from the capital amount directly. A revenue of $800 and an expense of $300 are shown in Figure 7.4. The difference is a net income.

TRANSACTION	ANALYSIS
Received $800 cash as revenue from the sale of services.	1. The asset *Cash* increases by $800 because the business now has more money. 2. Owner's equity increases by $800 because the business now has earned revenue.
Paid an expense, $300 for rent.	1. The asset *Cash* decreases by $300 because the business now has less money. 2. Owner's equity decreases by $300 because the business has incurred an expense.

		Assets			=	Liabilities	+		Owner's Equity	
Cash	+	Accounts Receivable	+	Furniture	=	Accounts Payable	+	Carl Case Capital	+	Net Income
$5,000	+	$500	+	$2,500	=	$600	+	$7,400		
+800										+$800
−300										− 300
$5,500	+	$500	+	$2,500	=	$600	+	$7,400	+	$500
		$8,500			=	$600	+		$7,900	

Figure 7.4

The T Account

When students have demonstrated their ability to analyze transactions and record their changes in the equation, the class is ready to move to the next topic, the use of accounts. The teacher might say, "If a business had many transactions each day, you can see that it would be very impractical to continue to add to or subtract from the basic elements and recopy the figures in the equation after each transaction. Therefore, a special device is used in accounting to record the changes resulting from transactions. This device is known as an *account.*

"Various forms of accounts are used in business, but for the present we shall use the simplest form. It is called a *T account* because it resembles the letter *T.*"

A large *T* is drawn on the chalkboard or transparency and the equation placed above it. The items (Cash, Furniture, etc.) shown on the equation for the Case Service Company are set up in T accounts, with the assets accounts placed on the left side and the liabilities and owner's equity accounts placed on the right as shown in Figure 7.5.

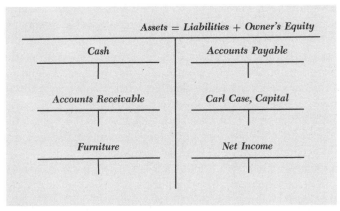

Figure 7.5

The amounts in each account would then be entered in the accounts as shown in Figure 7.6.

The purpose of this procedure is to relate the account and the account balance to the equation and to develop through the deductive process the following principle: Since assets are placed on the left side of the account-

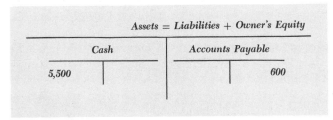

Figure 7.6

ing equation (A = L + OE), the amount of each asset account in the equation is entered on the left side of the appropriate account. Since liabilities and owner's equity are on the right side of the equation, the amount of each liability and owner's equity account in the equation is entered on the right side of the account.

ACCOUNT TITLES. A brief explanation of the account title should be made. The explanation might be given in the following way, referring to an illustration such as Figure 7.7.

Figure 7.7

"The heading written at the top of each account is known as the *title of the account.* Each account title should be brief but descriptive of the type of items to be placed under it. The title of an account with a creditor contains two parts—*Accounts Payable* (*Accts. Pay.*) and the name of the creditor. If someone owes the business money, the title of that account should also contain two parts—*Accounts Receivable* (*Accts. Rec.*) and the name of the person. The inclusion of the abbreviations *Accts. Pay.* or *Accts. Rec.* in the title of a customer or creditor account identifies whether the account is an asset (receivable) or whether it is a liability (payable)."

Another major advantage of the two-part heading is that it simplifies the teaching of the controlling account concept when subsidiary accounts receivable and accounts payable ledgers are introduced.

DEBITS AND CREDITS. Debits and credits and additions and subtractions to accounts might be explained in this manner:

"We will now learn two new terms [the terms *debit* and *credit* are placed on the chalkboard or transparency]. You have observed that an account has two sides. The left side is called the debit side. The right side is called the credit side.

"When amounts are entered on the left side of an account, they are called *debits* and the account is said to be *debited.* When amounts are entered on the right side, they are called *credits* and the account is said to be *credited.* Each amount entered on the left side of an account is called a *debit entry.* Each item entered on the right side of an account is called a *credit entry.*

"The increase side of an account is determined by the position of the account in the equation. Assets are on the left side of the equation; therefore, when an asset is increased, the entry is made on the left side of the asset account. Liabilities and owner's equity are on the right side of the equation; therefore, when a liability or the owner's equity is increased, the entry is made on the right side of the account.

"Addition and subtraction in accounting are indicated by position.

When an asset is decreased, the amount of the decrease is always written on the credit (minus) side. When a liability or owner's equity is decreased, the amount of the decrease is always written on the debit (minus) side. It is obvious now that debit does not mean *increase,* for in some cases, accounts are *decreased* by debiting them. Debit refers to the left side and has that meaning only."

You may then develop an illustration such as Figure 7.8. Point out that the difference between the two sides of an account is known as the *account balance* and then try to get the students to identify the balance of an asset account, a liability account, and an owner's equity account and to explain why the account has a debit or credit balance.

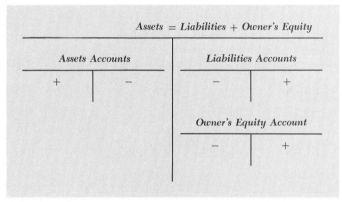

Figure 7.8

PROCEDURE FOR ANALYZING TRANSACTIONS.   The emphasis so far has been on helping students to understand "why"—why an asset account is increased by an entry on the debit side, why a liability account is increased by an entry on the credit side. It is this understanding that enables the student to apply knowledge from one type of transaction to another and from the classroom to work. The same emphasis on "why" should be continued when students begin recording transactions in T accounts. One way of achieving understanding, as opposed to memorization, is to continue to insist that students analyze each transaction before entering it. The teacher can assist students by writing these three analytical steps on the chalkboard or transparency:

1. What happens? What accounts are affected? What are the classifications of the accounts? How are they affected (increased or decreased)?
2. Which accounting rules apply?
3. What entry is to be made?

Figure 7.9 gives the analysis, according to these three steps, for the following transaction: The business placed $1,000 in a savings account.

Analysis of the Transaction: The business placed $1,000 in a Savings Account

WHAT HAPPENS?	ACCOUNTING RULE	ENTRY
The asset *Savings Account* increased by $1,000.	To increase an asset, debit the account.	Debit: Savings Account $1,000
The asset *Cash* decreased by $1,000.	To decrease an asset, credit the account.	Credit: Cash $1,000

Figure 7.9

The students are then drilled in analyzing transactions which include the following:

- Changing one asset for another asset.
- Obtaining an asset through incurring a liability.
- Paying a liability.
- Increasing and decreasing the owner's investment.

Transactions involving revenue and expense accounts would not be included. The method of handling revenue and expense transactions is discussed later in the chapter.

To get students to think about and analyze each transaction is not easy. They tend to take shortcuts, saying merely, "Debit Savings, credit Cash" or "Debit M&M Company, credit Cash." Such answers may be a guess or a parroting of a response they have heard. An effective but easy way to obtain a complete analysis of each transaction is to place on an infrequently used section of the chalkboard the following outline:

The _____ account _____ is _____
      (Classification)   (Name of   (Increased,
                         account)   decreased)

therefore, it is _____ for _____ .
          (Debited,   (Amount)
          credited)

Whenever a student takes a shortcut in the analysis, the teacher merely points to this outline as a reminder to the student to restate the analysis following the outline. If this outline is left on the board for several days and used as indicated, it will soon become unnecessary. Students will have developed the habit of following the desired sequence in the analysis.

To ensure that students analyze transactions when doing their out-of-class assignments, some teachers duplicate a form similar to Figure 7.10 and ask students to fill in this form for each transaction before they record the transaction.

CLASSIFICATION OF ACCOUNTS. Exclusive of arithmetic errors, errors in accounting are of two major types—errors in theory and errors in mechanics. A study of theory errors that were made by accounting students

TRANS-ACTION	WHAT HAPPENS?	ACCOUNTING RULE	ENTRY
1			
2			
3			

Figure 7.10

revealed that one of the most prevalent weaknesses pertained to account classification. Students debited or credited accounts incorrectly because they had classified the account incorrectly.

To emphasize account classification, many teachers follow these steps:

* *Always present each new account by showing its proper relation to the accounting equation.* The way to present a new account is to open the T account under the proper account classification in the accounting equation.
* *Always classify accounts when making entries.* The teacher not only follows this procedure, but also requires the students to do likewise during oral recitation.
* *Provide adequate practice.* The practice procedure must be varied to maintain interest and learning at a high level.

Before introducing revenue and expense accounts, students need to be given time to master the principles of debits and credits as they apply to assets, liabilities, and owner's equity.

Revenue and Expense Accounts

A suggested procedure is first to record all changes in the owner's equity (investments, withdrawals, revenues, and expenses) in the one account—Capital. This procedure develops the concept that the owner's investment and revenues are increases in the owner's equity and are recorded on the credit side of the account and that withdrawals and expenses are decreases in owner's equity and are recorded on the debit side.

After the basic concept of the relationship of the revenue and expenses to the owner's capital account has been established, the advantages of using separate revenue and expense accounts may be presented. This may be done by pointing out that separate accounts are used for the various types of assets and various types of liabilities so as to provide a better description of assets and liabilities. Likewise, separate accounts are used to record changes in the owner's equity resulting from changes in investment, from revenue, and from expenses. Thus, instead of having only one owner's

93

equity account (Capital) and recording all changes in this one account, separate and temporary owner's equity accounts are set up for revenue items and expense items. These temporary accounts are shown as subdivisions of the Capital account. A three-step development sequence such as the following is suggested.

1. All changes in owner's equity are recorded in one account. See Figure 7.11.

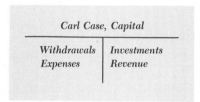

Figure 7.11

2. A separate temporary account for expenses and a separate temporary account for revenue are established, and *all* expenses and *all* revenue are recorded in these two accounts. See Figure 7.12.
3. A separate temporary account is used for each type of expense and revenue. See Figure 7.13.

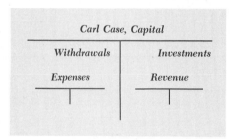

Figure 7.12

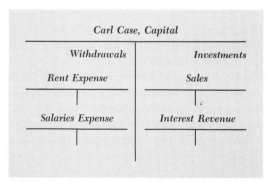

Figure 7.13

The relationship between the expense accounts and the debit side of the Capital account, as well as the one between the revenue accounts and the credit side, should be emphasized.

This slow but systematic sequence of development pays dividends when the class comes to the topic of closing entries. The students readily recognize that closing entries merely transfer the balances in these temporary revenue and expense accounts back to the owner's Capital account where they were initially recorded.

Suggested Drills

Much drill is necessary on such basic elements as whether an account (1) is an asset, liability, or owner's equity; (2) has a debit or credit balance; or (3) is increased by a debit or by a credit entry. The drill must be varied to maintain interest, and it must be well planned and executed so as to obtain the maximum benefit. A number of different drills employing various instructional media may be used. For example, a list of account titles might be placed semipermanently on the chalkboard, projected on an overhead projector, duplicated and distributed to the class, or individually printed on flash cards. No matter which medium is used, the students are asked to respond orally to the following questions:

1. Is the account an asset, liability, or owner's equity account?
2. Would the account have a debit or credit balance?
3. To increase the account, would you debit or credit it?
4. To decrease the account, would you debit or credit it?

Another type of drill that might be used is a completion drill. A list of incomplete statements is duplicated and distributed to the students, who are required to complete each of the statements. The list may contain statements such as the following:

1. The financial interest that an owner has in a business is called _____ .

2. You decrease an asset by placing the entry on the _____ side.

3. All asset accounts have _____ balances.

An effective drill on transaction analysis can be devised with a pegboard. The board may be used in two ways: (1) A transaction is given, and the students are asked to show the effect of the transaction on the basic elements. (2) An analysis is made on the pegboard, and the students are asked to indicate which transaction would result in these changes in the basic elements.

95

Visual Aids

The chalkboard and the overhead projector are indispensable to the presentation of this topic; the suggestions for the effective use of these instructional media presented in Chapter 4 should be observed. The transparencies can be either teacher-made or obtained from various suppliers. Those transparencies correlated to a specific text might be particularly useful for presentation and review purposes. Similarly, text-correlated filmstrips might be employed to present and review the topic, and flash cards, while not suitable for initial presentation, might be effective for drills and reviews.

Questions and Projects

1. One author states that accounting "is a pyramiding subject." What does this mean? What are the implications of the statement for teaching?

2. Some teachers criticize the use of the T-account form. They believe the regular ledger account form should be used from the beginning even though not all of the columns may be used at first. They say that if the T-account form is used, relearning is required once the regular account form is introduced. What is your reaction?

3. Some instructors place a plus sign and a minus sign at the top of each account when it is first introduced to assist the students in determining which side is the increase side and which side is the decrease side. What do you think of this plan? What are its advantages? disadvantages?

4. A student presents the following question, "Expenses represent decreases in the owner's equity. Decreases in liabilities and owner's equity are recorded on the debit side of the account. Yet to record *an increase* in an expense, you *debit* the account. Why is this?" Give your answer.

5. One author proposed what he calls the get and give concept. The students, according to the author, should ask the simple question, "What did the business *get* and what did the business *give*?" You debit the items you *get* and credit the items you *give.* What is your reaction to this approach?

6. What answer would you give a student who asked, "How can we tell if we are keeping our total debit amounts equal to the total credits?"

7. The chapter emphasizes the importance of the physical arrangement of the revenue and expense accounts when first introduced in relation to the debit and credit sides of the Capital account. Why is this important?

8. Complete one of the following projects:
   a. Create a set of flash cards and demonstrate their use.
   b. Prepare a demonstration on how you would use the overhead projector to drill on account classifications and on the rules of debit and credit.
   c. Devise a game or contest you could use for drill in account classification. Prepare copies for distribution to the class.

Case Problems

1. An experienced teacher uses the deductive method of teaching analysis of transactions.

Accounts and transactions are not analyzed on the basis of the basic equation or balance sheet. When accounts are first introduced, the students are told by the teacher that "when you receive cash, you debit the Cash account; when you pay out cash, you credit the Cash account; when you incur a liability, you credit the liability account; when you pay a liability, you debit the liability account."

The students then drill on recording transactions. The teacher illustrates each transaction on the chalkboard until the students are able to proceed on their own. After the students have learned how to record transactions, they develop the principles deductively. From practice, they deduce that assets are increased by debits; liabilities, by credits; and so on. At this point, the teacher directs the class discussion to show the relationship between the account and the basic equation and the balance sheet.

The teacher defends this procedure on the basis that learning is more effective and permanent when students develop the fundamental principles and rules through practice. Thus the rules grow out of practice instead of practice being an application of the rules.

What is your evaluation of this teacher's procedure?

2. To assist students in analyzing transactions, a teacher distributes a duplicated chart on which typical transactions have been fully analyzed and entered for student reference. When the chart is distributed, each transaction is explained by the teacher, the students following the chart. The students are instructed to place the chart in their notebooks and to refer to it when necessary in doing their homework. If students come across a transaction they do not know how to analyze and record, they refer to the chart, find the equivalent transaction, and study how it is analyzed and recorded. What do you think of this plan? Explain your answer.

CHAPTER 8

Teaching About Journals

As soon as it is evident that the students can analyze business transactions by identifying the account to be debited and the account to be credited and that they can record each transaction correctly in T accounts, the class can go on to the study of journals. It is often useful, however, to begin this topic with a discussion of the recording of transactions on source documents and the use of these source documents in making journal entries. But first, let us review some of the accounting fundamentals related to journalizing.

ACCOUNTING FUNDAMENTALS

1. Transactions that affect assets, liabilities, and owner's equity should be captured on source documents.
2. There are many kinds of source documents, but the two most important ones in accounting practice are invoices and checks (cheques).
3. The dollar results of each transaction are listed in strict chronological (or numeric) sequence in a daybook or diary called a *journal*.
4. Since transactions generally are captured on source documents, it follows that a journal is a chronological (or numeric) listing of all source documents.
5. Two types of journals are common to most accounting systems: (*a*) a specialized journal in which are recorded the dollar results of highly repetitive transactions and (*b*) a general journal in which are recorded the dollar results of transactions of a nonrepetitive type that are not recorded in a specialized journal.
6. Names and styles of specialized journals differ with special kinds of business enterprises. The following types of specialized journals are commonly used in merchandising (trading) and manufacturing businesses:
   a. *Cash receipts journal*—a chronological listing of all cash receipts (also common to service enterprises).

(*continued*)

      b. *Cash payments* or *disbursements journal*—a chronological listing of all cash payments (also common to service-type enterprises).

      c. *Sales* or *revenue journal*—a chronological listing of sales made on credit (also common to service enterprises).

      d. *Purchases journal*—a chronological listing of purchases of merchandise (raw materials in manufacturing) on credit from suppliers.

      e. *Payroll journal* or *register*—a chronological listing of all payrolls (also common to service-type businesses).

7. Where the volume of transactions is quite low, the general journal and all the special journals may be combined into a single journal called a *combination journal,* or *synoptic journal.*

8. Traditionally, the journal was considered a book of original entry, because the debits and credits for transactions that affect the general ledger are recorded in a journal before they are transferred to the book of secondary or final entry, that is, to the general ledger.

9. Because every transaction of the enterprise must be recorded in the form of a double entry, the total of the debit entries must be equal to the total of the credit entries.

Performance Goals

The performance goals for lessons on the various journals are offered here. Remember that only part of the suggested instructional objective may be appropriate for an individual lesson; for example, the teacher may select one or two of the definitions for a particular lesson. On the other hand, the teacher may prefer to delay the communication of a performance goal until all of the related accounting terms or all of the special journals have been covered.

1. Given a list of transactions involving sales, purchases, cash receipts, and cash payments, the student should identify correctly the source document that originated the particular transaction.

2. Given facsimiles of source documents or a list of source document names for cash and credit sales, cash and credit purchases, cash receipts from customers, and cash payments to creditors, the student should be able to (*a*) give the correct debit and credit analysis for the document and (*b*) identify the correct journal in which the source document would be recorded.

3. Given a list of definitions, the student should be able to identify the definition of each of the following terms: *accounting cycle, compound*

99

journal entry, journal, journalizing, opening entry, originating data, and *source document.*

4. Given a series of transactions, the student should be able to record each transaction in a two-column journal. All dates should be entered correctly, the correct accounts and amounts should be debited and credited, all items should be placed in the correct columns, and the indentations should be correct.

5. Given a list of definitions, the student should be able to identify the definition of each of the following terms: *special journal, cash receipts journal, general journal, memorandum entry, purchases journal, sales journal, cash payments journal, combination journal,* and *journal voucher.*

6. Given a series of transactions involving the receipt of cash, the student should be able to record each transaction in a cash receipts journal with all dates, accounts, explanations, and amounts entered correctly.

7. Given a series of transactions involving the payment of cash, the student should be able to record each transaction in a cash payments journal with all dates, accounts, explanations, check numbers, and amounts entered correctly.

8. Given a series of transactions involving purchases of merchandise, payments for merchandise, and purchases returns and allowances, the student should be able to record each transaction in correct form in the proper journal.

9. Given a series of transactions involving credit sales, cash received on account, and sales returns and allowances, the student should be able to record each transaction in correct form in the proper journal.

10. Given the required payroll data, the student should be able to enter the data in the payroll journal (register) with all data entered correctly in the appropriate columns.

11. Given a series of transactions to be recorded in a combination journal, the student should be able to indicate the accounts to be debited and credited and the columns to be used in making each entry.

12. Given any special journal for which entries have been recorded for a particular accounting period, the student should be able to prepare a journal proof of the column totals before the totals are posted to the general ledger.

Teaching the Concept of Originating Transaction Data

Traditionally, authors and teachers have delayed the study of source documents until the end of the first cycle when a practice set is introduced. In the presentation of the first cycle, therefore, the student associated the first step of the accounting cycle with the process of journalizing. Now authors and teachers support the early identification of originating transaction data through a study of common source documents, for the following reasons:

- The student is able to relate the transactions examined in the earlier topics with the concept that transaction data is generally supported by source documents.
- The student is able to define the journal as more than just a book of original entry. By introducing the concept of originating transaction data on source documents, the student can view the journal as a chronological listing of source documents.
- The student is able to identify that the first step in any analysis of an accounting cycle is to capture transaction data on source documents; thus journalizing may correctly be viewed as the second step in the accounting cycle.
- The student is able to better understand future source documents as they are introduced in relation to the study of new transactions.
- The student is able to better comprehend the relationship between the various steps in the accounting cycle and the overall accounting system.
- The student is able to respond more quickly to the study of the journalless system of posting directly from source documents to a subsidiary ledger.

Method of Presentation

One way to introduce the concept of originating transaction data is to review the transactions previously analyzed within the study of the accounting equation. For example, the teacher places on the chalkboard or overhead a transaction where the firm buys office equipment from a supplier on a 60-day credit basis. A student is then asked what evidence exists to prove that the transaction actually happened. If the student correctly responds that the buyer receives a copy of the sale—the sales invoice—the teacher should be prepared to show an actual example of the document. The document may be shown on an overhead projector so that the entire class can study it and review the debit and credit analysis of the transaction reflected by the document.

Additional transactions may then be presented so that the class can relate the transaction to a particular document or set of documents. It is important to emphasize that each document or set of related documents will contain all the facts about a particular transaction. Once the students have been introduced to the idea of originating transaction data through different source documents, student reinforcement of this learning may be applied in accordance with the first two performance goals suggested earlier in this chapter. The student should respond not only to a set of narrative transactions, but also to examples of actual source documents or facsimiles of such documents.

Introducing the Journal

The question is frequently raised whether journalizing should be introduced through the two-column journal or through multiple-column and special journals. Those accounting teachers who favor the latter maintain that the use of multiple-column and special journals is more realistic because the two-column journal is not extensively used in business. In a large business—one in which several persons are engaged in keeping the company's books—work can be done more quickly and efficiently when specialization is utilized; therefore, special journals are used. In a small business—one in which all records are kept by one person—the work can be expedited if all transactions are recorded in a single journal with several money columns.

Most accounting textbooks and teachers, however, introduce journalizing through the two-column journal for the following reasons:

- Students learn best when instruction proceeds from the simple to the complex. The simplest form of journal is the two-column journal, in which all types of transactions may be recorded. It has two money columns—the fewest that can be used for the double-entry system. It is the most effective journal medium for developing the meaning of double-entry accounting since every transaction will show an equal debit entry for an equal credit entry. It emphasizes the debit-credit relationship.

- The purpose of the first unit on journalizing is to develop an understanding of the basic principles of journalizing, and this can best be done through the two-column journal. The multiple-column journal is just an expansion of the two-column journal; whether the journal contains two, four, six, or twenty columns, the basic principles are identical. Moreover, special journals originated from the two-column journal and the need for special journals and their value can be shown only through comparison with the two-column journal. When students learn journalizing through the multicolumn- and special-journal approach, they tend to memorize procedures without understanding basic principles.

Avoid Unlearning

All too frequently this first two-column journal is referred to as the *general journal*. Later, when special journals are introduced, the student learns that the general journal is actually a book of original entry in which entries are made to record transactions that do not appropriately fit into one of the special journals. Although the true general journal is similar in form to the two-column journal to which the students are first introduced, its use is considerably different.

The name given to a journal is determined by its function and not by the number of columns it has. Any journal may have a varying number of columns; for example, although the general journal most frequently has two columns, it may have four columns. The term *general journal* is applied to that journal in which entries are made that do not fit into other journals. Therefore, the use of the term *general journal* is confusing when it refers also to a simple journal in which all types of entries are recorded. The term *two-column journal* is more appropriate when the principles of journalizing are first presented, and the use of the term prevents students asking what is meant by the term *general*. Thus there is no unlearning to be done later, because the term *general* can be introduced when the first special journal is presented.

Method of Introducing the Two-Column Journal

Up to the point that the journal is introduced, students have recorded transactions directly in T accounts. The first step in introducing the journal is to point out the need for the journal. One way that this may be done is to place on the chalkboard or overhead a series of T accounts with entries taken from a previous problem that the class has completed. Then ask such questions as the following:

- Can anyone tell me what transactions brought about this credit entry?
- On what date was the entry made?
- In which account was the corresponding debit recorded?
- Can anyone point out all the transactions that were completed on (specific date)?
- If we made an error in recording a transaction in the accounts, how would we locate it?

Point out that to answer these questions and to avoid the difficulties that arise from making entries directly to accounts, a day-by-day record of all business transactions captured on source documents is kept. This record is called a *journal*. The journal form is then placed on the chalkboard or overhead and explained.

One teacher uses the following method of showing the need for the journal. A series of T accounts containing many entries, one of which has an intentional error, is duplicated on a sheet of paper and distributed to the class. The students are then asked to prepare a balance sheet from the T accounts. After working with the problem for a short time, they soon discover that the fundamental equation will not balance. When the class concludes that there must be an error on the sheet, the students are asked to locate the error. The inability of the students to locate the error finally leads into the discussion of the need for a preliminary record (journal) of the transactions before they are recorded in the accounts. This discussion develops the following points:

- The need for a chronological record of business transactions to show the daily history of the business.
- The need for more complete information.

- The need for better means of locating errors.
- The need for a supporting system of providing evidence of the transactions should one or more source documents become lost.

Other Teaching Suggestions

The suggestions presented in the following paragraphs have been used successfully in the teaching of the initial journal.

USE FAMILIAR TRANSACTIONS. When the journal is first being introduced, avoid transactions with which the students are not familiar. Illustrate the journal through the use of transactions taken from problems which the students have completed in the previous unit.

ALWAYS REFER TO ACCOUNTS. Before demonstrating the recording of a transaction in the journal, always analyze the transaction in terms of the T accounts and then show how to record the entry in the journal to bring about the necessary change in the accounts. The nature of the journal entry is always explained in terms of the change desired in the ledger; therefore, each transaction must first be analyzed in terms of the ledger and then the journal entry should be recorded.

USE AN ANALYSIS CHART. To ensure that each student analyzes each transaction before making the journal entry, give each student a copy of a chart similar to Figure 7.10 or the more comprehensive one shown in Figure 8.1. The students are required to record each transaction on the chart before making the journal entry. The use of the chart, of course, is discontinued when the teacher is certain that the students have developed the sequence of first analyzing the transaction in terms of the fundamental accounting equation and the ledger accounts before recording the journal entry.

| TRANS- ACTION | ASSET | | LIABILITY | | OWNER'S EQUITY | | ACCOUNT | |
	INCREASE	DECREASE	DECREASE	INCREASE	DECREASE	INCREASE	DEBITED	CREDITED
1	✓					✓	Cash	Carl Case, Capital
2	✓	✓					Equip.	Cash

Figure 8.1

STRESS CORRECT PROCEDURE. Emphasize the correct sequence of recording transactions in the journal.

1. Record the date of the source document.
2. Record the debit account title, commencing at the date margin.

3. Record the amount in the Debit column. Emphasize that the word *debit* still means "left"; in the journal, the Debit column is the left-hand column.
4. On the next line, about a half inch (about 2.5 cm) from the date margin, write the title of the account to be credited. Then, on the same line, enter the amount credited in the Credit column (the right-hand money column). Explain that indenting the credit is a simple method of distinguishing the credit entry from the debit entry. It may also help the student to remember that credit here means "to the right."
5. Record the necessary explanation. Some teachers prefer to indent all explanations an additional one-half inch. Other teachers prefer to begin all explanations back at the date margin. Regardless of the technique they use, the majority of teachers support the principle that explanations should be included for all transactions at the initial stage of student learning. At a later stage, the explanation may be omitted whenever account titles reveal the reason for an entry.
6. Show only complete journal entries on a journal page. Stress the point that it is better to leave a line or two than to have a journal entry carried over to another page.
7. Finally, stress that a consecutive page number is required for each new page of the journal.

TEACH THE CLASSIFICATION OF JOURNAL ENTRIES. After several familiar transactions have been analyzed and correctly recorded, teach the students how to identify opening entries, compound entries, and adjusting and closing entries. The opening entry can also be analyzed as a compound entry when two or more debits and two or more credits are required. Emphasize that the source document for the opening entry is the beginning balance sheet of a business enterprise.

Introducing the Special Journals

At one time, teachers introduced as many as nine special journals to beginning accounting classes, but the trend today is to treat only the four or five most common special journals and the general journal. These are the cash receipts journal, the cash payments journal, the sales journal, the purchases journal, and the payroll journal.

Special journals is one of the easiest topics in accounting to present provided the class has a thorough understanding of the two-column journal and posting. The following teaching considerations should be included in the presentation of all special journals:

1. Emphasize the basic principles of all special journals.
   a. Transactions with a common debit or a common credit are recorded in one journal.

        b.   Special journal rulings are used to fit the special transactions and thus to facilitate journalizing.

        c.   Totals are posted to save time and improve accuracy.

        d.   The need for a special journal is determined by the frequency of any given type of transaction.

        e.   The types of special journals used are related to the types of subsystems used.

2.   Point out the advantages of special journals.

        a.   Special journals reduce the amount of space required to record transactions.

        b.   They facilitate division of labor and thus permit the use of more than one person in keeping the records.

        c.   They reduce the number of postings to ledger accounts.

        d.   They decrease the opportunity for errors.

        e.   They concentrate transactions of a similar nature in one place for easier analysis and retrieval of data.

3.   Teach the mechanics of all special journals.

        a.   Demonstrate how to record transactions.

        b.   Demonstrate how to prove, rule, and post.

Which Special Journal Should Be Introduced First?

If one excludes the payroll journal on the grounds that it is often used as a register from which the totals are recorded in the general journal, then which one of the other four special journals should be introduced first? Traditionally, teachers have introduced either the sales journal or the purchases journal as part of treating the second accounting cycle with a merchandising firm. Other teachers, however, prefer to introduce the cash receipts journal, followed by the cash payments journal, for these reasons:

- The individual cash journals are common to all types of firms. Therefore, teachers can introduce the concept of special journals through the use of the service firm, thereby avoiding the added problem of teaching the accounting of merchandise inventory.

- A spiral development of special journals can be initiated with the study of the cash receipts and the cash payments journals. In the second cycle with a service-type business, a one-column cash receipts journal and a one-column cash payments journal can be offered to give a simple format. Then, with the study of the merchandising firm in a third cycle, the use of special money columns within the special journals can more easily be introduced.

- An early use of cash receipts and cash payments journals allows the teacher to introduce the basic concepts of systems work in accounting. Of all of the internal control systems used in accounting, the control of cash is basic to all firms—large and small. This important area of teaching accounting systems is examined in more detail in Chapter 15.

Teaching the Cash Receipts Journal

The simplest type of cash receipts journal is the one-column journal. The multicolumn cash receipts journal should not be introduced until the students understand the concept of special journals and until there is a need for the use of special amount columns within the special journals.

PREPARATION FOR THE LESSON. Before the class begins, place on the overhead or on the chalkboard at the front of the room a two-column journal containing various types of transactions for a monthly accounting period. Included in these entries would be several transactions showing a debit to the Cash account. To the right of the two-column journal, place a large Cash T account and show the individual debit amounts posted from the two-column journal to the Cash account.

INTRODUCING THE LESSON. Call attention to the fact that in the two-column journal the debit to Cash is highly repetitive for the accounting period. In addition, emphasize the fact that Cash must be posted each time that the account appears in the two-column journal. For example, if Cash is debited eight times in the two-column journal, then eight separate postings must also be required to the Cash account. Call attention to the problem that would be faced in an actual business where Cash may be debited many more times, say ninety times during the month. Try to elicit from the class the need for a more efficient way to record only cash receipts and to post the total cash received only once at the end of the month. Now introduce the principle of a special journal, in this case a special cash receipts journal in which will be recorded all transactions that identify a debit to the Cash account.

RECORDING TRANSACTIONS IN A ONE-COLUMN CASH RECEIPTS JOURNAL. The next step is to demonstrate on the overhead or chalkboard how one of the transactions involving a debit to Cash is journalized in the cash receipts journal. An illustration similar to Figure 8.2 can bring out these points:

1. The relationship between the two-column journal entry and the special cash receipts journal entry.
2. The space saved by the use of the special journal (one line is used instead of three lines).
3. The convenience provided by the rulings in the special journal.

TEACHING THE POSTING OF THE MONTHLY TOTAL. After explaining and demonstrating how one cash receipt would be entered into the special journal, demonstrate how the remainder of the transactions are recorded, emphasizing the advantage of posting the total only once to the debit of Cash. A comparison should be made between the T account entries under the two-column journal and the new T account showing only the one total. It is also important to emphasize these points before the total is posted to the Cash account: (1) The single money column must be totaled and double-checked for arithmetic accuracy and (2) the journal must be

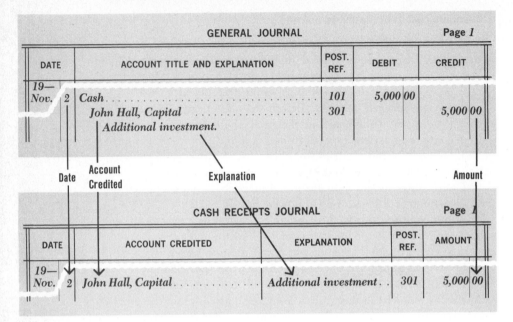

Figure 8.2

correctly ruled, as shown in Figure 8.3, to show that all of the cash receipts have been journalized for the month. And finally, it is important to have the students recognize that the double-entry system is sustained within the single cash receipts journal: The single total of Cash debit is in agreement with the total of the individual credit entries.

TEACHING THE MEMORANDUM ENTRY. After the students have been introduced to the advantage of posting only the total to the Cash account, pose this problem: If the Cash account is posted at the end of the month, how does one obtain a daily cash balance during the month from the accounting records? Although the cash payments journal has yet to be treated, an introductory explanation can be offered by introducing the idea of recording the beginning monthly balance of Cash as a memorandum entry in the cash receipts journal. The balance of cash at the end of any day during the month can be easily found by adding the daily cash receipts to and subtracting the daily cash payments from the memorandum entry. The teaching of a daily cash proof from the accounting records can be delayed until the cash payments journal is introduced in subsequent lessons. By introducing the concept of the memorandum entry here, however, the students are given some foundation for the future learning of the daily cash proof and a satisfactory response to any questions challenging the merit of posting the total of cash at the end of the month only.

TEACHING THE RECORDING OF THE OPENING ENTRY. A methods controversy arises regarding the correct recording of either an opening entry that consists of a cash investment only or an opening entry that combines a cash

CASH RECEIPTS JOURNAL   Page *1*

DATE		ACCOUNT CREDITED	EXPLANATION	POST. REF.	AMOUNT	
19—						
Nov.	1	Cash Balance................	$9,440 ←............	—		
	2	John Hall, Capital.............	Additional investment..	301	5,000	00
	5	Sales.......................	Cash sales for week....	401	400	00
	9	Accts. Rec./Wilson's Radio Center.	Received on account...	113	200	00
	12	Sales.......................	Cash sales for week....	401	350	00
	16	Accts. Rec./Jane Miller.........	Received on account...	111	75	00
	19	Sales.......................	Cash sales for week....	401	750	00
	25	Accts. Rec./Smith & Adams......	Received on account...	112	300	00
	26	Sales.......................	Cash sales for week....	401	400	00
					7,475	00
	30	Cash Debit.................	Total receipts........		7,475	00

	Cash		101
19—			
Nov.	1	9,440	
	30	7,475	

Figure 8.3

investment and other assets. Since there is no dogmatic rule to follow in practice, consistently use one of the following acceptable practices:

1. Record all opening entries, regardless of form, in the general journal only. In support of this rule, teachers argue that students will always associate an opening entry with a general journal recording. Furthermore, the argument is presented that the opening entry is nonrecurring; therefore, it should be recorded only in the general journal.
2. If an opening entry consists of a cash investment only, record this opening entry in the cash receipts journal. Record all other opening entries in the general journal. Supporters of this rule argue that this rule is consistent with recording all debits to Cash in the cash receipts journal.
3. If the opening entry consists of a cash investment and other assets, record the cash portion in the cash receipts journal and the other assets in the general journal. Record all other opening entries in the general journal.

All teachers agree that an additional investment of cash is always recorded in the cash receipts journal when such a special journal is part of the accounting system.

TEACHING THE MULTICOLUMN CASH RECEIPTS JOURNAL. The multicolumn form of cash receipts journal should not be introduced until the need for including special amount columns is made evident to the students. This need is easily identified when students are asked to respond to a cash receipts transaction when teaching recording procedures for a merchandising firm. Consider, for example, the students' oral analysis of the following double entry:

Cash	24.75	
Sales Discount	.25	
Accts. Rec./Wilson's Radio Center		25.00
Received customer's check in payment of account, less 1 percent sales discount.		

If the general ledger and the subsidiary ledger have been previously treated, the students can easily be shown the limitations of a one-column cash receipts journal: There are two debits to record and two ledgers to acknowledge. Thus a four-column design, as illustrated in Figure 8.4, can be used to demonstrate how to use special money columns within the special journal.

CASH RECEIPTS JOURNAL Page 3

DATE	ACCOUNT CREDITED	EXPLANATION	POST. REF.	GENERAL LEDGER CREDIT	ACCOUNTS RECEIVABLE CREDIT	SALES DISCOUNT DEBIT	NET CASH DEBIT
19— Jan. 26	Wilson's Radio Center	On account	√		25 00	25	24 75

Figure 8.4

The point should be made that additional money columns may be added when a highly repetitive account is acknowledged in the analysis of the transaction. The following additional points should then be made:

1. How each transaction must be supported by a source document that captures the cash receipt for accounting purposes; for example, cash register tapes, sales slips, remittance slips, and cash proof forms commonly used as part of the overall system to control cash receipts.
2. How the double entry must be recognized across each line of amount columns used to record the transaction. In other words, the student must be able to demonstrate the principle of debits equaling credits line by line by reading the amounts correctly from the special money columns.
3. How to post daily from the correct money columns to the appropriate ledgers.

4. How to prove the money columns before the totals are posted to the general ledger. (This topic is examined in detail in Chapter 10.)
5. How to rule the special journal for the month.
6. How to post the totals to the general ledger.

Teaching the Cash Payments Journal

After the cash receipts journal has been discussed in detail, the cash payments journal can be presented in much less time by comparing the two journals and showing that exactly the same principles are involved in each. The differences in the headings of the two journals should be noted, and the source documents that support the cash payments transactions should be examined.

RECORDING TRANSACTIONS IN A ONE-COLUMN CASH PAYMENTS JOURNAL. In a spiral development presentation of special journals, it would be logical to follow the unit on the one-column cash receipts journal with one on the one-column cash payments journal. This is especially true when students are led through a second accounting cycle with the use of the service firm.

Reinforcement problems on the cash payments journal should require students to learn not only how to record transactions that affect Cash credit, but also how to distinguish between those transactions that must be recorded in the cash receipts journal and those that must be recorded in the general journal. In other words, as each new special journal is introduced, both accumulative problems and simple problems should be provided to reinforce the learning of the new special journal.

RECORDING TRANSACTIONS IN A MULTICOLUMN CASH PAYMENTS JOURNAL. In keeping with the learning principle of moving from the simple to the complex, the multicolumn cash payments journal—which is ideally suited as part of the study of the accounting cycle for the merchandising firm—should be introduced after the one-column journal has been discussed. The need for requiring additional money columns can be easily seen in a compound cash payments transaction, such as the following:

Accts. Pay./Todd Electronics	360.00	
Purchases Discount		7.20
Cash		352.80
Issued Check 308 in payment of Invoice 0567, less 2 percent discount.		

If the general ledger and subsidiary ledger for accounts payable have been previously treated, the need for a multicolumn cash payments journal should become evident when students are asked to record the compound entry in the one-column cash payments journal. Obviously, at least three amount columns are required to record the compound entry on a single line. At this stage of the development of special journals, teachers generally favor a four-column design similar to the one shown in Figure 8.5. **111**

CASH PAYMENTS JOURNAL

DATE	ACCOUNT DEBITED	EXPLANATION	CHECK NO.	POST. REF.	GENERAL LEDGER DEBIT	ACCOUNTS PAYABLE DEBIT	PURCHASES DISCOUNT CREDIT	NET CASH CREDIT
19— Jan. 2	Mortgage Payable	January mortgage	304	231	310 00			310 00
2	Purchases	Fisher Company	305	501	100 00			100 00
4	Office Equipment	Typewriter	306	132	350 00			350 00
12	Transportation In	Eagle Freight Lines	307	502	50 00			50 00
18	Todd Electronics	Inv. 0567	308	✓		360 00	7 20	352 80
24	George Young	Inv. P876	309	✓		200 00	2 00	198 00
28	Dixon & Hicks	Inv. 82A	310	✓		1,204 00		1,204 00
31	Salaries Payable	January 29 payroll	311/314	225	930 00			930 00
31	Advertising Expense	Replenish petty	315	512	12 25			26 00
	Miscellaneous Exp.	cash fund	—	515	13 75			—

Figure 8.5

In a complete analysis of the multicolumn cash payments journal, stress the following points:

1. The double entry must be identified across each line of amount columns used to record the transaction.
2. Daily postings must be made from the correct amount columns to the correct ledger.
3. All money columns must be proved as to the equality of debits and credits *before* the journal is ruled and the totals posted.
4. The special journal must be double-ruled before posting the totals to the general ledger. Students often forget that this double rule indicates that all of the cash payments for the month have been journalized.
5. The totals that affect general ledger accounts must be shown as having been correctly posted.

Special Problems. Experienced teachers report the following errors as the most frequent ones made by students in using the multiple-column cash receipts and cash payments journals:

- Failure to check the equality of debits and credits across each line of entry.
- Failure to prove the journal by determining the equality of the total debits and total credits.
- Incorrect recording of the memorandum entry for the beginning cash balance in the cash receipts journal.
- Failure to post the totals of all columns requiring posting.
- Incorrect use of the general ledger debit and credit columns.

Each of these problem points requires special attention. Each should be demonstrated, and drill material should follow each demonstration.

Teaching the Purchases Journal

Traditionally, the teaching of a special journal to record only merchandise purchases on credit has been reserved for the coverage of the accounting cycle for a merchandising firm using the periodic inventory method of accounting. Before such a special journal is introduced, however, teachers generally agree that they must first teach certain important concepts: the nature of a merchandising firm, the calculation of net income under a periodic inventory method, and the need of a system to control the purchase of merchandise. Some teachers also take time to analyze merchandising transactions, using a T account or showing entries recorded in the two-column journal.

INTRODUCING THE ONE-COLUMN PURCHASES JOURNAL. When a preliminary coverage of transactions for a merchandising firm has been analyzed in the two-column journal form, the need for a special journal can easily be shown from a study of the repetitive nature of the purchases account for an

113

accounting period. For example, a compound entry recording three in-voices in one entry may first be studied as follows:

Purchases	1,764	
Accts. Pay./Todd Electronics		360
Accts. Pay./Dixon & Hicks		1,204
Accts. Pay./George Young		200
To record Purchases Invoices 0567, 82A, and P876 received today.		

To the right of the two-column journal, place a group of T accounts, and enter in these accounts the transactions recorded in this journal. To the right of these accounts, show a one-column purchases journal; and to the right of that, show another set of blank T accounts.

Call attention to the fact that in the completed T accounts there is a debit for every credit as entered in the journal and that the total debits equal the total credits, as they do in the journal. Then point out that the transactions to record purchases on credit are scattered throughout the two-column journal, but the three purchase invoices received on the same date could be recorded as one compound entry. This compound entry enables us to post to the ledger account only the total of the three pur-chases, $1,764, instead of each of the three figures.

Ask the students this question: "Why not enter all credit purchases in one compound entry?" The answer, of course, is that transactions are entered as they occur and that purchases invoices are received periodically. Then ask, "What would be gained if it were possible to enter all credit purchases as one compound entry?" The answer is that this would facilitate entering all credit purchases in one place instead of having them scattered on many pages. A compound entry would also enable the accounting clerk to post one figure to the Purchases account rather than many debits.

Then tell the class that a special journal known as a *purchases journal* makes it possible to record all credit purchases of merchandise in one place and to post only the total purchases to the ledger. The students are now ready to listen to the explanation of the purchases journal because they see the need of such a special journal. Also, the principle involved in the purchases journal is clarified even before the journal is introduced, because the class understands that in the compound entry the equality of debits and credits is maintained.

RECORDING TRANSACTIONS IN THE ONE-COLUMN PURCHASES JOURNAL. Next, enter in a one-column purchases journal on the chalkboard or overhead all transactions involving credit purchases of merchandise for a monthly accounting period and then post them to the T accounts to the right of the purchases journal on the chalkboard (or above the journal on the trans-parency). After completing the entries and posting the total, allow time to present the following points in review of the illustrations, which should resemble Figure 8.6.

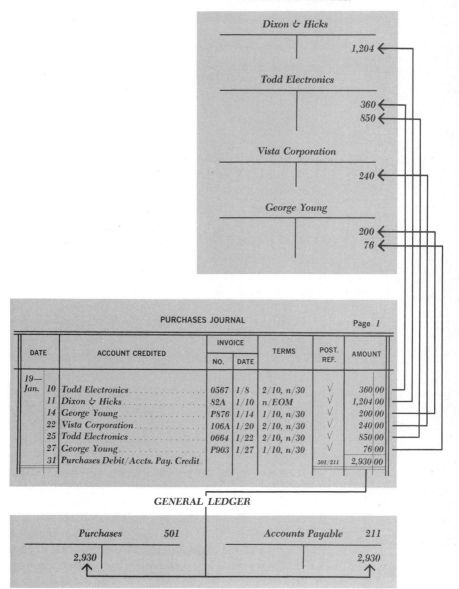

Figure 8.6

1. The rulings provided in the purchases journal are designed to record the six basic facts of each credit purchase: date of approving purchase invoice, creditor's name, invoice number, invoice date, terms, and invoice amount. Note that by having the students list the information needed on each credit transaction and then pointing

115

out how the purchases journal is custom-ruled to facilitate the recording of this information, the teacher is able to emphasize the convenience of the special journal.

2. All of the information previously analyzed in the two-column journal is maintained in the special purchases journal.

3. One line is used instead of three or more lines; therefore, space is saved by the use of the special journal.

4. After all of the credit purchases have been recorded for the month, only the total is posted to the debit side of the Purchases account; the individual credits have been posted to the creditor accounts during the month.

5. By maintaining a separate journal to record purchases on credit, a division of labor is possible. One clerk can be engaged to post to accounts payable accounts without interrupting the work of others.

6. The purchases journal may be defined as a chronological listing of purchase invoices since only merchandise purchased on credit is recorded in this special journal.

After sufficient reinforcement problems are given on the one-column purchases journal, students generally see the need for a subsidiary ledger for accounts payable. This topic will be examined in Chapter 9.

INTRODUCING THE MULTICOLUMN PURCHASES JOURNAL. Many teachers support the view that a multicolumn special journal to record all forms of purchases on credit should be included in a beginning accounting course for the following reasons. This special journal is sometimes known as the *columnar purchases journal* or *all-inclusive purchases journal*.

1. A one-column purchases journal rarely exists in modern accounting practice.

2. Many merchandising firms buy assets and incur many of their expenses through accounts payable; consequently, it is logical to account for all of the accounts payable in one special journal.

3. Some managers insist on having a record of the costs relating to each main class of merchandise; therefore, additional columns would be required to record the distribution of merchandise costs to various departments or other organized responsibility centers.

4. The introduction of a multicolumn purchases journal should follow the teaching of the one-column purchases journal to be consistent with the spiral development principle of presenting other special journals.

5. The recording of all accounts payable in one record lays the foundation for the future introduction of the voucher system of controlling all forms of purchases.

One illustration, similar to Figure 8.7, can bring out the following teaching points:

1. In a multicolumn purchases journal, all recorded transactions have one thing in common: they affect one account—a credit to accounts

PURCHASES JOURNAL
Page 14

DATE	ACCOUNT CREDITED	INVOICE NO.	INVOICE DATE	TERMS	POST. REF.	ACCOUNTS PAYABLE CREDIT	CHILDREN'S WEAR	MEN'S WEAR	WOMEN'S WEAR	ACCOUNT TITLE	POST. REF.	AMOUNT
19— Apr.												
2	Wilson Coat Co.	A811	3/29	2/10, n/30	√	1,264 80	1,264 80					
4	Ross Shoe Corp.	1612	4/3	1/10, n/30	√	846 10		356 42	489 68			
5	Bush Office Supply Co.	409	4/4	n/30	√	76 80				Office Expense	551	76 80
6	Wayne Manufacturing Co.	1014	4/5	2/10, n/30	√	269 80		257 15		Advertising Expense	541	12 65
30	Fun-Time Sportswear, Inc.	732	4/27	2/10, n/30	√	172 10			172 10			
30	Totals					36,865 92	12,033 42	12,467 21	12,275 84			89 45
						(211)	(501)	(511)	(521)			(√)

Debit Columns

Purchases:
Children's Wear........ $12,033.42
Men's Wear............ 12,467.21
Women's Wear......... 12,275.84
General Ledger........ 89.45
Total............. $36,865.92

Credit Column

Accounts Payable......... $36,865.92

Total......... $36,865.92

Figure 8.7

payable. A columnar purchases journal, therefore, may be regarded as a special journal to record transactions that are credits to accounts payable.

2. The individual debit money columns must add up to the total of the Accounts Payable money column. This proof of the debit and credit money columns must be made before the totals are posted to the general ledger.

3. The use of additional money columns allows the accounting system to provide management with a breakdown of purchases according to the merchandising departments established by the business.

4. The use of a special journal to record all forms of accounts payable enables management to hire one or more clerks to work only in the area of accounts payable. This division of labor not only permits a more efficient system in accounting, but also agrees with the principle that no one person should control an accounting transaction from beginning to end.

Teaching the Sales Journal

The principles involved in the teaching of the sales journal are identical with the ones presented for the purchases journal. In the initial step, teachers generally agree to present a view of a credit sales system for a merchandising firm so that students recognize the source document used to capture the accounting transaction. Next, the need is presented for a special journal to record credit invoices for each monthly accounting period. At this stage of the spiral development, many teachers favor the use of the one-column sales journal. As in the treatment of teaching purchases and accounts payable, the need for a subsidiary ledger to file all customer accounts is introduced along with the teaching of posting from the one-column sales journal. To complete the spiral development, teachers also introduce the need for a multicolumn sales journal. The following points are considered by many teachers to be vital in the teaching of any sales journal.

1. The sales journal is a chronological listing of source documents that have captured the dollar results of sales on a credit basis.

2. In accounting practice, the sales journal may take different forms and names. For example, one business may prefer to list all sales invoices in an invoice register, while another business may simply list all unpaid invoices in a special binder.

3. For nonmerchandising businesses, the design of the sales journal generally acknowledges the specific type of revenue-making transaction. For example, hotels and motels may extend short-term credit to customers, notably to established firms and to those carrying recognized credit cards. Their journal system will probably include a Rooms and Meals Register or Journal to record revenue derived from room rentals, restaurant and cocktail lounge.

4. Regardless of the form and name, the dollar results of the monthly listing of sales invoices are analyzed in the form of a double entry and posted to appropriate accounts in the general ledger.

INTRODUCING THE ONE-COLUMN SALES JOURNAL. If a previous spiral development of presenting special journals has been used, students react quickly to the need for a sales journal to list chronologically all credit sales. Once again, teachers find it useful to have students identify the highly repetitive nature of credit sales, especially for a wholesale merchandising firm, so that the advantages of using a special journal are easily acknowledged. In addition, many teachers prefer to have students do an oral or T-account analysis of each sales transaction before they actually record the credit sale in the sales journal. This technique reinforces the students' learning that only credit sales are recorded in the sales journal. And, finally, the teaching of posting of amounts to the subsidiary ledger and the general ledger is more easily understood when a one-column sales journal is initially used.

INTRODUCING THE MULTICOLUMN SALES JOURNAL. One method to introduce the need for additional columns in a sales journal is to consider a merchandising firm's credit sales that also include a sales tax to be collected by the seller. Consider, for example, the presentation of a compound entry as follows:

Accts. Rec./Jane Miller	82.40	
Sales Tax Payable		2.40
Sales		80.00
To record Invoice 102 for $80 plus sales tax of $2.40.		

From an analysis of the compound entry, students should grasp quickly the need for special columns to record three amounts: the accounts receivable, the sales tax payable, and the sales revenue. A three-column sales journal, such as the one shown in Figure 8.8, should then be presented.

These additional points should be considered in the teaching of the multicolumn sales journal.

1. During the month, the amounts in the Accounts Receivable Debit column are posted individually to the customers' accounts in the subsidiary ledger.
2. At the end of the month, the journal must be totaled and the equality of debit and credit must be proved *before* the totals are posted to the general ledger.
3. When a sales tax payable account is used, emphasize that, in general, the government levying the sales tax requires the seller to collect the tax from the customer. In other words, the seller is obliged under government law to account for the sales tax payable and to forward the collection at appropriate times to the government. A

SALES JOURNAL							Page 1
DATE	INVOICE NO.	ACCOUNT DEBITED	TERMS	POST. REF.	ACCOUNTS RECEIVABLE DEBIT	SALES TAX PAYABLE CREDIT	SALES CREDIT
19— Jan. 11	102	Jane Miller	2/10, n/30	√	83 20	3 20	80 00
31		Totals.			3,006 64 ⟨3,006 64⟩	115 64 ⟨115 64⟩	2,891 00 ⟨2,891 00⟩
					(111)	(216)	(401)

Figure 8.8

multicolumn sales journal, therefore, enables management to record the sales tax payable on each credit sale and then to post the total each month to the current liability account.

Cash Sales and Cash Purchases.   When only credit sales and credit purchases are entered, respectively, in the special sales journal and purchases journal, students frequently raise the question about the recording of cash sales and cash purchases. This situation provides an excellent opportunity to develop the basic principles upon which all multiple-column journals are based.

Place on the chalkboard or overhead projector a cash receipts journal containing a number of cash sales entries. Point out that the cash sales transaction occurs repeatedly. While the Sales account has only one posting for the total credit sales (because of the use of the special sales journal), it contains an individual posting for each cash sale.

Then raise the question about what can be done to have only one posting for all the cash sales. A student will generally suggest that a special cash sales journal be used. A discussion of this proposal, however, will show that cash receipts would be recorded in two places; however, this is impractical. The discussion will eventually lead to the suggestion that a special money column be placed in the cash receipts journal where all cash sales can be accumulated, and the total of the column posted to the credit side of the Sales account. Then add a special sales credit column to the cash journal, and demonstrate its use.

Follow the same procedure in handling the cash purchases.

Out of these class experiences, the following basic principles can be established:

1.   A special column may be added to either the cash receipts journal or cash payments journal whenever a debit or a credit item occurs so frequently as to make such a column a time-saver.

2.   The use of special money columns is not limited to either the cash receipts journal or the cash payments journal; special columns may be added to any journal.

120   3.   The use of the special column does not change the principles of debits and credits. It merely permits the accumulation of all items going to the one side of an account so that they may be posted in total instead of individually.

4. There is no limit to the number of columns that may be added to any one journal.

One teacher emphasizes these principles by duplicating for distribution to the class a one-column cash receipts journal containing several pages. The journal has a large number of recurring transactions. The students are requested to analyze the journal and develop an appropriate multiple-column journal to replace the duplicated one-column journal. To prove its practicality, they are to record the transactions in the journal they develop.

Teaching the Payroll Journal

For many years, teachers and authors have presented the topic of payroll either at the end of a beginning course in accounting or as part of a second or advanced course of instruction. Recently, however, they support an earlier introduction to payroll accounting for the following reasons:

1. Many of the students have part-time jobs; consequently, they can contribute their knowledge to the class discussion of the topic.
2. Payroll accounting is an area that appeals to all students; consequently, the topic should be introduced in a beginning course where many more students register than in a second course of instruction.
3. Payroll accounting is the most widely applied area in data processing; consequently, an earlier teaching of payroll allows the teacher to integrate accounting and data processing in one course. (A detailed treatment of integrating accounting with data processing is offered in Chapter 16.)

PAYROLL JOURNAL VERSUS PAYROLL REGISTER. In planning for the complete treatment of payroll accounting, teachers must consider the difference between the use of a payroll journal and the use of a payroll register. To state it briefly, in some accounting systems, the chronological listing of the firm's payroll is summarized in a journal; that is, the totals of the payroll listing are posted directly to the general ledger. On the other hand, many other accounting systems treat the payroll listing as a register; that is, the totals are taken from the payroll register and summarized in the form of a compound double entry in the general journal. A payroll journal, therefore, acts as both a chronological listing of the payroll and the source medium from which totals are posted to appropriate accounts in the general ledger. On the other hand, a payroll register merely lists the chronological summary of the payroll. A subsequent step of summarizing the totals in the form of a general journal entry is required before posting occurs to update the general ledger file.

Regardless of the system followed, the double entry presents little **121** difficulty once students are led through the study of an elementary accounting cycle. Two classes of accounts are easily identified from the payroll register or payroll journal: the total gross earnings is acknowledged as an expense to the business, while each payroll deduction and the total net pay is analyzed as a liability to be paid by the firm. Since the area of payroll accounting is a vital part of every firm's accounting systems and procedures, this important area is examined in detail in Chapter 15.

Introducing the Combination Journal

Once students are familiar with the general journal and special journals, and the general and subsidiary ledgers, the teacher may introduce the combination journal to demonstrate a special accounting application for a small firm where little or no internal control over cash and other assets is required. As the name suggests, a combination journal combines the general journal and the special journals for cash receipts, cash payments, purchases, and sales into one multicolumn journal. Since all the separate journals may be viewed on a single record sheet, the combination journal may also be known as a *synoptic journal*. The important teaching points to include in lesson plans to present the combination journal are:

1. Review the use of the special journals for cash receipts, cash payments, purchases, and sales. Review also the concepts of the general ledger and subsidiary ledgers for accounts receivable and accounts payable.
2. Introduce the combination journal as a journal that combines the general journal and special journals into one multicolumn journal.
3. Explain how combination journals are designed to meet the needs of individual businesses.
4. Show how to record entries in the combination journal. Analyze each transaction and discuss how it would be recorded in a special journal or the general journal before illustrating the entry in the combination journal.
5. Show how to prove the combination journal.
6. Show how to carry totals from one page to another.
7. Show how to close the combination journal.
8. Show how to post from the combination journal.
9. Discuss the advantages and disadvantages of the combination journal.

TEACH A COMPLETE EVALUATION OF THE COMBINATION JOURNAL SYSTEM. In general, some teachers present an excellent view of the advantages of the combination journal, but quite often forget to discuss the shortcomings of such a journal system. In presenting a fair evaluation, it is important to include both the advantages and disadvantages of the system. The advantages may be summarized as follows:

1. The time-saving, space-saving, and error-reducing features of a special journal are found because special money columns are used for highly repetitive transactions.
2. Since all the journals are combined into one multicolumn journal, all entries can be reviewed at any time from one source only.
3. Considerable saving can be realized by engaging only one person to record the dollar results of all the transactions.
4. It may be ideal in the early stages of a new enterprise; special journals can then follow as transactions become more numerous.

The disadvantages may be stated as follows:

1. The large number of columns increases the opportunity for error.
2. Recording often becomes cumbersome and awkward. For example, a payroll entry may require several lines of writing before it is completely recorded.
3. The principle of effective internal control (that no one individual should be permitted to handle any transaction, in either its physical or its recording aspect, from beginning to end) is violated. A one-person accounting system permits easy manipulation of the records.
4. Entries are usually recorded by hand (manually) and the combination journal does not lend itself to high-level data processing methods. A combination journal is part of a simplified accounting system and its use will vary somewhat from business to business. For example, some may retain a general journal to record the adjusting, closing and correcting entries; others may retain one or more special journals, to relieve congestion of columns in their combination journal.

Teaching the Journal Voucher

In teaching about journals, instructors often overlook the journal voucher. The journal voucher is a special device often used in accounting systems instead of the formal journal. In simple terms, a journal voucher is an authorization to prepare or make an accounting entry in the ledger. There are several reasons for using the journal voucher instead of the traditional journal in book form.

1. In many businesses, a bound journal is an awkward item to carry from office to office. Moving one bound journal within a large business often results in the journal not being available when entries have to be made. The journal voucher is a device for transferring journal entry information from one department to another or from branch offices to head office.
2. There are many occasions when it is desirable to have someone with special accounting knowledge and authority approve the analysis of

a transaction and the explanation which make up the journal entry. For example, an accountant would probably record the adjusting entries for depreciation and expired insurance on separate journal vouchers. The correct information could then be posted to ledger accounts by accounting clerks.

3. The journal voucher can be used to record specialized transactions, such as a weekly summary of a branch office's sales and cash receipts, end-of-period adjusting and closing entries, correction entries, and other miscellaneous transactions, that ordinarily would not be recorded in special journals. In this regard, the journal vouchers would replace the general journal.

4. In some instances, the journal voucher can be used to record periodic journal entries relating to a special journal. For example, it may be convenient for a particular firm to use journal vouchers to record periodic receipts of revenue. In this case, the vouchers might be used to record revenues from individual transactions, from daily summaries of receipts from several sources of revenue, or from monthly cash receipt recapitulations. When examined in total, the journal vouchers actually replace the cash receipts journal and, therefore, can properly be considered cash receipts journal vouchers.

5. The journal voucher often serves as an important internal control device when journal entries are being processed by a central computer data processing department. The journal voucher is prepared by the accounting department, which in turn gives the authorization to the computer department to post the journal entries to the proper ledger accounts.

In presenting the journal voucher, it is important to emphasize that, in actual practice, there will be a number of different forms of journal vouchers serving particular needs. Normally, the journal voucher will contain space for recording the following: journal voucher number, date of entry, account name, account number, debit amount of the entry, credit amount of the entry, particulars or description of the journal entry, and the signature or signatures to give accounting approval for posting the journal entry.

Several different forms of journal vouchers can contribute to an effective bulletin board display. However, an overhead transparency of a journal voucher, such as the one in Figure 8.9, can bring out the following important points in the preparation and processing of journal vouchers:

1. Only *one* transaction entry is journalized on any one journal voucher form. For example, adjusting entries for depreciation and prepaid insurance would require two journal vouchers.

2. Journal vouchers are generally handwritten, regardless of the method of data processing used; account names, account numbers, and especially the dollar results must be accurate and legible.

3. For the purposes of accounting control, each journal voucher must

JOURNAL VOUCHER	DATE *March 31,* 19—				NO. 8	
ACCOUNT		ACCT. NO.	✓	DEBIT	CREDIT	
Insurance Expense		514		30 00		
Prepaid Insurance		113			30 00	

EXPLANATION

To record the expired insurance for March.

PREPARED BY *E. Jones* AUDITED BY *J.W.* APPROVED BY *D.W.*

Figure 8.9

have the approval of someone in authority, and each voucher form must have a separate number.

4. Once prepared and authorized, the journal voucher is posted to the ledger accounts. In some accounting systems, two copies are prepared: the original is used for posting purposes, while the copy remains with the person who originated the entry. Where one copy only is used, the voucher is returned to the source for permanent filing.

5. In general, journal vouchers are posted on a monthly basis. Once posted, the vouchers are usually filed chronologically or in numeric sequence on a type of post or ring binder for future reference. The file of journal vouchers then actually becomes the journal in book form.

WHEN SHOULD THE JOURNAL VOUCHER BE PRESENTED? Some teachers consider the topic of journal voucher basic to any introductory study of accounting systems; therefore, the topic is generally deferred until sometime after the teaching of the first accounting cycle and after all of the special journals have been covered. On the other hand, other teachers are just as strong in their view that the journal voucher should be introduced as early as possible so that accounting applications can be studied in relation to computer data processing. It is interesting to observe that the journal voucher has become the main source medium for transmitting accounting data to computer centers for processing the general ledger file. It is also revealing that the majority of general journal vouchers are two-column formats; consequently, the early teaching of journalizing on a two-column journal provides a good foundation for the later study of the journal

125

voucher. (For a treatment of teaching the journal voucher in conjunction with updating a computer general ledger file, refer to Chapter 10.)

Questions and Projects

1. Visit two small business firms and obtain copies of the journal sheets they use. Combine these with the forms gathered by other class members for a tackboard exhibit.

2. How would you reply to the following question asked by a student: "Why do we need to use both a journal and a ledger; isn't the same information recorded in both?"

3. Is journalizing the first step of an accounting cycle? Explain why or why not.

4. In demonstrating how to record a credit entry in a two-column journal, what explanation would you give for indenting the title of the account to be credited?

5. Would you include the teaching of special journals in the first accounting cycle? Explain your answer.

6. With what special journal would you begin the teaching of special journals? Give reasons for your answer.

7. Prepare a lesson plan for teaching one of the following:
    a. Recording the opening entries in a journal.
    b. Recording a series of typical transactions in a two-column journal.
    c. Introducing the need for a one-column special journal.

8. What factors determine whether or not a specific special journal is used in an accounting system?

9. Prepare a chalkboard or overhead demonstration showing how to do one of the following:
    a. Prove the equality of the total debits and total credits in a four-column cash receipts or cash payments journal.
    b. Record the beginning cash balance in the cash receipts journal.
    c. Prove the equality of the totals in a payroll register (payroll journal).

10. When all special journals are combined into one multicolumn journal, is the process of recording an individual transaction any different from that followed when individual special journals are used? Explain your answer.

11. Prepare a lesson plan on introducing the multicolumn sales journal to a beginning accounting class.

12. Explain the difference between a payroll journal and a payroll register. Which term would you use with an introductory accounting class? Give reasons for your answer.

13. At what point would you introduce the teaching of the combination journal? Explain your answer.

14. In simple terms, define the term journal voucher, and explain why this device is used in modern accounting practice. At what point would you teach the concept of a journal voucher? Explain your answer.

Case Problem

To help develop the idea that the use of special journals permits more than one person to work on the books at one time, a teacher divides his class into groups. Each group contains five students. The teacher assigns from the textbook a problem requiring the use of these journals: purchases, sales, cash receipts, cash payments, and general. Each student is given the assignment of keeping a specific journal and the group collectively completes the problem. Each group completes the problem five times, rotating the journal assignments so that each student will have the experience of keeping each of the five journals.

    a.   What advantages and disadvantages do you see in this plan?
    b.   If you were using the plan, how would you group your students?
    c.   How frequently would you use the plan?

CHAPTER 9

Teaching About Ledgers

In the traditional presentation of an elementary accounting cycle, the step of posting transaction data to the ledger logically follows the teaching of journalizing. In keeping with the spiral development principle, teachers generally favor the introduction of only one ledger for the first accounting cycle. As the merchandising firm is studied in a subsequent cycle, however, teachers generally support the introduction of controlling accounts and the three-ledger system. In this chapter, we shall treat the methodology of presenting not only the traditional view of posting transaction data from the journals to the ledgers, but also of posting directly from source documents to the subsidiary ledgers. Before examining the methods of teaching the various ledgers, let us first review some of the important accounting fundamentals related to the study of ledgers.

ACCOUNTING FUNDAMENTALS

1. Traditionally, the ledger is a book of accounts. In contemporary accounting practice, however, the ledger is appropriately viewed as a file of accounts because the accounts may be stored in accordance with the method of data processing adopted by the accounting system. For example, a ledger file may be stored on magnetic disk or magnetic tape when a computer is used to process an accounting ledger.
2. The ledger may be considered a record of final entry because the debits and credits of the dollar results of transactions end up in ledger accounts.
3. In any accounting system, the general ledger is the key ledger because it contains the accounts from which information is obtained to prepare the financial statements of the business.
4. To assist in the preparation of financial statements, general ledger accounts are usually classified to a plan known as the *chart of accounts*.
5. A chart of accounts generally provides for five classifications:

(continued)

asset accounts, liability accounts, owner's equity accounts, revenue accounts, and expense accounts.

6. Traditionally, *posting* is defined as the operation of transferring transaction data from the journals to ledgers.

7. To facilitate posting, general ledger accounts are usually identified by some number code.

8. In the majority of accounting systems, transaction data is posted monthly from the general journal and special journals to appropriate accounts filed in the general ledger.

9. To keep the accounts in the general ledger at a practical number, many accounting systems adopt a system of controlling accounts and subsidiary ledgers.

10. A subsidiary ledger is a group of like accounts that have been separated from the general ledger for the purpose of providing significant details relating to a single category of accounting information.

11. An accounting system that has many charge account customers and creditors usually moves all these accounts from the general ledger to separate subsidiary ledgers known as the *accounts receivable ledger* (or *customers' ledger*) and the *accounts payable ledger* (or *creditors' ledger*) respectively.

12. Other common subsidiary ledgers are the inventory ledger, the fixed asset ledger, and various expense ledgers.

13. Once any group of accounts is removed from the general ledger, a controlling account must be maintained in the general ledger.

14. Controlling accounts show only the total of the balances contained in the corresponding subsidiary ledger.

15. Accounts filed in a subsidiary ledger are identified by an alphabetic arrangement or by an account code distinct from codes in the general ledger.

16. Posting transaction data to subsidiary ledger accounts generally is performed daily and may be done from the journals or directly from the accounting source document.

17. In a fairly large accounting system, the general ledger and the various subsidiary ledgers are organized under the responsibility of separate departments to facilitate greater internal control. Hence the general ledger would be controlled by the general accounting department, the accounts receivable ledger by the accounts receivable department, the accounts payable ledger by the accounts payable department, and so on.

18. In contemporary practice, the form of ledger account will vary with the needs of summarizing useful information and in ac-

(continued)

cordance with the method of data processing adopted by the accounting system.

19. In some accounting systems, a subsidiary ledger may be replaced by a file of source documents; hence an accounts receivable file of unpaid invoices would replace the accounts receivable ledger. In all accounting systems, however, a general ledger is maintained in order to accumulate account balances for the preparation of financial statements.

Performance Goals

Some of the more important performance goals for appropriate lessons on the various ledgers are suggested below. Some of these performance goals must be stated in sequence with similar ones on journalizing, since journalizing and posting are closely related operations within many accounting systems.

1. Given a plan for a chart of accounts, the student should be able to assign correct account numbers to a series of ledger accounts.
2. Given a two-column journal with entries recorded in it and given a series of ledger accounts, the student should be able to post the journal entries to the appropriate ledger accounts.
3. Given a journal and the ledger accounts to which the journal entries were posted, the student should be able to answer a series of questions about them.
4. Given a ledger account, the student should be able to balance the account. This operation involves pencil-footing the total debits and total credits, determining the account balance, and entering the account balance in pencil.
5. Given a one-column cash receipts journal with entries recorded in it and given a series of ledger accounts, the student should be able to post the journal entries and the total to the ledger accounts.
6. Given a one-column cash payments journal with entries recorded in it and given a series of ledger accounts, the student should be able to post the journal entries and the total to the ledger accounts.
7. Given a purchases journal and a cash payments journal with entries recorded in them and a series of general ledger and subsidiary ledger accounts, the student should be able to post the journal entries to the accounts.
8. Given a sales journal, cash receipts journal, purchases journal, cash payments journal, and general journal with entries recorded in them and a series of general ledger and subsidiary ledger accounts, the student should be able to post the journal entries to the ledger accounts.

9. Given a batch of sales invoice copies and an adding-listing machine, the student should be able to, first, alphabetize the source documents by customer's name and, second, prepare a prelist on an adding machine tape.

10. Given a batch of similar source documents and a series of subsidiary ledger accounts, the student should be able to post correctly the dollar results of each transaction document to the appropriate account.

11. Given a computer printout of the general ledger, the student should be able to identify the account name, the account balance at the beginning of the month, the current listing of debits and credits, the posting media for the current listing of debits and credits, and the account balance at the end of the month.

12. Given a computer printout of the general ledger, the student should be able to rewrite the information contained in one or more accounts in the balance ledger form.

Introducing the One-Ledger System

Under the balance sheet and equation approaches, the student is introduced to the T account as a useful device to record changes in the various elements of the accounting equation. At that point, be careful to emphasize that the T account form is not used in accounting practice, and that a more practical design will be introduced at a subsequent stage of the accounting cycle. The students, therefore, are ready to accept a new form of account as part of learning how to post transaction data from the two-column journal to the ledger.

Standard Versus Balance Ledger Forms

Teachers and textbook authors differ about which of the several types of ledger forms is most appropriate at this point. Some opt for the standard ledger form—the one most similar to a T account—while others argue that since the balance ledger form has to be used in subsequent accounting cycles, the student should be introduced to it now rather than later. The advantages and disadvantages of each of the various ledger forms are summarized below.

THE STANDARD FORM OF LEDGER ACCOUNT. The standard form of ledger account, sometimes known as the two-column or two-sided ledger account, has been in use longer than any other form. This form is illustrated in Figure 9.1.

Advocates of this form point to the following advantages.

1. An effective spiral development is maintained because students are led from the T account (something they know) to a form similar to a T account.

					Accts. Rec./King Stores				Account No. 102	
DATE		EXPLANATION	POST. REF.	DEBIT	DATE		EXPLANATION	POST. REF.	CREDIT	
19—					19—					
Sept.	30	Opening entry .	J1	1,000 00	Oct.	2	. . . .	J1	1,000 00
Oct.	29	. . . . 800.00	J1	800 00		31	Balance	√	800 00
				1,800 00						
				1,800 00					1,800 00	
19—										
Nov.	1	Balance	√	800 00						

Figure 9.1

2. Students require additional time for reinforcement of the concepts of debit and credit as these concepts are related to the left side and right side of a formal ledger account.

3. The standard form can be replaced with other account forms in the study of the accounting cycle for a merchandising firm.

4. Some accounting systems operating under the traditional pen-and-ink method still employ the standard form of ledger account.

Opponents urge the elimination of the standard ledger form for the following reasons:

1. Under any modern data processing method—from manual to mechanical to computer—the standard ledger form just does not exist.

2. In determining account balances, students must be taught how to pencil-foot the total debits, pencil-foot the total credits, and enter the account balance as a small pencil notation on the proper side of the account.

3. In completing the accounting cycle, students must be taught the extra step of balancing and ruling accounts and, for all permanent accounts, bringing down the account balance on the correct side.

THE BALANCE LEDGER FORM. The balance ledger form, sometimes called the *three-column ledger account,* has three money columns—Debit, Credit, and Balance. This form is illustrated in Figure 9.2.

Supporters of this form point to the following advantages:

1. The balance ledger form is the most commonly used form in practice today. It can easily be adapted to manual, mechanical, or computer processing methods.

2. The use of a running balance column eliminates the necessity of adding and subtracting pencil footings continually in order to determine account balances during and at the end of an accounting period.

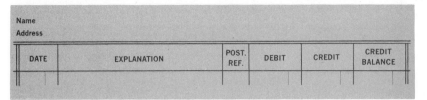

Figure 9.2

3. The use of the balance column also eliminates the extra steps of balancing, ruling, and bringing down account balances at the end of each accounting period.

4. The three-column form forces the readers to relate normal balances to the sides of the accounting equation; consequently, the students are constantly aware of the requirement to classify all accounts in relation to the sides of the accounting equation.

5. Any abnormal balance may be identified only once either by encircling the amount or by placing the abbreviations *Dr.* or *Cr.* opposite the figure.

Critics of the balance ledger form offer these views:

1. Students are introduced to the balance column too early; consequently, the use of three columns confuses many of them.

2. The three-column form should be introduced only after the students have acquired a thorough knowledge of the T account and the standard ledger form. A better alternative, critics believe, is to introduce the balance ledger form after teaching the first accounting cycle.

3. Students often misinterpret the balance in the account because the balance column is not qualified as either Debit or Credit.

THE BALANCE LEDGER FORM WITH DEBIT AND CREDIT BALANCE COLUMNS. Some teachers believe that a variation of the three-column balance ledger form—one that provides a narrow column to acknowledge each debit or credit running balance—not only offers the first three advantages listed above, but also eliminates student confusion in identifying the balance. On the other hand, some teachers point to the unnecessary redundancy in qualifying obvious account balances. For example, the Cash account would normally have only debit balances; therefore, no learning value is achieved by having the students write "Dr." before each running balance. Furthermore, these teachers point out that ledger forms processed through mechanical and computer methods do not have a narrow column for qualifying the type of balance.

OTHER VARIATIONS OF THE BALANCE LEDGER FORM. Teachers who support the use of the standard form of ledger account in the first accounting cycle generally turn to one or more variations of the balance ledger **133**

form when a merchandising firm is treated in the accounting cycle. One type of variation is the four-column balance ledger form illustrated in Figure 9.3.

Cash						Account No. *101*	
						BALANCE	
DATE		**EXPLANATION**	**POST. REF.**	**DEBIT**	**CREDIT**	**DEBIT**	**CREDIT**
19—							
Nov.	*1*	*Balance*	—			*9,440 00*	
	30	. . . .	*CR1*	*7,475 00*		*16,915 00*	
	30	. . . .	*CP1*		*1,800 00*	*15,115 00*	

Figure 9.3

For the most part, teachers who use the four-column balance ledger form restrict its application to general ledger accounts. When the subsidiary ledgers for accounts payable and accounts receivable are introduced, however, a second variation of the balance ledger form is usually applied. For example, many teachers use a three-column format that shows the balance column labeled "Credit Balance" in an accounts payable subsidiary ledger account and "Debit Balance" for an accounts receivable subsidiary ledger account. These formats are illustrated in Figures 9.4 and 9.5, respectively.

ACCOUNTS PAYABLE LEDGER

Name	*Todd Electronics*					
Address	*22 Elmwood Avenue, Cincinnati, Ohio 45218*					
DATE		**EXPLANATION**	**POST. REF.**	**DEBIT**	**CREDIT**	**CREDIT BALANCE**
19—						
Jan.	*10*	*Inv. 0567; (1/8); 2/10, n/30*	*P1*		*360 00*	*360 00*
	18	. . . .	*CP3*	*360 00*		*— 00*
	25	*Inv. 0664; (1/22); 2/10, n/30*	*P1*		*850 00*	*850 00*
Feb.	*3*	*Inv. 0703; (2/1); 2/10, n/30*	*P2*		*120 00*	*970 00*

Figure 9.4

When presenting the three-column balance ledger form with a qualified balance column, emphasize that the accounts payable subsidiary ledger account is headed "Credit Balance" because the normal balance of such an

ACCOUNTS RECEIVABLE LEDGER

| Name | Jane Miller | | | | Credit Limit | $1,000 |
| Address | 89 Liberty Avenue, Ashley, Ohio 43015 | | | | Telephone | 369-3031 |

DATE		EXPLANATION	POST. REF.	DEBIT	CREDIT	DEBIT BALANCE
19—						
Jan.	11	Inv. 102; 2/10, n/30	S1	80 00		80 00
	26	Inv. 106; 2/10, n/30	S1	160 00		240 00
	27	Cash	CR3		80 00	160 00

Figure 9.5

account is a credit balance. Similarly, the accounts receivable subsidiary ledger balance column is headed "Debit Balance" because normal balances for such accounts are debit balances. A final instruction is usually given to overcome the problem of recording an abnormal balance. For example, some teachers recommend encircling a credit balance in a customer's account and encircling a debit balance in a creditor's account. On the other hand, some teachers prefer students to place the abbreviation *Dr.* or *Cr.* next to the amount that represents a balance opposite to the one indicated by the column heading.

THE YEAR-TO-DATE BALANCE LEDGER FORM. When teaching the updating of a general ledger file by means of a computer, many teachers point to the need for an account form that not only shows the monthly balance of an account, but also the accumulation of monthly balances to print the year-to-date balance. As stated earlier, many variations exist in account forms to meet the needs of management information and also the computer method adopted by the accounting system. In general, however, a computer printout of general ledger accounts may take a form similar to the illustration in Figure 9.6.

Observe that three general ledger accounts are shown: Account 101 for Cash, Account 102 for Petty Cash, and Account 111 for Accounts Receivable (the controlling account). With the aid of an overhead projector and a transparency of the illustration, emphasize the following points:

1. The general ledger is produced on one continuous roll of printout paper. Several accounts may appear on one page of the continuous form.
2. In a computer printout, entries are printed in capital letters.
3. In this computer printout, no account names are used; only the account codes are shown.
4. The principles of debit and credit for a ledger account have not changed. What has changed is the format of debits and credits.
5. Each general ledger account shows the opening balance (known as the *previous year-to-date*), the current debits and credits, and the closing balance (known as the *new year-to-date*).

135

ACCT NO	CENTRAL DIVISION JV-NO	DATE	PREV Y-T-D	PAGE 001 CURRENT	NEW Y-T-D
101	01	12/31/--	.	8,005.80	.
101	02	12/31/--	.	6,715.20CR	.
101	B101	12/31/--	2,460.70	.	.
101		12/31/--	2,460.70	1,290.60	3,751.30*
102	B102	12/31/--	50.00	.	.
102		12/31/--	50.00	.	50.00*
111	01	12/31/--	.	4,780.00CR	.
111	06	12/31/--	.	2,977.73	.
111	07	12/31/--	.	110.50CR	.
111	11	12/31/--	.	150.75	.
111	12	12/31/--	.	80.15CR	.
111	B111	12/31/--	6,740.18	.	.
111		12/31/--	6,740.18	1,842.17CR	4,898.01*

Figure 9.6

From *Elements of Accounting: A Systems Approach, Advanced Course* by Kaluza, Leonard, and Furneaux. Copyright © 1971. Reprinted by permission of McGraw-Hill Ryerson Limited.

6. The current month's debits and credits are listed in one column—here, the middle column.

7. To analyze the printout of any single account, the reader of the computer form must group all the lines that are identified by the account number. For example, the Cash account on page 001 of the printout shows four lines with the Account 101 (Cash). Similarly, two lines are shown for Account 102 (Petty Cash) and seven lines for Account 111 (Accounts Receivable).

8. Only credit amounts are qualified by the letters *CR* after every credit. Obviously, the unqualified amounts will represent debit figures. In a computer printout, therefore, all credits will usually be programmed to show the letters *CR* immediately after the dollar amount, while the debit is understood for all other dollar amounts.

9. To analyze how any balance was obtained through the computer, one must first read the balance between the debits and the credits in the Current column. For example, in Account 101, the difference between the debit and credit in the Current column is $1,290.60. Next, the difference is added to the previous year-to-date balance ($2,460.70), shown on the line immediately before the last printed line of that account. On the final line, the computer prints out the entire calculation of the new balance: the previous year-to-date ($2,460.70), the difference between the debits and credits in the Current column ($1,290.60), and the resulting new balance ($3,751.30) in the column marked "NEW Y-T-D."

10. In a computer method of updating the general ledger file, the entries are journalized on journal vouchers; consequently, the JV-NO. column is the posting reference column on this printout.

After the computer printout is analyzed, reinforce the students' understanding of earlier account forms by requiring the complete rewrite of one or more accounts. For example, if the Cash account were rewritten in the four-column balance ledger form, it would appear as shown in Figure 9.7.

CONCLUSIONS. Additional illustrations could be offered to prove the point that other ledger account forms do exist in accounting practice. In the main, however, these would be variations of the ones already presented. What conclusions, therefore, can be drawn from the study of the various forms previously illustrated?

1. In the initial accounting cycle, the T account is used to teach the analysis and recording of transactions in debit and credit form.

2. After the journal is presented, some teachers introduce the standard ledger form while other teachers proceed directly to a form of the balance ledger form.

3. There is a decided trend in favor of restricting the use of the standard ledger form to the study of the first accounting cycle or eliminating it altogether from accounting instruction.

4. One or more variations of the balance ledger form should be used

					BALANCE	
DATE	EXPLANATION	POST. REF.	DEBIT	CREDIT	DEBIT	CREDIT
19-- Dec. 1	Balance	—			2,460 70	
31	. . . .	CR1	8,005 80		10,466 50	
31	. . . .	CP2		6,715 20	3,751 30	

Cash   Account No. 101

Figure 9.7

when account forms are related to the study of subsidiary ledgers and the general ledger in a subsequent accounting cycle.

5. When an account form is applied to a data processing method, as through a computer, the form may change greatly; however, the principles of debiting and crediting do not change.

6. In accounting practice, the form of ledger account will vary according to the needs of management information and to the method of data processing used by the accounting system.

7. One effective method to study a variety of ledger forms is to gather actual examples of ledger account forms and present these on a bulletin-board display. When such a display is presented, point out the facts that support what the students have previously learned. In particular, the students should be able to translate the principles of debiting and crediting on any ledger account form.

Teaching the Need for the Balance Ledger Form

At some point, teachers must plan for the introduction of the balance ledger form of account. One teacher introduces the need for the three-column form as follows.

1. Before class, a summary of three transactions affecting Cash is placed on the overhead or on the chalkboard. Below the transactions, four T accounts are prepared for an oral review of the transactions. The Cash account is placed at the extreme right to allow space for the later addition of a third column.

2. When the class begins, the teacher reviews the analysis of each transaction and records the entries in the T accounts.

3. After the final transaction is recorded, the teacher asks the class to calculate the balance in the Cash account. Students are then asked to explain how the balance of Cash was obtained. And, finally, the class is asked to suggest an alternative method of showing a balance in the Cash account when many more transactions have to be recorded to the account.

4. At this point, the teacher draws a vertical line after the credit column in the Cash account and explains how to calculate and record a balance immediately after each entry. (If an overhead is used, the Balance column may be masked and then uncovered at this point.)

5. The teacher now directs the class to a different section of the chalkboard where the balance ledger form is to be introduced. If an overhead is used, the form may be masked and uncovered at this point, or a separate transparency may be prepared showing the expanded T account and the balance ledger form.

6. Each section of the balance ledger form is analyzed and related to the T-account form. Care is taken to emphasize that *debit* still means "left-hand column" and *credit* means "right-hand column." The only significant change is the addition of a Balance column to record the running balance after each transaction.

7. The teacher explains that in manual systems of processing information the running balance is calculated by hand. In mechanical and computer systems, however, this balance is calculated automatically by a machine. To prove this point, the teacher demonstrates the automatic calculation of the balance on an adding machine by using the subtotal key for each running balance.

8. Finally, the teacher emphasizes that there are several different forms of balance ledger accounts, and that these different forms must be tailored to the actual method of processing account information. (Several transparencies of actual forms of accounts may be shown to emphasize the main teaching points of a balance ledger form.)

Teaching the Chart of Accounts

Regardless of what account form is used for the teaching of the first ledger, the instructor must consider the introduction of the chart of accounts prior to the teaching of the mechanics of posting. At this early stage of using only one ledger for all accounts, many teachers prefer to present only three points: (1) the need for a chart of accounts; (2) a simple plan for grouping accounts; and (3) a simple plan for coding accounts.

In presenting the need for the chart of accounts, the students' attention should be drawn to the question of organizing all accounts under some efficient plan to facilitate the efficient preparation of financial statements. Then explain that such a plan is known as the *chart of accounts*.

Next, review the main sections of the balance sheet and the income statement. Students should have little difficulty identifying five headings: Assets, Liabilities, and Owner's Equity for the balance sheet; Revenue and Expenses for the income statement. Since the primary purpose of the ledger is to facilitate the preparation of these statements, the students should grasp the logic of grouping or classifying all accounts under these five headings.

The final step is to present a number code for identifying not only the five sections, but also all of the accounts under each of the five groupings. The teacher can explain that, in practice, different numbering codes exist to accommodate each firm's accounting system. One popular plan is the three-digit code, which may be presented as shown in Figure 9.8.

PLAN FOR A CHART OF ACCOUNTS

ASSETS (100 through 199)

101	Cash
102	Accts. Rec./King Stores
103	Accts. Rec./Frank Long
111	Furniture
112	Office Equipment
Etc.	

LIABILITIES (200 through 299)

201	Bank Loan
202	Accts. Pay./Modern Products
203	Accts. Pay./Oak Repair Shop
Etc.	

OWNER'S EQUITY (300 through 399)

301	Roy Bell, Capital
Etc.	

REVENUE (400 through 499)

401	Sales
Etc.	

EXPENSES (500 through 599)

501	Repairs Expense
502	Salaries Expense
Etc.	

Figure 9.8

Some teachers, of course, expand the plan to accommodate a further classification. For example, teachers at the college and university levels would probably introduce the distinction between current assets and fixed assets, and between current liabilities and long-term liabilities with the presentation of the chart of accounts. Other teachers, however, prefer to add to the chart's classification as each new account and account classification is introduced in their treatment of subsequent accounting cycles. Regardless of how soon subclasses of accounts are introduced in the ledger, teachers generally agree that the same coding plan should be used consistently throughout the course if the numbering system is to aid students in classifying accounts.

When presenting account codes, remember to stress their importance in data processing. For example, emphasize the fact that in a computer method of processing the ledger codes are essential to identify each account and even each class of accounts. In a fully classified ledger, for example, the title "Current Assets" may be assigned code 100, while the first current asset would be given code 101. Similarly, the title "Fixed Assets" may be given code 120, while the first fixed assets account is given 121, and so on. Such a presentation would help students to understand why gaps are deliberately left among different numbers in any account code system. The teacher who wishes to integrate accounting with computer data processing can present several examples of ledger codes to underline the importance of a chart of accounts in the data processing of the ledger.

Teaching the Mechanics of Posting

Teachers agree that the best way to teach the mechanics of posting from the two-column journal to ledger accounts is through the teacher explanation-demonstration method. Under this method, students are led through a series of logical steps to learn how to transfer data from the journal to the ledger. In presenting these steps, teachers often disagree on two areas: (1) the order of the steps in posting and (2) the date of posting.

Order of Posting

Before the introduction of data processing, many teachers presented the steps of posting in the following order. Some teachers still prefer this method. However, the second method listed should be emphasized in light of the posting methods used in business today.

1. Locate the ledger account for the first debit in the journal entry.
2. Enter the amount of the debit in the Debit column of the account. At this point, take time to emphasize that the amount is usually transferred first because it is the most important part of the entry.
3. Enter the date of the journal entry in the Date column of the ledger account.
4. Enter an explanation if one is needed to clarify the entry. Give an example of transferring an opening entry and demonstrate how the words *Opening entry* are written in the Explanation column.
5. In the Posting Reference column of the journal, enter the letter *J* (for *journal*) and the number of the journal page from which the entry is used. Explain that this step identifies an important cross-reference between the journal and the ledger account. (If a standard ledger form is used, the Posting Reference column on the debit side would be emphasized; similarly, the credit-side column would be singled out when a credit entry is being posted.)
6. In the Posting Reference column of the journal, enter the number of the ledger account to which the journal entry has just been posted. Explain that this cross-reference is necessary to show that the transaction was completely posted. Furthermore, emphasize the

importance of entering this cross-reference as the final step so that the posting clerk can resume posting quickly after any interruption.

7. Locate the ledger account for the next entry. If the next entry is a debit, then repeat the same procedure. If the next entry is a credit, apply the procedure on the credit side of the account.

With the introduction of data processing methods, especially in mechanical and computer posting, teachers generally favor presenting the mechanics of posting by emphasizing the logic of moving from the left side of the account to the right side. The steps are as follows:

1. Locate the ledger account for the first debit in the journal entry.
2. Enter the date of the journal entry in the Date column on the debit side of the ledger account.
3. Enter an explanation if one is needed to explain the entry.
4. Enter the journal initial and journal page number in the Posting Reference column.
5. Enter the debit amount in the Debit money column.
6. Enter the number of the account in the Posting Reference column of the journal to show that the information has been posted.
7. Locate the ledger account for the next entry. If the next entry is a debit, then repeat the same procedure. If the next entry is a credit, apply the procedure on the credit side of the account.

Some teachers favor a compromise solution to the problem of identifying the order of posting. Where a standard ledger form is used, some teachers identify the posting steps under a manual accounting method; therefore, they favor the order of transferring the amount as the first step. When the standard ledger form is replaced by the balance ledger form, teachers emphasize that this form is often used in machine and computer data processing; consequently, the left-to-right order is followed. Many other teachers argue that only one consistent method should be used to avoid later confusion. Furthermore, these teachers point to the fact that even under manual methods there is merit in transferring data from left to right to avoid errors and omissions in any posting procedure.

The Date of Posting Versus the Date of the Transaction

The controversy over which date to use in posting should cause little difficulty when the principle of transferring the dollar results of the financial transaction from the journal to the ledger is emphasized. Since the dollar results of transactions are captured on source documents, it follows that the date of such transactions is the source document date and the journal date. Under no circumstances should the date entered in the ledger be the actual date on which transaction data is transferred from the journal to the ledger. Emphasize this point by explaining the importance of identifying the transaction date in both books of entry. When the purchases journal is used, the journal often has the date of the transaction—the date on which the purchase invoice was approved for accounting purposes—and the date of the vendor's invoice. Students must be taught to use the date of the transaction in the ledger account and to enter the invoice number and invoice date in the Explanation column as a further reference.

Posting from Special Journals

When special journals are introduced, care must be taken to teach one or more additional posting procedures related to the special journal being used as the posting medium.

1. When a one-column special journal is used to post transaction data to a one-ledger system, two points must be emphasized: the posting of the individual entries and the posting of the journal total. For example, if a one-column cash receipts journal is the posting medium, explain that the individual credit entries are transferred to appropriate ledger accounts at some convenient time during the month; the posting date for these individual entries must be the transaction date. For posting the total to Cash debit, however, the month-end date is used.

2. Two additional points must also be emphasized when posting is taught from a multicolumn special journal: the procedure for preparing a proof of the column totals before posting these totals and the method of cross-referencing the column totals after they are transferred to ledger accounts. In demonstrating the concept of proving the column totals, some teachers use the pencil-footing procedure. Other teachers, however, prefer to use adding machine tapes to demonstrate a journal proof. (Teaching suggestions for presenting journal proofs are treated in detail in Chapter 10.) In teaching the cross-referencing of column totals, instructors agree that students must relate column totals to ledger accounts; consequently, an account number must appear immediately below each column total posted to the ledger accounts.

ORDER OF POSTING. When the balance ledger form is used to teach students how to post from special journals and the general journal, the question is often raised as to the correct order of posting from various journals to ledger accounts. Consider, for example, the use of special journals for sales, purchases, cash receipts, and cash payments in addition to the general journal. In what order should students post transaction data from journals to ledger accounts?

Some teachers argue that any order is acceptable as long as students transfer information correctly. Other teachers, however, point to the necessity of avoiding abnormal account balances in the ledger; consequently, they teach the following order: (1) from the sales journal, (2) from the cash receipts journal, (3) from the purchases journal, (4) from the cash payments journal, and (5) from the general journal. These teachers also prefer to maintain that order when subsidiary ledgers are introduced.

Introducing Subsidiary Ledgers and Controlling Accounts

At some convenient point in an introductory accounting course, teachers face the problem of moving from a one-ledger system to a two- or three-ledger system. In general, many teachers support such a move when the instruction is presented in relation to the merchandising firm. Furthermore, to keep the material simple, subsidiary ledgers and controlling accounts for only accounts payable and accounts receivable are introduced. One way to introduce these subsidiary ledgers is given here.

Present the Need for a Subsidiary Ledger

This need may be brought out by reviewing a balance sheet in which only a few creditors and a few customers are listed, as shown in Figure 9.9.

Central Sales Company
Balance Sheet
January 31, 19—

Assets			
Cash		12,100 00	
Accounts Receivable:			
Jane Miller	$130.00		
Smith & Adams	90.00		
Wilson's Radio Center	25.00		
Winston, Inc.	160.00	405 00	
Land		6,000 00	
Building		20,000 00	
Office Equipment		7,200 00	
Stockroom Equipment		12,100 00	
Total Assets			57,805 00

Liabilities			
Loans Payable		4,000 00	
Accounts Payable:			
Dixon & Hicks	$1,204.00		
Todd Electronics	1,210.00		
Vista Corporation	240.00		
George Young	276.00	2,930 00	
Mortgage Payable		10,000 00	
Total Liabilities			16,930 00

Owner's Equity			
John Hall, Capital			40,875 00
Total Liabilities and Owner's Equity			57,805 00

Figure 9.9

Then raise the problem of having many more creditors and many more customers, perhaps hundreds more of each. If the teacher questions effectively, students should be able to single out the problem of an overcrowded ledger, as well as the problem of producing a very lengthy balance sheet. As a result of identifying these problems, students are ready to respond to a more efficient system of accounting for accounts payable and accounts receivable.

Demonstrate and Explain How One Subsidiary Ledger Is Created

If purchases is being examined, then accounts payable can be treated. On the other hand, some teachers prefer to begin with sales; therefore, the subsidiary ledger for accounts receivable can be presented. For example, one effective illustration similar to the one shown in Figure 9.10 may be used to introduce important concepts for a subsidiary ledger of accounts payable.

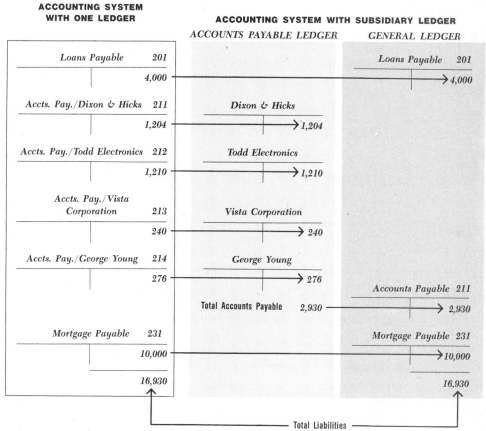

Figure 9.10

From the illustration, observe that only the basic concepts are presented. The actual mechanics of posting from the various journals to the two ledgers should be delayed at this stage. It is essential to emphasize the following points:

- When the creditors' accounts are placed in an accounts payable ledger (or creditors' ledger), an accounts payable controlling account is opened in the general ledger.
- Two ledgers are now part of the accounting system—a subsidiary ledger for the individual creditor accounts and a general ledger to house accounts to provide information for the preparation of the financial statements.
- The controlling account summarizes the balances of the individual creditors' accounts in the subsidiary ledger, and it keeps the general ledger in balance.
- The two ledgers identify their respective accounts differently from each other: the general ledger identifies all accounts according to the chart of accounts, while the accounts in the subsidiary ledger are usually arranged in alphabetic order. The teacher may explain that in some accounting systems the accounts of a subsidiary ledger may also be number coded. When such a coding system is used, however, the numbers must be quite distinct from the general ledger accounts. To avoid confusion, teachers generally agree to present the accounts in the accounts payable ledger in alphabetic order.
- By creating separate ledgers, the accounting system adds a measure of effective internal control. For example, persons working on individual accounts payable would be housed in the accounts payable department, while personnel assigned to work on the general ledger would be placed in a separate general accounting department. At this point, bring out how the controlling account actually "controls" the subsidiary ledger. In simple terms, one person in general accounting, separated from others, strikes a balance in the controlling account at the end of the month. On the other hand, another person in the subsidiary ledger department provides a total of the balances of individual accounts also at the end of the month. When the total of subsidiary ledger account balances is in agreement with the balance of the controlling account, then the accounting system has gained one more effective measure of providing internal control over its accounting information.

To visualize the relationship between the general ledger and the subsidiary ledger, one teacher uses a loose-leaf notebook containing a large number of ledger account pages. He directs the attention of the class to the bulkiness of the ledger and mentions that only one person can work on it at a time. The ledger is shown to contain approximately 100 pages of accounts receivable, 60 pages of accounts payable, and 40 pages of other assets, liabilities, and owner's equity accounts. The teacher then takes the 60 accounts payable pages out of the ledger and places them in another loose-leaf binder, called the accounts payable ledger. He then asks whether or not the general ledger will balance now that the accounts payable have been removed. The students readily recognize that it will not. The teacher then suggests that they insert one account in the general ledger to represent all the accounts removed. This account would show the balance of the accounts removed. This procedure is demonstrated, and the general ledger is balanced. The same procedure is followed with the accounts receivable.

Introduce a Ledger Account Form Appropriate for the General Ledger and the Subsidiary Ledger

As explained earlier, teachers prefer the balance ledger form at this stage over the standard ledger form.

Teach the Mechanics of Posting From the Journals to the Subsidiary Ledger

In addition to the points presented earlier on posting, emphasize the point that the concept of controlling is largely accomplished by the posting procedure. Posting to subsidiary ledger accounts is generally done daily, whereas totals affecting those same accounts are transferred from the columns of special journals to the controlling account monthly. When all postings are completed, the balance in a controlling account should be equal to the sum of the balances of the accounts found in the related subsidiary ledger.

It follows logically that, after presenting one subsidiary ledger, the same techniques would apply to the teaching of the second subsidiary ledger. In the final analysis, therefore, students would conclude that a three-ledger system would consist of one general ledger, and separate subsidiary ledgers for accounts payable and for accounts receivable.

Teaching Short Cuts in Journalizing and Posting

Teachers who present only the conventional view of journalizing all transactions and then posting these transactions from the journals to various ledgers usually encounter criticism from some of their future graduates who gain employment in various accounting positions. Perhaps the most often heard remarks follow along these lines:

1. "I did not enter each invoice in a sales journal; I was required to journalize only batch totals."
2. "I did not use a journal at all; I posted directly from source documents to the customer accounts."
3. "The business for which I worked did not use a journal to record sales invoices; our accounting system filed all sales invoices in a sales invoice binder."
4. "Our accounting system did not have an accounts receivable ledger; instead, we were required to file each source document in the customer's folder."

Many firms employ short cuts to process their accounting data, and several of these can be taught after the conventional view is learned by students. The three most common of these short cuts are batch processing, journalless accounting, and ledgerless accounting.

Introducing the Journalizing of Batch Totals

The concept of journalizing batch totals generally applies to any accounting system that reduces the amount of journalizing formerly done through the conventional procedure of journalizing each separate document. The concept can be introduced in this manner.

1. Give a short review of conventional journalizing and posting of a sale on credit for a merchandising business. In this review, take care to emphasize the use of two copies of the sales invoice: Copy 1 is sent to the customer; Copy 2 is used to record the transaction in the sales journal and then is filed in the unpaid accounts receivable file. In addition, emphasize the procedure of posting, at regular intervals, the entries from the sales journal to the individual customers' accounts in the subsidiary ledger. And, finally, review the procedure at the end of the month, when the sales journal is totaled and the double entry of this total is posted to the Accounts Receivable controlling account and the Sales account in the general ledger.

2. Give a short explanation to introduce the idea that some firms, especially those which process a large number of sales invoices on a regular basis, reduce the time-consuming job of copying the data from each sales invoice to a journal. An example may be given to identify a firm that has an average of twenty sales invoices a day. Then ask the class to respond to the question of how many entries would be required in the sales journal for one week and for one month. After responding, the students are ready to learn one method of reducing the number of entries in the sales journal.

3. Introduce the concept of preparing a batch of invoices and recording only the batch total. Present a second example to simplify the procedure. Suppose that the accounting system receives five sales invoices every hour to process. Explain that, instead of journalizing each invoice separately, the five source documents are arranged first in numerical order and then the amount of each invoice is listed on an adding machine tape. Once a total is obtained, emphasize that the group of invoices represents a batch, and that the batch total is now ready for journalizing. Students will have little difficulty in concluding that much time is saved by recording only the batch total in the sales journal. Take care to identify the general concept of batching; that is, a batch may consist of invoices for a part of a day, for a whole day, for a week, or for any other period of time, depending on the number of invoices to be processed.

4. Next, present the posting of the monthly total of all the batches recorded in the journal. An illustration such as the one in Figure 9.11 can not only present the procedure of posting the total but also can tie in the earlier procedures.

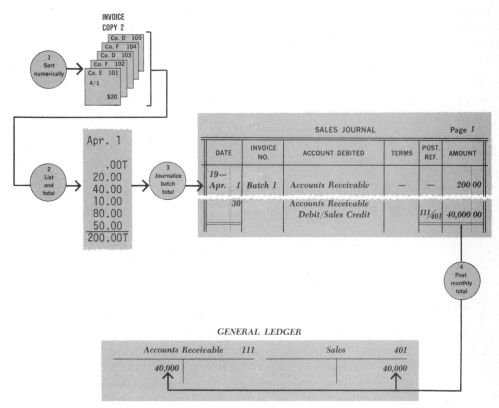

Figure 9.11

5. Referring to the illustration, emphasize three key points. First, point to the importance of preparing the adding machine tape. The adding machine tape is an important control document because it is the only independent record at this point of the number of invoices in the daily batch and the amount of each. Second, emphasize the importance of storing the batch of invoices with the adding machine tape for future reference. And, finally, single out the problem of the lack of posting to the individual customer accounts. Students should conclude that, although the general ledger has been updated by the process of posting the monthly total of all of the batched invoices, no provision has been made to post to the subsidiary ledger. This shortcoming allows the introduction of the concept of direct posting.

Introducing Direct Posting From Source Documents

Begin with a review of the use of the earlier invoice copies under a batching system. Since Copy 1 was mailed to the customer, and since Copy 2 was used to form the batch for the sales journal, explain that a third copy is required for use as the source medium for posting to the accounts receivable ledger. At this stage, present an illustration, similar to Figure 9.12, to show how the third copy is processed.

Referring to the illustration, emphasize these key points.

1. All third copies of the sales invoices are arranged in alphabetic sequence by customer name. The students should readily conclude that this step is required since individual customer accounts are usually filed in alphabetic order in many accounting systems.

2. A preliminary list of the batch of invoices is taken before posting occurs. This list is merely a listing of all invoices to be posted on an adding machine tape. It will be used later to check the accuracy of posting amounts to each individual customer's account. (In some accounting systems, the preliminary list may be omitted; consequently, proceed directly to the next point.)

3. The accounting clerk then posts the amount of each invoice to the appropriate customer's account in the subsidiary ledger. A check mark is made on the invoice, or the clerk initials it to indicate that it has been posted.

4. After all the invoices have been posted, a check is often made of the accuracy of the postings. The accounting clerk goes through the accounts in the subsidiary ledger and lists on an adding machine each amount that was posted that day. This listing becomes the proof tape, which must agree with the total of the batch tape recorded in the journal, as well as with the total of the preliminary list when such a list is also used. It is important to emphasize that the proof tape is prepared from the amounts posted to the ledger and not from the invoice (see the proof tape in Figure 9.12). Of course, if the totals do not agree, the error must be located before the next batch of invoices is posted.

5. When the totals of the tapes agree, all third invoice copies are placed in filing folders by customer's name. These folders are filed alphabetically in the accounts receivable filing cabinet.

In summarizing the concepts of journalizing batch totals and of posting directly from source documents, emphasize three important advantages. First, journalizing the batch total of sales invoices is much faster than recording in the sales journal the date, customer's name, amount, and other data for each sales invoice. Second, the system of direct posting from copies of the sales invoice to individual customer accounts can be done by a separate clerk, who quickly provides management an up-to-date picture of its accounts receivable ledger. And, third, the process of batching source

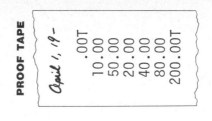

April 1, 19—

```
        .00T
      10.00
      50.00
      20.00
      40.00
      80.00
     200.00T
```

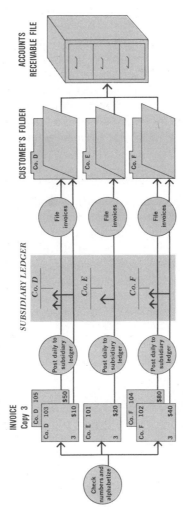

Figure 9.12

151

documents lends itself ideally to mechanical and computer methods of data processing.

One final point should be noted in presenting an analysis of any firm's batching system. Work in journalizing can be reduced in a similar manner when subsidiary ledger accounts are affected frequently by a single type of transaction. Thus the teacher may consider the presentation of other possibilities. For example, the processing of cash receipts may be done by journalizing only the batch totals of collections on account in the cash receipts journal. Individual credits to customers' accounts in the subsidiary ledger may then be posted directly from duplicate copies of the receipts or from other source documents that report the collections. Similarly, the teacher may present the processing of accounts payable by journalizing only the batch totals of purchases invoices. These changes in procedure and the increasing use of direct posting from source documents should prove to the student that accounting records and systems must be designed to meet the needs of the particular business enterprise.

Introducing Journalless Accounting

The teacher who has presented the concepts of journalizing batch totals and of posting directly from source documents can easily introduce the next short cut, which involves eliminating the use of the formal journal altogether. Perhaps the best method of teaching the journalless concept is to present the previous example with changes in the illustration as shown in Figure 9.13.

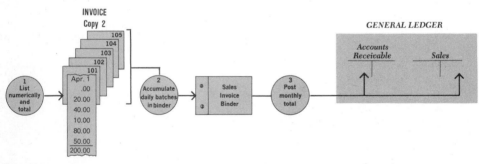

Figure 9.13

Before the illustration is analyzed, point out that Copy 1 and Copy 3 of the sales invoice are handled as before. Copy 1 is mailed to the customer, while Copy 3 is used as the source medium for direct posting to the subsidiary ledger. Now present an analysis for Copy 2 as follows. The duplicate copies of a group of invoices are sorted in numerical order to form a batch; then a batch total is prepared with the aid of an adding machine.

Instead of recording the total of the batch in a journal, the accounting clerk simply places each batch of invoices, with its own adding machine tape attached, in a sales invoice binder. The accounting clerk simply totals the individual batch figures on an adding machine to obtain a monthly total of credit sales. Using this new adding machine tape as the source document medium, the accounting clerk posts the monthly batch total as a debit to Accounts Receivable and a credit to Sales in the general ledger.

In summarizing the features of the journalless system, emphasize these points. First, the binder containing the sales invoices takes the place of the sales journal. Second, although no formal journal is used in journalless accounting, the concept of a journal still remains in the form of the binder. Third, there is no change in the double-entry principle and in the posting to the general ledger and the subsidiary ledger. And, finally, a similar system can be used for credit purchases, for paying invoices, for receiving cash on account from customers, and indeed in any situation where a large number of *like* source documents affects a firm's accounts receivable and accounts payable.

When concluding the teaching of journalless accounting, a fair evaluation of the system should be presented. On the positive side, the teacher can single out these advantages: (1) A journalless system of processing sales on credit saves time and money, particularly when there is a large volume of sales transactions. (2) Direct posting eliminates the chance of error in recording the information from the source document to a journal. (3) The necessity of copying the name of the customer or creditor and other details which are commonly found in the journal is eliminated, saving considerable time. (4) Time saving by division of labor is possible because invoices can be divided into a number of alphabetical batches and assigned to several posting clerks.

On the other hand, a fair evaluation acknowledges the fact that many accountants do not support journalless accounting for these reasons: (1) The journalizing of batch totals for later posting to the general ledger provides a greater degree of security than the use of a binder alone, so that any transaction can be accurately and quickly traced back if a source document, or a batch of documents, is lost. (2) Eliminating the journal for posting to the general ledger also eliminates a valuable check on the accuracy of the complete double entry. If transactions are recorded directly in the general ledger, there is the danger of omitting the debit or the credit side of the entry, or of making two debit or two credit entries. (3) Eliminating the journal also eliminates the real advantage gained through the use of special columns in a special journal. For example, if sales taxes are charged on the invoices, a separate adding machine tape must be made to obtain the amount of the sales tax payable to the government. Similarly, a separate analysis of department sales must be made on adding machine tapes when management requires such a sales analysis. Thus, in some cases, a multicolumn sales journal may still be helpful. **153**

Introducing Ledgerless Accounting

The teacher who has presented the earlier short cuts of journalizing batch totals, of posting directly from source documents, and of eliminating the journal altogether may wish to introduce one further refinement in processing a firm's accounts receivable and accounts payable. This further refinement introduces the ideal of eliminating the subsidiary ledger for customers and creditors.

As with the presentation of the previous short cuts, begin with a review of processing the earlier examples, for accounts receivable, for example. In this case, explain that some firms eliminate not only the sales journal, but also posting to individual customers' accounts in a subsidiary ledger; hence, the idea of a journalless and a ledgerless accounting system. In support of the explanation, prepare overhead transparencies to present at least five sets of illustrations.

The first illustration can show three copies prepared for the accounting system as in Figure 9.14.

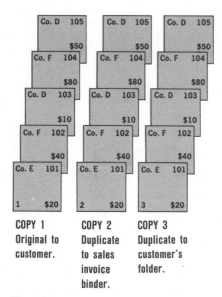

COPY 1
Original to customer.

COPY 2
Duplicate to sales invoice binder.

COPY 3
Duplicate to customer's folder.

Figure 9.14

The second illustration, shown in Figure 9.15, is a repeat of an earlier one for the handling of Copy 2 under the journalless approach. When repeating what the student has learned earlier about journalless accounting, it is critical to emphasize that the general ledger does *not* disappear from a ledgerless system. Take care to stress that only the traditional subsidiary ledger is being eliminated and that a traditional general ledger is important for the preparation of financial statements.

The third illustration, shown in Figure 9.16, introduces the concept of the ledgerless system for accounts receivable. From the illustration, students

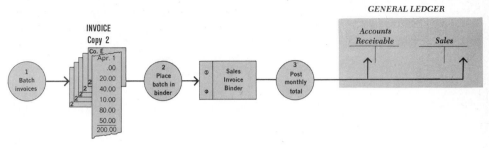

Figure 9.15

should conclude that all third copies of the sales invoices are alphabetized according to customer name and are then placed in the customers' folders in the accounts receivable file. Emphasize two points at this stage: (1) To find the total owed by any customer, the customer's folder is removed from the file, and the amounts of the invoices are added (usually on an adding machine). (2) While the source documents filed in folders have replaced the accounts receivable ledger, they have not replaced the need for the controlling account in the general ledger. Return to the second illustration to make this point clear.

A fourth illustration presents the first of two other procedures affecting accounts receivable: how to handle sales returns and allowances. Begin by identifying the source document that has captured the transaction, that is,

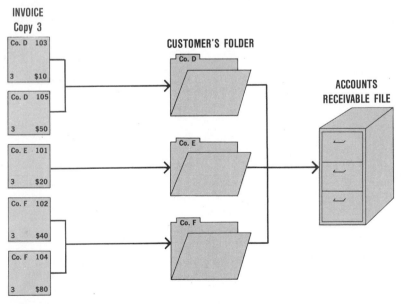

Figure 9.16

155

the credit memorandum. In addition, have the students review the analysis of the double entry in the general journal. Once again, it is important that students conclude that double entries must be posted to the general ledger; otherwise, it would be most difficult to prepare an accurate set of financial statements. For handling the credit memorandum itself, use again the third illustration, altered so that the credit memorandum is placed in the customer's folder in the accounts receivable file. Of course, a separate illustration can be prepared showing the processing of one or more actual credit memoranda to the file folders. Explain that the credit memorandum is usually attached to the invoice on which the merchandise was originally billed; therefore, an examination of both documents can quickly lead to the calculation of the net amount owed by the customer.

By now, the students should have learned how to process credit sales and sales returns and allowances without the use of the formal accounts receivable ledger. What remains is an analysis of a transaction showing cash received "on account." A separate overhead transparency, similar to Figure 9.17, showing the processing of one customer's check may be prepared.

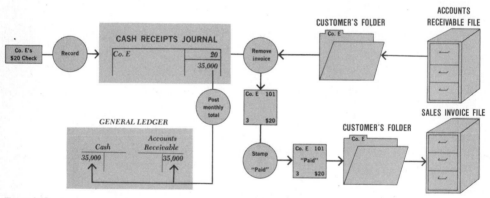

Figure 9.17

From the illustration, again emphasize the need for a journal to serve as the source medium for updating the general ledger accounts. In this case, the cash receipts journal is being used to update both Cash and the controlling account for Accounts Receivable. Also trace through the steps of removing the invoice from the customer's folder, marking the invoice "Paid," and refiling the paid invoice under the name of the customer in a permanent file, called a *sales invoice file*.

A point of accounting systems terminology can now be presented. Explain that because a separate record of each unpaid invoice is maintained in an open file, the ledgerless method of accounting for accounts receivable is known as an *open-item system*. Compare this open-item system with the formal treatment of maintaining a subsidiary ledger for accounts receivable. The key point to teach is the difference between the two methods. The open-item system is different from the *balance-forward approach* in which a record of the customer's total outstanding balance is maintained, and payments are applied against the balance rather than individual invoices. General examples may be given to reinforce the students' learning of the two methods. For example, although there are exceptions, the open-item accounts receivable system is widely used by businesses which sell to other businesses (manufacturers and wholesalers) because they prefer to pay invoices on an individual basis. On the other hand, the balance-forward system will more usually be found in businesses that deal with consumers as individuals (department stores, specialty shops, oil companies) because consumers prefer to pay the amount owing on the balance due in their account.

It should be self-evident that the same principles for processing accounts receivable without a formal ledger for customer accounts can also be applied to the teaching of accounts payable. After the teaching of one or both ledgerless systems, it is critical that students prepare an evaluation of the method by offering both advantages and disadvantages.

Teaching About Other Subsidiary Ledgers

In presenting an introductory course, teachers are generally satisfied that students grasp reasonably well the concepts of subsidiary ledgers for accounts receivable and accounts payable, as well as understand the function for the related controlling accounts in the general ledger. When testing students on applying these concepts to other possible subsidiary ledgers, however, many teachers report that their students are still very much in doubt on how another subsidiary ledger works. One may conclude, therefore, that beginning accounting students should be introduced to one and possibly two subsidiary ledgers in addition to accounts receivable and accounts payable.

One subsidiary ledger that may be considered is the fixed asset ledger. (For teaching suggestions on introducing the fixed asset ledger, refer to Chapter 12.) Another possibility is presenting a merchandise inventory ledger, which is ideally suited when the perpetual inventory method is being examined for a merchandising firm. In more advanced topics, teachers will find other possibilities. For example, subsidiary ledgers for raw materials, goods in process, and finished goods are ideally suited in the presentation of manufacturing accounting. Similarly, a stockholders' subsidiary ledger may be presented when the capital stock account is being analyzed in corporation accounting.

Regardless of the type of subsidiary ledger being considered, successful teachers agree that students must learn not only how to construct subsidiary ledgers, but also how to distinguish between ledgers. These general guidelines may be helpful to students.

General Rules for Constructing Subsidiary Ledgers

First, divide the ledger into several very definite parts. Second, search the ledger for certain account groups. Third, analyze the accounts within each group to learn which are sufficiently numerous to warrant their own separate ledgers. Fourth, set up the separate new ledgers, which will be known as subsidiary ledgers. Fifth, replace the accounts transferred to the subsidiary ledger with an appropriate controlling account. And, finally, rename the original ledger as the general ledger.

General Rules for Distinguishing Between Ledgers

First, identify the ledger in which all accounts are kept for the preparation of financial statements as the general ledger. Second, identify any ledger which contains accounts of a like nature as a subsidiary ledger. And, finally, check that the accounts in the subsidiary ledger are summarized and controlled in the general ledger by a controlling account.

Questions and Projects

1. Prepare a lesson plan for teaching one of the following:
   a. Posting from the two-column journal to ledger accounts.
   b. Posting from a single-column special journal.
   c. Posting from a multicolumn special journal.

2. Suppose you were faced with the decision of introducing a ledger form after completing the study of journalizing in a two-column journal. What ledger form would you select? Give reasons for your answer.

3. Would you use the standard form of ledger account with your introductory class? Explain why or why not.

4. What ledger form would you use for teaching posting **(a)** to the general ledger, **(b)** to the accounts receivable ledger, and **(c)** to the accounts payable ledger? Give reasons for each answer.

5. Describe one account form that is used in the updating of a general ledger file through computer data processing. Would you present such a form to an introductory accounting class? Explain why or why not.

6. Do the principles of debiting and crediting change when an account form is applied to a computer method of processing accounting data? Explain your answer.

7. Describe one method for teaching the need for the balance ledger form.

8. At what point of accounting instruction would you teach the chart of accounts? Give reasons for your answer.

9. Assume that you will present the lesson on the chart of accounts to an introductory accounting class. Show a sample chart that you would use to demonstrate the basic concept related to such a chart. Would you classify assets and liabilities in your chart? Explain why or why not.

10. In presenting the mechanics of posting, some teachers emphasize that the first step is to enter the amount journalized to the correct amount column of the account; then the date, explanation (if any), and the posting references are entered. Do you agree with this order of posting from the journal to the ledger account? Give reasons for your answer.

11. Describe your favorite teaching procedure for showing students the need for, and value of, posting references.

12. In checking posting work, a teacher finds that students are entering the wrong date in the ledger. What important principle should be emphasized to the students to eliminate any error regarding the date that must appear for the posted entry?

13. What teaching points must be emphasized when posting is taught from a multicolumn special journal?

14. A lengthy merchandising problem involving special journals, the general journal, and posting to three ledgers is assigned to a beginning accounting class. In what order should students be instructed to post from the journals to the ledgers? Give reasons for your answer.

15. Prepare a lesson plan for teaching one of the following:
  a. Introducing the subsidiary ledger for accounts receivable.
  b. Introducing the subsidiary ledger for accounts payable.

16. If possible, prepare an overhead transparency to support the presentation of the concepts related to the teaching of a two-ledger system involving the general ledger and a subsidiary ledger for accounts receivable or accounts payable. What teaching points should be brought out in support of this visual aid?

17. In what way does a controlling account actually "control"?

18. In discussing the arrangement of accounts in the accounts receivable subsidiary ledger, one teacher argues strongly for teaching an alphabetic arrangement only. Another teacher, however, argues for presenting an alphanumeric code because he has seen many customer accounts updated through a computer. Which method would you use with your beginning accounting class? Give reasons for your answer.

19. Prepare a series of overhead transparencies for presenting the topic of introducing ledgerless accounting for processing accounts receivable or accounts payable.

20. Suppose that, after having taught the topic of ledgerless accounting, you tested the knowledge of the students by requiring them to produce a written comparison between the short cut and the conventional use of the subsidiary ledger. What advantages and disadvantages would you accept for a complete answer to a fair evaluation of the ledgerless system?

Case Problem

Mary Cowens, a student in a beginning accounting class, works in the accounting office of a local department store. Mary reported to her accounting teacher that journals are not used in her office. Sales slips are posted directly to the customers' accounts and no entries are made in journals. She expects to work in the same office when she is graduated from school, and she does not see why she should record entries first in journals and then post to accounts, for that is not the way she does it on the job. In fact, Mary more or less refuses to make any journal entries.

Mary's instructor told her that he does not care what she does on the job, but in the accounting class journals will be used. If she expects to pass the accounting course, she is to do what she is told.

Do you think the instructor has handled the situation correctly? How would you have handled it?

CHAPTER 10

Teaching the Trial Balance and Other Accounting Proofs

Once the students understand journalizing and posting, they are ready to be introduced to the third stage of the accounting cycle: the trial balance. Since the trial balance is basically an accounting proof—it proves that the ledger is in balance—it is often convenient to follow a discussion of the trial balance with similar coverage of other accounting proofs. Some accounting proofs are only touched upon in this chapter because they have been introduced in earlier chapters. For example, journal proofs are covered in the chapter on journalizing, and account balance proofs are treated in the chapter on posting. Cash proofs and journal voucher proofs, however, warrant fuller explanation; therefore, they are examined here in greater detail.

As usual, let us begin with a review of the accounting principles fundamental to an understanding of trial balances, cash proofs, and journal voucher proofs.

ACCOUNTING FUNDAMENTALS

Trial Balance

1. There is an equality of total debit amounts and total credit amounts in the journal. Therefore, this should also be true in the ledger. The trial balance is a check to see whether or not this equality has been maintained in the ledger.
2. The trial balance merely indicates that the totals of debit and credit balances in the ledger accounts are equal. It does not prove the accuracy of the original journal entries.

(continued)

3. Accounts in the ledger are assigned numbers which are in accordance with the chart of accounts.
4. Accounts are listed on the trial balance in the order in which they appear in the ledger—assets, liabilities, capital, revenue, and cost and expense.
5. The normal balance of any account would appear on the same side as it is established in the accounting equation.
6. Most errors that prevent the trial balance from balancing result from errors in posting—copying figures incorrectly or placing them on the incorrect side of the appropriate account in the ledger.

Cash Proofs

1. Cash is the most valuable asset of any firm and is, therefore, more susceptible to fraud and theft than any other asset.
2. All efficient accounting systems include internal controls to prevent losses of cash from fraud and theft.
3. To provide for the efficient control of cash, accurate accounting records must be maintained for cash receipts, cash payments, and cash balances.
4. One important internal control principle is to separate the function of handling cash from the maintenance of accounting records. For example, the cashier should not maintain the accounting records and should not have access to those records. On the other hand, accounting personnel should not have access to the asset itself.
5. A second internal control measure is to separate the function of receiving cash from that of disbursing cash. It follows, therefore, that the same person should not handle cash receipts and also make cash payments.
6. A third important area of internal control is to enforce a comprehensive policy that includes depositing all cash receipts intact and on a daily basis in a bank account; making all cash payments (except for petty expenses) by check; and maintaining a petty cash imprest system to pay minor expenses.
7. A final but important principle to safeguard cash is to require that a series of accounting cash proofs be maintained to control the receipts of cash, the payments of cash, and the balance of cash.

Journal Voucher Proofs

1. In a large-scale business enterprise, the accounting function is generally organized around specialized departments, such as Accounts Receivable, Accounts Payable, Payroll, and General Accounting.
2. General Accounting may be considered the key area in the

(continued)

organization of the overall accounting activity because it is responsible for the general ledger.

3. The general ledger is the important ledger in any accounting system because the information contained therein is used to prepare financial statements on a monthly and on a yearly basis.

4. The general ledger is organized around a chart of accounts. Each account in this chart is given a short descriptive name in order to reveal the function and purpose of that account.

5. Where accounts are updated through a computer method, each account in the chart of accounts is given an account code. This code consists usually of a three-digit number, which permits a more precise identification of the account for data processing purposes.

6. As applied to the processing of the general ledger, it is widely held that general accounting is the functional responsibility of the financial system, while the computer department is essentially the service center that provides the method of processing the financial information.

7. As a functional responsibility, general accounting is held responsible to provide accurate information to update the general ledger accounts and the accounting reports that are generated as a result of this updating. To ensure that accurate information is maintained, general accounting must control the source media that are used to update the general ledger. One method of effective control is to insist on a proof of journal vouchers—the source media—before computer data processing updates the general ledger and prints the set of financial statements.

Performance Goals

Some performance goals for lessons on the trial balance and on cash proofs and journal voucher proofs are given below:

1. Given a standard ledger account, the student should be able to balance the account. This involves pencil-footing the total debits and total credits, determining the account balance, and entering the account balance in pencil.

2. Given heading data and a list of accounts with their balances, the student should be able to prepare an accurate trial balance.

3. Given a list of errors in journalizing, posting, balancing accounts, and entering items in a trial balance, the student should be able to identify the errors that will be revealed by the trial balance and the errors that will not be revealed by the trial balance.

4. Given a trial balance that does not balance, the student should be able to locate the errors and correct the trial balance.
5. Given a ledger and an adding-listing machine, the student should be able to prepare a "quick" trial balance with a zero proof.
6. Given subsidiary ledgers for accounts receivable and accounts payable, the student should be able to prepare trial balances for each of the subsidiary ledgers and prove them against their controlling accounts in the general ledger.
7. Given the data for cash receipts, the student should be able to prepare cash proofs for procedures using cash registers and sales slips received for cash in person and remittance slips for cash received through the mail.
8. Given a series of questions about the procedure for verifying the cash account balance and the checkbook balance during the month and at the end of the month, the student should be able to answer the questions.
9. Given the data in a special cash receipts journal, cash payments journal, and checkbook, the student should be able to prepare a cash proof during the month and at the end of the month.
10. Given all the required data, the student should be able to reconcile a bank statement.
11. Given a series of questions about journal voucher proofs, the student should be able to answer questions about receiving general ledger source data, preparing journal vouchers, batching journal vouchers, and preparing the journal voucher proof list.

Teaching the Trial Balance

To set the scene for the trial balance, first review the nature of each account illustrated in the accounting equation and how the accounts are established within the equation. Generally, very few teaching problems are encountered in the review of accounts for assets, liabilities, and the owner's equity Capital account. What usually troubles students is the accounting of revenue and expense; therefore, a thorough review of revenue and expense accounts and their effect on the accounting equation is essential. At least the following three accounting fundamentals should be reviewed.

First, revenue is identified as an inflow of assets in the form of cash and/or accounts receivable as a result of the sale of goods and/or services. Since assets are increased, the left side of the accounting equation must similarly be increased. On the right side of the equation, some element must be increased by an identical amount because the equation must balance. Since liabilities are not affected, the revenue causes the third element (owner's equity) to increase. Revenue is, therefore, a plus factor under owner's equity. Any revenue account is shown as a credit because owner's equity accounts must be increased on the same side as owner's equity appears in the accounting equation.

Second, expense is identified as an outflow of assets in the form of cash as a result of incurring costs in the process of creating revenue. Of course, this outflow of cash may be delayed if the expense incurred is identified through a liability. For example, a bill is received for advertising the firm's services or products, and the bill gives credit of 30 or 60 days. It is essential to communicate the concept that an expense cannot be identified without relating the activity to the revenue process. Assuming a direct cash expense, the left side of the equation decreases as a result of a cash decrease. Similarly, the right side of the equation must decrease by the amount of the expense. Since liabilities are not affected, expenses under owner's equity causes the third element in the equation to go down. Since owner's equity in the equation is decreased by the expense, the record of the expense is shown as a debit in the Expense account, because any decrease to owner's equity must be reflected on the opposite side to the one where owner's equity is established in the equation. Note that this does not mean that expenses are decreasing; the minus sign before the Expense account simply reflects the effect of the transaction on the elements of the accounting equation. Review also the effect of that expense transaction which affects a liability as, for example, the advertising bill given earlier. Here again, liabilities are increased while expenses decrease owner's equity on the right side of the equation.

Third, once revenues and expenses are identified for an accounting period, both are matched in order to determine the net income (or net loss) for that period. An excess of revenue over related expenses will cause owner's equity to increase, because the net income is added to the owner's equity capital (investment) in the equation. On the other hand, an excess of expenses over revenue will decrease owner's equity, and this decrease will be shown as a minus factor opposite the owner's equity capital in the accounting equation.

Once these three accounting fundamentals are reviewed, the teacher can demonstrate the basic concept that all debit account balances must be equal to all credit account balances. This demonstration is easily achieved by shifting the T account for Expense (shown as a minus factor on the right side of the equation) to the left side of the equation. By moving the expense accounts to the left side, all debit balances can be added together, while all credit (right side) balances can similarly be added. Of course, the students should conclude that the equation still remains in balance under such a simple transfer arrangement.

Launching the Topic

One way to introduce the trial balance is to emphasize the need for proving the accuracy of postings that students have already completed. Point out the following facts:

1. The students enter a series of transactions in a two-column journal and post these entries to a ledger. Each entry is a double entry

METHODS OF TEACHING ACCOUNTING

containing one or more debits and credits. The debit entries are posted to accounts in the ledger different from those to which the corresponding credit entries are posted.

2. If the debits and credits are equal in the journal and if these figures are all correctly transferred to the ledger, the total of the debit entries in the ledger will be equal to the total of the credit entries.

3. In accounting, there is a device for verifying the accuracy of the work in posting from the journal to the ledger. This device, or proof, is known as a *trial balance* and means exactly what the two words imply—a preliminary or trial adding of all the figures in the ledger to see if the total of all debit entries equals the total of all credit entries.

4. It is advantageous to take a trial balance at frequent intervals. If errors have been made, they can be found more readily. If, for example, 5,000 journal entries were to be posted to one ledger—and all were posted correctly—the total of all the debit entries in the ledger would equal the total of all the credit entries in the ledger. If, however, errors were made during the posting process, the total debits might not equal the total of the credits. If all 5,000 entries were posted before checking the accuracy, it might be necessary to check over the entire 5,000 entries before finding the errors.

Another method that might be used to introduce the trial balance is to show a journal page containing approximately a dozen entries and a ledger in which these journal entries have been posted. Then point out that the equality of the debit and credit amounts entered on each page of the journal can be proved rather easily by footing the two money columns. Following this step, show that the debit amount and the credit amount of any one entry in the ledger are one or more pages apart. Next ask how the equality of all the debits and all the credits entered in the entire ledger might be proved. In response to this question, some student may suggest a procedure similar to that used in the journal—add all the debit amounts and all the credit amounts entered on each page and then add all these page totals together. From here it is just one step forward to suggesting that this might be done for each account instead of for each page.

Preparing an Accurate Trial Balance

The solution of an actual problem will do more to help students understand how a trial balance is prepared than an extended series of questions and answers. Place on the chalkboard or transparency the ledger for one of the problems the students have already completed, one which they have previously journalized and posted to the ledger.

The objective at this point is to teach students how to prepare an accurate trial balance, and this objective may be taught more effectively by requiring the students to consider the logic of the following steps:

1. Preparing a proof of each journal page.
2. Preparing a proof of each account balance in the ledger.
2. Copying the account titles, account numbers, and balances in proper form.
4. Adding the trial balance and checking the accuracy of the trial balance totals.

If students perform these operations as separate steps, completing one before beginning another, many mechanical errors which throw trial balances out of balance will be eliminated. When students go through the ledger adding the debits and credits, calculating the account balances, and writing the name and balance of each account on the trial balance—all as one operation—they are more likely to make arithmetic and placement errors than if they perform the operations as four separate steps. It is difficult, however, to explain this in such a way as to make believers of all students.

All accounting teachers have had the experience of observing students preparing a trial balance by merely listing two columns of figures as shown in Figure 10.1.

Debit	Credit
293.43	408.00
82.90	678.43
13.56	416.43
3,870.09	1,000.00
1,400.00	3,908.57
338.50	
113.50	6,411.43
130.57	
29.88	
6,272.43	

Figure 10.1

The same information, put in proper trial balance form, results in the arrangement shown in Figure 10.2.

The student errors are now obvious. Notes Receivable is an asset account and should have a debit balance; Sales, a revenue account, should have a credit balance. Correct placement of these two figures will give a correct trial balance.

Students who come for assistance on a trial balance similar to the one in Figure 10.1 should be told to "put the trial balance in proper form, list account titles, numbers, and balances on a sheet of two-column paper, and then bring it back." Teachers who follow this procedure find that many

	Debit	Credit
Cash	$ 293.43	
Notes Receivable		$ 408.00
Accts. Rec./C. J. Adams	82.90	
Accts. Rec. / R. S. Peters	13.56	
Merchandise Inventory	3,870.09	
Delivery Equipment	1,400.00	
Notes Payable		1,000.00
Accts. Pay./ J. W. Davis, Inc.		678.43
Accts. Pay./ Harold's Supply Co.		416.43
R. M. Randle, Capital		3,908.57
Sales	338.50	
Salary Expense	113.50	
Supplies Expense	130.57	
Miscellaneous Expense	29.88	
	$6,272.43	$6,411.43

Figure 10.2

students do not return to ask for help: the process of putting the trial balance in its proper form focuses the students' attention on errors.

Students often ask about listing an account with no balance in the trial balance. The students' question can be answered by emphasizing the nature of the trial balance: a trial balance is a summary or schedule of all ledger accounts that have balances. An account that is "in balance," therefore, is generally omitted from the trial balance.

Locating Errors
When the Trial Balance
Is Out of Balance

Students should be taught the procedures to be followed when the trial balance does not balance. Certain procedures will aid students in locating errors. These procedures should be demonstrated for students by means of several illustrations of each. (This would not be done the first time that the procedure of taking a trial balance was presented to the class but at a subsequent class period, after the students have had an opportunity to prepare several trial balances for themselves.) These ideas should preferably be presented in the order that one would normally follow in trying to correct a trial balance. An outline which might be used in part or in its entirety is presented here.

Throughout the outline the amount by which the trial balance is out of balance will be referred to as the *error amount*. In teaching the finding and correcting of errors, begin by assuming that only one error has been made. After the different types of errors have been considered in this way, problems involving two or more errors may be considered.

1. Read the trial balance. If an adding machine is used, check the figures on the tape against those on the trial balance.
2. Determine exactly by how much the trial balance is out of balance. Look for an entry of this amount that may not have been posted.
3. Divide the error amount by two. Look for an entry of this amount that may have been posted as a debit when it should have been posted as a credit, or vice versa.
4. Apply certain tests of arithmetic accuracy.
   a. If the error amount is 1 cent, 10 cents, $1, $10, or $100, or some other round number, an error in addition or subtraction may have occurred.
   b. If the error amount is divisible by 9, the error could be the result of one of three causes:
      (1) Two errors in addition or subtraction (as described in point *a*) operating against each other. When this occurs, the error amount will be 9, 90, 900, 999, 909.
      (2) The sliding of all digits one column to the right or to the left—*$2,706.50* written as *$27,065.00* or *$270.65.*
      (3) Transposition of figures—*$64* written as *$46;* or *$38.47* written as *$83.47, $34.87* or *$38.74.*
   c. If the error amount is divisible by 99, a double slide might be the cause, that is, a shift of two columns to the right or left—*$36.00* written as *$3,600.00* or as *36 cents.*
5. Examine the trial balance for reasonableness.
   a. Check to see if the Purchases account balance and the Sales account balance appear reasonable in terms of the inventories and in terms of each other.
   b. A customer's account with a credit balance might be the result of an overpayment but most likely this situation would indicate that an error has been made.
6. Skim through the ledger rapidly, checking to see if any accounts not in balance have been omitted from the trial balance. Check the balances shown on the trial balance against those shown in the ledger, both as to amount and whether or not it is a debit or a credit balance.
7. Check the calculation of the account balances in the ledger.
8. Check the posting.
   a. Some prefer to check from the ledger to the journal account, rather than from the journal to the ledger account.
   b. Make sure that the totals of the special journals have been posted. When subsidiary ledgers are used, check to see that the total of

169

              sales and purchases journals are posted to the control account as well as to the Purchases and Sales accounts.

c.   If control accounts and a two-column general journal are used, make sure that the amounts are double posted—that is, to both the general ledger and the subsidiary ledger.

d.   Place a check mark by each figure in the ledger and the corresponding figure in the journal. When all posting is checked, there should be a check mark by every entry in the journals and in the ledger.

e.   Watch carefully to see that debit journal entries are posted as debits in the ledger and that credit entries are posted as credits.

Errors Not Shown
by the Trial Balance

Students need to recognize that, even though the trial balance is in balance, this fact is no assurance that the books are accurate. The trial balance merely indicates that the ledger accounts balance. The following kinds of errors will not show up on the trial balance:

1.   Journal entries that are (a) incorrect as to the account debited or the account credited, (b) correct but are posted to the *correct* side of the *wrong* account, (c) incorrect as to amount in both debit and credit figures, or (d) not posted.

2.   Transactions that are omitted completely from the journal.

3.   Transactions that are journalized more than once.

4.   Two errors for the same amount that offset each other.

Illustrations and test problems provide two excellent means of assurance that students understand the types of errors that the trial balance will and will not reveal. For example, place on the chalkboard or overhead the T accounts representing a ledger and a copy of the trial balance prepared from that ledger. By referring to some of the original entries and posting them incorrectly, illustrate that the ledger may be in error, even though the trial balance is in balance. Thus, a journal entry charging a customer for an amount might be posted to the debit side of some other customer's account. By erasing the correct entry from one account and posting this incorrectly as suggested, show that the ledger still balances. Give a greatly exaggerated example by posting a journal entry debiting Sales to the debit side of Purchases, and then later posting it to the debit side of Salary Expense. In each case, trace the effect of the posting error through to the trial balance, showing that it still balances because each time the debit was posted as a debit. Then post a debit entry to the credit side of the correct account and show that this throws the trial balance out of balance by *an amount equal to twice the amount of the entry.* Unless such illustrations and demonstrations are used, the student may not clearly understand what a trial balance proves and what it does not prove.

Determining the Missing Balance

There is another type of illustrative problem that will help to drive home the lesson of the trial balance. Supply the student with the balances of all accounts except one. Do not indicate whether the accounts have debit balances or credit balances. Ask the student for the balance of the one account whose balance is not given. For example:

Cash	$ 293.43
Notes Receivable	408.00
C. T. Adams	82.90
R. S. Peters	13.56
Merchandise Inventory	3,870.09
Delivery Equipment	1,400.00
J. W. Davis, Inc.	678.43
Harold's Supply Co.	416.43
Notes Payable	
R. M. Randle, Capital	3,908.57
Sales	338.50
Salary Expense	113.50
Supplies Expense	130.57
Miscellaneous Expenses	29.88

The problem here is to determine which accounts have debit balances and which have credit balances. If no error is made, the difference between these two totals is the amount of the account whose balance is not supplied—in this case, Notes Payable.

Preparing a "Quick" Trial Balance

Adding-listing machines can be used in conjunction with the teaching of the trial balance. For example, students will respond positively toward an assignment that requires them to prepare a lengthy trial balance in proper form and which includes an accompanying adding machine tape to prove the addition of the debit and credit totals in the trial balance. When a formal trial balance is not required, however, the teacher can communicate the idea that an accounting clerk may be asked to use an adding-listing machine to check the equality of debits and credits directly from the ledger. This is known as taking a "quick" trial balance. The following steps can be demonstrated on the majority of adding-listing machines.

1. Clear the machine register of any previously entered figures. A clear symbol must be shown on the tape.
2. Begin with an examination of the first account in the ledger and list in order all accounts with debit balances as *additions.*
3. Return to the beginning of the ledger and then list all accounts with credit balances as *subtractions.*
4. When the final account balance has been listed, clear the register

with the total key or bar. Since the debits (additions) and credits (subtractions) have been listed in one column—that is, within the same machine register—the final printout must give a zero.

If the final result is a *zero proof,* then the ledger is considered to be in balance. If it is not a zero, an error has been made and the tape can be used as the clerk checks back through the ledger in an attempt to locate the error.

Interpreting Different Trial Balances

Once students are taught the unit on the trial balance, they very often conclude that only one trial balance or ledger proof exists in accounting. In the main, students do remember that the first trial balance taught to them has two functions: (1) to prove the equality of the debits and credits within the ledger and (2) to provide in a convenient form the data needed for preparing the worksheet, financial statements, and adjusting and closing entries. What they fail to realize, however, is that this first trial balance is a general ledger proof and that other ledger proofs are just as functional. At least two other trial balances should be considered in any introductory accounting course.

TRIAL BALANCE OF ACCOUNTS PAYABLE. Once the units on the accounts payable ledger and the accounts payable controlling account have been taught, introduce the concept of the proof of the subsidiary ledger. Again, this proof of accounts payable is usually prepared formally as a schedule or summary of all creditors' accounts filed in the related subsidiary ledger. At this stage, an important accounting proof concept can be communicated. Simply stated, the total of the account balances in the accounts payable ledger at the end of an accounting period must agree with the balance in the related controlling account of the general ledger. In other words, the figure shown for accounts payable in the general ledger trial balance must agree with the total of the separate creditor accounts as shown by the trial balance of accounts payable.

TRIAL BALANCE OF ACCOUNTS RECEIVABLE. Obviously, one would teach the same proof idea about accounts receivable as was given for accounts payable. One added concept, however, can be considered. Accounting proofs not only promote a high degree of mathematical accuracy, but also support management's need for internal control. For example, the proofs of the general ledger and of the accounts receivable must be done independently of each other. One clerk would be assigned the task of preparing a general ledger trial balance, while a second clerk would be restricted to the preparation of the summary for accounts receivable. It is only at the point of comparing the two independent proofs that students will realize the importance of accounting as a subject that goes beyond simply the record-keeping function. Without this concept of independent proofs, the students could easily conclude that little control exists over accounts receivable—an important asset since it represents a future source of cash to the business enterprise. Accounting proofs, therefore, should be taught with the idea of controlling valuable assets within any firm.

Cash Proofs

There are many different types of cash proofs. However, the major principle underlying all can be adequately conveyed to students by concentrating discussion on three topics: accounting proofs for handling cash, proof of the cash balance, and bank reconciliation.

Accounting Proofs for Handling Cash

Three simple but very effective accounting proofs may be taught in relation to the broad area of analyzing an accounting system for handling cash receipts: (1) proof of cash through a cash register system, (2) proof of cash acknowledged on cash sales slips, and (3) proof of cash received through the mail.

PROOF OF CASH THROUGH A CASH REGISTER SYSTEM. Students of accounting at all levels are generally familiar with the use of a cash register for recording the amount of cash received when goods or services are sold over the counter. In a discussion of a cash register system, emphasize the difference between the two copies of the tape that are generated by the machine: one copy is ejected from the cash register and given to the customer as a receipt; and the other copy remains locked inside the cash register and is used as a source document for accounting control. Once the difference between the two tapes is explained, explain and demonstrate the following cash proof system for a cash register.

At the end of the day the amount of cash that is in the cash drawer should equal (1) the amount of the change fund, plus (2) the total of the cash sales recorded on the cash register tape, plus (3) the total of the amount received on account (if any) from customers, less (4) any money taken from the cash drawer (if any) for cash refunds. This cash proof may be demonstrated on the overhead projector with an illustration similar to Figure 10.3.

The following teaching suggestions are offered to help reinforce the students' learning of the cash register proof system:

1. Assign a bulletin board project displaying actual samples of various cash register tapes with accompanying explanatory notes. Ideally, sample cash proof blanks should also be displayed.

2. Arrange a field trip to a local store where a cash register system is employed. If a field trip is not possible, arrange to have a representative of a local store visit the class to explain the procedures for controlling cash receipts through a cash register system.

3. Simulate problems where students are required to prepare a cash

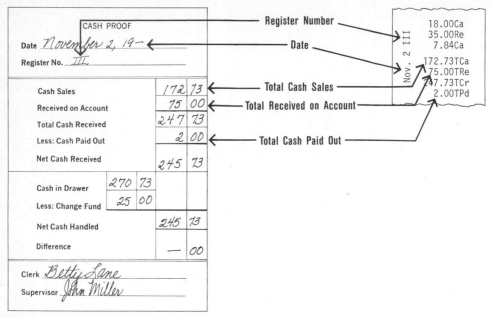

Figure 10.3 Cash Proof Prepared for Cash Register

proof given information from a cash register system and a cash proof blank.

4. Present a management case problem to force attention on the inefficient use of the cash register. Encourage students to conclude their discussion of any case with a written report of their recommendations to improve the system.

CASH PROOF OF SALES SLIPS. Students are also quite familiar with the use of sales slips to record the receipt of cash, especially when they are applied to specialty shops. In discussing such a sales slip system, care should be taken to emphasize the importance of prenumbering all sales slips. In addition, the teacher should communicate the difference between sales slips that are found in a padded sales book and those that are used in forms registers. These points should be underscored when teaching a cash proof system that includes prenumbered sales slips to record the receipt of cash.

1. A person other than the salesclerk, usually the supervisor, arranges the sales slips in numeric order. Any missing slip must be accounted for with a proper explanation from the salesclerk.
2. The totals of the sales slips from cash sales are listed on an adding machine tape. Again, the supervisor, not the salesclerk, should perform this listing.
3. Next, the supervisor lists and totals on the adding machine tape the individual cash amounts received from customers on account.

4. The two totals are then relisted to determine the total cash receipts for the day.

5. If cash was paid out, these amounts are listed from the sales slips, totaled, and subtracted on the tape to determine the net cash received for the day.

6. Finally, the supervisor must total the amount of cash in the cash drawer, subtract the amount of the change fund, and then check the net cash count against the net figure disclosed on the adding machine tape. Obviously, the net amount of cash in the drawer should be equal to the net cash calculated from the sales slips. The entire cash proof system can be taught most effectively by showing an illustration similar to Figure 10.4 on the overhead projector.

PROOF OF CASH RECEIVED THROUGH THE MAIL. Very few students are aware of any system for proving checks and currency received through the mail. Briefly, these points should be emphasized to all students who are introduced to this topic.

1. As a general principle two or more employees should participate in the procedures.

2. One employee should open the mail and prepare a list in duplicate of the amounts received. The duplicate list may be prepared on duplicate adding machine tapes in the mail room. Duplicate pre-numbered remittance slips may be used instead of adding machine tapes.

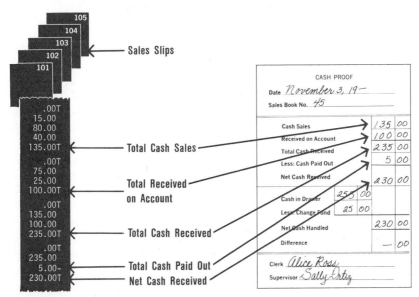

Figure 10.4 Cash Proof Prepared for Sales Slip

3. The checks and other currency received, together with the original tapes or remittance slips, are then forwarded to the cashier, who will deposit the cash in the bank.
4. The duplicate tapes or duplicate remittance slips are sent to the accounting department, which will record the cash collections.
5. For a proof of cash received, the total cash receipts recorded from the duplicate tapes or remittance forms must agree with the total deposited in the bank, as shown by the original tapes or remittance forms.

Proving the Cash Balance

Another important cash proof measure is to compare the cash balance in the checkbook with the balance as shown in the Cash account. Ideally, this proof should be made each day. Under an accounting system that includes special journals, however, the Cash account in the ledger may not be updated until the end of the month. Where such a cash proof is required on a more frequent basis, students can be taught the following procedures to verify the Cash account balance with the checkbook balance.

1. Begin the cash proof by showing the Cash account balance at the start of the month. This balance figure may be obtained directly from the Cash account, or it may be more conveniently acquired from the memorandum entry in the cash receipts journal.
2. Add all the amounts recorded in the cash receipts journal between the first day of the month and the day of preparing the cash proof. This total, representing the accumulated debits to Cash during the month, may be entered as a pencil footing in the cash amount column of the journal.
3. On a cash proof form, add the debit balance at the start of the month and total the accumulated debits to date; the total will represent the total debits to Cash as of the proof date.
4. Add the amounts recorded in the cash payments journal between the same time period. This figure represents the total credits to Cash during the month and may also be pencil footed in the special journal.
5. On the cash proof sheet, subtract the total credits from the total debits to determine the balance of the Cash account. Of course, this balance should equal the amount shown on the checkbook record for the same date.

The entire cash proof may be prepared on a standard cash proof form, or it can be prepared on an adding machine tape. Regardless of what method is used, it is important to emphasize that the Cash balance in the ledger must be checked against the checkbook record balance at frequent intervals during the month.

Teaching Bank Reconciliation

Students are generally surprised to learn that bank reconciliation is an integral part of any firm's overall system for the effective control over its cash. In developing this topic, therefore, teachers should recognize the importance of teaching the cash control aspect as well as the mechanics of preparing an actual bank reconciliation. The teaching method generally involves a five-step development: (1) teaching the need for bank reconciliation, (2) verifying the internal cash balance, (3) locating and listing discrepancy items, (4) preparing the bank reconciliation statement, and (5) adjusting records to update the cash balance.

TEACHING THE NEED FOR BANK RECONCILIATION. Preliminary to any discussion of the need for bank reconciliation, review the principles of using a bank checking account as part of any firm's system for the control of its most valuable asset. In this regard, it is important to emphasize these points:

1. The bank acts as a custodian of the spendable funds of the business.
2. The funds of the enterprise on deposit with its bank represent a debt owing by the bank to the business. On the records of the bank, therefore, this debt is a liability which is payable on demand.
3. The liability on the bank's records increases each time the business makes deposits, and this debt decreases each time the business writes checks on the bank (in effect, the bank is making cash payments on behalf of the enterprise).
4. On the records of the business, this amount of indebtedness of the bank to the enterprise naturally appears as an asset (as reflected by the account Cash).
5. Two independent records of Cash, therefore, are maintained to obtain control over the asset. At any point of time, theoretically, an identical figure for cash should appear in both sets of books.

After these preliminaries have been covered, proceed to the stage of comparing a copy of the bank's record—the monthly bank statement—with the records of the business: the checkbook and the ledger account for Cash. By selecting one item, such as outstanding checks, show that both records will rarely reveal an identical amount for the cash balance and, consequently, the need for proving the cash balance by bringing the two amounts into agreement at the time the bank provides a copy of its record of the depositor's account.

VERIFYING THE INTERNAL CASH BALANCE. It should be quite obvious to students that no reconciliation can begin until the cash balances shown within the records of the business are in agreement. Since the cash proof between the checkbook and the Cash account has been treated earlier, this proof will not be developed further.

LOCATING AND LISTING DISCREPANCY ITEMS. It is important that students be taught how to analyze a monthly bank statement and the returns enclosed with the statement. Otherwise, this next stage of locating and listing discrepancy items is of no value. Discuss the significance of outstanding checks, canceled checks, deposits in transit, dishonored checks, bank memorandums, bank service charges, and bank errors. With this background knowledge, students can be taken through a problem checking and comparing a monthly bank statement against the information contained in the checkbook record. In this sorting process, the students may find it most helpful to list all discrepancy items found under two headings: "Items Unknown by the Bank" and "Items Unknown by the Business." In this sorting process, students should be taught to do the following:

1. Compare the amounts of the deposits listed on the bank statement with the amounts of the deposits listed on the checkbook records. Place check marks in the company's checkbook records and on the bank statement beside the items that agree. Check the previous month's reconciliation statement to make sure that any deposits then in transit have been recorded on the current month's statement. Any unchecked item in the company's records of deposits will be deposits not yet recorded by the bank and should be listed as deposits in transit under the heading, "Items Unknown by the Bank."

2. Take the bundle of canceled checks and check off each one against the bank statement. The bank may have made an error in posting these checks. Then, arrange the paid checks in numeric order and compare each one with the corresponding entry in the checkbook records. (Some authorities prefer to have these checks compared with the corresponding entries in the cash payments journal as well.) Place a check mark in the checkbook record (and cash payments journal, if required) opposite each entry for which there is a canceled check. The unchecked entries would be acknowledged as outstanding checks and should be listed as discrepancy items under the heading, "Items Unknown by the Bank." Of course, last month's reconciliation statement should also be examined to learn whether there still are outstanding checks from the last reconciliation. If so, then these too would be added to the list of outstanding checks.

3. Examine carefully the bank statement and any attachments for items unknown by the business. For example, list all debit memorandums issued by the bank that have not been recorded by the business under the heading, "Items Unknown by the Business." Similarly, list all credit memorandums issued by the bank that have not been recorded by the business under this same heading.

4. List under "Items Unknown by the Business" items that were not disclosed by actual bank debit and bank credit memorandums. For example, monthly bank service charges may have appeared on the bank statement in coded form only.

5. And finally, list any other discrepancy item under the appropriate

discrepancy heading. For example, show any errors discovered in the checkbook records and in the bank statement.

Once all of the discrepancy items have been identified and listed, explain the basic principle of reconciling the various items directly on the form. The following guide may help students to make this reconciliation: treat each discrepancy item according to the way in which the known party has recorded the item in his records. For example, outstanding checks under Items Unknown by the Bank are treated as a minus or subtraction because the checks were recorded as deductions from Cash in the records of the business (the known party). Similarly, a bank debit memo under Items Unknown by the Business are treated as a minus quantity in reconciliation because the known party, the bank, has deducted the amount of the memo from the cash balance of the bank's records. It is useful to review the significance of "debit" in a debit memorandum. Point out that debiting the cash in the bank's records has the effect of decreasing the liability account. The final analysis of the discrepancy items may appear on a working form like the one shown in Figure 10.5.

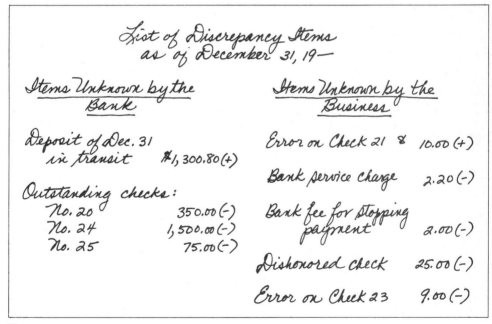

Figure 10.5

PREPARING THE BANK RECONCILIATION STATEMENT. Teaching the actual preparation of a bank reconciliation statement presents few problems if the previous stage has been learned by students. Use either the standard reconciliation form that is found on the reverse side of many bank statements, or two-column paper. Whatever form is used, however, it is important to show a reconciliation of the cash balance; that is, the adjusted bank balance must agree with the adjusted checkbook balance as at the date of reconciliation. This reconciliation is shown quite clearly in Figure 10.6.

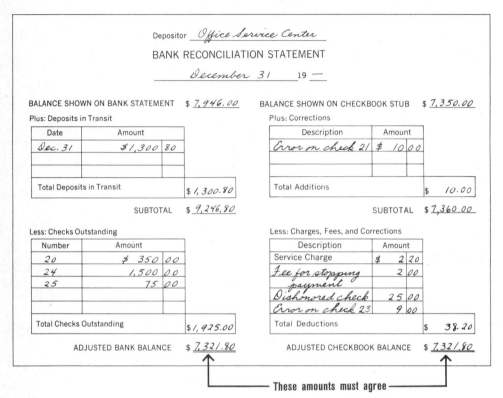

Depositor *Office Service Center*

BANK RECONCILIATION STATEMENT

December 31 19 —

BALANCE SHOWN ON BANK STATEMENT $ *7,946.00*   BALANCE SHOWN ON CHECKBOOK STUB $ *7,350.00*

Plus: Deposits in Transit

Date	Amount
Dec. 31	*$1,300 80*

| Total Deposits in Transit | $ *1,300.80* |

SUBTOTAL $ *9,246.80*

Plus: Corrections

Description	Amount
Error on check 21	$ *10 00*

| Total Additions | $ *10.00* |

SUBTOTAL $ *7,360.00*

Less: Checks Outstanding

Number	Amount
20	$ *350 00*
24	*1,500 00*
25	*75 00*

| Total Checks Outstanding | $ *1,925.00* |

ADJUSTED BANK BALANCE $ *7,321.80*

Less: Charges, Fees, and Corrections

Description	Amount
Service Charge	$ *2 20*
Fee for stopping payment	*2 00*
Dishonored check	*25 00*
Error on check 23	*9 00*

| Total Deductions | $ *38.20* |

ADJUSTED CHECKBOOK BALANCE $ *7,321.80*

↑ └─────── These amounts must agree ───────┘ ↑

Figure 10.6

ADJUSTING RECORDS TO UPDATE THE CASH BALANCE. Two adjustments must be taught after the reconciliation statement has been completed: (1) the balance on the latest checkbook record (usually the check stub) must be brought into agreement with the adjusted checkbook balance on the reconciliation statement; (2) the Cash account in the ledger must be updated by journalizing and posting adjusting entries. It is important to emphasize that the source of these entries is the section of the bank reconciliation statement that reconciles the cash balance of the business and not of the bank. Where necessary, it is also important to reteach any difficult correcting entry. For example, students will find it helpful to review the background of all the transactions that led to a check returned for insufficient funds. By tracing the entries back to the beginning, students will realize that Accounts Receivable must be redebited and Cash credited for a dishonored check. The use of T-account analysis is especially helpful.

The Journal Voucher Proof

Although it is true that computers are used to process accounting data primarily for large-scale business enterprises, computers may, in time, almost entirely replace the manual bookkeeping and accounting functions as we know them today. It is important, therefore, that teachers not only acquire an exposure to computer methods of processing financial information, but also teach computer concepts in relation to traditional accounting topics. One topic that allows the teacher to relate to what the student has learned and that also bridges the gap between manual and computer methods is the accounting proof of transmitting journal vouchers to computer data processing before the general ledger is updated.

No attempt will be made to develop the teaching of the hardware or software sides of computer data processing, just the treatment of processing general ledger information up to and including the stage where the journal entries are verified. The teaching of these steps may be identified as follows: (1) receiving general ledger source data, (2) preparing journal vouchers, (3) batching journal vouchers, and (4) preparing the journal voucher proof list. But, before one can develop each one of these stages, it is important that the learner understand the meaning and function of a journal voucher. If the concept of the journal voucher has not been covered, introduce the topic along the format suggested in Chapter 8. On the other hand, a brief review is desirable if the topic has been previously treated.

Receiving General Ledger Source Data

In an organization where the accounting function is divided into specialized departments, the various accounting activities such as invoicing, accounts receivable, accounts payable, and others must report the dollar results of their financial transactions on a regular basis, usually monthly, to the general accounting department. These transactions obviously affect the general ledger accounts in the form of debits and credits. For example, the regular payroll register provides the source data to debit an expense account such as Payroll, Wages, or Salaries, and also to credit a variety of current liability accounts. In some cases, however, the summary of payroll may be transmitted to general accounting on individual payroll journal vouchers. Similarly, the sales register or individual sales journal voucher provides monthly totals debiting Accounts Receivable (the controlling account) and crediting Sales.

The first step in updating a general ledger file, therefore, is to receive in the general accounting department source data that affects the general ledger.

Preparing Journal Vouchers

The various documents received by general accounting are first audited for accuracy; then, the general ledger source data is prepared in a form for transmittal to computer data processing. As suggested earlier, a common system used by many firms is to prepare general journal vouchers, or simply journal vouchers. In this case, journal vouchers would be prepared by personnel in the general accounting department which, in turn, would authorize the computer department to post the journal entries to the proper ledger accounts. Before this updating occurs, however, it is important to teach the concept that general accounting must devise a plan to ensure complete control over the journal entries. Here is one control system that has been used successfully by several large firms.

A common journal voucher form is designed, and this form becomes the only recognized source for updating the general ledger. There are many types of journal voucher forms in use today. A collection of several different types would make an excellent bulletin board display at this point of the discussion. The one illustrated in Figure 10.7 is in wide use today. An overhead transparency of the illustration would be an ideal aid from which to teach students the basic concepts of the journal voucher. From an internal control viewpoint, it is important to teach that the journal entries must originate with responsible employees, and that these entries must be properly reviewed and approved. In this case, entries that affect the general ledger must originate in general accounting and not in the computer data processing center.

A second measure to obtain control over journal entries is to prepare complete sets of standard journal entries under an assigned number. These standard journal entries provide the structure for the recording of all recurring transactions, adjustments, and closing entries. When numbers are given to specific transactions, general accounting can easily recognize the type of entry that must be made each month. For example, Journal Voucher No. 6 might be assigned to the transactions that have originated in the Sales Journal. Any omission of this number during the processing stage of the general ledger would remind persons charged with completing the data not to overlook the corresponding journal entry that affects Accounts Receivable (to be debited) and Sales (to be credited). Similarly, No. 1 might be assigned to the transactions that originate in the Cash Receipts Journal. The omission of this number would mean that the Cash account has not been debited and other accounts have not been credited. All journal vouchers are numbered in accordance with a related journal entry.

Beginning students do not always realize that these journal vouchers are usually handwritten by personnel in the general accounting department. Since the journal vouchers will have to be read by a keypunch operator for computer data processing, it is essential that this handwritten information be not only accurate, but also legible. It is interesting to conclude that the teaching of the first two-column journal (and later the two-column general journal) provides an excellent relationship to the future teaching of this two-column journal voucher. And what is most revealing is the fact that even within a computer system some handwritten accounting methods still prevail.

5841-3	JOURNAL VOUCHER					No. 9			
ACCOUNT NAME	**ACCOUNT NUMBER** CONTROL DETAIL DEPT.			**DEBIT**			**CREDIT**		
Depreciation Expense on Building	09	522	12	80	00				
Accumulated Depreciation on Building		123						80	00
TOTAL									

PARTICULARS

To record the standard monthly depreciation.

PREPARED BY E. Jones NOTED BY	APPROVALS J.W. D.W. SUPERVISOR DEPT. MANAGER GEN ACCTG MANAGER CONTROLLER ASST. CONTR ACCOUNTING	IDT. REF.	DATE Dec 3/19 — LOCATION Central NO. 1086

Figure 10.7

Batching Journal Vouchers

Two other points should be considered before analyzing the stage where journal vouchers are transmitted to data processing. First, that general ledger source data are not received by general accounting all at the same time. While general accounting may have a schedule to update the general ledger by a specific date, it does not usually wait until all the source data are received. In most accounting systems, the journal vouchers are sent to keypunching in batches; for example, there may be 15 or 20 journal vouchers in a batch. The concept of batching journal vouchers, therefore, is an important part of the procedures for preparing journal vouchers for transmittal to data processing.

The second point to consider at this time is the principle of accounting control. No batch of journal vouchers should ever be sent to data processing without first preparing some form of control record. This control record may take the form of a Journal Voucher Control Sheet which lists the journal voucher numbers and the entries by debits and credits. In other systems, the control record may simply be an adding machine tape which lists all the entries in the batch by debit or credit amounts. It is important that the department originating and submitting the source data (general accounting in this case) has a record of the financial information to be processed. Without such a control record it would be impossible to check the accuracy of the total entries to be processed.

Preparing the Journal Voucher Proof List

Once the journal vouchers are batched and a control sheet or control tape is prepared, the batched vouchers are sent to computer data processing for keypunching. Here the vouchers are usually keypunched onto general ledger transaction cards. At this point it must be taught that the general ledger file (usually a magnetic tape) cannot be updated until the general accounting department is satisfied that all of the batches of journal vouchers have been keypunched, and that no entry has been omitted. To provide this proof, the transaction cards are processed through the computer, where a stored program provides instructions to print a journal voucher proof list for each batch of journal vouchers. This journal voucher proof list serves one primary purpose: to furnish the general accounting department with a control listing of all entries that affect general ledger accounts, proving that nothing has been omitted. A typical journal voucher proof list might appear printed as in Figure 10.8.

Note that in Figure 10.8 the computer program produces printed information which general accounting can use to check against their own journal voucher control sheet or against an adding machine control tape if used. Observe in Page 2 of the journal voucher proof list, illustrated in Figure 10.9, that the computer program has printed out a journal entry that does not balance. From this, general accounting can easily see that the error must be traced back to journal entry 01 (a cash receipts transaction). It is now the responsibility of the general accounting department to locate the error and provide the correction before the general ledger file is updated. Herein lies the main advantage of the journal voucher proof list: computer data processing helps the general accounting department to find any out-of-balance conditions before the actual general ledger accounts are updated (posted).

Once the general accounting department is satisfied that all errors have been located and that the appropriate corrections have been made, a final

JOURNAL VOUCHER PROOF LIST

12/31/--

PAGE 01

BATCH NO	JV-NO	DATE	ACCT NO	JOURNAL ENTRY DESCRIPTION	DEBIT AMOUNT	CREDIT AMOUNT	DIFFERENCE
01	03	12/31/--	516	SALARIES EXPENSE	8,561.50		
		12/31/--	211	CPP DED PAYABLE		118.85	
		12/31/--	212	INC TAX DED PAYABLE		851.10	
		12/31/--	213	UIC DED PAYABLE		79.20	
		12/31/--	214	GROUP INSUR PAYABLE		145.00	
		12/31/--	210	SALARIES PAYABLE		7,367.35	
	06	12/31/--	111	ACCOUNTS RECEIVABLE	2,977.73		
		12/31/--	203	SALES TAX PAYABLE		86.73	
		12/31/--	401	SALES		2,891.00	
	09	12/31/--	522	DEP EXP-BLDG	80.00		
		12/31/--	123	ACCUM DEP-BLDG		80.00	
01		BATCH TOTALS			11,619.23*	11,619.23*	

Figure 10.8
From *Elements of Accounting: A Systems Approach, Advanced Course* by Kaluza, Leonard, and Furneaux. Copyright © 1971. Reprinted by permission of McGraw-Hill Ryerson Limited.

BATCH NO	JV-NO	DATE	ACCT NO	JOURNAL ENTRY DESCRIPTION	DEBIT AMOUNT	CREDIT AMOUNT	DIFFERENCE
				JOURNAL VOUCHER PROOF LIST			
				12/31/--			PAGE 02
02	01	12/31/--	101	CASH	8,005.80		
		12/31/--	403	SALES DISCOUNT	68.20		
		12/31/--	111	ACCOUNTS RECEIVABLE		4,780.00	
		12/31/--	203	SALES TAX PAYABLE		194.00	
		12/31/--	401	SALES		3,080.00	
		12/31/--	511	CASH SHORT AND OVER		2.00	
				ENTRY DOES NOT BALANCE	8,073.00	8,056.00	17.00
	07	12/31/--	402	SALES RET AND ALLOW	110.50		
		12/31/--	111	ACCOUNTS RECEIVABLE		110.50	
02	BATCH TOTALS			ERROR COUNT 01	8,183.50*	8,166.50*	17.00*
	FINAL TOTALS			ERROR COUNT 01**	19,802.73**	19,785.73**	17.00**

Figure 10.9

From *Elements of Accounting: A Systems Approach, Advanced Course* by Kaluza, Leonard, and Furneaux. Copyright © 1971. Reprinted by permission of McGraw-Hill Ryerson Limited.

journal proof list can be printed. General accounting can now advise computer data processing to update the general ledger magnetic tape file and to produce the required printouts. These outputs usually consist of the general ledger, the general ledger trial balance, the income statement, and the balance sheet.

Suggested Student Reinforcement Activities

Students' understanding of a basic general ledger application through a computer method may be reinforced by one or more of the following activities.

1. Prepare a systems flowchart. Students may welcome the opportunity to prepare a systems flowchart of the entire general ledger application. This systems flowchart would commence with the receipt of general ledger source data by the general accounting department and would proceed to the final stage of identifying the outputs by the computer.

2. Batch journal vouchers and prepare a control tape. A practical simulation would involve a project whereby students would receive prepared general ledger source data, check the source data for mathematical accuracy, prepare journal vouchers, batch the journal vouchers, and finally, prepare a control tape of the batched journal vouchers in readiness for transmittal to computer data processing.

3. Given the complete set of journal vouchers, students can prepare a simulated computer printout of the journal voucher proof list.

4. Given a general ledger listing of "last month's balances," and a completed set of journal voucher proof lists for transactions of the "current month," students can prepare the simulated computer outputs consisting of the general ledger update, the trial balance, the income statement and balance sheet. Provide sample sheets to illustrate how this output looks when printed on a computer.

5. The ideal objective is to process a simulated general ledger application through an actual computer. It is important to note that one does not require a computer within the school. Nor does the accounting teacher have to instruct the students how to write various computer programs. What is critical, however, is that access be made available to have computer cards processed through a previously written computer program. Given a set of journal vouchers, students would prepare transaction cards which would then be processed through a computer to print the journal voucher proof list according to the computer's stored program. The same transaction cards can then be reprocessed together with the aid of a second stored program to produce the outputs of the general ledger update, the trial balance, and the financial statements. Of course, it would be necessary to teach students how to either keypunch transaction

cards or mark sense the cards according to the limitations of the computer method, and finally, to have access to a computer that has been programmed to process the transaction cards. Accounting students can then analyze the return of the various printouts.

Problems, Questions, and Projects

1. What background should a teacher review before he or she introduces the lesson on the trial balance?
2. Describe an interesting way to introduce the trial balance to your class.
3. At what stage of the teaching development would you introduce procedures to follow when a trial balance does not balance? Give reasons for your answer.
4. What steps would you have your students follow when preparing a trial balance?
5. If a cash sale for $375 were entered correctly in the Cash Receipts Journal but posted to the debit of the Sales account as $357, by how much would the trial balance be out of balance? What type of error is this? If this were the only error made, what test would give a clue that this type of error had been made?
6. The discussion in this chapter explains how the equality of the account balances in the ledger may be proved on an adding machine without the preparation of a formal trial balance. Would you recommend teaching this technique to beginning accounting students? Why or why not?
7. Discuss two methods of evaluating the students' knowledge of the work on the trial balance.
8. Describe two accounting proofs for handling cash. Discuss how you would teach one of these proofs to a first-year accounting class.
9. The teaching of bank reconciliation generally involves a five-step development. Name each of these stages in their respective teaching order.
10. What points would you emphasize in teaching the need for bank reconciliation?
11. After having examined the debits and credits on a monthly bank statement, Jonathan addresses this question to his teacher: "I still don't understand why the bank has credited the customer's account for increases and debited the account for decreases. Is bank accounting backwards?" How would you reply to the student's question if you were his teacher?
12. In learning the mathematics of reconciling discrepancy items on a bank reconciliation form, many students are tempted to memorize the items to add and the ones to subtract. What guide can you teach to help students reason the simple mechanics of reconciliation? Give two examples to support your rule.

13. How would you teach the effect of a certified check in bank reconciliation?

14. What is a journal voucher? Explain four reasons why a journal voucher system would probably be used in a large business enterprise.

15. What points would you emphasize when teaching the difference between accounting and computer data processing in the analysis of a computerized general ledger application?

16. Name and discuss briefly the different stages that are recognized in updating the general ledger through a computer method.

17. Explain the significance of the journal proof list in a computerized general ledger application.

18. "Computers may, in time, almost entirely replace the manual bookkeeping and accounting functions as we know them today." Do you agree or disagree with this statement? Explain your answer.

19. Prepare overhead transparency masters as teaching aids to develop the method of teaching any one of the topics included in this chapter. Construct your teaching aid so that there is one base transparency and at least two overlays or two masks. If possible, prepare transparencies from your masters and display your finished product to your methods instructor.

20. Prepare as many functional performance goals as possible for the various accounting proof topics given in this chapter. Keep in mind that these performance goals must be stated in behavioral terms and, where possible, include the conditions under which the terminal behavior takes place.

Case Problems

1. Carla Weisberger received her students' solutions to her "review problem, first assignment" concerning the trial balance. As she examined them, she discovered that they could be classified into three groups: (1) correct solutions, (2) trial balances that were not correct but which did balance, and (3) completed solutions but trial balances that were out of balance. The two questions that faced her immediately were:

   a. How to grade the incorrect solutions—what kinds of grades to give students whose answers fell in groups two and three above.

   b. Whether to mark the errors (thus making it easy for students to correct their errors) or to return incorrect solutions and require the students to find and correct their errors.

What advice would you give her regarding these two questions?

2. Four teachers were asked to express their views on the question of introducing data processing into their respective accounting programs. Comment briefly on each of the speakers' points of view as summarized on page 190. Offer supporting arguments for your position in each case.

a. "I cannot see the value of teaching any data processing as part of the accounting curriculum. In my opinion, the teaching of machine accounting, computing, and other forms of data processing should be restricted to the graduate school level."

b. "I believe in the principle of teaching both machine accounting and computerized accounting, but because the equipment is so costly to buy or to rent, I have decided to exclude both areas from my accounting instruction."

c. "My accounting students do have access to two-register posting machines, one-write boards, and a complete IBM 1130 computer system. In my opinion, all future accounting students should take at least one semester's work in business data processing before they register in a beginner's course in accounting. At our school, we require all of our accounting exercises to be done through one or more of the hardware systems and, in particular, through stored computer programs."

d. "I believe in the principle of integrating accounting and data processing in any form of accounting instruction. As I see it, however, a solid base of accounting principles and concepts should precede any unit that integrates accounting with data processing. Furthermore, I believe that only the computer method of data processing should be used because all other methods are on the verge of being obsolete."

CHAPTER 11

Teaching the Worksheet and End-of-Period Adjustments

Until now students have dealt only with transactions that begin and end in the same accounting period. Some transactions, however—such as those involving merchandise inventory—begin in one accounting period and end in another. Others, like those involving prepaid expenses, cover more than one accounting period.

Since managers and outsiders use the financial statements of a business to judge both its financial position and the results of its operation, it is important that each statement reflect all items owned, all debts, and all ownership, as well as all revenues and costs and expenses as of a specific cutoff date. The balance sheet must show all assets, liabilities, and owner's equity as of the last day of the accounting period. The income statement must show all revenue and costs and expenses for the current period—none for future accounting periods.

Accounts that involve transactions spread over more than one accounting period are updated by means of adjusting entries. This chapter discusses methods of teaching adjusting entries for prepaid expenses and merchandise inventory and introduces the worksheet. Before proceeding, let us review the relevant accounting principles.

ACCOUNTING FUNDAMENTALS

1. The worksheet is a columnar device consisting of related debit and credit columns used to gather the data for the end of the accounting period.
2. It shows the effect of various adjustments which are made in the general journal.

(continued)

3. It shows the basic data needed to prepare both the balance sheet and the income statement.
4. The worksheet sorts accounts into their respective classifications so they may appear on the appropriate financial statement.
5. It provides a preliminary calculation of the net income (or net loss) for an accounting period.
6. It shows the information needed to record the closing entries to be made at the end of the accounting period.
7. Prepaid expenses are normally carried on the books as current assets.
8. As supplies are consumed, the asset amount decreases and the expense resulting from the use of supplies must be recorded at the end of the accounting period.
9. As time passes, the amount of insurance still prepaid is continuously reduced. At the end of each accounting period, the expense due to expired insurance must be recorded.
10. The purpose of an adjusting entry to a prepaid expense account is to divide the account balance into its asset amount and its expense amount.
11. Under a periodic inventory system, the inventory account is updated only at the end of the accounting period.
12. The inventory amount on the books, recorded in the account Merchandise Inventory, is the amount of the beginning inventory.
13. The ending inventory is determined by a physical count of goods on hand on the last day of the accounting period. (This represents the current asset amount of merchandise on hand.)
14. The account Merchandise Inventory is updated to show the current asset amount. This is done by an adjusting entry at the end of the accounting period.

Performance Goals

Some performance goals for lessons on the worksheet and on adjustments are offered below.

1. Given a series of incomplete statements related to the steps in the accounting cycle and the adjustments for merchandise inventory and prepaid expenses, the student should be able to complete each statement.
2. Given a series of transactions involving (*a*) increases and decreases in merchandise inventory, (*b*) purchases, and (*c*) prepaid expenses (supplies and insurance), the student should be able to indicate

which account would be debited and which account would be credited to record each transaction.

3. Given a trial balance and data about the adjustments for merchandise inventory, supplies on hand, and prepaid insurance, the student should be able to enter the adjustments on the worksheet.

4. Given a list of accounts that appear in the Adjusted Trial Balance section of the worksheet, the student should be able to indicate whether the balance of each account would be extended to the Income Statement section or the Balance Sheet section of the worksheet.

5. Given a worksheet with data extended to the Income Statement section and the Balance Sheet section, the student should be able to compute the net income or net loss on the worksheet.

The Worksheet

The primary purposes of the worksheet are (1) to compute adjustments to the trial balance accounts before the financial statements are prepared, and (2) to sort accounts into the principal account classifications for the financial reports. For these reasons, some teachers prefer to present the worksheet after students have studied financial statements. They reason that if students know what balance sheets and income statements are and if they know the types of accounts that appear on each, students can more readily see why they are sorting the accounts by using the worksheet. Other teachers present the worksheet before they teach financial statements, thus presenting the units in the same sequence as the steps in the accounting cycle. From the very beginning of their accounting course, students have had to classify accounts, prepare balance sheets, and establish and use revenue and cost and expense accounts. Therefore, although students have not had the income statement, they may have the necessary background for understanding the function of the worksheet whether it is presented before or after financial statements.

In addition to its two primary purposes, the worksheet performs other functions.

1. It brings all the end-of-period calculations together on one sheet of paper for the convenience of the accountant. In no other place is there found a picture of the effect of the adjusting entries on the balance sheet and income statement accounts.

2. It is the basis for the adjusting entries which are entered in the journal. The data for these adjusting entries are shown in the Adjustment columns of the worksheet.

3. It is the basis for making the closing entries. These entries are based on the data that are shown in the Income Statement columns of the worksheet.

4. It is a means of calculating and proving the profit or net income. **193**

Introducing the Ten-Column Worksheet

Although there are several multicolumn worksheets available, the ten-column worksheet is the most suitable for classroom use. It best exemplifies the concepts of (1) sorting accounts according to their classification and (2) adjusting all accounts whose balances have to be updated. An example of a ten-column worksheet is shown in Figure 11.1.

Central Sales Company
Worksheet
For the Month Ended March 31, 19—

	ACCOUNT TITLE	ACCT. NO.	TRIAL BALANCE DEBIT	TRIAL BALANCE CREDIT	ADJUSTMENTS DEBIT	ADJUSTMENTS CREDIT	ADJUSTED TRIAL BALANCE DEBIT	ADJUSTED TRIAL BALANCE CREDIT	INCOME STATEMENT DEBIT	INCOME STATEMENT CREDIT	BALANCE SHEET DEBIT	BALANCE SHEET CREDIT	
1	Cash	101	9,500				9,500				9,500		1
2	Petty Cash	102	30				30				30		2
3	Change Fund	103	70				70				70		3
4	Accounts Receivable	111	3,300				3,300				3,300		4
5	Merchandise Inventory	112	5,000			(a) 400	4,600				4,600		5
6	Prepaid Insurance	113	360			(b) 30	330				330		6
7	Supplies on Hand	114	400			(c) 100	300				300		7
8	Land	121	5,000				5,000				5,000		8
9	Building	131	12,000				12,000				12,000		9
10	Office Equipment	132	2,200				2,200				2,200		10
11	Stockroom Equipment	133	2,778				2,778				2,778		11
12	Loans Payable	201		2,000				2,000				2,000	12
13	Accounts Payable	211		4,600				4,600				4,600	13
14	Employee Income Taxes Payable	221		242				242				242	14
15	FICA Taxes Payable	222		218				218				218	15
16	Federal Unemployment Taxes Payable	223		34				34				34	16
17	State Unemployment Taxes Payable	224		184				184				184	17
18	Mortgage Payable	231		10,000				10,000				10,000	18
19	John Hall, Capital	301		22,000				22,000				22,000	19
20	John Hall, Drawing	302	400				400				400		20
21	Sales	401		9,260				9,260		9,260			21
22	Sales Returns and Allowances	402	160				160		160				22
23	Sales Discount	403	37				37		37				23
24	Purchases	501	4,955				4,955		4,955				24
25	Transportation In	502	60				60		60				25
26	Purchases Returns and Allowances	503		185				185		185			26
27	Purchases Discount	504		50				50		50			27
28	Cash Short and Over	511	8				8		8				28
29	Delivery Expense	513	65				65		65				29
30	Miscellaneous Expense	515	24				24		24				30
31	Payroll Taxes Expense	516	176				176		176				31
32	Salaries Expense	518	2,100				2,100		2,100				32
33	Utilities Expense	520	150				150		150				33
			48,773	48,773									34
35	Revenue and Expense Summary	399			(a) 400		400		400				35
36	Insurance Expense	514			(b) 30		30		30				36
37	Supplies Expense	519			(c) 100		100		100				37
38					530	530	48,773	48,773	8,265	9,495	40,508	39,278	38
39									8,265				39
40									1,230			1,230	40
41	Net Income										40,508	40,508	41

NOTE: The cents columns have been omitted in order to show the entire worksheet.
Figure 11.1

Place a ten-column worksheet on the chalkboard or overhead projector and explain the following items.

1. The worksheet consists of five main sections: (a) the Trial Balance section, (b) the Adjustments section, (c) the Adjusted Trial Balance

section, (*d*) the Income Statement section, and (*e*) the Balance Sheet section.

2. The worksheet is not a statement. It is only an accountant's working tool; therefore, it is completed in pencil and can be changed and erased.

3. The worksheet covers a specific accounting period because it is used to compute net income or net loss for the period.

COMPLETING THE TRIAL BALANCE SECTION. Before the class period, place a worksheet with a filled-in Trial Balance section on the chalkboard or overhead projector. Review the classification of accounts, pointing out that all accounts on the worksheet may be classified as either permanent accounts or temporary owner's equity accounts. Then explain the following statements.

1. Each account with a balance is listed just as it appears in the ledger.

2. The account balance is entered in the appropriate Debit or Credit money column.

3. After all account balances are entered, a single rule is drawn across both money columns and the amounts are totaled.

4. If the two amounts agree, double rules are drawn across both money columns. If there is an error, it must be located before the worksheet is completed.

COMPLETING THE ADJUSTMENTS SECTION. Some of the accounts on a trial balance may have to be adjusted to show the correct balance. Methods for computing adjustments for prepaid expenses and merchandise inventory will be discussed later in this chapter. At this point, either go on to a full discussion of adjustments or briefly explain the concept of adjusting entries. Then tell the students that after the adjustments have been entered on the worksheet, they are to do the following:

1. Draw a single rule across the money columns in the Adjustments section.

2. Total the columns. The two totals must be equal. If they are not, the error must be located before completing the worksheet.

3. When the two amounts agree, draw double rules under the totals.

COMPLETING THE ADJUSTED TRIAL BALANCE SECTION. After the Adjustments section has been completed, the students can move on to the Adjusted Trial Balance section. Show the students that they can complete this section by doing the following:

1. Combine each account balance in the Trial Balance section with its adjustment in the Adjustments section. Enter the combined new balance in the Adjusted Trial Balance section.

2. If there is no adjustment for an account, simply move the balance from the Trial Balance section to the Adjusted Trial Balance section.

3. After all the balances have been entered, draw a single rule across both amount columns.

4. Total each column. If the amounts agree, draw a double rule across both money columns. If they do not, locate the error before proceeding further.

COMPLETING THE INCOME STATEMENT AND BALANCE SHEET SECTIONS. Explain to the students how each balance in the Adjusted Trial Balance section is moved to one of the four remaining columns:

1. Move the balance of all the assets, liabilities, and owner's capital and drawing accounts to the appropriate Debit or Credit column in the Balance Sheet section.

2. Move the balances of all revenue and cost and expense accounts (including the Revenue and Expense Summary account) to the appropriate Debit or Credit column in the Income Statement section.

3. Draw a single rule across all money columns.

4. Total each column. It should be explained to the students that the two columns in the Income Statement section do not agree because the business has either a net income or a net loss. The two columns in the Balance Sheet section do not agree because the net income or net loss for the period has not been transferred to the capital account. (This is discussed in Chapter 15.)

5. Compute the net income or net loss. If the total of the Credit column of the Income Statement section is greater than the total of the Debit column, the business has a net income. Place the debit amount under the credit amount, draw a rule, and enter the difference—the net income for the business. If the total of the Debit column is greater than that of the Credit column, place the credit amount under the debit amount, draw a rule, and enter the difference—the net loss for the business.

6. If the Income Statement section shows a net income, extend the amount to the Credit column of the Balance Sheet section and add it to the total of that column. If this new total agrees with the total of the Debit column, draw a double rule across all four money columns in the last two sections. If the totals do not agree, locate and correct the error.

7. If the Income Statement section shows a net loss, extend the amount to the Debit column of the Balance Sheet section and add it to the total of that column. If this new total agrees with the total of the Credit column, draw a double rule across all four money columns in the last two sections of the worksheet. If the totals do not agree, locate and correct the error.

SUGGESTIONS FOR TEACHING THE TEN-COLUMN WORKSHEET. Many teachers find that the following suggestions are helpful when introducing the ten-column worksheet:

- Have the students complete the worksheet at their seats at the same time it is being shown on the chalkboard or transparency. To save class time, duplicate for distribution to the class forms with the trial balance filled in. Use the same trial balance shown on the chalkboard or transparency.
- When first introducing the worksheet, use round numbers in the trial balance to both eliminate arithmetic problems and permit full concentration on the procedure. Use realistic numbers when students show an understanding of the worksheet process.
- When adjustments necessitate the opening of new accounts, they may be opened at the bottom of the sheet.
- If the trial balance is a long one and requires the use of more than one sheet of paper, have the students skip to the second sheet when they come to the revenue accounts. (The two sheets may be fastened together with tape.)
- Before giving a test on the worksheet, run off duplicated copies of problems, and distribute these to the class on the test day. This plan saves time since the students need not copy the trial balance before solving the problems.

Visual Aids

Overhead transparencies, film slides, and filmstrips are particularly effective for introducing the ten-column worksheet. If these aids are not available, however, premade chalkboard headings, chalkboard masks, and colored chalk can both facilitate and enhance the lessons.

CHALKBOARD HEADINGS. The worksheet column headings and rulings may be preprinted on heavy cardboard or hardboard which has been painted white. When a worksheet is to be used, the prepared headings are mounted at the top of the chalkboard with tape, with clips (storm-window clips permanently mounted at top of board), or by magnets if the board is magnetized. The headings may be cut or folded for easy storing.

CHALKBOARD MASKS. Time can be saved by having the entire worksheet, including all account titles and amounts, placed on the chalkboard before the class period. Using wrapping paper or cloth, mask all parts of the worksheet except the trial balance, thus directing the class attention to the trial balance. After the trial balance has been reviewed, remove the masking paper from the adjustment columns, and discuss the adjustments. Then remove the mask from the financial statement columns to discuss these columns. This procedure focuses the attention of all class members on the specific section of the worksheet being discussed and avoids the delay required to fill in the details during the class period.

COLORED CHALK. The worksheet also lends itself to color coding with chalk. Prepare the bulk of the worksheet on the chalkboard in white; however, use colored chalk to highlight the particular topic on which attention is being focused. For example, when teaching the Supplies adjustment, use red chalk throughout for the adjusting entry for Supplies. When Depreciation is being taught, use blue chalk for that adjusting entry. When the corresponding amounts are carried over to the Balance Sheet and Income Statement sections, follow through with the same colors.

End-of-Period Adjustments

Accounting is taught on a spiral, with the accounting cycle first completed in a very elementary fashion. Additional principles are presented each time through the cycle, and problems especially designed to focus attention upon the applications of the new principles are taught. A service business is generally used for the first cycle; thus the necessity of teaching end-of-period adjustments is avoided. The next time through, the cycle adjustments for prepaid expenses and merchandise inventory are usually presented, and these are treated in this chapter. Adjustments for depreciation and for bad debts and the accruals are discussed in subsequent chapters.

Prepaid Expenses

Explain to the students that some items and services—office supplies and insurance, for example—are bought for use in operating a business in one accounting period but are either not used or not completely used at the end of that accounting period. Point out that the generally accepted accounting principle is that revenue must be matched with the expenses incurred in earning that revenue; therefore, only the expense for those office supplies used (or for that portion of the insurance premium expired) in a period should be considered expenses for that period. The unused office supplies (or unused portions of the premium) will not become expenses until they are used in a future accounting period.

ADJUSTING SUPPLIES. Demonstrate that to correct the balance in the Office Supplies account, the Office Supplies account is credited to reduce the balance in the account to the amount of unused supplies, or the supplies on hand. The current amount of office supplies is found by taking a physical count of the supplies on hand. If, for example, the balance in the assets account Office Supplies is $88 and the current inventory of supplies on hand is $32, the amount used would be $56. Show the students that the journal and ledger entries would be as illustrated below and in Figure 11.2.

Supplies Expense	56	
Office Supplies		56
To record the expense due to supplies		
used and reduce the Office Supplies		
account to its unexpired cost amount.		

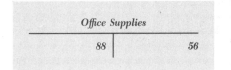

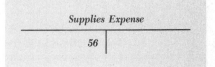

Figure 11.2

The amount of the adjustment is entered in the Credit column of the Adjustments section of the worksheet, on the same line as Office Supplies. Key the adjustment by using a letter; in Figure 11.3, the letter (*a*) is used. Then debit the expense to the Supplies Expense account by entering the amount in the Debit column of the Adjustments section, using the same letter to key the adjusting entry. In the example shown, the account Salaries Expense was not listed in the Trial Balance section; therefore, the account title and number were entered on the first available line.

ADJUSTING INSURANCE. Most students have more trouble determining how much of an insurance premium should be charged against the account Insurance Expense for a specific accounting period than they have actually making the adjusting entry itself. It is wise, therefore, to allow ample time for reviewing the arithmetic involved in such problems. Ask the class this question: If a one-year insurance premium of $72 was paid on June 1, what part of that premium has expired on June 30? If they understand that one twelfth of the premium has expired, they should realize that $6 has to be transferred from the Prepaid Insurance account to the Insurance Expense account. Show the students that the journal entry would be as follows:

Insurance Expense	6	
Prepaid Insurance		6
To record expense resulting from		
expired insurance and reduce Prepaid		
Insurance account to its unexpired cost amount.		

Enter the amount of the adjustment in the Credit column of the Adjustments section on the worksheet, on the same line as Prepaid Insurance. Key the adjustment with a letter—in Figure 11.2, the letter (*b*) is used. Debit the expense to the Insurance Expense account by entering the amount in the Debit column of the Adjustments section, using the same letter to key the adjusting entry. In the example shown, the account Insurance Expense was not listed in the Trial Balance section; therefore, the account title and number were entered on the first available line.

ADJUSTING MERCHANDISE INVENTORY. When merchandise inventory is adjusted, the merchandise inventory figure as recorded on the books has to be brought into agreement with that of the physical inventory taken at the end of a fiscal period. The inventory may be adjusted in a variety of ways. In this chapter, four different methods are discussed and illustrated. In

199

Frank Dalton
Worksheet
For the Quarter Ended June 30, 19—

	ACCOUNT TITLE	ACCT. NO.	TRIAL BALANCE		ADJUSTMENTS		ADJUSTED TRIAL BALANCE		INCOME STATEMENT		BALANCE SHEET		
			DEBIT	CREDIT	DEBIT	CREDIT	DEBIT	CREDIT	DEBIT	CREDIT	DEBIT	CREDIT	
1	Cash	101	1,000				1,000				1,000		1
2	Accts. Rec. . . .	131	2,450				2,450				2,450		2
3	Office Supplies .	141	88			(a) 56	32				32		3
4	Prepaid Ins. . . .	142	72			(b) 6	66				66		4
5	Office Equip. . .	151	1,900				1,900				1,900		5
6	Accts. Pay. . . .	210		150				150				150	6
7	F. Dalton, Cap. .	301		3,981				3,981				3,981	7
8	Commissions . .	401		2,045				2,045		2,045			8
9	Sal. Exp.	501	200				200		200				9
10	Rent Exp.	502	120				120		120				10
11	Misc. Exp.	503	346				346		346				11
12			6,176	6,176									12
13	Supplies Exp. . .	504			(a) 56		56		56				13
14	Insurance Exp.. .	505			(b) 6		6		6				14
15					62	62	6,176	6,176	728	2,045	5,448	4,131	15
16										→728			16
17	Net Income . . .								1,317		→1,317		17
18											5,448	5,448	18
19													19

Figure 11.3

each instance, the beginning inventory is $8,600; the ending inventory is $7,700; and the balance in the Purchases account is $9,500.

Using a Single Adjusting Entry. A single adjusting entry procedure can be followed. In this procedure, the Merchandise Inventory account is increased (by a debit entry) or decreased (by a credit entry) to bring the account into agreement with the correct merchandise inventory amount at the end of the accounting period. The corresponding debit or credit entry is made to the Revenue and Expense Summary account, where it will become a plus or a minus amount in determining the cost of goods sold.

In this example, the adjustment is made as a credit to the Merchandise Inventory account for $900 to reduce the account balance from $8,600 to $7,700, the amount of the ending inventory, and is shown on page 201 and in Figure 11.4 as entry (1).

(1) Revenue and Expense Summary	900	
Merchandise Inventory		900
Adjusting entry to correct the balance		
in the inventory account.		

The entry is made for the amount of the difference in the two inventories.
When the ending inventory is larger than the beginning inventory, the Merchandise Inventory account must be increased; therefore the Merchandise Inventory account is debited, and the Revenue and Expense Summary account credited.

The closing entry for Purchases is shown as entry (2) below and in Figure 11.4. After the adjusting entry to update the Merchandise Inventory account and the closing entry to close the Purchases account have been made, the three accounts would appear as follows.

(2) Revenue and Expense Summary	9,500	
Purchases		9,500
Closing entry to transfer the Purchases		
account balance to the Revenue and		
Expense Summary account.		

Merchandise Inventory		Revenue and Expense Summary		Purchases	
8,600	(1) 900	(1) 900		9,500	(2) 9,500
		(2) 9,500			
Debit balance		Cost of Goods Sold		Account is closed.	
is now $7,700.		is $10,400.			

Figure 11.4

Using Two Adjusting Entries. Explain that this method requires two adjusting entries: the first entry transfers the beginning inventory to the Revenue and Expense Summary account, and the second entry records the ending inventory. The third entry shows the closing entry for the Purchases account. When demonstrating this method, show both the journal and ledger entries as follows and as in Figure 11.5.

(1) Revenue and Expense Summary	8,600	
Merchandise Inventory		8,600
Adjusting entry to transfer the		
beginning inventory to the Revenue		
and Expense Summary.		
(2) Merchandise Inventory	7,700	
Revenue and Expense Summary		7,700
Adjusting entry to record the ending		
inventory.		

(3) Revenue and Expense Summary	9,500	
Purchases		9,500
To transfer the balance in the		
Purchases account to the Revenue		
and Expense Summary.		

Merchandise Inventory	Revenue and Expense Summary	Purchases
8,600 (1) 8,600	(1) 8,600 (2) 7,700	9,500 (3) 9,500
(2) 7,700	(3) 9,500	
Debit balance is now $7,700.	Balance is $10,400, Cost of Goods Sold.	Account is closed.

Figure 11.5

Using a Cost of Goods Sold Account. Explain that this method is identical to the preceding methods, except that a new ledger account—Cost of Goods Sold—is used rather than the Revenue and Expense Summary account. Show that when this new account is used with the single-entry adjusting method, the journal entry is as follows:

(1) Cost of Goods Sold	900	
Merchandise Inventory		900
To correct the inventory account.		

The Purchases account is closed to the Cost of Goods Sold account as part of the closing entries. The result is that the Cost of Goods Sold account will then show purchases plus or minus any increase or decrease in the merchandise inventory. The Cost of Goods Sold account is then closed into the Revenue and Expense Summary account as below and in Figure 11.6.

(2) Cost of Goods Sold	9,500	
Purchases		9,500
Closing entry to transfer the Purchases		
account balance to the Cost of Goods		
Sold account.		

(3) Revenue and Expense Summary	10,400	
Cost of Goods Sold		10,400
Closing entry to transfer the Cost of		
Goods Sold account balance to the		
Revenue and Expense Summary		
account.		

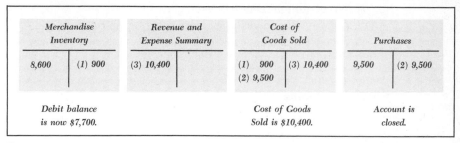

Figure 11.6

Using Two Closing Entries. The entries to correct the Merchandise Inventory account can also be recorded as closing entries instead of as adjusting entries. The entries used in this method are identical to those made in the preceding two-entry adjusting method, except that they are recorded as closing entries instead of as adjusting entries.

ENTERING THE ADJUSTMENT ON THE WORKSHEET. Explain to the students that when the beginning inventory is greater than the ending inventory, the Merchandise Inventory account has a debit balance and it must be credited to decrease the balance. Thus, the difference is entered in the Credit column of the Adjustments section on the same line as the Merchandise Inventory account. Point out that this entry is keyed with a letter. This amount is then entered in the Debit column of the Adjustments section on the same line as the Revenue and Expense Summary account; this entry is also keyed with a letter. Remind the students that if the Revenue and Expense Summary account is not listed in the Trial Balance section, the account title and number should be entered on the first available line.

Questions and Projects

1. Some teachers like to teach the worksheet before teaching the financial statements and vice versa. What are the advantages of each of these methods?

2. What are the various functions that a worksheet performs?

3. List a number of teaching suggestions for use when presenting the worksheet to students—for example, the keying of adjustments.

4. When the income statement columns show a credit balance, the balance sheet columns always show a debit balance. Why is this true?

5. Do the entries made in the adjustments columns of the worksheet ever change the balance of an account as shown in the trial balance from a debit to a credit or vice versa?

6. Describe what background information you would include in your classroom explanation of prepaid expenses.

7. Under the periodic inventory plan, why must the record of merchandise inventory as recorded in the ledger be adjusted at the end of each fiscal period?

8. What are the relative advantages of the one-entry adjusting method and the two-entry adjusting method for adjusting merchandise inventory?

9. What is the relationship of the amount of the inventory adjustment to Purchases and to Cost of Goods Sold?

Case Problems

1. One teacher has used a plain sheet of paper divided into four sections as a simple worksheet, as shown below.

Assets	Revenue
Liabilities and Owner's Equity	Expense

Accounts and their balances are taken from the trial balance and placed in the appropriate section on this sheet. What do you think of using such a form before presenting the formal worksheet in columnar form? What do you see as its values and weaknesses?

2. George Seamons, an experienced accounting teacher, prepares his students for the worksheet by classifying the accounts on the trial balance and writing a letter in front of each account to show what kind of account it is (A, L, OE, R, and E). After each account is so classified, each amount is extended to the proper column on the worksheet. What do you think of this procedure?

CHAPTER 12

Teaching Bad Debts and Depreciation

Two important topics that usually follow the teaching of adjustments for prepaid expenses are the handling of bad debts (doubtful accounts) and depreciation. Traditionally, both topics are treated in one chapter because of the marked similarities in their methodologies; however, there have been developments in recent years that update the generally accepted principles underlying the accounting treatment of each. Teachers should ensure that their students know well not only the similarities but also the clear differences that exist between them. Before going further, let us first review the accounting fundamentals relevant to bad debts and depreciation.

ACCOUNTING FUNDAMENTALS

Bad Debts

1. *Revenue* may be defined as the inflow of cash and accounts receivable as a result of sales. In many businesses, the greatest inflow of revenue by far results from sales on short-term credit.
2. For accounting purposes, the inflow of revenue resulting from credit sales is recognized at the time the sale is transacted; therefore, a credit sale is recorded as a debit to Accounts Receivable and a credit to the Sales Revenue account.
3. The probability that some accounts receivable will prove uncollectible is recognized by most enterprises that pursue an aggressive policy of deriving revenue from short-term credit sales. It follows, logically, that uncollectible accounts receivable are treated as one of the regular operating costs (expenses) of these businesses.
4. It is a generally accepted accounting principle that revenues must be matched against related expenses for a specific ac-
(continued)

counting period to present fairly the net income (or net loss) for that period.

5. Unsuccessful attempts to collect amounts due from customers are logically expenses and, therefore, should be matched against the sales of the accounting period that recognized this revenue.

6. Since uncollectible accounts cannot be predicted during the same accounting period in which the revenue derived from accounts receivable is recorded, an adjusting entry is required to match the revenue against an estimated amount of bad debts expense.

7. Failure to make an adjusting entry to create an allowance for bad debts will probably result in an overstatement of both revenue and accounts receivable for the accounting period; therefore, the reported figures for net income (or net loss) and accounts receivable will not be presented fairly to readers of the financial statements.

8. In subsequent accounting periods, whenever management learns that the amounts due from customers cannot be collected, the appropriate accounting principle is to write the accounts off as bad debts. The correct accounting procedure to write off an account as a bad debt is to debit the Allowance for Bad Debts account and to credit Accounts Receivable—the individual customer's account.

Depreciation

9. Fixed assets such as buildings, machinery, office equipment, and so on, are acquired for one reason only—to generate revenue for the business enterprise over a series of future years.

10. It is a generally accepted accounting principle that all fixed assets are entered in accounting records at the dollar amounts required to acquire these assets. The accounting basis for reporting fixed assets, therefore, is the cost at the date of their acquisition.

11. Until fixed assets are used (expired) in revenue-making activities, they are considered to be a bundle of unexpired costs and, therefore, are reported as assets under an appropriate heading in the balance sheet. Unexpired costs and assets thus are synonymous terms in accounting.

12. Except for land, fixed assets have a limited life in their use for revenue-making activities. This limited life is due to factors such as physical wear and tear and obsolescence.

13. Except for land, all fixed assets put to use in the production of revenue must have their costs included in the match-up with the other operating expenses to determine the net income or net loss

(continued)

for the accounting period. Since the useful life of fixed assets extends well beyond one accounting period, it is a generally accepted accounting principle that the costs of fixed assets be spread fairly over their useful life.

14. The cost of any fixed asset when matched against revenue in an accounting period becomes an expired cost. In the language of accounting, the expired cost of a fixed asset is known as depreciation expense.

15. In simple terms, depreciation in accounting refers to the process of converting the unexpired costs of fixed assets into expenses over a series of accounting periods.

16. Depreciation, in accounting, does not refer to the physical deterioration of any asset. Nor does it refer to the decrease in the market value of the fixed asset over a period of time. In terms of generally accepted accounting principles, depreciation is a process of allocation, not valuation.

17. Land is considered to be a nondepreciable property because it is not used in the production of revenue. Land costs, therefore, must not be converted into expenses to be matched against the revenue of any accounting period.

18. There are three steps in the allocation process: (a) to establish the amount to be allocated (that is, the depreciation base); (b) to estimate the useful life of the fixed asset over which the amount is to be allocated; and (c) to select a method of allocating the amount.

19. There is no one method of spreading the cost of the fixed asset over its useful life. The basic objective of the various depreciation methods is to allocate the cost of the asset over its service life in a systematic and rational manner.

20. To allocate the cost of a fixed asset, correct accounting procedures require an adjusting entry at the end of each accounting period to debit a descriptive depreciation expense account, and to credit a contra account showing the accumulation of expired costs.

21. The depreciation expense account records the allocation of cost for one accounting period. It must be included with other related operating expenses to be matched against the revenue of the same accounting period.

22. A descriptive accumulated depreciation account is credited to record the accumulation of expired cost (depreciation expense) over the useful life of the fixed asset. At the end of each accounting period, the total of expired cost (credit balance to date) will be shown on the balance sheet as contra to the related fixed asset in order to reveal the unexpired cost of that asset.

Teaching Bad Debts

The methods of teaching bad debts may be developed around the following order of topics: (1) introducing the concept of bad debts; (2) teaching the need for matching; (3) analyzing the matching entry; (4) analyzing bad debts through the accounting cycle; (5) teaching the methods of estimating bad debts; (6) recording actual bad debt losses; and (7) recording collection of debts written off.

Introducing Bad Debts

In almost every class, there will be one or more students who have had paper routes. These students know what it means to fail to collect from some of their customers. Here is a possible beginning that is based on the previous knowledge and experience of the students.

Another possible opening is to display a nonadjusted balance sheet to the class. Point to Accounts Receivable and ask the students to review the meaning of this asset. Then ask whether the amount reported for accounts receivable will be fully realized in cash. In a discussion of the answer, students generally have little difficulty in identifying bad debts as uncollectible accounts. What they usually overlook, however, is the fact that the balance sheet figure reported for accounts receivable is in all likelihood an overstatement and, therefore, requires some accounting treatment to adjust the figure to an amount that can be realized.

A third possibility is to discuss the role of a credit department for a large, well-known retail enterprise. In the discussion of granting credit, two points can be emphasized: (1) many businesses sell on short-term credit to increase their volume of revenue through credit sales and (2) as a result of granting this credit, a certain amount of risk-taking is involved in order to generate that revenue. This second point of risk-taking should logically identify the likelihood that some customers will fall into financial difficulty and find themselves unable to honor their promises, in full or in part. Once it is established that risk-taking leads to some bad debts, offer this conclusion: most businesses that pursue an aggressive policy of selling on credit recognize the probability that some accounts receivable will prove uncollectible and, therefore, the amounts uncollected are treated as one of their normal operating costs (expenses). Now, direct the students' attention to a nonadjusted income statement in order to underscore two points: (1) revenue derived from accounts receivable is probably overstated and, consequently, the net income is similarly overstated (or the net loss is understated) and (2) the operating expenses of any business transacting sales on credit must include a provision for bad debts expense in order to present a fair reporting of revenues and net income (or loss).

Regardless of the method used to introduce the concept of bad debts, it is important to offer the following summary *before* the next topic is introduced to the students:

1. Many businesses sell on short-term credit to increase their volume of revenue.
2. Regardless of how thoroughly management checks the credit reliability of prospective customers, some uncollectible accounts will arise as a result of errors in judgment or because of unforeseen customer financial difficulty.
3. Credit risk-taking is recognized by most businesses that pursue an aggressive policy of credit selling; therefore, any resulting uncollectible accounts must be considered part of the regular operating costs of these businesses.
4. An analysis of current-year sales on credit would indicate that there is a strong likelihood that an overstatement exists in the year-end reporting of accounts receivable and of revenue.

Teaching the Need for Matching

One effective way to teach the need for matching revenues against related expenses is to introduce the students to the direct write-off method of recording the bad debts expense when it occurs. A series of related transactions can be analyzed for one customer's account as follows.

1. Assume that the yearly accounting period ends December 31. Review the analysis of one credit sale as part of the total credit sales for the month of December. This analysis can be presented most effectively by an illustration relating the double entry in the subsidiary ledger and the general ledger as in Figure 12.1.

GENERAL LEDGER

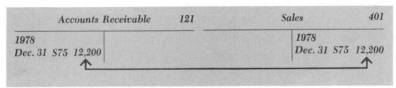

*ACCOUNTS RECEIVABLE
SUBSIDIARY LEDGER*

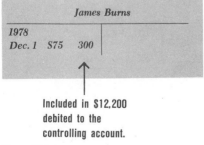

Included in $12,200
debited to the
controlling account.

Figure 12.1

In analyzing the transaction with the class, emphasize the fact that the customer has been given a short-term credit period of 30 days. As a conclusion to this analysis, it is important that the students understand that the revenue has been recorded in the last month of the accounting period and that the customer has been given until the end of the accounting period to discharge the debt.

2. Next, assume that the customer, James Burns, has not paid on December 31, the year-end. By referring to the year-end financial statements, the students should conclude that the amount owed by this customer, $300, is part of the figure shown for Accounts Receivable under the Current Assets section of the balance sheet and part of the total sales as shown under the Revenue section of the income statement.

3. Assume that within the following few months all attempts to collect from the customer fail and, as a result, management decides in June of the next accounting period to write off the $300 balance of Burns' account as a bad debt expense. The direct write-off can now be illustrated as shown in Figure 12.2.

ACCOUNTS RECEIVABLE
SUBSIDIARY LEDGER

James Bence

1978			1979		
Dec. 1	S75	300	June 15 Un- J46 300		
			collectible		

Entry made to write off an uncollectible account under the direct write-off method.

GENERAL JOURNAL   Page 46

DATE	ACCOUNT TITLE AND EXPLANATION	POST. REF.	DEBIT	CREDIT
1979				
June 15	Bad Debts Expense	511	300 00	
	Accounts Receivable/James Bence	121/√		300 00
	Write off the account as			
	uncollectible.			

GENERAL LEDGER

Accounts Receivable	121		Bad Debts Expense	511
	1979		1979	
	June 15 J46 300		June 15 J46 300	

Figure 12.2

With the posting of this direct write-off entry, the students should conclude that the customer's account in the subsidiary ledger is reduced to zero and that the Accounts Receivable controlling account in the general ledger is decreased by $300. Furthermore, they can see that an operating expense account called Bad Debts Expense (or Uncollectible Accounts Expense) must be debited to reflect the decrease of owner's equity in the accounting equation.

4. This next phase of the development is critical. Allow the students to react to a comparative view of the year-end income statements at the end of the first and second years. By means of careful examination and questioning, the students can be led to identify a violation of the matching principle: that is, the operating expenses of the second accounting period contains an expense—Bad Debts Expense—that has resulted from the revenue of the first year's accounting period. In other words, revenues of the second accounting period have been matched not only with the expenses incurred in securing that revenue, but also with an expense incurred in securing the revenue of the previous year. This mismatch can be emphasized through an analysis of an illustration similar to Figure 12.3.

Glen Scott Company
Comparative Income Statements

For the Year Ended	1978	1979
Revenue:		
Sales	12,200	12,200
Gross Profit	4,000	4,000
Operating Expenses:		
Bad Debts Expense	-0-	300
Net Income	4,000	3,700

Overstated because no expense was subtracted for the loss caused by the bad debt.

Understated because an expense from another period was subtracted from gross profit.

Figure 12.3

Before the next teaching stage is developed, it is important that the following generally accepted accounting principle be reemphasized: *Revenue must be matched with the expenses incurred in securing that revenue.*

Analyzing the Matching Entry

Students should now be receptive to an entry that would adjust the probable overstatement of both sales revenue and accounts receivable at year-end. Two questions, however, must be posed. First, since the exact amount of uncollectible accounts cannot be known until accounts are declared bad, what amount of expense should be matched against the revenue of the period? And second, since customer accounts cannot be identified as uncollectible until they are written off, what accounts receivable should be reduced?

A discussion of both questions must lead to the accounting concept that an *estimate* is taken and recorded for the amount of the probable overstatement of both revenue and accounts receivable. Students will want to know whether this estimated amount is based on guesswork or on some facts. At this stage of the development, it may be sufficient to generalize the answer along these lines. "Based on the experience of the business in granting credit, management can estimate more accurately than through guesswork. Later on, we shall examine several of these facts that assist management to estimate as accurately as possible the amount of probable bad debts. For the time being, let us assume an estimated amount so that we can analyze the adjusting entry."

Once the idea of the estimate is accepted, the debit side of the adjusting entry rarely provides a problem. As a result of earlier discussion, students will accept that the account Bad Debts Expense must be debited for the estimated amount. The effect of this debit entry will, of course, be to match the expense against the revenue of the same accounting period. The matching principle is, therefore, sustained and may easily be illustrated by referring to the income statement with the addition of the bad debts expense.

Now direct attention to the credit side of the adjusting entry. As a result of earlier discussion, students are ready to accept the point that the total amount of accounts receivable is probably overstated. Therefore, they are prepared to accept a reduction in this asset. And since the accountant does not know at this time which of the customer accounts are uncollectible, the concept of an Allowance for Bad Debts account to reduce accounts receivable can be introduced. The complete analysis for the adjusting entry may now be presented on the chalkboard or overhead projector as shown in Figure 12.4.

Since the Allowance for Bad Debts account will be new to the students at this time, it is very important to teach them how to classify this particular type of account. In previous work on the accounting equation, students have been referred repeatedly to five broad classes of accounts: Assets, Liabilities, (Owner's Equity) Capital, (Owner's Equity) Revenue, and (Owner's Equity) Expense. Under which of these five groups of accounts does the Allowance for Bad Debts belong? The correct answer should be taken from the analysis of the credit side of the adjusting entry. Since the credit side of the entry attempts to correct the overstatement of accounts receivable, then it is logical to suggest a name such as *minus asset account, asset reduction account,* or *contra account.* Of the three, contra account may be favored because *contra* means "contrary to the normal balance." And, in this case, the immediate reference would be contrary to the normal bal-

DECEMBER 31, 1978: The Glen Scott Company records an estimated loss from bad debts of $550 for the accounting period.

WHAT HAPPENS	ACCOUNTING RULE	ENTRY
The expense for bad debts decreases owner's equity by $550.	To decrease owner's equity, debit the account.	Debit: Bad Debts Expense, $550.
The realizable amount of *Accounts Receivable* decreases by $550.	To decrease an asset, credit the account.	Credit: Allowance for Bad Debts, $550.

Figure 12.4

ance of accounts receivable. The teacher can now show the relationship of the contra account to Accounts Receivable by referring to the Current Assets section of both the Chart of Accounts and the partial balance sheet.

Analyzing Bad Debts Through the Accounting Cycle

In teaching any new adjusting entry, the teacher should be careful to trace the entry from the point of origin to the end of the accounting cycle. Two methods are generally employed. After discussing the theory of the adjusting entry, some teachers illustrate the handling of the adjustment on the worksheet. Then they require the preparation of the financial statements to reflect the adjustment. Next they show the adjusting entry recorded in the general journal and posted to the general ledger. They then illustrate the closing entries correctly journalized and posted. Finally, they prepare the postclosing trial balance to reveal the Accounts Receivable controlling account and its related contra account.

On the other hand, some teachers prefer to delay this formal treatment until one set of adjustments—for example, prepaid expenses, bad debts, and depreciation—has been covered. In this case, these teachers may wish to show only a T-account analysis of the adjusting and closing entries and only a partial section of the financial statements, in order to reveal the effects of the adjustment. Once the theory of these adjustments has been covered, the teachers then present all of the adjustments through the accounting cycle, beginning with the ten-column worksheet and ending with the postclosing trial balance. Regardless of the method they use, the majority of teachers support the principle that some continuity be maintained for the teaching of each new adjusting entry. This continuity should include at least the analysis of the adjustment from the point of its origin; next an analysis of the adjustment on the specific sections of the financial statements; and finally an analysis of the closing entry.

Teaching the Methods of Estimating Bad Debts

Up to this point, the students have examined the adjustment for bad debts through a basic spiral development. As you will recall, the treatment of estimating the actual amount of the adjustment was avoided to keep matters as simple as possible. Once the teacher is satisfied that the students have grasped the basic concept of bad debts through a few reinforcement problems, then the next phase of the spiral development can be tackled. This next stage includes the methods of estimating the amount of uncollectible accounts.

To introduce this next topic, most teachers first offer a brief review in order to reemphasize two main points: (1) that at the point of establishing the estimate of allowance for bad debts, management does not know which debts will prove uncollectible, but merely that a statistical probability exists that some unknown amount will not be collected and (2) that the estimate is based upon known facts. Stated in general terms, these known facts are based on the business's past experience with uncollectible accounts and on the experience of similar businesses. In more specific terms, students can be introduced to one, two, or three methods of computing the estimates: (1) as a percentage of net sales, (2) as a percentage of total outstanding accounts receivable, and (3) as a percentage of the aged accounts receivable.

PERCENTAGE OF NET SALES. When management estimates the cost of bad debts as a percentage of net sales, the estimates in percentage terms are usually based upon past experience. For example, for one type of business this estimate may be 0.5 percent of the net sales. Four points must be taught when the percentage of net sales method is used.

1. The meaning of net sales must be emphasized. Review the meaning of this concept by pointing to the revenue section of an income statement for a merchandising firm. What students may forget to do is to deduct both the sales returns and allowances and the sales discount from the gross sales.
2. If the business has many cash sales, only the net credit sales should be considered in determining the loss due to bad debts.
3. The mathematics of calculating a percentage of a base number must be reviewed. Do not take for granted that all students will remember how to calculate 1 percent of net sales or 0.5 percent of net sales.
4. The amount of the adjustment will be the amount computed regardless of any balance in the Allowance for Bad Debts account.

Consider this problem to demonstrate the percentage of net sales method. X Company estimates its bad debt loss on the basis of 1 percent of net sales. Assume that the year-end general ledger shows the following account balances: Sales, $120,000; Sales Returns and Allowances, $9,000; Sales Discounts, $1,000; Accounts Receivable, $7,200; and Allowance for Bad Debts, $200 credit. (Note the use of round numbers for account balances in order to demathematize the problem.) Show the adjusting entry and the

T accounts as they would appear posted for Accounts Receivable, Allowance for Bad Debts, and Bad Debts Expense.

The students may well ask why the existing balance in the Allowance for Bad Debts account was ignored in computing the amount of the adjusting entry. Under the percentage of net sales method, the estimate is made on the basis of the relationship between bad debts expense and net sales rather than on that between bad debts expense and the year-end accounts receivable. This question will be resolved when the next two methods of estimating the bad debts are considered.

PERCENTAGE OF TOTAL OUTSTANDING ACCOUNTS RECEIVABLE. Under this method management, from past experience, would estimate that a certain percentage of accounts receivable, say 7 percent, will be uncollectible. When this method is introduced, four teaching points must be considered.

1. The base figure must be the balance of accounts receivable at the end of the accounting period.
2. The actual percentage calculation must be reviewed. Again, the ability of students to perform a percentage calculation should not be taken for granted.
3. If the Allowance for Bad Debts has a credit balance before the percentage calculation is made, then the actual estimate of bad debts expense must be the difference between the percentage calculation and the credit balance. In other words, the balance in the Allowance for Bad Debts account after posting the adjusting entry must be *equal to* the percentage of total outstanding accounts receivable. Explain that the estimate is made on the basis of the relationship between bad debts expense and accounts receivable at the end of the accounting period.
4. If the Allowance for Bad Debts has a debit balance before the percentage calculation is made, then this debit balance must be added to the percentage calculation in order to maintain an estimate equal to the percentage of total outstanding accounts receivable. It is wise to offer sufficient reinforcement problems to cover calculations involving the Allowance account with both debit and credit balances.

PERCENTAGE OF AGED ACCOUNTS RECEIVABLE. Many businesses, especially those with large numbers of credit customers, are estimating the cost of uncollectible accounts by computing a percentage of the aged accounts receivable. The teaching of the adjusting entry by aging accounts receivable generally involves a four-stage development.

First, prepare a schedule of accounts receivable by age. This schedule provides a breakdown of the total accounts receivable into age groups. It is interesting to observe that the actual preparation of such a schedule is ideally suited to a computer application; however, a computer is not required to teach the basic concepts inherent in an aging schedule. A transparency of an illustration similar to the one in Figure 12.5 can be analyzed very effectively on an overhead projector.

Glen Scott Company
Schedule of Accounts Receivable by Age
December 31, 1978

ACCOUNT WITH	BALANCE	1–30 DAYS	31–60 DAYS	61–90 DAYS	91–120 DAYS	OVER 120 DAYS
Adams Machine Company . . .	200 00	200 00				
James Burns	300 00	300 00				
Charles Bakery	400 00				250 00	150 00
Ross and Needham	700 00	600 00		100 00		
Salem Corporation	1,400 00	1,000 00	400 00			
Albert Smith, Inc.	100 00					100 00
Totals	7,200 00	4,400 00	800 00	900 00	600 00	500 00

Figure 12.5

Second, estimate the percentage of probable losses. After the total of accounts receivable outstanding is broken down into age groups, the estimated loss from bad debts can then be determined by taking a percentage of the total of each age group. The theory of striking a percentage for each age group is based on a simple principle: the further past due an accounts receivable becomes, the greater the likelihood that it will not be collected in full. For example, management may decide from past experience that 50 percent of accounts that are more than 120 days past due might be considered uncollectible, while only 1 percent of those with a current account balance might be considered a risk. Demonstrate a percentage schedule of probable losses by referring to an illustration such as Figure 12.6.

PERCENTAGE OF PROBABLE LOSSES

1–30 Days 1%
31–60 Days 2%
61–90 Days 10%
91–120 Days 25%
Over 120 Days 50%

Figure 12.6

Third, apply the percentages to the schedule of aged accounts receivable. Now that the percentages have been estimated for each age group, they can be applied to calculate the estimated bad debt expense. This calculation would naturally be taken in relation to the individual totals obtained through the schedule of accounts receivable by age. A transparency master similar to Figure 12.7 could be prepared in order to teach this step on an overhead projector.

Age Group (in days)	Total	Estimated Percentage	Estimated Loss
1–30	$4,400	1%	$ 44
31–60	800	2%	16
61–90	900	10%	90
91–120	600	25%	150
Over 120	500	50%	250
	$7,200		$550

Figure 12.7

Fourth, record the adjusting entry. The teaching of the adjusting entry is no different from the method presented in relation to calculating the estimate as a percentage of total outstanding accounts receivable. What must be emphasized again, however, is the preliminary step of either adding the debit balance in the Allowance account or subtracting the credit balance of the Allowance account, as the case may be. The main point here is that the calculated estimate is based on the relationship between bad debts expense and accounts receivable. The actual adjustment, therefore, must be a desired amount equal to the calculated estimate based on the aging of accounts receivable.

Choosing a Method

A methodology question may be raised at this point. Should one, two, or all three methods of estimating the allowance for bad debts be taught? The use of all three methods can be justified. Where the lack of time indicates that a choice must be made, however, most teachers support the presentation of two: the estimate as a percentage of net sales and the estimate as a percentage of the aged accounts receivable. In particular, teachers are quite open to support of the aging method for these reasons:

1. Aging accounts receivable is regarded as a more accurate calculation of the estimate.
2. Aging accounts receivable is in common use by the management of many firms that transact a large volume of credit sales. Briefly, management requires an aged analysis of accounts receivable, generally on a monthly basis, in order to control the most valuable asset next to cash, that is, the accounts receivable. With a monthly reporting of accounts receivable by age, management is continually informed of the trend of collections and can take appropriate action in the granting of credit terms to present and future customers.
3. An aged schedule of accounts receivable is a common application of both machine accounting and computer data processing. Students

should be given the theory of aging before they employ their knowledge to the actual hardware method.

4.   Where computerized applications are available, many manufacturing and wholesaling firms now prepare a customer's monthly statement in the form of an aged schedule. This "aged" monthly statement is mailed to the customer in order to reveal a more accurate accounting of the customer's credit rating on each individual invoice.

Recording Actual Bad Debt Losses

The principle to teach under this next stage should be simple to grasp. Whenever management learns that the amount receivable from a particular customer cannot be collected, the acceptable accounting procedure is to write the account off as a bad debt. What must be emphasized to students is the debit side of the entry. The Allowance for Bad Debts account, and *not* Bad Debts Expense, is always debited to record the offsetting credit to Accounts Receivable (and to the appropriate customer's account in the subsidiary ledger). To avoid any possibility of making an error in the debit entry, emphasize the following points:

• The only time Bad Debts Expense is debited is at the end of the accounting period. The student should always associate this entry with the need for matching revenues and relating expenses within the same accounting period.

• When a particular account receivable is written off, the entry does not represent any additional expense because the Allowance for Bad Debts account has been set up to receive the actual bad debts when they are so declared. The Allowance account, therefore, acts as a sort of clearinghouse for recording all bad debts written off.

• If any bad debt were to be written off against Bad Debts Expense, then there would be a double counting of uncollectible accounts receivable expense (bad debts expense).

Another point must be taught in conjunction with any actual write-off entry. Observe that the net amount of accounts receivable—the amount of accounts receivable management expects to realize in cash—does not change as a result of recording an actual bad debt loss. Consider this example. Before any write-off entry, assume that the balance of Accounts Receivable was $10,000, and that the Allowance for Bad Debts was $700. Now assume that after the adjusting entry was made a customer's account was declared as a bad debt and was written off for $300. Notice in Figure 12.8 that no change has occurred in the *net* amount of accounts receivable.

By showing this comparative view to students, a point made earlier can be emphasized. Because of the need for matching, the expense of uncollectible accounts belongs in the period in which the sale is made. For this reason, the Allowance for Bad Debts account must be used to reduce the Accounts Receivable whenever a customer's account is actually written off.

	Before the Write-Off	After the Write-Off
Accounts Receivable	10,000	9,700
Less: Allowance for Bad Debts . .	700	400
Net amount of receivables	9,300	9,300

Figure 12.8

To use the expense account would not only violate the matching principle but also affect the relationship between Accounts Receivable and the related contra account.

One final point may be questioned by students in respect to the relationship between the total write-offs during the subsequent accounting period and the calculated estimates at the end of the previous accounting period. In answering, emphasize that the exact amount of bad debts can never be estimated in advance. The best that is possible is to provide an estimate based on a statistical probability. In the final analysis, refer students to the next year-end when accounting takes care of any debit or credit balance in the Allowance account through a new adjusting entry.

Recording Collection of Debts Written Off

The final phase in the methodology of teaching bad debts is to present the recovery of an account previously written off. One or two transactions should be sufficient to teach the accounting procedures involved. Consider this example. Assume that James Burns pays $300 on May 31, which is a little over a year after the decision was made to write off his account as a bad debt.

To begin the correct analysis of this transaction, review the history of the customer's account prior to the collection. The important point to note here is that before the receipt of the $300, the customer's account was reduced to zero (and a corresponding amount of reduction was made to the controlling account). Collection of Burns' amount due, therefore, must prove that the write-off was an error. To correct this error, accounting generally records first a reversing entry that may be shown in the general journal as in Figure 12.9.

GENERAL JOURNAL				Page 55
DATE	ACCOUNT TITLE AND EXPLANATION	POST. REF.	DEBIT	CREDIT
1980 May 31	Accounts Receivable/James Burns	121/√	300 00	
	Allowance for Bad Debts	122		300 00
	Reverse entry of June 15, 1979 writing off this account, which was collected in full today.			

Figure 12.9

With the posting of the above reversing entry, the customer's account will once again show the original debt. A separate entry can now follow in the cash receipts journal to record the collection of $300 from Burns. The posting of this receipt will bring the customer's account back to zero. In the final analysis, the customer's account, as shown in Figure 12.10, will reveal an accurate record of his credit history.

Name		James Burns				Credit Limit		$500	
Address		32 Peabody Street, Milford, Illinois 60953				Telephone		932-3148	
DATE		EXPLANATION	POST. REF.	DEBIT		CREDIT		DEBIT BALANCE	
1978 Dec.	1	. . . .	S75	300	00			300	00
1979 June	15	Uncollectible	J46			300	00	—	00
1980 May	31	Reverse write-off	J55	300	00			300	00
	31	. . . .	CR91			300	00	—	00

Figure 12.10

Performance Goals for Bad Debts

The following are suggested performance goals for the unit on bad debts.

Given a nonadjusted trial balance showing year-end balances for Sales, Sales Returns and Allowances, Sales Discount, and Accounts Receivable, the student will be able to analyze in T-account form the adjusting entry to estimate the bad debts loss as 1 percent of the net sales.

Given a nonadjusted trial balance showing year-end balances for Sales, Sales Returns and Allowances, Sales Discount, Accounts Receivable, and a credit (or debit) balance for Allowance for Bad Debts, the student will be able to record correctly the adjusting entry in the general journal to estimate the bad debt loss as 0.5 percent of net sales.

Given a year-end trial balance showing a debit balance for Accounts Receivable and a credit (or debit) balance for Allowance for Bad Debts, the student will be able to analyze correctly in general journal form the estimate of uncollectible accounts as 2 percent of the total outstanding accounts receivable.

Given an aged trial balance of accounts receivable and a percentage schedule of probable losses, the student will be able to (1) compute the total amount of the expected bad debt loss; (2) record the adjusting entry for bad debts expense in the general journal assuming a zero balance for the Allowance for Bad Debts account; (3) record the adjusting entry if Allowance for Bad Debts has a credit balance; and (4) record the adjusting entry if Allowance for Bad Debts has a debit balance.

Given a list of ten customers and their respective subsidiary ledger balances at year-end, and given the invoice information for each customer, the student will be able to prepare on a standard form a schedule of accounts receivable by age which is correctly verified by column totals.

Given general ledger information for account balances at the end of an accounting period and given similar information for accounts in the accounts receivable ledger, the student will be able to correctly (1) open general ledger and subsidiary ledger accounts; (2) record the adjusting entry in the general journal for a given amount of estimated bad debts for the accounting period; (3) post the adjusting entry to ledger accounts; (4) record the entry in the general journal to close Bad Debts Expense; and (5) post the closing entry to the accounts. Using the same working papers, the student will be able to journalize and post correctly transactions writing off two customer accounts as bad debts in the second accounting period; the adjusting entry to record a given estimated amount of bad debt loss for the second accounting period; and the closing entry showing the transfer of the expense account into the summary account.

Given a set of working papers that includes completed ledgers, a year-end trial balance, and information on adjustments to prepaid insurance, prepaid supplies, inventory of goods, and the estimated bad debts loss for the accounting period, the student will be able to correctly (1) prepare a ten-column worksheet; (2) prepare a set of financial statements in classified form; (3) record and post adjusting entries; (4) record and post the closing entries; and (5) prepare a postclosing trial balance.

Teaching Depreciation

Of all the adjustments to teach to any level of accounting class, depreciation offers perhaps the most difficulty and the greatest challenge. The difficulty lies primarily in the deep-rooted meaning of the word in common usage; the challenge is to teach depreciation in proper accounting context and especially in accordance with generally accepted accounting principles. The following suggested sequence of presentation helps meet this challenge:

1. Review the adjustments for prepaid expenses.
2. Bring out the real business reason for acquiring fixed assets.
3. Introduce the concept of the limited useful life of fixed assets in terms of generating revenue for the business.
4. Teach the concept of spreading the cost of the asset over its useful life.
5. Teach the concept of estimating depreciation.
6. Teach the way depreciation is recorded by adjusting entries, using the straight-line method of recording depreciation.
7. Teach the entries disposing of a fixed asset.
8. Introduce the concept of a fixed asset ledger.
9. Analyze depreciation through the steps of the accounting cycle.
10. Teach one or several more methods of depreciation.
11. Teach a comparison of accounts for Accumulated Depreciation and Allowance for Bad Debts.

Review Prepaid Expenses

A review of the adjustments for prepaid expenses is recommended before you launch the topic of depreciation. In particular, two areas should be emphasized. First, the terms *unexpired cost* and *expired cost* should be brought out so that they can easily be transferred to depreciation accounting. As you will recall, one good example to emphasize the distinction between expired and unexpired cost is prepaid insurance. It is important that all students relate the unexpired cost of insurance to the current asset account and the expired cost of insurance to the operating expense account. Second, the principle of matching must be reviewed so that students automatically associate the term *expired costs* with the expenses to be matched against the revenue. Keep in mind that the entire area of recording adjusting entries is largely the process of accounting to match fairly revenues with related expenses for the same accounting period. With a good review of prepaid expense adjustments, the move can be made from the known to the unknown.

Acquiring Fixed Assets

One effective way to launch the topic of depreciation is through a series of well-developed questions. Three objectives are essential at this early stage. First, avoid posing the traditional definition question. There is no need to rush into the meaning of depreciation at this early stage. Second, bring out the real reason for the business acquisition of fixed assets. And third, review the principle of the cost base in acquiring these assets. It is most important to help the students to understand that assets such as buildings, machinery, and delivery trucks are acquired to produce revenue for the business.

To give added strength to this principle, it is convenient to think of such assets as a bundle of services to be received by the business over a period of future years. These two examples can be used to reinforce the idea.

The acquiring of a building may be regarded as payment in advance for several years' supply of housing services. For any business, the building houses the sales personnel who sell goods or services; it houses the equipment and office personnel required to support the operations of the business; it houses the inventory to be sold to customers; and it houses the customers who prefer to shop at the business location. Clearly, the building has been acquired to support revenue-making activities for a number of years to come. Of course, it must be stressed that the building was not acquired for the purpose of resale. If this were intended, then the business would cease to operate the moment the building was sold.

The purchase of a delivery truck offers a bundle of transportation services to the business for a period of years or so many thousands of miles. Here again, the objective in acquiring such a truck is to support the revenue-making activities of a business. The truck has not been acquired with the intention of resale; it is hoped that the truck will deliver goods sold to customers for several years to come.

At this point, you have accomplished two of the three objectives: the word *depreciation* and its common meaning have been avoided and the real reason for acquiring fixed assets has been emphasized. To accomplish the third objective, introduce the cost principle related to fixed assets, if it has not been introduced before. Without an understanding of the cost basis for reporting fixed assets, the concepts of unexpired costs and expired costs become meaningless.

It is worth mentioning here that teachers of college-level courses would probably expand on the cost principle to introduce the concept of "laid-down" cost. For example, the cost of acquiring a machine from a manufacturer located many miles away would include all expenditures reasonable and necessary to place the asset in a position and condition for use in the operations of the business. A specific example such as the one that follows will reinforce this concept.

A manufacturing plant in New Jersey orders a machine from a Mississippi tool manufacturer. Details of acquisition are list price, $15,000; terms, 2/10, n/30; sales tax, 5 percent; freight charges to New Jersey rail station, $1,200; transportation charges from the rail station to the factory, $200; labor costs to install machinery, $500. The cost base of the machine to be recorded as a debit to Machinery would be calculated as shown in Figure 12.11.

List price of machine	15,000
Less cash discount (2% of 15,000)	300
Net cash price	14,700
Add sales tax (5% of 14,700)	735
Add freight	1,200
Add transportation from rail station to factory	200
Add installation labor	500
Cost of machine	17,335

Figure 12.11

The Concept of Limited Useful Life

The next step is to lead the students to form the concept of the limited useful life of the asset in terms of generating revenue for the business. Ask the class how long a building, acquired at a cost of $80,000, must last in order to produce revenue for the business. Most students will respond that the building cannot last forever and that physical wear and tear will shorten its life. Point out that a second factor, obsolescence, also affects the building's life. In the discussion, again avoid the pitfall of using the traditional meaning of the word *depreciation.*

The Concept of Allocation

Now proceed to develop the concept of spreading the cost of an asset over its useful life. Ask the class to make two assumptions: that management decides that the estimated useful life of the building is 20 years and that the building will be worthless at the end of that time. Then pose this question: Should the business charge this year's profits with the entire cost of the building? By this time the students should agree that since the building is to generate revenue for 20 years, a fair proportion of the cost of the building must be allocated in each of those 20 years. Remind the students of the generally accepted accounting principle of matching revenues and related expenses within the same accounting period. Demonstrate that if the cost of the building is to be equally spread over its 20-year life, the expired cost at the end of the first year would be $\frac{1}{20}$ of $80,000, or $4,000. The unexpired cost would be the difference between the cost and the expired cost, or $76,000. At this point, explain the following accounting concepts:

1. The entire process of spreading the cost of the fixed asset over its useful life is called *depreciation.*
2. The expired cost is matched against revenue, just as are all other expenses incurred to generate revenue for that accounting period. This expired cost is called *depreciation expense.*
3. The accumulated expired costs over the years of using the asset are called *accumulated depreciation.*
4. The unexpired cost of the asset is known as the *net book amount.*

It is important at this juncture to mention that there is one fixed asset, land, that does not depreciate. Explain that there are two reasons why land does not depreciate: land is acquired solely with the idea of serving as a site on which a depreciable building will be constructed, and land is regarded as having unlimited life because its cost can be recovered once a building on it is eliminated from further use.

In the teaching development so far, note that no journal has yet been used, no accounts have been introduced, and the common definition of depreciation has been avoided. In other words, the proper foundation has been constructed for the correct accountant's meaning of the term and for the later introduction of the adjusting entry. But, before analyzing the debits and credits, develop the concept of estimating depreciation further so that students can react to the idea of disposal value.

Estimating Depreciation

One additional concept related to depreciation accounting is recommended before the actual accounting entries are presented to the students. This important concept is, of course, that depreciation of any depreciable fixed asset must be estimated. The following important points should be emphasized in teaching the estimating of depreciation.

1. In acquiring a depreciable fixed asset, management has no way to measure exactly how long the asset will be useful. At best, an estimate must be made as to the useful life of the asset.

2. One other estimate must be considered. For many fixed assets, management must make an estimate as to the prospective disposal value (salvage value, scrap value, trade-in value). It is important to emphasize that whatever disposal value is estimated, the amount must be deducted from the original cost of the asset *before* most methods of depreciation are applied. The remaining amount will be known as the *depreciable cost* or the *cost base of depreciation*.

3. With the two estimates given—the estimated useful life and the estimated disposal value—a method of estimating the amount of depreciation expense for each accounting period can be applied.

4. It is important to stress that there are several recognized methods of estimating the depreciation expense. Since the foundation for the straight-line method has already been developed, this method should be the first one to be presented.

5. To illustrate the straight-line method, use a simple example of a fixed asset that has a rather short useful life and some disposal value. For example, a typewriter purchased at a cost of $800 has been given an estimated useful life of six years and an estimated disposal value of $80. The estimated calculation for the annual and monthly depreciations may be shown as follows:

$$\frac{\text{Original unexpired cost} - \text{Disposal value}}{\text{Estimated useful life (in years)}} = \text{Annual depreciation}$$

$$\frac{\$800 - \$80}{6} = \$120 \text{ a year}$$

$$\$120 \div 12 = \$10 \text{ a month}$$

The students may then be assigned a series of similar problems.

The question arises as to whether other methods of calculating depreciation should be presented in addition to the straight-line method. However, to explain two or more methods at this point might be confusing. Later in the course, and especially in college-level courses, other methods may be presented and some of the better students encouraged to do library study and prepare papers presenting the pros and cons of various methods.

Recording the Adjusting Entry

Before presenting the way depreciation is recorded, review the importance of the matching principle. By this stage of the development, and especially after having seen adjustments for prepaid expenses (and possibly for bad debts), all students should recognize the importance of matching revenues and related expenses for the same accounting period. Of course, depreciation expense must be included with other expenses of earning revenues.

A series of T accounts may be used to present an effective analysis of the accounting for fixed assets. Once again, select a fixed asset like a typewriter so that the entire accounting of its useful life can be easily illustrated. A procedure such as the following might be observed.

Review the entry recording the purchase of the office typewriter shown in Figure 12.12 as Office Equipment in the general ledger.

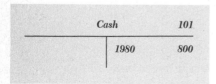

Figure 12.12

Explain that the typewriter was purchased exactly one year ago and that management has estimated a disposal value of $80 after six years of use. The class should determine easily the depreciation expense and unexpired cost of the typewriter at the end of the first year of operation (current date).

Through class discussion, develop the entry that should be made at the end of the year to record the depreciation expense. Make the entry first in T accounts and then show the journal entry. (The accounting term *allowance for depreciation of office equipment* is sometimes used instead of *accumulated depreciation*, although the latter is the more modern usage. Note that the term *reserve* is now regarded with disfavor.)

Depreciation Expense on Office Equipment	120	
Accumulated Depreciation on Office Equipment		120
To record the annual depreciation expense		
on office typewriter.		

Several questions may come up in the discussion.

Should Depreciation Expense or Depreciation Expense on Office Equipment be debited? To answer this question, point out that accounting principles support the policy of disclosing as much information about reporting expenses as possible. In this case, therefore, depreciation on office equipment is usually considered to be an administrative or management expense. Similarly, the depreciation expense relating to owned buildings used as retail stores or sales warehouses and to equipment contained in these structures is a selling expense.

Why not place the credit for the depreciation directly into the Asset account instead of establishing the separate Accumulated Depreciation account? In theory, there would be nothing wrong with a practice of crediting depreciation directly to the related asset accounts. However, in keeping with the principle of disclosing useful information to readers of financial statements, it is customary to show both the unexpired cost and accumulated expired costs of fixed assets on balance sheets. This concept can be easily reviewed by returning to the first set of examples showing the process of depreciating the building. It is extremely important to avoid the temptation to describe the credit entry as having the effect of decreasing the value of the asset. An accumulated depreciation account has no independent meaning or significance; it is merely a contra account that describes the accumulation of expired costs (depreciated amounts) of the depreciated property. To conclude, ask the class this question: "If you were owners of businesses, would you prefer to know only the balance of the fixed asset or both the original cost figure and the total accumulated depreciation?"

Does the accumulated depreciation account represent money set aside to replace the equipment? This type of question would not be raised if a proper foundation of depreciation in accounting had been treated. Some students, however, may have been influenced by what they may have read in newspapers and what was said to them by ill-informed persons. If the question is raised, return to the double entry to emphasize this point. The contra account, accumulated depreciation, represents the credit side of the equipment account and the two accounts are, in a sense, inseparable. The accumulated depreciation account remains on the books as long as the equipment still has a useful life. When the equipment is no longer useful or is sold, the account is closed.

As in the presentation of all previous adjusting entries, it is always helpful to the student to see the complete picture. Therefore, the effects of depreciation should be shown first on the financial statements; then the closing entry may be analyzed in T-account form. To show the complete depreciation of the fixed asset, however, a set of T accounts similar to those shown in Figure 12.13 may be used.

Office Equipment		156
1980	800	

Accumulated Depreciation— Office Equipment		157
	1980	120
	1981	120
	1982	120
	1983	120
	1984	120
	1985	120

Depreciation Expense— Office Equipment		514
1985	120	

Figure 12.13 Depreciation for the sixth year.

The scene has now been set for presenting the next topic, disposing of the fixed asset.

Disposal of Fixed Assets

In introducing the unit on the disposition of a fixed asset, teachers generally agree that unnecessary complications should be avoided. Thus the first presentation should analyze an asset that is fully depreciated and that shows no loss or gain on disposal. For example, in the case of the typewriter, let us assume that the office equipment is sold early in the seventh year. The following procedure may be used to teach the disposition and sale of the fixed asset.

Review the position of the general ledger accounts for Office Equipment and Accumulated Depreciation—Office Equipment at the end of the sixth year. The student must be aware that the typewriter is fully depreciated; that is, except for the disposal value of $80, the original cost of the asset has been spread over six years.

Stress the principle of accounting for the disposal or retirement of any depreciable asset. In simple terms, the cost of the property is removed from the asset account, and the accumulated depreciation is removed from the related contra account. This principle would suggest the following double entry on sale of the fixed asset.

Cash	80	
Accumulated Depreciation: Office Equipment	720	
Office Equipment		800
To remove from the accounts the cost and the accumulated depreciation on a fully depreciated office typewriter, which was sold for the disposal value of $80.		

The complete account analysis, similar to Figure 12.14, may now be shown.

Cash		101
1986	80	

Office Equipment		156
1980	800	1986	800

Accumulated Depreciation—Office Equipment		157
1986	720	1980	120
		1981	120
		1982	120
		1983	120
		1984	120
		1985	120
	720		720

Figure 12.14

In a discussion of the disposal of a fixed asset, college students in particular will raise several important questions. In this text, we shall identify and suggest a brief treatment for the following four: (1) How does accounting handle the disposal of a fixed asset where the disposal price is above the net book amount (often referred to as the *book value*)? (2) How is it handled where the disposal price is below the net book amount? (3) How does accounting record the disposal of a fixed asset at any date other than the end of the accounting year? (4) How does accounting handle the problem of management's decision to use the fully depreciated asset in subsequent accounting periods?

Disposal Price Above Book Value. Where a fixed asset is disposed of at a price above the net book amount, generally accepted accounting principles recognize a gain on the disposal of the fixed asset. For example, assume that a fixed asset costing $100,000 has been depreciated at the rate of $5,000 a year on a straight-line basis over a 10-year period. At the end of ten years, it is replaced by a newer machine and sold for $60,000. The calculation of gain on disposal is as follows:

Original cost	$100,000
Less accumulated depreciation	50,000
Net book amount	50,000
Less proceeds from disposal	60,000
Gain on disposal	$ 10,000

The double entry to record the disposition of the asset would be as follows:

Cash	60,000	
Accumulated Depreciation: Machinery	50,000	
Machinery		100,000
Gain on Disposal of Fixed Assets		10,000
To record the sale of machinery at		
a price above the net book amount.		

Theoretically, this gain may be said to represent an overstatement of depreciation expense recorded in the past ten years. Hence the entry to record the gain corrects an understatement of ten years' recorded earnings (other things being equal). Where the gain is material in amount, it should be shown separately in the income statement under a heading such as "Extraordinary Items." This category is generally found near the bottom of the income statement after the income (or loss) from operations has been shown.

Disposal Price Below Net Book Amount. For disposal of a fixed asset at a price below the net book amount, there would be a loss on the disposal of the fixed asset. Assume, for example, that the same machinery were sold for $40,000. Students should be able to provide the analysis that shows a debit to "Loss on Disposal of Fixed Assets" for $10,000. They should also be able to state how this loss is reported on the income statement.

Disposal at a Date Other Than Year-End. When a depreciable asset is disposed of at any date other than the end of the accounting year, an entry is usually made to record the depreciation for the fraction of the year ending with the date of disposal. For example, assume that in the case of the machinery, management decides to dispose of the asset six months before the end of the tenth year of useful life. Furthermore, assume that the machinery is sold for $40,000 cash immediately after the decision is made to retire the asset. The teaching of this transaction would require a three-step development as follows.

1. An analysis of the ledger accounts at the end of the ninth year for Machinery and the related contra account.
2. An accounting entry to record depreciation for the six months prior to the disposal of the machinery.
3. An accounting entry to record the sale of the machinery at less than the net book amount.

Continued Use of a Depreciated Fixed Asset. The question of what to do when management decides to continue the use of a fixed asset after it has been fully depreciated will interest the students. In general, the asset account and the related accumulated depreciation account may be permitted to remain on the books without further entries until the asset is discarded. Furthermore, no useful purpose is served by disclosing a fully depreciated asset and, therefore, it is usually omitted from the balance sheet.

Teaching the Fixed Asset Ledger

A topic that is generally overlooked in teaching depreciation is the concept of the subsidiary ledger for fixed assets. In general, the student is given an excellent development on accounts receivable and accounts payable subsidiary ledgers but fails to see the importance of applying the principle of the control device to other general ledger accounts. Time permitting, this short development of the fixed asset ledger can be presented.

First, review the concept of subsidiary ledgers in relation to accounts receivable and accounts payable. Do not forget to reemphasize the importance of each controlling account.

Second, teach the concept that the general ledger contains a separate asset account and related depreciation account for each major class of fixed assets. For example, it would be impractical to open a separate general ledger account for each piece of furniture or each piece of office equipment a business owns.

Third, teach the need for a separate subsidiary ledger for each major class of fixed assets. For example, a subsidiary ledger should be established for office equipment. Discuss the relationship between the controlling account, Office Equipment, and the individual subsidiary ledger accounts such as typewriters, filing cabinets, dictating machines, office calculators, copiers, duplicators, and desks. To assist in the students' understanding of a fixed asset record, prepare a transparency of a typical fixed asset record card as shown in Figure 12.15.

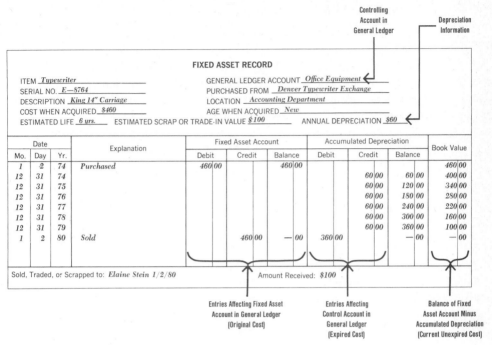

Figure 12.15

And finally, discuss the advantages of maintaining a fixed asset ledger. In addition to the obvious advantage of greater efficiency in maintaining general ledger accounts, there is greater internal control over the fixed assets and improved efficiency in acquiring immediate information about any asset for insurance and tax purposes.

Analyzing Depreciation Through the Accounting Cycle

It goes without saying that the teaching of any new adjusting entry should be analyzed through the individual steps of the accounting cycle. As outlined earlier under the methods of teaching bad debts, two methods are generally used by teachers. The first method, an abbreviated one using T-account forms, has already been suggested. The second method would offer the grouping of a number of adjustments to provide for the following type of instructional objective:

Given a set of working papers, a year-end nonadjusted trial balance, and year-end information on inventory of goods, supplies unused, unexpired insurance, estimated bad debts, and depreciation data on depreciable fixed assets, students will prepare correctly (1) a ten-column worksheet; (2) a set of financial statements; (3) the recording and posting of adjusting entries; (4) the recording and posting of closing entries; and (5) a postclosing trial balance.

Methods of Depreciation

As mentioned earlier, one or more other methods of estimating the amount of depreciation expense may be presented. For example, the teacher of college-level or advanced high school courses may wish to introduce one or more of the following acceptable methods in addition to straight-line: units-of-output method; fixed-percentage-on-declining-balance method; and the sum-of-the-years'-digits method.

In presenting any one of these additional methods of estimating depreciation, develop the topic around the following plan:

1. Use a simple example to demonstrate the meaning of the method. Be sure to indicate when the disposal value is not a consideration in a specific method.
2. Review the accounting entry for the depreciation expense.
3. Discuss the advantages and limitations of each method.
4. Discuss the methods that are approved for income tax purposes. Canadian teachers will note that the only acceptable method of writing off certain depreciable assets is the fixed-percentage-on-declining-balance method (often known as simply the *capital cost allowance method*). On the other hand, the Internal Revenue Code of the United States recognizes several acceptable methods of "rapid write-off" of certain depreciable assets. Since the Code is revised periodically, the American teacher is advised to check with the nearest Internal Revenue office.
5. Finally, point out that many methods are generally acceptable in accounting practice so long as one is followed consistently by the business enterprise.

Comparing the Two Contra Asset Accounts

At the beginning of this chapter the need was indicated for teaching a comparative analysis of the accounting treatment of bad debts with that of depreciation. One way to accomplish this objective is through a comparison of the two contra asset accounts: accumulated depreciation and allowance for bad debts. At the outset, notice that the traditional use of the term *valuation accounts* has been avoided in an attempt to comply with the accounting profession's recommendation to eliminate any misunderstanding of the "value" concept.

In any comparative analysis, insist on the indentification of both similarities and differences between the two contra asset accounts. The following common identifications can be underscored:

1. Both accounts appear on the balance sheet as deductions. The accumulated depreciation is shown as a deduction from depreciable assets, such as buildings or office equipment, and the allowance for bad debts as a deduction from Accounts Receivable.

2. Both are created by adjusting entries.

3. Both are based on estimates rather than on precisely determined amounts.
4. Both show that the debit side of the adjusting entry affects an expense account (Depreciation Expense or Bad Debts Expense).

On the other hand, the striking differences between the two contra asset accounts must also be taught. These are shown in Figure 12.16.

ACCUMULATED DEPRECIATION	ALLOWANCE FOR BAD DEBTS
1. This account does *not* reduce the related fixed asset to a realizable value. It merely shows what portion of the original cost has expired and has been recorded as expenses.	1. This account serves to reduce the accounts receivable to the amount of cash expected to be obtained through the collection of accounts receivable.
2. This account is debited only at the time the related fixed asset is disposed of.	2. This account is debited each time an individual customer account is written off.
3. This account will have only a credit balance during the lifetime of the related fixed asset.	3. This account may have either a debit balance or credit balance at the end of each accounting year. The specific type of balance will depend on the extent of bad debts written off during the accounting period.
4. This account is "contra" to a fixed asset account.	4. This account is "contra" to a current asset account.

Figure 12.16 Differences of contra asset accounts.

Problems, Questions, and Projects

1. Describe two methods that may be used to introduce the concept of bad debts to a beginning accounting class. Would you prefer one method over the other, or would you use both? Explain your answer.

2. In teaching bad debts, what method would you use to demonstrate the effects of the adjusting entry through the accounting cycle? Give reasons for your answer.

3. In applying any one of the three methods of calculating the actual amount of the estimate, students often fail to consider the existing balance in the Allowance for Bad Debts account. How would you explain when to consider the balance in the Allowance account, and when to avoid this balance?

4. Of the three methods in common use for calculating the estimate of uncollectible accounts, which one would you make sure is taught to students? Give reasons.

5. Prepare as many functional performance goals as possible for the various topics in the area of depreciation accounting.

6. What danger exists in presenting the meaning of depreciation as a decrease in the value of a fixed asset?

7. Discuss a plan for introducing the first lesson in depreciation accounting.

8. A new piece of office equipment was purchased by the Philips Company at a list price of $46,000 with credit terms of 2/10, n/30. Payment was made within the discount period; it also included a 5 percent sales tax on the net price. To acquire the new equipment, the firm paid transportation charges of $1,800 and labor costs of $3,200 for installing the equipment. During the unloading and installation work, some of the equipment fell from a loading platform and was damaged. The Philips Company paid $200 to have the equipment repaired. Calculate the cost base of the machine to be recorded as a debit to the Office Equipment account. Discuss the reasoning behind your answer.

9. To what area of depreciation accounting should the teacher relate the factors of physical wear and tear and obsolescence?

10. The accounting profession supports the principle that depreciation is a method of allocation, and not of valuation. Discuss the meaning of this principle.

11. Use an example to illustrate the allocation process of depreciation.

12. Explain why land does not depreciate in accounting of fixed assets.

13. Develop a teacher's plan for introducing the topic of disposal of fixed assets.

14. Where would an accountant report a sizable gain (or loss) on the disposition of a fixed asset? Explain the rationale involved.

Case Problems

1. One accounting teacher introduced the topic of depreciation by accompanying his class to a parking lot. He had previously selected three automobiles of different makes and models. Each student was asked to estimate the present value of each of the three cars. The class then returned to the classroom, calculated the value of each car (by using the average of all students' estimates), and figured the annual depreciation of each. (The age and cost price of each car had been determined earlier.)

What is your opinion of this teacher's procedure?

2. One accounting teacher introduced her students to the topic of depreciation by bringing to class a new dress and one that was out of style, a new pair of skates and a worn-out pair, a new book and a used one. She displayed each set of articles, then asked the class what the differences between the two articles were and why there was so much variance. What do you think of her presentation? Does it bring out the fact that depreciation results from both time and use?

CHAPTER 13

Teaching Accruals, Deferrals, and Reversing Entries

Two other types of adjusting entries—those for accruals and deferrals—still have to be introduced to the students. In addition, at this point some teachers also discuss a third type of adjustment: the reversing entry. Before going further, however, let us briefly review the relevant accounting fundamentals.

ACCOUNTING FUNDAMENTALS

1. Accrued and deferred items are closely tied to services. Accruals pertain to services received (or rendered) but not yet paid for. Deferrals relate to services that have been paid for in advance but not yet received (or rendered).
2. Entries for accruals record either revenue or expense items and usually set up new current asset or current liability accounts.
3. Entries for deferrals reduce certain revenue or expense accounts, thus postponing their effect until a future fiscal period.
4. Both accruals and deferrals are recorded at the end of the accounting period and have an effect on both the income statement and the balance sheet.
5. Adjusting entries that record accrued revenue and expenses may have to be reversed. Entries to record deferrals are usually not reversed. (Reversing entries are made on the first day of the new accounting period.)

Introducing Accruals

Because many students have difficulty understanding the meaning of the word *accrued,* teachers often first introduce the underlying principles of accruals and defer a definition of the word until after these principles have

235

been understood. The following problem provides a good vehicle for launching the topic.

Mr. Cole operates a small office. He employs two typists whose combined salaries total $300 for a five-day week. On Friday, June 25, he paid the typists and entered the transaction in his cash payments journal by debiting Salaries Expense for $300. The following week payday fell on July 2. Normally Mr. Cole would again pay them the week's salaries totaling $300; however, the accounting period ended Wednesday, June 30. Should Mr. Cole pay his typists twice that week, once on Wednesday and again on Friday, or should he just wait and pay them on Friday as usual?

After the class correctly responds that Mr. Cole should pay his typists only on Friday, point out that this transaction involves expenses for two different accounting periods, and remind them of the important accounting principle of matching revenue for a period with expenses incurred in earning that revenue. The salaries for Monday through Wednesday ($180) are an expense of the accounting period ended Wednesday, June 30. Because this expense will not be paid until a future period, an adjusting entry must be made on June 30 for this unrecorded expense. Now explain to the class that expense items that have been incurred during an accounting period but have not been paid or recorded are called *accrued expenses.* Similarly, a revenue item earned during an accounting period but not received until a future period is known as *accrued revenue.*

Recording Accrued Expenses

Since in the example given above none of the accrued expense has been recorded, the Salary Expense account must be debited by $180 to show that salary expense for the period. Because that expense will not be paid until July 2, it is a liability; therefore $180 is credited to the liability account Salaries Payable to show the increase in liabilities.

The ledger entry is shown in Figure 13.1.

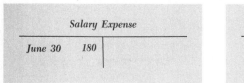

Salary Expense		*Salaries Payable*	
June 30 180			June 30 180

Figure 13.1

The journal entry would be:

Salary Expense	180	
Salaries Payable		180
To record salaries that have been earned but not paid.		

Recording Accrued Revenue

A common form of accrued revenue is the interest earned on notes receivable. As the basis for the discussion of accrued interest, place on the chalkboard or overhead projector a notes receivable account similar to Figure 13.2.

DATE		EXPLANATION	POST. REF.	DEBIT	CREDIT	BALANCE DEBIT	BALANCE CREDIT
		Notes Receivable				Account No. *111*	
Apr.	1	Note 1; 30-day; 6%	G.4	700 00		700 00	
	16	Note 2; 3 mo.; 4%	G.4	600 00		1300 00	
	30	Note 3; 60-day; 5%	G.4	1500 00		2800 00	
May	1	Note 4; 3 mo.; 4%	G.5	900 00		3700 00	
	1	Coll. Note 1	CR 6		700 00	3000 00	
	16	Note 5; 70-day; 6%	G.5	400 00		3400 00	
	20	Note 6; 1 mo.; 7%	G.5	900 00		4300 00	
June	20	Coll. Note 6	CR 7		900 00	3400 00	
	29	Coll. Note 3	CR 7		1500 00	1900 00	
July	1	Note 7; 60-day; 6%	G.5	1200 00		3100 00	
	15	Note 8; 30-day; 6%	G.7	250 00		3350 00	

Figure 13.2

Point out that Notes 1, 3, and 6 were collected before June. Also show the class that interest has been earned on Notes 2, 4, and 5, but that this interest will not be collected until the notes fall due and are paid by their makers—which will be during the following fiscal period.

Students find explanations to be rather vague when they do not fully understand the meaning of the amounts being used in recording transactions. Accrued interest is a good example. However, by using a Notes Receivable account in which several notes are recorded, and by actually calculating the amount of interest that has been earned on each note, the students see what is meant by accrued interest.

The interest that has been earned on Notes 2, 4, and 5 should be reported as revenue for the fiscal period ended June 30 rather than during the following period. In other words, the revenue should be recorded during the period in which it was earned, not during the one in which it is collected. Note 2 has earned $5 interest from its date of April 16 to June 30, a period of 75 days; Note 4 has earned $6 by June 30; and Note 5 has earned $3. This makes a total of $14 interest ($5 + $6 + $3) that has been earned but not collected. The revenue from interest earned is recorded by crediting the Interest Revenue account. Since the interest has not been collected, it is owed by the signers of the notes. The interest is therefore an asset (a receivable) and is recorded by debiting the asset account Interest Receivable. The entry in T-account form would be as shown in Figure 13.3.

Figure 13.3

The journal entry is the following:

Interest Receivable	14	
Interest Revenue		14
To record the interest earned on notes		
receivable but not yet collected.		

The examples given were based on an accounting period ended June 30 rather than December 31 to avoid the complication that arises because January 1 is a holiday. The January 1 date is especially confusing in the explanation of reversing entries. If June 30 has been used for the adjusting entries, the discussion of reversing entries can be built upon the same examples. This makes it easier to understand the principles related to reversing entries because the students are already familiar with the basic adjusting entries.

Introducing Deferrals

In a sense, a deferral is the opposite in meaning to an accrual. Whereas accruals are concerned with services rendered but not yet paid for, deferrals are concerned with services paid for but not yet rendered. The purpose of any adjusting entry that would be called a *deferral* is to postpone a revenue or expense item to the next accounting period.

One example is that of interest that has been prepaid on notes. The rule regarding interest is that it is usually recorded as interest revenue or interest expense even though it is paid or received in advance.

In the case of a note receivable, assume that a customer, J. Akin, has paid $18 interest in advance at the time his note is received. This would have been recorded at the time as follows:

Cash	18	
Notes Receivable	400	
Accounts Receivable/J. Akin		400
Interest Revenue		18
To record receipt of promissory note		
and interest paid in advance.		

If at the end of the fiscal period $5 of this interest has now been earned and $13 represents the amount still paid in advance, the adjusting entry needed would be:

Interest Revenue	13	
Unearned Interest Revenue		13
To record the liability due to interest		
revenue received in advance but not yet		
earned.		

The above treatment illustrates only one method of analyzing deferred revenue. Other teachers prefer to present the same example as follows:

Cash	18	
Notes Receivable	400	
Accounts Receivable/J. Akin		400
Unearned Interest Revenue		18
To record receipt of promissory note		
and interest unearned.		

Notice that this entry sets up the liability account Unearned Interest Revenue right from the beginning. In support of this presentation, teachers explain that the interest should not be recorded as revenue because the amount covers more than one accounting period. The $18 is therefore credited to a liability account because the interest has not been actually earned.

At the end of the fiscal period, if $5 of this interest has now been earned, an adjusting entry would be made to transfer the revenue earned from the liability account to a revenue account. This adjusting entry may be shown as follows:

Unearned Interest Revenue	5	
Interest Revenue		5
To record the amount of interest		
earned on J. Akin's promissory note.		

Another good example of a transaction for deferred revenue is deferred rental revenue. For example, a firm may rent property to a customer and receive rent paid in advance. Assuming that this payment covers more than one accounting period, adjusting entries would be required at the end of each accounting period to record the actual amount of rent earned. The choice of one of the methods described is a matter of personal preference.

Similar adjusting entries must be made for prepaid expenses such as supplies and insurance when the expense method, rather than the asset method, was used to record them originally. Adjusting entries would be needed to set up the asset amounts and to defer certain expense charges to the next accounting period.

Consider this example. Suppose that the business initially did not debit the asset account for the purchase of supplies; instead, it recorded the cost of acquiring the supplies as follows:

Supplies Expense	500	
Cash		500
Issued Check 625 for supplies.		

If, at the end of the accounting period, only $100 of the supplies were actually used (that is, an actual physical count showed $400 of supplies on hand), an adjusting entry could be presented as follows:

Supplies on Hand	400	
Supplies Expense		400
To record the amount of supplies on hand, and to adjust the Supplies Expense for the true cost of the supplies used during the accounting period.		

In presenting the analysis of the adjusting entry, emphasize that a debit is required to the asset account to record the amount of supplies on hand at the end of the accounting period. Secondly, stress that the credit entry must be made to Supplies Expense to adjust this account so that the correct expense is shown. Of course, only $100 of supplies expense would appear on the income statement, since this is the balance shown in the account. And since $400 has been recorded to the Supplies on Hand account, this amount of the prepaid expense would be disclosed on the firm's balance sheet. Since the Supplies Expense would be closed into the Revenue and Expense Summary at the end of the accounting period, only the current asset would be carried forward into the next accounting period. If all additional purchases of supplies are to be recorded as expenses in this next accounting period, the adjusting entry to record the prepaid asset for supplies will have to be transformed into an expense at the beginning of the new accounting period.

Introducing Reversing Entries

The principle of reversing entries is one that very frequently confuses students. Most of their trouble can be traced to two weaknesses: (1) they do not realize why they are making the reversing entry—they do not understand exactly the function it performs—and (2) they do not know which adjusting entries are to be reversed and which are not. The discussion given here describes the explanation you might make to clarify these two points and also explains when the entries should be made.

Why Make Reversing Entries?

Reversing entries are fundamentally convenience entries. They are not necessary, but their use makes it possible to forget that one accounting period has ended and a new one started. When reversing entries are used, the payment of an expense following the end of an accounting period can be recorded in the normal way as a debit to the expense, rather than the amount being split by debiting part to a payable and part to an expense. Similarly, the receipt of revenue can be recorded as a credit to the revenue account rather than the amount being split by crediting part to a receivable and part to a revenue account.

What Adjusting Entries Are Reversed?

Not every adjusting entry is reversed; therefore, students need to have some rule of thumb to help them determine which entries are reversed and which are not. The most comprehensive rule is this: Reverse all adjusting entries that open new balance sheet accounts. This rule includes all adjusting entries that record accruals and all others as well.

When Are Reversing Entries Made?

Adjusting and closing entries are made on the last day of the accounting period. Reversing entries, on the other hand, are made the following day—the first day of the new accounting period. They are made on this day so that the new asset and liability accounts opened by the adjusting entries can be closed and normal entries entered during the new fiscal period.

Problems, Questions, and Projects

1. How would you introduce the topic of accruals and deferrals?

2. Is it better to present accruals in all its phases and then explain reversing entries as another lesson, or to take an item such as salaries and carry it all the way through the reversing entry?

3. Secure a large calendar sheet for a particular month and prepare an accruals and deferrals problem that fits that calendar.

4. Show in journal entries and T acounts the solution to the above problem.

5. Two methods for analyzing deferred revenue were presented in this chapter. Which method would you use to teach the concept of deferred revenue? Give reasons for your answer.

6. Prepare an overhead transparency for use in the teaching of a transaction for deferred revenue. Support the preparation of this visual aid with a written lesson plan.

7. In presenting the expense method of handling the adjustment for supplies, one teacher argues that the method merely confuses students and that only the asset method should be taught. On the other hand, a second teacher argues just as strongly for teaching both methods to ensure a better understanding of adjusting entries. State your view on this methods controversy.

8. In teaching reversing entries, one teacher gives the following rule:

"Reverse all adjusting entries that recorded accruals." Do you agree with the teaching of this rule as a student aid in learning what adjusting entries have to be reversed? Give reasons for your answer.

9. Prepare as many functional performance goals as possible for teaching accruals, deferrals, and reversing entries.

Case Problem

Ursula Sloop is an experienced accounting teacher who has had difficulty explaining the theory of making reversing entries. She suggests that reversing entries be eliminated and that the liability accounts, Salaries Payable and Interest Payable, be left as open accounts in the ledger. Then, when the payroll is made at the end of the first pay period in the new accounting period, a divided entry debiting both Salary Expense and Salaries Payable can be made. Based on the illustration used early in this chapter this entry would be as follows:

Salaries Payable	180	
Salary Expense	120	
Cash		300

Utilizing this scheme for interest payable resulting from owing several notes payable requires making split entries every time a note is paid on which accrued interest was recorded. These split entries would be made periodically over several weeks at the beginning of every new accounting period. The same would be true for accrued interest on notes receivable.

Mrs. Sloop suggests that if her idea were adopted the accountant could simply write memorandum entries on the calendar or in the notes register on the due date for every note on which accrued interest was recorded.

What is your reaction to this suggestion? Explain why you like it or object to it.

CHAPTER 14

Teaching the Financial Statements

The class members have now learned to analyze transactions, journalize, post, and prepare a trial balance and a worksheet. They have also studied briefly the balance sheet and the income statement as formal presentations of the fundamental elements in the accounting equation. In addition, they have analyzed the balance sheet as the basis for the opening entry for a business enterprise.

The students have reached the point at which they are ready to prepare formal financial statements for a business enterprise in relationship to the sequence of steps of the accounting cycle. We shall assume in this treatment that the worksheet with adjustments has been covered.

Some teachers prefer to teach the balance sheet first and to follow with the income statement. Others like to present the income statement first. Two reasons suggest that the income statement be prepared first: First, since the income statement columns on the worksheet come before the balance sheet columns, it seems logical that the income statement be the first statement prepared. Second, since the net income (or loss) ascertained on the worksheet is used on the balance sheet, it is practical to prepare the income statement first. Before going further, let's review the accounting fundamentals.

ACCOUNTING FUNDAMENTALS

The Income Statement

1. The income statement shows the results of operating a business—net income or net loss.
2. It covers a period of time as stated in the heading.
3. The temporary owner's equity accounts for revenue and expense are shown on the income statement.

(continued)

The Balance Sheet

1. The balance sheet is a statement of the financial position of a business.
2. It is an enlargement of the fundamental accounting equation $(A = L + OE)$.
3. It is true as of a specified date.
4. Only permanent accounts appear on the balance sheet.
5. The generally accepted accounting principle is that assets reported on the balance sheet should be classified into at least two groups: current assets and fixed assets.
6. The generally accepted accounting principle is that liabilities reported on the balance sheet should be classified into at least two groups: current liabilities and long-term liabilities.
7. The generally accepted accounting principle is that a balance sheet does not presume to show either the present values of assets to the business or the values that might be realized if the assets are sold. The accepted accounting basis for recording assets is the cost at the date when they were acquired.

Periodic Inventory System

1. The (Merchandise) Inventory account is updated only at the end of the accounting period.
2. A policy of maintaining an accounting system that relies on periodic inventory-taking alone is a policy that accepts the risks of loss through fraud and pilferage with considerable out-of-pocket saving of recording and administrative costs.
3. Prior to end-of-year stocktaking, accounting under a periodic system assumes that all merchandise purchases represent cost of goods sold until this expense amount is reduced by the end-of-year inventory. Consequently, the end-of-year inventory operates to reduce the amount that otherwise would be treated as expense.
4. Only *selling* prices are used in the accounting records when a sales transaction is recorded. No attempt is made to do a costing entry for the goods sold, nor is there a ledger account for cost of goods sold.
5. To assist in the calculation of the cost of goods sold at the end of an accounting period, accounts are kept for Purchases, Freight-in (Transportation-in), Purchases Returns and Allowances, and Purchases Discount.

Perpetual Inventory System

1. A policy of maintaining a perpetual inventory system accepts extra accounting and extra administrative costs in the expectation that worthwhile savings will result from loss minimization.

(continued)

2. The Inventory account is updated each time goods are purchased and sold.
3. In perpetual inventory systems, a separate subsidiary ledger account is kept for each type of merchandise. The various subsidiary ledger accounts are controlled by a general ledger account known as *Merchandise Inventory,* or simply, *Inventory.*
4. Two entries are required each time a sale is made. One entry records the normal recognition of revenue; the other is a costing entry to record the cost of the goods sold and to decrease the Inventory account.
5. A purchase of goods is recorded in the asset account. No account is kept for Purchases. In addition, all other costs involved in acquiring the goods are debited to the Inventory account.
6. A separate expense account, called Cost of Goods sold, is maintained in the ledger to receive the costs of goods sold. The balance of the Cost of Goods Sold account will be matched against the Sales revenue for the period to determine the Gross Margin (Gross Profit on Sales).

Presenting the Income Statement

Two basic principles may be followed in the teaching of the income statement: (1) build upon the knowledge that students already possess and (2) teach first those procedures that are most easily understood. Most textbooks observe these principles by using a service type of business for the first accounting cycle. This permits the most difficult section of the income statement, the cost of goods sold section, to be delayed until the students have had an opportunity to prepare a number of statements.

A Service Business

A restaurant or laundry makes an excellent beginning illustration. Almost any student in the class can tell you that the income for a laundry is found by subtracting the expenses from the total revenue. This introduces the first of a series of formulas that are used within the income statement. This formula may be written in two forms:

$$\text{Revenue} - \text{Expenses} = \text{Profit}$$
$$3,500 \quad - \quad 1,240 \quad = 2,260$$

or

Revenue	3,500
− Expenses	1,240
Profit	2,260

The form on the top emphasizes the relationship of the three items as an equation with which the students are familiar from their study of mathematics and of the fundamental accounting equation. The formula on the bottom shows these relationships in the form in which they appear on the income statement. The income statement for a service business may be prepared from the trial balance data without the use of a formal worksheet.

Profit Versus Income

Some teachers prefer to use the term *profit* over *income,* especially when the concept is first introduced. On the other hand, other teachers will argue for the use of *income,* since the term can be associated with the name of the financial statement. In general, most teachers do use the term *profit* to introduce the residual concept in order to go from the known to the unknown. They then quickly teach the synonym *income* to point out that current usage in accounting favors this term. It should also be emphasized here that one other term, *earnings,* is gaining acceptance. In other words, the three terms—*profit, income,* and *earnings*—all have the same meaning, but *income* is currently favored. (For current trends, consult *Accounting Trends & Techniques,* published yearly by the American Institute of Certified Public Accountants, 666 Fifth Avenue, New York, New York 10019. Canadian teachers are referred to *Financial Reporting in Canada,* published by the Canadian Institute of Chartered Accountants, 250 Bloor Street East, Toronto, Canada M4W 1G5.)

One other troublesome area can be identified. Some teachers often have difficulty introducing the term *net* in relation to net income, net earnings, or net profit. To solve this problem at the level of presenting the income statement for a service firm, teachers simply emphasize that *net* refers to the remaining figure after all revenues are matched with all related expenses for the same accounting period. Later on, the students can be introduced to other preliminary concepts such as *gross margin* (*gross profit on sales*) and *income before taxes.*

Data From Worksheet

When adjustments have been introduced, prepare the income statement through class discussion from a worksheet that is placed on the overhead projector or chalkboard. As will be seen later, the worksheet is especially important for preparing the financial statements of a merchandising business. Complete the income statement using the ruled form on the chalkboard or transparency while the students complete the same statement at their seats. Demonstrate the heading, placement of each item, and correct rulings as students write them on their copies.

NET INCOME FIGURE. It is extremely important that students see the relationship between the financial statements. For this reason, emphasize that the net income (or loss) as shown on the worksheet is the same as that obtained from the income statement. Also point out that the net income as shown on the income statement is the same as that which will appear on the balance sheet.

The Heading

Students tend to minimize the importance of headings in business statements. The heading of a statement is as important a part of the statement as any other information it may contain. When placing statements on the chalkboard or overhead, give status to this aspect by always placing a proper heading at the top of each statement.

The distinction between the date shown on the balance sheet and the dates shown on the income statement should be pointed out. The balance sheet is prepared as of a specific date, while the income statement covers a period of time and therefore must show inclusive dates, such as, "from July 1 to September 30, (Year)," "For Month of April, (Year)," or "For Year Ended December 31, (Year)." Note that the accounting period must have been "ended" and not "ending."

Terms such as *Income Statement, Statement of Revenue and Expenses,* or *Statement of Earnings* are the most commonly used titles for the income statement among businesses today. Statement headings may be either two-line or three-line headings.

The Merchandising Business

Later in the course, usually after the first cycle has been presented, the students will meet the problem of preparing an income statement for a merchandising business. The cost of goods sold section is the new element in this statement. However, the fact that the students understand the basic elements of the income statement and have prepared a number of such statements for service-type businesses simplifies the presentation and permits concentration on the cost section.

The first problem used in the demonstration should be a simple one, with the cost figures supplied rather than left to be calculated. Most students will know that the profit on the sale of any article is found by subtracting the cost price from the sales price. This rule or formula applies to the total sales of a business in the same way that it does to the sale of a single article. The formula is developed as follows:

$$\text{Sales Price} - \text{Cost Price} = \text{Profit}$$
$$\$25{,}000 \quad - \quad \$13{,}000 \quad = \$12{,}000$$

or

Sales Price	25,000
Cost Price	13,000
Profit	$12,000

Immediately the question of expenses is raised: these are subtracted from the profit. After they have been subtracted, the remainder is labeled *net income,* since it is now necessary to distinguish between the two profits— gross margin and net income.

Sales	$25,000
Cost Price	13,000
Gross Margin	12,000
Expenses	6,600
Net Income	$ 5,400

Thus the formula must be restated and a second one is introduced:

(1) Sales − Cost of Goods Sold = Gross Margin
(2) Gross Margin − Expenses   = Net Income

In order to emphasize these relationships, have the students work a few problems before introducing the method of determining the Cost of Goods Sold when it is not known. Problems such as the following could be used.

The Marjorie Duncan Shop sold merchandise during May totaling $14,000. The cost price of this merchandise was $8,000, and the expenses were as follows: Salaries, $2,000; Rent, $400; Utilities, $50; Office Expense, $300. Determine the gross margin and the net profit.

GROSS MARGIN VERSUS GROSS PROFIT. The traditional term to indicate the difference between revenue from sales and the cost of goods sold has been *gross profit.* Some teachers have also used the term *gross income.* In more recent times, however, writers have suggested two alternatives in the interest of clarity. One alternative is to use a qualified term such as *gross profit on sales.* On the other hand, accountants point to the fact that a business does not make a profit (income, earnings) until all expenses have been deducted from revenue. Therefore, there is a trend to accept the accounting profession's term *gross margin* as the difference between sales revenue and cost of goods sold.

THE COST OF GOODS SOLD SECTION. One plan that has proved helpful in presenting the cost section is to use titles that describe quite fully the various figures used. Rather than using the conventional terminology at first, use more descriptive wording such as the following:

Cost of goods we had at the beginning	$ 5,000
Cost of goods that we purchased	18,000
Cost of goods we could have sold	23,000
Cost of goods we did not sell	10,000
Cost of goods we sold	$13,000

After the students master the principle involved, the wording can be changed to the conventional titles. Terminology can be made quite clear if the new titles are written to the right of the figures used, as follows:

Cost of goods we had at the beginning	5,000	Beginning Inventory
Cost of goods that we purchased	18,000	Purchases
Cost of goods we could have sold	23,000	Merchandise Available for Sale
Cost of goods we did not sell	10,000	Ending Inventory
Cost of goods we sold	13,000	Cost of Goods Sold

At this stage the following formula is presented:

$$\text{Beginning Inventory} + \text{Purchases} - \text{Ending Inventory} = \text{Cost of Goods Sold}$$

Here again is a good place to have the class solve a few problems that will help them master this procedure.

Use Simple Examples. Provide a simple example from everyday life, one that has been observed by every class member. For instance, everyone has seen watermelons or baskets of fruit being sold directly from a farmer's truck backed up to the curb along the sidewalk. Drawing on this common experience, use an example such as the following.

Suppose a farmer begins one Saturday morning with 80 watermelons; by noon he has only 22 melons left. His experience has shown that his afternoon sales nearly always exceed those of the morning. Therefore, he places his 22 melons on the curb and sends his son back to the farm with the truck for more merchandise. Two hours later the son returns with 80 additional melons. That night when they leave for home they have only 6 melons left. Most members of the class can tell you how many melons were sold (80 + 80 − 6 = 154).

The principle in this example is identical to that used in the figuring of the Cost of Goods Sold for a business. In each case, the merchandise on hand to start with, plus the new merchandise received, minus that on hand at the end, represents the goods sold during the period. If students have trouble working with dollars, suggest that they work the problem using melons, bicycles, or radios.

Use Blocks. The calculation of the Cost of Goods Sold can be visualized by the use of wooden or plastic blocks. Assume, for example, that the beginning inventory is $4,000, the purchases $9,000, and the final inventory $5,000. Letting each block represent $1,000, stack four blocks together. To these add nine more blocks, making a total of 13, representing the total merchandise available for sale. Point out that both of the inventories and the goods purchased are all valued at cost prices. Also point out that the records kept of goods sold were at selling prices—no records at cost prices were made. At this point, identify the term *periodic inventory system* to apply to firms that update their inventory cost figures at the end of the accounting period. Several members of the class can tell you that the amount of the sales at cost prices can be determined by subtracting the five blocks representing goods still on hand. This will leave eight blocks as the amount of the sales at cost figures.

249

Consolidate the Inventory and the Purchases. One of the principles to emphasize is that the goods still on hand may represent part of the beginning
inventory and part of the purchases. As goods are purchased, they are
placed in the stock room and are later placed on shelves in the salesrooms.
No effort may be made to separate the merchandise that was purchased
during the fiscal period from that on hand at the beginning. (Point out that
some stores always place the new stock at the back of the shelf and move
the old to the front, so the old is sold first. Other stores do not follow this
practice. The practice followed depends upon the type of merchandise
handled, and upon the type of inventory system adopted.) As merchandise
is sold, it might be taken from stock included in the inventory at the
beginning of the fiscal period or from that purchased during the period, or
from both. In other words, the $4,000 worth of goods on hand at the start
and the $9,000 worth of merchandise bought during the period lose their
identity as such and become one figure—$13,000 worth of merchandise
available for sale. Thus, the $5,000 worth of goods on hand at the end of
the fiscal period also represents part of the beginning inventory and part of
that purchased during the period.

Separate the Cost of Goods Sold Section. It has become common practice to
show the cost section as a supporting schedule to the income statement.
Presenting the cost section as a supporting schedule has several advantages.
Some students question the inclusion of an asset (merchandise inventory)
on the income statement: since this is a statement of revenue, expenses, and
net income, why show an asset on it? Showing the Cost of Goods Sold
section as a supporting schedule meets this objection.

Many teachers have reported that their students have little or no trouble
with the mechanics or the arithmetic of the cost section when they attack it
separately. The preparation of an income statement is also quite a simple
matter when the cost of goods sold is supplied to the student. However,
students seem to become confused when asked to figure the cost of goods
sold and incorporate the results into the income statement as one combined
job. Thus, separating the cost section into a supporting schedule breaks the
income statement into two different calculations and seems easier for
students to manage.

The Marjorie Duncan Shop problem, showing the Cost of Goods Sold as
a supporting schedule, would appear as shown in Figure 14.1.

Test the Answer by Inspection. Encourage students to test their Cost of
Goods Sold figure by inspection. Point out that if a person begins business
with a given amount of merchandise, purchases additional goods, and has
less goods on hand at the end, more goods were sold than were purchased.
For example, a business starts with merchandise costing $4,000 and ends
the period with only $2,500 on hand. The business has sold $1,500 more
merchandise than it purchased. A business that starts with merchandise costing $4,000 and ends the period with $6,000 of goods on hand
has sold $2,000 less merchandise than it purchased. Thus, the amount
of merchandise sold will differ from the amount purchased during the

Marjorie Duncan Shop
Income Statement
For the Month Ended May 31, 19—

Revenue from Sales	14,000 00		
Cost of Goods Sold (Schedule 1)	8,000 00		
Gross Margin		6,000 00	
Expenses			
Salaries	2,000 00		
Rent	400 00		
Utilities	50 00		
Office Expense	300 00		
Total Expense		2,750 00	
Net Income		3,250 00	
Schedule 1			
Cost of Goods Sold			
Beginning Inventory (April 30, 19—) . .	4,000 00		
Purchases (May)	9,000 00		
Merchandise Available for Sale		13,000 00	
Ending Inventory (May 31, 19—) . . .		5,000 00	
Cost of Goods Sold		8,000 00	

Figure 14.1

period by an amount equal to the difference between the two inventories.

The Cost of Goods Sold figure can be tested by determining the difference between the two inventories and adding or subtracting this difference from the amount of the purchases (all at cost figures). Illustrate this by taking the figures from the Marjorie Duncan Shop Income Statement:

Ending Inventory	5,000
Beginning Inventory	4,000
Difference (amount by which ending	1,000
inventory exceeds beginning inventory)	

Since the business has $1,000 more merchandise at the end of May than it had at the beginning, the business purchased $1,000 more goods than it sold. The Cost of Goods Sold figure, therefore, should be $1,000 less than the amount of goods purchased.

Purchases	9,000
Differences in Inventory	1,000
Cost of Goods Sold	8,000

Show the One-Step Adjusting Procedure. Another approach to presenting the cost of goods sold section follows the one-entry adjustment method, which uses only one entry to adjust the merchandise inventory. The adjusting entry simply increases or decreases the Merchandise Inventory account with an offsetting debit or credit to the Revenue and Expense Summary account.

The cost of goods sold section on the income statement or the schedule is shown according to the procedure discussed in the previous *Test the Answer by Inspection* section. The increase or decrease in the inventory amount (the difference between the ending inventory and the beginning inventory) is determined from the adjusting entry. On the schedule, the cost of goods sold is computed by adding a decrease in inventory to the purchases amount and by subtracting an increase in inventory from the purchases amount. Using the figures from the Marjorie Duncan Shop, the cost of goods sold figure would be shown as follows:

Schedule of Cost of Goods Sold

Purchases (May)	9,000	
Less: Decrease in Inventory	1,000	
Cost of Goods Sold		8,000

The ending inventory balance is shown on the balance sheet. Since the change in inventory is shown in the cost of goods sold section, the beginning inventory balance can easily be determined.

Other Factors Affecting Cost of Goods Sold. At some point in the course, Purchases Returns, Purchases Discount, and Freight-In are to be included in the cost section of the Income Statement.

Freight adds to the cost of goods purchased from firms other than local ones. Most of the class members have had experience ordering articles from large mail-order houses. They know that an amount must be added for postage. Ask them to assume, for example, that a garden tool that can be purchased for $3.35 requires a charge of 65 cents for shipping, which increases the cost to $4—the price that must be used when comparing its cost with the cost of tools of equal quality bought locally. Explain that the situation with a business is exactly the same. If there is no local wholesaler from whom the merchant may purchase merchandise, the freight must be included as a part of the cost price of the goods purchased. It is obvious that returned merchandise has the same net result as goods never purchased. The business does not have the goods; therefore, returned merchandise should not be included in the net purchases figure.

Show that Purchases Discount also reduces the net cost of goods purchased and that, like Purchases Returns, the amount of the Purchases Discount is subtracted from the amount of Purchases as a part of the calculation to determine Net Purchases. Illustrate this expanded Cost of Goods Sold Section as in Figure 14.2.

Select Your Procedures. Some procedures used by successful teachers to help students understand the cost of goods sold section of the income statement have been presented. All of them would not be used with the same group of students, of course. Through experimentation, determine the methods that can be used best. Also remember that one plan may work well with one

Schedule of Cost of Goods Sold			
Beginning Inventory		4,000 00	
Purchases 9,000			
Freight-In 225			
Cost of Delivered Goods 9,225			
Less: Purchases Returns . . 350			
Purchases Discounts 180	530		
Net Purchases		8,695 00	
Cost of Goods Available			
for Sale		12,695 00	
Less: Ending Inventory		5,095 00	
Cost of Goods Sold			7,600 00

Figure 14.2

group, and some other scheme may be better with a different class. For example, with some classes, a better understanding of cost of goods sold can be given by showing a comparative view of the periodic and perpetual inventory systems. We offer a method of teaching this comparison following the treatment of the balance sheet.

FACTORS AFFECTING SALES REVENUE. At some point in the course—usually in conjunction with the development of the sales of a merchandising firm—both Sales Returns and Sales Discounts will be included under the Revenue section of the income statement.

In general, Sales Returns (and sales allowances) and Sales Discounts offer little difficulty, especially when they are treated after the factors affecting cost of goods sold. What must be emphasized is that both factors have the effect of decreasing the sales revenue and, therefore, must be grouped on the income statement as shown in Figure 14.3.

Revenue From Sales:		
Sales		9,260
Less: Sales Returns and		
Allowances . . . 160		
Sales Discount . . 37	197	
Net Sales		9,063

Figure 14.3

Presenting the Balance Sheet

When planning teaching procedures, always keep in mind the purposes to be accomplished in the lesson. The following objectives might be used for the unit on the balance sheet.

1. To build upon what the students know about the balance sheet from their early lessons in the course.
2. To explain how to prepare the account form of balance sheet—types of accounts appearing on the Balance Sheet, the arrangement of those accounts, and the proper form and rulings to be used.
3. To show that a balance sheet balances when the Owner's Equity account is brought up to date.
4. To teach the importance of a correct heading for the balance sheet.
5. To teach in simple terms what a balance sheet says and what it does not say.

Preparing for the Lesson

Place a simple account form of balance sheet, similar to Figure 14.4, on the chalkboard or overhead projector before the class session begins. In addition, the proper form for a new balance sheet that will be prepared during the class period should be ruled on the board or transparency. Students should have their solutions to certain problems that have been completed through the worksheet, and this worksheet should also be on the chalkboard or transparency. The students should have at hand paper on which they can make an account form of balance sheet as the solution is worked on the board or overhead projector.

Office Service Center
Balance Sheet
October 31, 19—

Assets			Liabilities		
Cash		7,050 00	Accounts Payable:		
Accounts Receivable:			Modern Products .	$1,000.00	
King Stores	$800.00		Oak Repair Shop .	50.00	
Frank Long	600.00	1,400 00	Total Liabilities		1,050 00
Furniture		4,000 00			
Office Equipment		10,000 00	Owner's Equity		
			Roy Bell, Capital . .	$20,000.00	
			Net Income	1,400.00	
			Total Owner's Equity . . .		21,400 00
Total		22,450 00	Total		22,450 00

Figure 14.4

Introducing the Lesson

Begin by relating an incident similar to the following.

Mr. Roland Baker is considering buying a small cleaning establishment. The present owner, who also owns a dairy, now wishes to give all his time to the dairy. He told Mr. Baker that the dry cleaning establishment has a large volume of business and makes a favorable profit each month. Mr. Baker wants to know more about the financial position of the company and the amount of profit earned. How can he obtain this information?

The class response to this question should bring forth the suggestion that the information Mr. Baker wants to know is shown on the balance sheet and that the balance sheet is a statement of assets, liabilities, and owner's equity.

Developing the Lesson

Review the placement of the various types of accounts, the rulings used, and the heading of the completed elementary balance sheet that is on the board. For a service type of business, which does not sell goods and therefore has no merchandise inventory to be adjusted, the balance sheet may be prepared from the data shown on the trial balance. But for a merchandising business where several adjustments are to be entered, the balance sheet is prepared from the worksheet on the screen or chalkboard. Prepare the balance sheet, working together with the class. The heading, the worksheet source for each item, the placement of each item, and the correct rulings should be discussed, demonstrated, and recorded by both you and the students. Place the balance sheet on the ruled form on the chalkboard or overhead while the students complete the same at their seats.

THE NET INCOME. Most students can identify the assets and liabilities items from the worksheet and list them in proper order on the balance sheet; however, the owner's equity section may not be clear. Before recording the owner's equity section on the balance sheet, review the fundamental accounting equation $(A = L + OE)$ with the class. Show that the total assets and the total liabilities are obtained from the partially completed balance sheet, and the equation is then used to obtain the present owner's equity. Point out that if the balance sheet is to balance, the owner's equity must equal the amount as shown by the equation. Explain that owner's equity is the sum of the beginning capital and the net income as shown on the worksheet. Direct attention to the capital figure shown on the worksheet, pointing out that it is not up to date because transactions involving revenue and expenses are entered in temporary accounts rather than in the owner's capital account. The net income figure on the worksheet summarizes the balance of these accounts and is the amount to be added to (or subtracted from) the capital to bring it up to date.

FOLDING THE WORKSHEET. When the financial statements are prepared from the worksheet, errors may be made in transferring the account title and figure from the worksheet to the financial statement. In following across from the account title to the amount in the Income Statement or Balance Sheet columns, the incorrect figure may be picked up. Pleating or fan-folding the worksheet is one means of avoiding such errors.

Classifying the Balance Sheet

There is common agreement among most teachers that a classified balance sheet should be introduced at some point in an introductory accounting course. Some teachers, especially in college-level courses, will present the concept of classifying assets and liabilities at some stage of the first accounting cycle. On the other hand, other teachers will delay classification until the end-of-period adjustments have been covered. Regardless of the timing, it is important that classification of assets and liabilities be presented in accordance with generally accepted accounting principles.

CLASSIFYING ASSETS. According to generally accepted accounting principles, assets reported on a balance sheet should be classified into at least two groups: current assets and fixed assets. For accounting purposes, two definitions for current assets may be considered.

Traditionally, the term *current assets* is used to identify cash and those assets that are reasonably expected to be realized in cash or sold within one year of the date of the balance sheet. Obviously, this definition places a heavy emphasis on the idea of liquidity, or converting assets into cash. For example, students are generally given such assets as cash, accounts receivable (less allowance for bad debts), notes receivable, inventory, and marketable securities.

Unfortunately, the first definition does not cover the inclusion of prepaid expenses. Therefore, an expanded concept of current assets is required to include not only the first definition above, but also the idea that some assets are to be "consumed" within one year of the date of the balance sheet. Another way to teach this second concept is from a cost viewpoint. As you will recall, prepaid expenses are unexpired costs. They are classified as current assets because their costs are expected to expire (to be used or consumed) during the next accounting year.

Classifying fixed assets presents little difficulty. By this stage of the instruction students respond well to the concept that certain tangible assets are acquired to contribute to the revenue-making operations of the business. Since these assets are neither converted into cash nor intended to be sold, the idea of permanent or fixed assets can be communicated. In addition, some teachers will emphasize the cost viewpoint. Excepting land, fixed assets may be defined as unexpired costs that are expected to be expired over a period much longer than one year from the date of the balance sheet. The point that no one designation of this category has been accepted may also be emphasized. In addition to fixed assets, other acceptable captions are *property, plant, and equipment,* or simply, *plant and equipment.*

One minor methods controversy does exist in listing the order of fixed assets on a balance sheet. Some teachers prefer an alphabetic arrangement. On the other hand, many others support the concept of permanency and, therefore, will insist that land must be listed first. Other fixed assets can then be listed in order of their useful service life.

CLASSIFYING LIABILITIES. Accounting also supports the generally accepted principle that liabilities reported on the balance sheet should be classified into at least two groups: current liabilities and long-term liabilities. In general terms, *current liabilities* can safely be defined as those debts that will come due within one year from the date of the balance sheet. In listing the order of these current debts, bank loans should be listed before accounts payable. Students frequently forget to do this. In this situation, review or teach the principle of granting bank loans to businesses on a demand basis.

Little difficulty is encountered in the teaching of the second group of liabilities. Students generally grasp quickly the idea that long-term liabilities are debts that are not due within a year of the balance sheet date. What must be emphasized, however, is the required listing under current liabilities of any long-term debt due within a year. For example, bonds payable may mature within one year and, therefore, should be noted under current liabilities as "bonds payable due (show due date)."

Account Form Versus Report Form

Teachers are generally agreed on the use of the account form of balance sheet to introduce this financial statement early in the first accounting cycle. Two strong arguments tend to support the early use of the account form. In the first place, the account form reveals the equation in proper form: $A = L + OE$. The equation approach, therefore, can be used to introduce the balance sheet. Second, the account form can be used to advantage in a later stage of the cycle when the need for the T account is introduced.

Teachers are also agreed on the introduction of the report form of balance sheet, but only after the account form has been well established. In general, many teachers will present the report form when the complete sequence of procedures is established for the students. In other words, the students will have a knowledge of early accounting concepts as well as journalizing, posting, and the trial balance. In presenting the report form, the usual advantage is that it is easier to typewrite the balance sheet when liabilities and owner's equity are listed vertically beneath the assets. When the students are assigned to do a few report form exercises (usually in handwritten form), they quickly see the advantages of avoiding account form problems such as having inadequate writing space and having to show the totals on the same line.

With these advantages, however, many students conclude that the report form of balance sheet is the "customary" form in common usage. To dispel this misconception, refer students to a cross-section of published annual reports or to either *Accounting Trends & Techniques* (American practice) or *Financial Reporting in Canada* (Canadian practice).

Teaching the Statement of Owner's Equity

Some teachers will argue in favor of introducing the statement of owner's equity as part of the first accounting cycle. They point to the fact that a separate statement showing the detailed changes in owner's equity is in common use. On the other hand, other teachers prefer to delay this statement until a later cycle. In defense of this position, they point to the need for simplifying concepts as much as possible in the first cycle. It would appear that the timing is a matter of personal preference.

Regardless of when the statement is introduced, it is important to teach the need for the separate statement and the correct format. In presenting the need, emphasize the fact that the owner of a business will desire more detailed information in owner's equity, especially after transactions have been recorded for additional investments, withdrawals, and the calculation of net income (or loss) for the accounting period. And in presenting a correct format, it is important to show the order of details similar to the order shown in Figure 14.5.

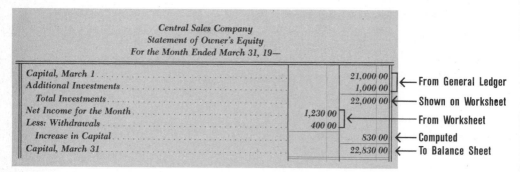

Figure 14.5

Interpreting the Balance Sheet

In presenting the balance sheet, the final suggested objective is to teach in simple terms what this financial statement says and what it does not say. It is important to recognize that no sophisticated ratio analysis is suggested. What is essential, however, is to present a few principles that emphasize clearly a basic understanding of the balance sheet. The traditional ratio analysis can be deferred until a later stage of the course. After the students learn how to prepare early balance sheets, present an elementary interpretation under two headings: (1) What a Balance Sheet Says and (2) What a Balance Sheet Does Not Say.

WHAT A BALANCE SHEET SAYS.   A good place to begin an interpretation of a balance sheet is to analyze what a balance sheet says. To keep matters simple, avoid a formal ratio analysis. At least five points can be discussed with the students following their preparation of several early balance sheets.

Reveals Firm Name.   Review the balance sheet heading. Direct the students' attention to the firm name. Emphasize that not only does the balance sheet disclose the firm name, it also reveals the fact that the firm is an accounting entity. In simple terms, bring out the meaning that accounting separates the business enterprise from the owner or owners. One or two examples should be given to drive home this principle. For example, when the owner invests personal money into a business, only the amount of the investment is included in the assets of the balance sheet for the firm. As a second example, the owner may have contributed an office desk to the business. Here, only the cost of the desk would be included in the assets of the balance sheet. Obviously, the point to emphasize is that in preparing the balance sheet for the business enterprise, accounting is not concerned with the owner's other personal assets such as homes, cars, boats, and so on; nor is accounting interested in the owner's personal liabilities. For accounting purposes, therefore, the proprietor as an individual and the business enterprise are treated as separate entities, but only the firm is an accounting entity.

Provides a Summary of Assets and Claims. Review the meaning of the accounting equation within the balance sheet. In simple terms, the equation provides the reader with a summary of what the business owns in the way of economic resources (assets), and the claims against those resources as at a specific date. Of course, these claims are divided into two groups: creditors and the owner's equity.

Reveals Firm's Financial Position. A balance sheet does provide the reader with a view of the firm's financial position as to its ability to pay debts. Direct attention to any one of the previously prepared balance sheets, and then pose a question such as: "Is this firm in a good or poor financial position to pay those debts that would ordinarily be due within one year of the balance sheet date?" Ask students to explain the answer.

Observe that the above question does not require a formal ratio analysis. All that is required of the students at this stage is to compare the available assets that can be used to pay off debts. No current ratio analysis need be mentioned. Drive home the importance of this simple analysis by providing one or two unfavorable financial position balance sheets. In any discussion, students should conclude that, to be in a favorable position, a business should at least have cash or potential cash not only to clear immediate debts, but also to pay for expenses in operating the business.

Shows Firm's Ability to Conduct Business. A balance sheet shows the reader a view of the enterprise's ability to carry on its business operations. Such an interpretation may be made by forcing an analysis of those assets ordinarily not converted into cash. A question could be raised on any asset that is obviously missing from the balance sheet. For example, in the absence of land and buildings listings, the reader should be led to the conclusion that the business must rent office space. For listed assets such as furniture and office equipment, however, emphasize the point that these are regarded as permanent economic resources; they are not intended for resale but are kept in order to support the operations of the business.

Assesses Owner's Claim Against Assets. One final point of simple analysis can be taught from a balance sheet at this time. From an analysis of the accounting equation, a balance sheet does reveal the relative strength or weakness of the owner's claim against the assets of the business. For example, where A = $20,000, L = $5,000, and OE = $15,000, this claim would appear to be a strong one since the owner has 75 percent of the total claims. Now turn the figures around so that the class can respond to allow L to equal $15,000 and OE to equal $5,000. In the discussion of the weak claim here, emphasize the fact that this claim is a residual one because the claims of creditors must always be satisfied first. It is essential for this reason that one write the correct order of the elements in the equation as $A = L + OE$ and *not* $A = OE + L$.

WHAT A BALANCE SHEET DOES NOT SAY. One of the most important problems facing many readers of a balance sheet is that of misinterpreting the financial statement altogether. At least four things that a balance sheet does *not* say can be taught early to students.

1. A balance sheet does not give the reader a picture of how profits were made by the business enterprise. While the net income is usually revealed on the balance sheet, the details of how this net income was calculated are provided by the income statement.

2. A balance sheet does not show the claims of creditors and the owner(s) against specific assets. The students should be reminded that the claims are against the assets in general, that is, against the total assets only.

3. One of the traditional misconceptions involves the interpretation of the word *Capital*. What must be emphasized is that Capital under owner's equity does not represent cash. Through discussion, remind the class that although the owner may have invested only cash, in all probability some or all of this original cash investment has been used to acquire additional economic resources for the business. In short, no balance sheet reveals how money originally invested by the owner has been used by the enterprise. Because balance sheets do not disclose actual transactions, it is important that the meaning of capital be restricted only to the word *investment*. A correct interpretation of Capital, therefore, simply refers to the owner's claim against total assets through investment.

4. This final point is very important to teach. A balance sheet does not report the so-called market value or worth of any business. Unfortunately, many readers believe that the total assets represent a bundle of future cash resources. While there is little difficulty in assigning a dollar value to Cash and Accounts Receivable, the students must be reminded that there are assets that have been acquired *not* for the purpose of being converting into cash. Through questions, have the students identify several examples such as typewriters and other office equipment, land, and buildings as economic resources that will be used to generate revenue through the sale of goods and/or services. To avoid any reader misunderstanding of assets and other information in financial statements, emphasize that the accounting profession has set out a number of guidelines called *generally accepted accounting principles*. One very

important principle has been widely supported for interpreting the "value" of assets ordinarily not converted into cash, that is: A balance sheet does not purport to show either present values of assets to the enterprise or values that might be realized in liquidation. The accepted accounting basis for assets is the cost at the date of their acquisition.

Through discussion, the students should draw out the simple meaning that accountants prefer to record such assets on the basis of the dollars that have been used to acquire these economic resources; the dollar amounts listed do not indicate the prices at which the assets could be sold. In the language of accounting, therefore, the *value* of an asset simply means the "cost of that asset," and not the present value or worth of that asset. With this principle in mind, students should conclude that a balance sheet is a position statement that gives the reader three main pieces of information: it summarizes the position of assets, liabilities, and owner's equity at a specific point of time; it allows the reader to analyze the financial position of the firm's ability to meet its debts; and finally, it allows the reader to analyze those economic resources to be used to generate revenue for the firm. A balance sheet, therefore, may properly be defined as a statement of financial position.

Periodic Versus Perpetual Inventory Systems

As indicated earlier, teachers can give a better understanding of the cost of goods sold for a merchandising business by showing some classes a comparative view of the periodic and perpetual inventory systems. In fact, a basic knowledge of both will go a long way toward eliminating confusion in basic transaction analysis. Consider, for example, the problem facing students in the required analysis of the following transaction: The proprietor, T. Black, withdrew goods (merchandise for resale) costing $85 for his own use.

If one assumes that the drawing account has been previously presented, then teachers would probably receive the account analysis shown in Figure 14.6 in T-account form.

T. Black, Drawings 85

Inventory 85

Figure 14.6

In discussing this response, most students would support their analysis by pointing to the fact that some inventory was removed from stock and, therefore, the asset Inventory must surely decrease. And yet, under the traditional periodic method, teachers will require the students to learn the second answer shown in Figure 14.7.

T. Black, Drawings		Purchases	
85			85

Figure 14.7

Obviously, students become most confused not with the debit entry, but with the credit to Purchases. Many cannot understand why Inventory is not affected when some stock is removed. This underscores the fact that little emphasis is given in traditional accounting courses to the understanding of both a periodic inventory system and a perpetual inventory system.

In teaching a comparative view of both inventory systems, it is logical to present first what the students already know, that is, a review of the periodic inventory system. Several important teaching points are worth considering in the development of this review.

1. Use a short accounting period, say one month.
2. Use only the basic accounts that will enable the students to calculate quickly and accurately the cost of goods sold. Such factors as freight-in, purchases returns and allowances, and purchases discount should be eliminated from the review problem.
3. To expedite and simplify matters, use a T-account analysis of all transactions.
4. Again to simplify the review exercise, use only monthly credit transactions for both purchases and sales. In addition, analyze only the general ledger accounts.
5. In keeping with a basic teaching principle, use very simple dollar amounts so that the mathematics difficulty is removed from the accounting problem.
6. And finally, require the students to prepare a partial income statement showing the calculation of the gross margin. As will be observed later, this partial income statement is to be compared with a similar one for the treatment of the perpetual inventory system.

Review of Periodic Inventory System

Follow closely the suggested review exercise below, which is offered in individual stages. Keep in mind that the data provided in the review will be used again in the subsequent treatment of the perpetual inventory system.

To begin, it is important to emphasize the principle that the inventory at the beginning of an accounting period is the inventory on hand at the end of the last accounting period. Assume, for example, a merchandising firm that shows on May 1, the beginning of a new accounting period, 10 items costing $100 each in the Inventory account (Figure 14.8).

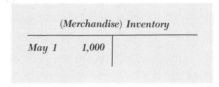

(Merchandise) Inventory

| May 1 | 1,000 |

Figure 14.8

Next, assume purchases of merchandise for the month of May of 20 items at the same cost of $100 each (assume also that all merchandise purchases are acquired on account). The general ledger entry, in T-account form, would be shown as in Figure 14.9.

| *Purchases* | | *Accounts Payable* | |
| May 31 | 2,000 | May 31 | 2,000 |

Figure 14.9

As part of the above analysis, review the basic principle of any periodic inventory system: The Inventory account is updated only at the end of the accounting period. This principle will explain the use of the Purchases account at this time, but it may not answer the question of why the Inventory account cannot be used. If the question is raised, then simply explain that firms using this periodic method cannot afford the luxury of buying or renting machines and hiring extra personnel to update all inventory items as each change occurs.

Calculate the cost of goods available for sale. As suggested under the earlier treatment for calculating the cost of goods sold, you may wish to use wooden or plastic blocks. In this case, let each block represent $100, so that the total of 30 blocks (10 + 20) can now be shown. The students should have little difficulty in concluding that the 30 items at a cost of $100 each would give $3,000, or the cost of all goods available for sale.

Now consider the sales aspect of the problem. Assume that all sales are on a credit basis and that sales for the month of May consisted of 22 items at a selling price of $250 each. The students should now show a T-account analysis of the general ledger as in Figure 14.10.

If blocks or similar items are used, then remove 22 from the original pile representing the cost of all goods available for sale. The remaining pile, of course, shows the cost of the goods *not* sold or, simply, the final inventory. **263**

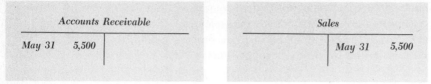

Accounts Receivable		Sales	
May 31 5,500			May 31 5,500

Figure 14.10

As suggested earlier, a short accounting period of one month is used in the review exercise. Assume that on May 31 a physical stocktaking showed eight items counted on hand at a cost of $100. Of course, these eight items would agree with the pile of blocks unsold. Under a periodic inventory system, the students must realize that the main objective in taking stock at the end of any accounting period is to use the final inventory amount for the calculation of the cost of goods sold.

From the information given, students should be able to prepare a partial income statement down to the Gross Margin figure as illustrated in Figure 14.11.

Revenue from sales	$5,500
Cost of Goods Sold:	
Inventory, May 1	$1,000
Purchases	2,000
Cost of Goods Available for Sale	$3,000
Less Inventory, May 31	800
Cost of Goods Sold	2,200
Gross Margin	$3,300

Figure 14.11 Periodic inventory method: partial income statement for the month ended May 31.

Teaching the Perpetual Inventory System

The stage is now set for the teaching of the perpetual inventory system. In developing the complete unit, it is important to consider the following objectives.

1. Students must be able to compare the perpetual system with the one they know; therefore, it is critical that the same data be used in order to reveal a partial income statement under a perpetual system.
2. As in the development of the periodic inventory system, students should use only T-account analysis for the basic transactions.
3. Students must be able to compare both T-account ledgers. It is important that students visualize the similarities and the differences between the general ledgers under both systems.
4. Students must classify correctly the Cost of Goods Sold accounts in the general ledger of the periodic inventory plan. With this knowl-

edge, they will be able to interpret correctly Cost of Goods Sold (Cost of Sales) in any financial statement.

5. Students must be able to recognize the importance of inventory control under the perpetual inventory system, and the lack of inventory control under the periodic plan. One suggested method here is to consider an added problem wherein the physical stock-taking reveals an amount of goods on hand quite different from the "book" records.

6. Students must have a conceptual knowledge of a subsidiary inventory ledger under the perpetual inventory method.

7. And finally, students must be able to offer a final evaluation of both inventory methods. In each case, both the strengths and limitations must be acknowledged.

DEVELOPING THE LESSON. The following development is suggested in order to achieve the objectives stated above:

Step 1. Begin with the same opening data in the Inventory account, but this time indicate to the class that the study of all transactions will affect a merchandising firm that prefers to use a perpetual inventory system. In basic terms, explain that this system involves an immediate updating of the inventory account each time goods are purchased and sold. Once again, the students should reveal a T account for the Inventory account showing the basic principle that the inventory at the beginning of an accounting period is the inventory on hand at the end of the last accounting period. In this case, the T account will show on May 1 an opening balance of $1,000. It is also important to emphasize that this balance refers to 10 items costing $100 each. Again, blocks may be used to represent all transactions visually.

Step 2. Next, show purchases of merchandise for the month of May: 20 items at $100 each (assume that all merchandise purchases are acquired on account). This next transaction will require that the students present a T-account analysis for the perpetual inventory system. The correct analysis is illustrated in Figure 14.12. Of course, it is very important for the students to conclude that under the perpetual inventory system a purchase of goods is recorded in the assets account. No account is kept for Purchases. In addition, the students must realize that the Inventory account, once updated (posted), reveals a new balance. This new balance must represent the cost of all goods available for sale, or the $3,000. Again, the use of blocks can reinforce the concept quite easily.

Step 3. Next, analyze the same sales for the month of May: 22 items at a selling price of $250 each. Under a perpetual inventory system, students must learn to analyze two entries instead of one. These entries, in T-account form, may be illustrated as shown in Figure 14.13.

In analyzing the two entries above, several important points need emphasis. First, no change occurs in the recording of the sales revenue as such. Second, the cost of the goods sold is charged to the Cost of Goods Sold account, while the Inventory account is decreased by the same cost amount. The second entry allows you to introduce a simple and yet very impor-

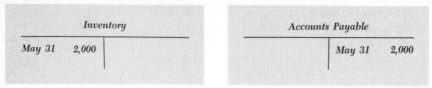

Figure 14.12

tant concept. Under a perpetual inventory system, costing clerks are usually employed to perform a costing calculation on a duplicate copy of each sales invoice. Very briefly, costs of each kind of merchandise sold are recorded by transferring data from the invoice copy to the inventory card or sheet maintained for that class of item. Since the review problem deals with only one hypothetical item, the concept of a subsidiary ledger for inventory can be delayed until later. It should be pointed out, however, that in actual practice many large firms now employ a computer system to perform the costing operation automatically.

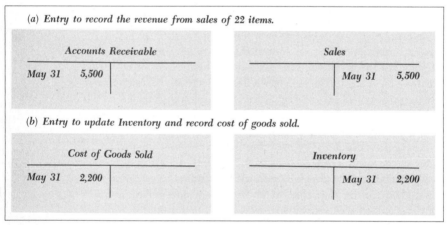

Figure 14.13

One other point is worth considering at this time. Since Cost of Goods Sold is new in the sense of a general ledger account, students will want to learn how to classify it correctly. Will it be classified as Asset, Liability, Capital, Revenue, or Expense? Obviously, Cost of Goods Sold is an expense account. Students must remember that under a perpetual system, sales invoices are costed and entries are subsequently made to transfer costs of goods sold out of inventory accounts into an expense account entitled *Cost of Goods Sold.* What may confuse students is the fact that this account is not present under the periodic inventory method. On the other hand, they have learned the concept of cost of goods sold in the income statement; therefore, explain the correct accounting theory that Cost of Goods Sold (or simply, Cost of Sales) is an expense to be matched against related sales revenue in order to calculate the gross margin (gross profit on sales) for a definite period of time. As the students will soon realize, no indirect calculation for cost of goods sold is necessary under a perpetual plan. The amount is taken directly from the general ledger account when required.

One methods controversy is worth mentioning here. Some teachers are under the impression that cost of goods sold is a cost account. When debating the proper classification, keep in mind that costs in accounting are correctly defined as either unexpired or expired. When inventory is acquired, then accounting correctly records the unexpired cost as a current asset. On the other hand, when the goods are sold, then the unexpired cost of those goods becomes expired. As you know, an expired cost in accounting is correctly classified as an expense. This theory is consistent with all other so-called cost treatments.

Step 4. In this next part of the development, it may be desirable to have students visualize all of the entries so far in a T-account general ledger. Once they have this view, then the students may compare the accounts under a perpetual inventory system with accounts under a periodic method. You may wish to prepare an overhead transparency or place on the chalkboard a comparative illustration similar to Figure 14.14. Assume that a physical check on May 31 showed a total cost of inventory on hand of $800 (eight items at $100).

These points should become quite evident in a comparison of the two general ledgers. Under a periodic inventory system, the cost of goods sold must be calculated from information taken from the Inventory account (for the beginning inventory amount), the Purchases account, and the final inventory amount that had to be provided through a physical stocktaking at the end of the accounting period. On the other hand, the general ledger for the perpetual plan shows not only the amount of cost of goods sold directly from the account, but also the balance of inventory on hand in the Inventory account. Of course, both ledgers show identical information for Sales, Accounts Receivable, and Accounts Payable.

Step 5. The next step should be an easy one for the students. From the general ledger of the perpetual inventory system, students should prepare a partial income statement down to the calculation for the gross margin. This partial income statement should then be compared with the earlier one developed for the periodic inventory system. The students will easily conclude that the income statement under the perpetual plan is quite simplified since the cost of goods sold is taken directly from the general ledger account.

Step 6. Now direct the students' attention to the importance of inventory control that exists under the perpetual inventory system, and the lack of inventory control under the periodic plan. This objective can be attained by presenting an additional problem along the following lines.

Suppose that on May 31 the actual count of stock showed only seven items at a cost of $100 each instead of the eight previously reported. With this new information and the comparative general ledger, require the

Periodic Inventory System

Accounts Receivable
May 31 | 5,500

Sales
| May 31 | 5,500

Inventory
May 1 | 1,000

Purchases
May 31 | 2,000

Accounts Payable
| May 31 | 2,000

Perpetual Inventory System

Accounts Receivable
May 31 | 5,500

Sales
| May 31 | 5,500

Inventory
May 1 | 1,000 | May 31 | 2,200
31 | 2,000 |

Cost of Goods Sold
May 31 | 2,200

Accounts Payable
| May 31 | 2,000

Figure 14.14 General ledgers compared.

students to prepare partial income statements for both inventory systems as in Figures 14.15 and 14.16. Then, instruct the students to consider these three questions: (1) How do you account for the difference between the two statements? (2) Under a perpetual system, how does accounting reconcile the balance in the Inventory account with the actual count on May 31? (3) What obvious weakness is found in the periodic method of inventory control?

Revenue from sales		*$5,500*
Cost of Goods Sold:		
Inventory, May 1	*$1,000*	
Purchases	*2,000*	
Cost of Goods Available for Sale	*$3,000*	
Less Inventory, May 31	*700*	
Cost of Goods Sold		*2,300*
Gross Margin		*$3,200*

Figure 14.15

By comparing the two partial income statements and taking part in a teacher-led discussion, students should be able to give interesting replies to the three questions. For the first question, students will easily provide the answer that the difference of $100 in the comparative gross margins can be explained by the differences in the amounts reported for the cost of goods sold. Under the periodic plan, the cost of goods sold was taken as a result of deducting the ending inventory figure of seven items at $100 each. On the other hand, the cost of goods sold under the perpetual system shows the actual cost of the 22 items sold, that is, the correct amounts taken from costing each invoice copy.

Revenue from sales	*$5,500*
Cost of goods sold (expense)	*2,200*
Gross margin	*$3,300*

Figure 14.16

Before the second question is considered, provide this brief but important background. Under the periodic plan, the purpose of the stock-taking at the end of the accounting period is simply to obtain the amount of final inventory so that the cost of the goods sold can subsequently be calculated. Under the perpetual plan, however, the physical count at the end of the accounting period serves the important function of inventory control. Simply stated, the balance in the Inventory account is used to check against the actual physical count of goods on hand. Since the book record shows eight items on hand ($800) and the physical count shows only seven items ($700), then the obvious step is to account for the difference. If the one item cannot be accounted for, then one would conclude that it probably has been stolen from stock. How, then, does accounting reconcile the difference between the book record and the actual physical count? The answer is through an adjusting entry such as the following.

Loss, Theft, Pilferage of Inventory (Expense)	100	
Inventory (Current Asset)		100
To record the loss of one inventory item		
at a cost of $100.		

In the income statement for the firm using the perpetual system, the reported loss would be shown as part of the operating expenses or under "Other Expenses." It is important to teach that the loss would not be shown as part of the calculation of the gross margin figure; it is reported separately so that management can initiate action to control the loss of valuable stock. The students should consider the importance of accounting for inventory control in relationship to high-priced items such as color televisions and automobiles. One missing item could mean a loss of several hundreds or even thousands of dollars.

With the first two questions thoroughly discussed and answered correctly, students should have little difficulty with the last question. The obvious weakness with the periodic inventory method is the lack of inventory control. And the reason? At this stage students will conclude that the costs lumped under the heading Cost of Goods Sold are likely to reflect not only the cost of goods actually sold but inventory losses of unknown amounts. Before students become too critical, however, provide a proper perspective. Would a small firm selling many low-priced items want a perpetual inventory accounting system? Obviously, a policy of maintaining an accounting system that relies on periodic inventory-taking alone accepts the risks of loss with considerable out-of-pocket saving of extra accounting and administrative costs.

Step 7. One of the important teaching objectives in presenting the perpetual inventory method is to give students a conceptual knowledge of a subsidiary inventory ledger. In all probability many more students will find employment in subsidiary ledger departments than in general accounting where the general ledger is updated.

Teaching the concept for an inventory subsidiary ledger is no more difficult than teaching the need for a separate accounts receivable ledger, a separate accounts payable ledger, or a separate fixed asset ledger. The students should be receptive to the basic idea that the general ledger could not possibly keep a record of hundreds of different inventory items. A more efficient system would suggest that costs of each kind of merchandise bought and sold are recorded on the inventory card or sheet maintained for that class of item. These cards or sheets will comprise the subsidiary ledger whose balances should equal in total the inventory controlling account in the general ledger. This idea can be reinforced by showing several examples of subsidiary stock ledger cards.

One other related point is worth teaching. As with any subsidiary ledger, accuracy of the accounting is tested by listing the balances of the subsidiary stock ledger cards and totaling the list. Of course, the total should agree with the balance of the general ledger controlling account.

From a discussion of the subsidiary ledger for inventory items, students should conclude that this extra accounting work involves extra expense. In the end, management must decide between (a) the prevention of losses that might otherwise occur to be derived from perpetual inventory accounting and (b) the extra clerical and machine costs involved in the perpetual inventory method.

Step 8. The last objective in the suggested development is to have the students offer a final evaluation of both inventory methods. From the stages presented so far, the students should be able to identify several key points. In the case of the periodic inventory system, for example, there are these features: (1) the required calculation of cost of goods sold at the end of each accounting period; (2) the lack of inventory control; and (3) the expectation of cost savings by eliminating much of the accounting for inventory items. On the other hand, the students should be able to single out these points on behalf of the perpetual inventory system: (1) a more direct method of arriving at the figure for cost of goods sold; (2) an attempt to control inventory, especially of high-priced items; (3) the acknowledgment of extra expense to hire costing clerks and maintain machines in order to keep a subsidiary ledger for valuable inventory items; and (4) the expectation that the extra expense will be absorbed by minimizing the losses in valuable stock items.

ADDITIONAL BENEFITS OF PERPETUAL INVENTORY. There are two other important points that should be offered on behalf of the perpetual inventory system. These may be presented as follows.

Perpetual inventory records provide management with needed information for such operations as purchasing and production.

In the event of a fire or other disaster covered by insurance policies, the independent operation of perpetual inventory records may greatly assist management in their responsibility to prove the amount of loss recoverable from insurance companies, particularly in cases of partial loss, such as loss of goods stored in a specific location.

Problems, Questions, and Projects

1. Prepare as many functional performance goals as possible for the units on the income statement, the balance sheet, and periodic versus perpetual inventory systems.

2. Assume that you have taught the unit on the worksheet and that your next development is to teach the preparation of financial statements from

the worksheet. Do you prefer to teach the balance sheet or the income statement first? Why?

3. For the date on the heading of the income statement, one student writes: For the Year Ending December 31, 19—. Would you criticize this heading in any way? Explain.

4. In your opinion, what is the clearest and best way to teach the Cost of Goods Sold section of the income statement?

5. The suggested method of showing the Cost of Goods Sold section as a supporting schedule to the income statement to help students understand how this section is computed is criticized as being unrealistic. It is argued that students should not be shown a method that is inconsistent with practice. Do you find the criticism justified? Explain your answer.

6. Why is the term *gross margin* favored over *gross profit* in today's accounting practice?

7. Why is the owner's equity figure that is shown on the worksheet out of date for balance sheet purposes?

8. The suggestion was made in this chapter that while the teacher demonstrates and prepares the balance sheet on the overhead projector or at the board, the students should complete the same statement at their seats. Why is this a good practice? Can you think of any disadvantages to the procedure?

9. Prepare a lesson plan for the presentation of one of the following:
   a. The balance sheet.
   b. The income statement for a service type of business.
   c. The development of the Cost of Goods Sold section of the income statement for a firm using the periodic inventory method.

10. When would you introduce a classified balance sheet in accordance with generally accepted accounting principles? Explain your answer.

11. What definition for current assets would you communicate to your first-year accounting students? Would this definition change in any way in a later development of the topic? Explain why or why not.

12. In listing current liabilities on a balance sheet, many students memorize the order that makes accounts payable the first listed debt. Are they correct? Explain your view.

13. When would you introduce the report form of the balance sheet? Would you eliminate the use of the account form after the report form has been presented? Explain your answers.

14. Traditionally, many teachers delay any form of interpreting the balance sheet until the end of the first-year course or include it in a second-year course. Do you agree with this view? Explain your answer.

15. Would you teach the perpetual inventory method to your first-year accounting students? Explain why or why not.

16. Explain the meaning of this important accounting fundamental: A policy of maintaining an accounting system that relies on periodic inventory-taking alone accepts the risks of loss through fraud and pilferage with considerable out-of-pocket saving of recording and administrative costs.

17. If your merchandising firm were selling home appliances such as stoves, refrigerators, and color televisions, would you recommend a periodic or a perpetual inventory accounting system? Explain your answer.

18. In teaching proper account classification, one teacher insisted that his students learn to identify the following six classes: Assets, Liabilities, Capital, Revenue, Costs, and Expenses. On the other hand, another teacher supported the view that there are only five main classes of accounts: Assets, Liabilities, Capital, Revenue, and Costs and Expenses. Do you agree with either view? Explain your answer.

19. Prepare a simple schematic to illustrate the relationship between a subsidiary ledger for inventory items and the related controlling account in the general ledger.

20. Prepare overhead transparency masters as teaching materials to develop the method of teaching any one of the topics included in this chapter. Construct your teaching materials so that there is one base transparency and at least two overlays or two masks. If possible, prepare actual transparencies from your masters and display your finished product to your methods teacher or methods class.

Case Problems

1. Two accounting teachers were overheard debating the correct placement on the Income Statement of discount off purchases and discount off sales. One teacher argued strongly in favor of reporting both items under the separate headings "Financial Income" and "Financial Expense" respectively. The other teacher countered by stating that discount off sales should be grouped with sales returns and allowances in order to calculate the net sales. With whom do you agree? Give reasons for your answer.

2. A teacher of one introductory accounting class drafted the case problem shown below as part of the mid-year examination paper.

Mr. Ron Florendine is in the cattle business in an oil-producing region of the country. He owns 1,000 acres of land for grazing purposes. Originally this land cost the owner $60 an acre. For accounting purposes, the land was listed correctly in the asset section of the first and subsequent balance sheets with a dollar amount of $60,000. Recently, substantial oil reserves were discovered by a large oil company in a tract of land adjacent to the Florendine ranch; consequently, an official of the large oil development and exploration company offered Mr. Forendine $10,000 an acre for his entire tract of land. Although Mr. Florendine refused this offer, he called his accountant into his office and said, "I've recently been offered $10,000 an acre for my land and yet you continue to show the land to be worth only $60 an acre in the financial records. Why don't you report the true value of the land in my business's balance sheet?"

How would you answer the owner-manager's question if you were his accountant? Justify your position to management.

CHAPTER 15

Teaching End-of-Cycle Activities

Understanding of the procedure followed in making the closing entries depends upon mastery of an earlier lesson. When the revenue and expense accounts were first introduced, they were presented as temporary accounts used to record changes in the owner's equity resulting from revenue and expense transactions. Since that time, those transactions that directly affected the profit have been recorded in the various temporary accounts.

The result is that the capital account is grossly out of date and must be updated. This is accomplished by transferring the data that has been recorded in the temporary revenue and expense accounts to the capital account. This transferring is accomplished by making what are called *closing entries.* First, let us review the relevant accounting principles and procedures.

ACCOUNTING FUNDAMENTALS

1. The purpose of making closing entries is to bring the capital account up to date.
2. All temporary accounts—revenue and expenses—are closed.
3. The balances of these accounts are transferred to the Revenue and Expense Summary account. The balance left in this account is the amount of the net income (or loss) for the period.
4. The balance of the Revenue and Expense Summary account is transferred to the owner's capital account.
5. The balance of the owner's drawing account is usually transferred to the owner's capital account.
6. Closing entries are made as of the last day of the accounting period.
7. The accuracy of the balances in the ledger are then proved by preparing a postclosing trial balance.

The discussion in this chapter covers two areas: the teaching procedure to be followed and the explanation of the basic reasoning that underlies the idea of making closing entries. The basic questions that must be answered regarding closing entries are these:

1. What accounts are closed? Are the same accounts closed in each accounting period?
2. Why are these accounts being closed?
3. How are the entries made that close these accounts?
4. When are closing entries made?
5. How are the accounts that have been closed ruled?
6. What accounts remain open after the closing entries are made?

What Accounts Are Closed?

All temporary owner's equity accounts are closed. Two principal classes of accounts are involved: revenue accounts and expense accounts. All accounts in these classes are closed at the end of each accounting period.

The term *closing* frequently confuses students. Therefore, you should not only identify the accounts that are closed, but also explain what is meant by closing an account. In the language of accounting, the term *closing* means "to transfer the balance of an account, and thus to close the account." How the balance of an account is transferred needs to be demonstrated and explained, and this may be done by placing a number of accounts with debit and credit balances on the chalkboard or overhead. Demonstrate, and have the students practice, identifying (1) the amount needed to balance the account, (2) the side of the account the entry would be made on to balance the account, and (3) the corresponding debit or credit entry necessary to transfer the balance.

Why Are Temporary Accounts Closed?

To demonstrate to the class why temporary accounts are closed, start with an analysis of the owner's capital account. From a look at this account in the ledger (or trial balance), it is readily seen that its balance is not up to date with the figure shown on the balance sheet. Another way to teach the need for closing is to review an accounting equation that has been expanded to include revenue and expense transactions. From this equation, the students must conclude that the Owner's Equity comes from two sources: the initial investment—the owner's capital— and the excess of revenues over expenses (net income). Since both the balance sheet and the expanded accounting equation show the net income added to capital, the students will conclude that some method is necessary to transfer the net income within the ledger so that the result can be added to the Capital account. And since net income involves the use of revenue and expense accounts, the students will recognize that only these accounts are affected by the closing process. Now introduce the concept of the Revenue and Expense Summary account, which acts as a "clearinghouse account" in order to transfer the net income (or loss) to the owner's Capital account at the end of the accounting period.

In addition to transferring the excess of revenues over expenses to the Capital account, the closing of temporary accounts serves another useful purpose. Some accounts such as the Sales account and the Miscellaneous Expense account contain many entries. Closing these accounts eliminates the need to deal with the figures of previous accounting periods when calculating account balances. This considerably simplifies the mathematics involved in future accounting periods.

Emphasize that closing these ledger accounts is a means to an end, not an end in itself. Two purposes of closing, therefore, are: (1) to have the ledger show the same information that is contained on the balance sheet, as far as the owner's equity section is concerned, and (2) to prepare the ledger to receive revenue and expense transactions of the next accounting period.

How Are the Accounts Closed?

Early in the study of the accounting cycle for a service firm, students become familiar with the idea that the net income for the period is found by matching the revenue with related expenses. What follows should be a simple demonstration of how this matching occurs within the ledger to facilitate the transfer of net income to the owner's Capital account. The following procedure is suggested for teaching concepts of closing for a service enterprise in the first cycle.

Step 1. In T-account form on the chalkboard or overhead, show three expense accounts, one revenue account, and the owner's Capital account with balances identified before closing. Leave space before the Capital account for the insertion later of the Summary account. In this first presentation, the balance in the revenue account should be greater than the total of all balances in expense accounts to ensure the transfer of the net income.

Step 2. Review the need for updating the Capital account by comparing the balance to the owner's equity section of the balance sheet.

Step 3. Explain that the balances of the revenue and expense accounts could be transferred directly to the Capital account, but that it is preferable to transfer the balances to a special account that first summarizes all revenues and expense; hence the account Revenue and Expense Summary may be added on the chalkboard or overhead directly before the Capital account.

Step 4. Demonstrate and explain how the revenue account balance is transferred to the Revenue and Expense Summary account. Students should conclude that the transfer requires the revenue account to be brought down to zero; hence the debit entry. And, secondly, the students should conclude that the Revenue and Expense Summary account now contains the revenue account balance on the credit side. Emphasize that the entry must be journalized before it can be posted to the accounts; however, since a T-account analysis only is being used here, the formal journalizing and posting of the closing entry will be delayed until after all the steps in closing have been presented.

Step 5. Demonstrate and explain how the expense accounts are transferred to the Revenue and Expense Summary account. At this stage, students should have little difficulty following the logic of crediting each expense account to bring each to a zero balance and of debiting the Revenue and Expense Summary account with the total expenses. Emphasize the point that a compound entry is usually made: one debit for the total expenses to the Summary account, and individual credits to each expense account.

Step 6. Draw attention to the amounts now contained in the Revenue and Expense Summary account. Ask the students to identify the nature of the debit figure and the credit figure. Reinforce the students' answers by writing "total expense" on the debit side and "total revenue" on the credit side. Then ask the students to identify the balance in the Summary account. Students should have little difficulty recognizing that the credit balance is the net income for the accounting period. Offer the observation that the Revenue and Expense Summary account is like an income statement in T-account form.

Step 7. For this step, ask the students how the balance of the Summary account can be transferred to the Capital account. Students should offer the answer that the Summary account balance is closed to the Capital account. When the transfer is made, emphasize the point that the Capital account now contains the amount of the owner's investment plus the net income; thus, the owner's equity account in the ledger is in agreement with the owner's equity section of the balance sheet.

Step 8. Review the steps of closing by emphasizing their order: first, close the revenue; second, close the expenses; and third, close the balance of Revenue and Expense Summary to the Capital account. This review can be shown on the chalkboard or overhead in an illustration similar to Figure 15.1.

Step 9. Repeat the steps by showing how a net loss is transferred to the Capital account. Of course, the same T accounts may be used, but the revenue balance should be changed to a lower amount to effect a subsequent net loss.

Step 10. Introduce a problem for closing by demonstrating the entries in a journal and posting them to formal ledger accounts.

Three Methods Controversies

In discussing the methods of presenting closing entries for the first time, some teachers disagree on three questions: (1) What name should be given to the Summary account? (2) When first introducing closing entries, should

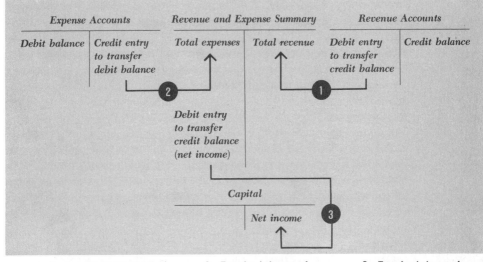

1. Transfer balances of revenue accounts to summary account.
2. Transfer balances of expense accounts to summary account.
3. Transfer balance of summary account (net income) to capital account.

Figure 15.1

the accounts be closed directly to the Capital account? and (3) Should individual or compound entries be used?

SUMMARY ACCOUNT NAME. When the name *Profit and Lost Statement* was in popular usage, the clearinghouse account used to transfer the profit (or loss) was called *Profit and Loss Summary*. However, with the adoption of the name *Income Statement* in contemporary practice, authors have replaced the term *Profit and Loss Summary* with names such as *Income and Expense Summary*, *Revenue and Expense Summary*, and *Income Summary*. The first term, *Income and Expense Summary*, appears to be a contradiction of accounting principles, since only revenues and expenses can be summarized to produce a net result called *net income* (or *net loss*). The second name, *Revenue and Expense Summary*, leaves no doubt as to the nature of the account; it suggests that revenues and expenses are to be summarized within the account. The last name, *Income Summary*, attempts to emphasize the end result of clearing; that is, it conveys the residual concept of income. In selecting the account name, the trend today is to favor either the term *Revenue and Expense Summary* or *Income Summary*.

CLOSING DIRECTLY TO CAPITAL ACCOUNT. The second controversy identifies the question of whether the accounts should be closed directly to the owner's Capital account. Some teachers prefer this procedure when first introducing the closing entries, thus delaying the use of the Summary account. In support of this method, these teachers emphasize that students have previously been shown that the revenue and expense accounts are only subdivisions of the owner's Capital account; therefore, the purpose of

279

closing entries is to transfer their balances back to the Capital account. On the other hand, many other teachers claim that the direct method of closing leads to future unlearning. Secondly, these teachers point out that the direct method clutters the capital account with revenue, expenses, investments, and capital withdrawals. For these reasons, they prefer to introduce the Summary account right from the beginning. Since both methods achieve the end result of teaching closing, the choice can be made by the instructor.

INDIVIDUAL OR COMPOUND ENTRIES. On the question of whether individual or compound entries should be taught, one may again conclude that the choice is a matter of personal preference. Current trends in textbooks, however, point to the use of compound entries only. To avoid confusion, follow whatever pattern is used in the textbook.

Closing Treatment for the Merchandising Firm

Several added points must be considered when closing is reintroduced as part of the study of the accounting cycle for a merchandising firm. Teachers generally favor the use of the service firm in the presentation of the first cycle. To keep matters simple, the study of worksheets, adjustments, and the drawing account are reserved for study with the merchandising firm. Each of these new topics, therefore, must be considered in teaching closing procedures for a merchandising firm.

After presenting a review of closing for a service firm, draw the students' attention to the worksheet as the source for journalizing the adjusting and closing entries. First, ensure that students learn to journalize and post the adjusting entries from the Adjustments section of the worksheet. Second, direct students to the Income Statement section of the worksheet as the source for journalizing the closing entries. In general, teachers favor two compound entries. One entry would debit the Summary account with the total of the Income Statement debit column, while a credit would be made to each individual account recorded as a debit in the worksheet column. A second compound entry would debit each account shown as a credit in the Income Statement section, while the total of the credit column would be credited to the Summary account. After both entries have been posted, direct the class to compare the figures in the Summary account with the totals of the Income Statement section of the worksheet. Obviously, the amounts must be identical; otherwise, the net result would not be the same.

One teaching problem usually arises in the treatment of inventory for a merchandising firm that uses the periodic inventory method. Some teachers employ the adjustment method to account for the difference between the beginning and ending inventories. For example, if the beginning inventory account was $5,000 and the ending inventory was only $4,600, then the difference of $400 may be identified as an additional cost to the business. This cost may be transferred directly from the Merchandise Inventory account by the following adjusting entry:

Revenue and Expense Summary	400	
Merchandise Inventory		400
To adjust inventory.		

When the adjustment method for treating inventory is used, Revenue and Expense Summary appears as one of the adjustments on the worksheet. In directing students to the closing procedure, emphasize that the Revenue and Expense account must be excluded from the compound closing entry because the entry has already been made as part of the adjustments.

Other teachers prefer to avoid the adjustment method by showing both the beginning and ending inventories on the worksheet. The beginning inventory is entered as a debit to the Income Statement section, while the ending inventory is entered as a double entry: a credit to the Income Statement section and a debit to the Balance Sheet section. When this method is analyzed, the beginning inventory is shown as a debit to the Income Statement section to reflect the expense part of the cost of goods sold. On the other hand, the current inventory entered as a credit in the Income Statement section is analyzed as having the effect of decreasing the cost of goods available for sale to arrive at the true cost of goods sold. Under this method, both inventories are included in the two compound closing entries to the Summary account.

After all revenue, contra revenue, expense, and contra expense accounts have been closed to Revenue and Expense Summary, the teacher must consider how to present the transfer of the net income (or net loss) to the owner's Capital account. Since the drawing account has been introduced by this stage of treating the accounting cycle, two questions are often debated. First, should the balance of the Summary account be closed to the owner's drawing or capital account? And, second, should the drawing account be closed at all?

The first question often arouses a good methods discussion. The answer is found by a careful analysis of the owner's drawing account. Briefly, it is a generally accepted accounting principle that withdrawals of cash or other assets by the owner are not considered as an expense of the business; consequently, such withdrawals must not be considered in any calculation of the net income for the accounting period. In fact, the withdrawals must be considered as advance distributions of profits. Since withdrawals do not constitute an expense, it logically follows that the owner's drawing account must *not* be closed into the Revenue and Expense Summary account; rather, it must be closed directly to the owner's capital account after the net income is transferred to the owner's capital account. Under this theory, therefore, the final steps in closing are these:

Close the Summary account by transferring the net income (or net loss) to the owner's capital account.

Close the owner's drawing account by debiting the capital account and crediting the drawing account.

On the second question of whether the drawing account should be closed at all, some teachers argue that the intention of the owner regarding the earnings determines whether the drawing account should remain open or should be closed into the capital account. These teachers offer the following rationale.

If the proprietor intends to withdraw the profit for personal use, it should be left in the drawing account. Consequently, the final step in closing should be a double entry to debit the Summary account and to credit the drawing account. This entry would have the effect of transferring the net income to the drawing account, where it may be decreased as each withdrawal is subsequently identified. On the other hand, if the owner wishes to increase investment in the business by the amount of the profit, it should be transferred to the capital account. In fact, the owner might choose to reinvest a portion of the year's earnings and to withdraw the balance. In this case, the amount to be invested should be transferred to the capital account, and the balance of the profit left in the drawing account to be withdrawn as desired.

In settling the controversy of keeping the drawing account open or closed, current writing supports the view that the drawing account should be closed at the end of the accounting period. To avoid student confusion, therefore, most teachers simply follow the trend presented in their adopted textbook.

When Are Closing Entries Made?

During the course of instruction, students are taught to prepare closing entries at the end of each accounting period; and to simplify problems, the accounting period is often measured in terms of one month. The question often arises: Are monthly closing entries made in accounting practice?

This question can be answered briefly and in simple terms. In general, closing entries are made as part of the firm's year-end procedures. Each revenue account runs for one year only and shows the revenues realized up to date for a twelve-month period. At the end of each year, the revenue account is reduced to a zero balance by a closing entry. At the beginning of the next year, the same revenue account is used to receive next year's revenues on a month-by-month basis. Similarly, each expense account runs for one year only and shows the cost of a specified category of expense for a single year. At the end of each twelve-month financial year, the expense account is reduced to a zero balance by a closing entry. At the beginning of the next year, the same expense account is used to receive next year's expense on a month-by-month basis.

If, in practice, revenue and expense accounts are closed at year-end only, then why teach closing to students on a monthly basis? The answer is to present a simplified version of the closing procedures and the accounting cycle. Students can now be provided with the following information.

1. In practice, it is customary among large firms to prepare monthly financial statements for management use. These statements are

generally prepared from information summarized on a worksheet. In many cases, these monthly statements are prepared through a computer from journal vouchers prepared by the general accounting department.

2. In practice, all general ledger accounts are usually updated at the end of each month. There is no need to close the accounts, since financial statements can be prepared without closing the books. For this reason, the accounting cycle is correctly analyzed with closing entries coming *after* the preparation of financial statements.

3. In practice, where monthly financial statements are required, the general ledger form often provides for columns showing the results of the previous month's entries, the current month's entries, and the year-to-date results. An example of such a ledger form was introduced in Chapter 9.

4. In practice, all revenue and all expense accounts are closed following the preparation of the year-end financial statements. This year-end closing is required not only to prepare the accounts for the next financial year, but also to comply with various legal requirements. One excellent example of a legal requirement is the preparation of annual financial statements for filing income tax returns. Another example occurs in the case of corporations when a set of financial statements must be included in the company's annual report to stockholders. It should be evident that the revenue and expense accounts must be closed at year-end so that annual financial statements can be prepared to meet legal requirements.

How Are the Accounts That Have Been Closed Ruled?

After the closing entries have been journalized and posted to the accounts, all the temporary accounts have zero balances. The remaining ledger accounts—assets, liabilities, and owner's investment—have balances to begin the new accounting period. When a balance ledger form is used for the accounts, they do not have to be balanced and ruled.

On the other hand, if the standard ledger form is used, all the accounts in the ledger with more than one entry are ruled to separate clearly the entries of one accounting period from those of the next period. This step appears to be such a simple procedure that all too frequently it is not taught, with the result that some students never balance and rule accounts properly.

Teach balancing and ruling by placing a few simple rules on the chalkboard or overhead and then illustrating each while the students make similar balancing and rulings at their seats. For example, the procedure for balancing and ruling the Cash account, as in Figure 15.2, may be illustrated with teaching points as follows:

1. In the money column on the side with the smaller total, record the balance of the account on the first available line. Write the last day of the accounting period in the Date column and the word *Balance* in

				Cash				Account No. *101*

DATE		EXPLANATION	POST. REF.	DEBIT	DATE		EXPLANATION	POST. REF.	CREDIT
19—					*19—*				
Sept.	*30*	*Opening entry* .	*J1*	*6,000 00*	*Oct.*	*1*	. . . .	*J1*	*2,000 00*
Oct.	*2*	. . . .	*J1*	*1,000 00*		*5*	. . . .	*J1*	*4,000 00*
	14	. . . .	*J1*	*9,000 00*		*21*	. . . .	*J1*	*3,000 00*
	28	. . . .	*J1*	*1,600 00*		*30*	. . . .	*J2*	*1,550 00*
		7,050.00		*17,600 00*					*10,550 00*
						31	*Balance*	✓	*7,050 00*
				17,600 00					*17,600 00*
19—									
Nov.	*1*	*Balance*	✓	*7,050 00*					

Figure 15.2 Several debits. Several credits. Debit balance. **1** **2** **3** **4** **5**

the Explanation column. Put a check mark (✓) or dash (—) in the Posting Reference column to show that this is not a journalized item.

2. Under the last amount in either money column, draw a single rule on the same line across both money columns.

3. Enter the totals of both money columns beneath the single rule. (Because the account balance has been added to the smaller side of the account, the totals should be equal.)

4. Draw a double rule across all the columns except the Explanation columns. (This divides the information of the old accounting period from that of the new period.)

5. On the side that originally had the larger amount, write the starting date of the new accounting period (including the year) in the Date column. Enter the word *Balance* in the Explanation column, and put a check mark (✓) or dash (—) in the Posting Reference column (again, to show that this is not a journalized item). Enter the balance in the money column. Be sure to bring down the account balance (the amount recorded in step 1), not the total of the columns.

As a result of this balancing procedure, students should conclude that each permanent account (assets, liabilities, and owner's equity) begins the new accounting period with a single amount—its balance. In addition, students should conclude that balancing is not necessary for permanent accounts that have only one entry.

One other set of guidelines must be presented for handling temporary accounts in the standard ledger form. At the outset, emphasize the principle that all revenue and all expense accounts have been closed; therefore, there is no balance to be brought down below the double rule. Then present the following guidelines with appropriate illustrations as offered on the following page.

If a closed account has two or more entries on either side of the account (as illustrated in Figure 15.3), draw a single rule across both money columns, total the columns, and then draw a double rule across all columns except the Explanation column.

			Sales				**Account No. 401**	
DATE	EXPLANATION	POST. REF.	DEBIT	DATE	EXPLANATION	POST. REF.	CREDIT	
19—				*19—*				
Oct. 31	*To R & E Summary*	J2	3,000 00	*Oct.* 28	. . . .	J1	*1,600 00*	
				29	. . . .	J1	*1,400 00*	
							3,000 00	
			3,000 00				*3,000 00*	

Figure 15.3 One debit. Several credits. Zero balance.

If a closed account has only one debit and one credit (as illustrated in Figure 15.4), draw a double rule across all columns except the Explanation column.

			Salaries Expense				**Account No. 502**	
DATE	EXPLANATION	POST. REF.	DEBIT	DATE	EXPLANATION	POST. REF.	CREDIT	
19—				*19—*				
Oct. 30	. . . .	J2	1,550 00	*Oct.* 31	*To R & E Summary*	J2	1,550 00	

Figure 15.4 One debit. One credit. Zero balance.

Postclosing Trial Balance

What accounts remain open after the closing entries are made? This question leads to the presentation of the postclosing trial balance. Briefly, after the ledger is closed and, where necessary, the accounts are balanced and ruled, a trial balance of the ledger is taken. The purpose of this postclosing trial balance is to see if the ledger is in balance before the recording of transactions for the next fiscal period.

Point out that nothing appears on the postclosing trial balance except permanent accounts. In fact, the accounts listed on the postclosing trial balance and their balances will be identical to those appearing on the balance sheet. A student sometimes asks why the postclosing trial balance must be taken since it is just like the balance sheet. Such a question indicates that the student does not understand the function of the trial balance. The postclosing trial balance is prepared to see if the ledger is in balance after it has been closed. If the picture obtained is like that of the balance sheet, it is correct. The purpose of the postclosing trial balance is to check the accuracy of the entries made during the ledger-closing process.

Questions and Projects

1. One could make a closing entry for each account that is to be closed; the revenue, contra revenue, expense, and contra expense accounts might be closed as groups (compound entries); or they could all be closed as one long compound entry. Which method do you recommend and why?

2. What do you consider to be the most important idea to be put across when teaching the closing entries?

3. What title would you give to the Summary account? Give reasons for your answer.

4. Would you close the balance in the Summary account to the owner's drawing or capital account? Give reasons for your answer.

5. What are the differences in the items and amounts shown on the trial balance and on the postclosing trial balance?

6. When a standard ledger form is used, what is the difference in ruling an account and balancing an account? Illustrate the difference by showing examples. Which accounts are ruled, and which are balanced?

7. Prepare a lesson plan for the opening lesson on closing entries.

8. Explain how you would teach the closing of Merchandise Inventory for a firm that uses the periodic inventory method. Defend your method by presenting a rationale.

9. One teacher argues strongly for keeping the drawing account open at the end of the accounting period. Another teacher argues just as strongly for closing drawings into capital at the end of the accounting period. What is your opinion on this controversy?

10. How would you answer a student who raises the question of when are closing entries made?

11. Prepare performance goals for the topics of closing entries and the postclosing trial balance.

12. We have now completed the accounting cycle. List in order the steps in completing the cycle.

Case Problem

John Aleska likes to teach the closing entries by using a larger T account on the chalkboard with the various temporary accounts shown under it as follows:

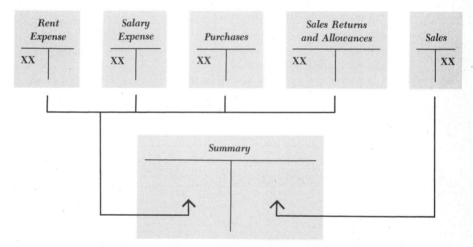

Helene Summons prefers to show these account balances in small T accounts with arrows showing where they would appear in the summary account, as follows:

Roger Barker prefers to go to the informal worksheet illustrated in Chapter 10 and work from there.

Describe your favorite method of introducing this topic and explain what you think is its chief value.

CHAPTER 16

Teaching Systems and Procedures

Suppose the following question were posed to a beginning class that has just completed the study of the first accounting cycle: "Now that you have learned the steps of an elementary accounting cycle, how would you define the term *accounting system?*"

Experienced teachers agree that students relate the idea of an accounting system to a number of activities required to produce a set of financial statements. Included in their descriptions of this accounting system would also be the forms and procedures for journalizing and posting transactions. While maintaining journals and ledgers and preparing financial statements are part of every accounting system, experienced teachers also agree that this explanation does not go far enough. Many successful teachers, therefore, introduce a more expanded meaning of an accounting system when subsequent accounting cycles are presented to the class.

There have been several attempts to define concisely what constitutes the systems and procedures that form the basis of the ideal accounting system for any business. It is a fact, however, that an accounting system must be tailored to meet the needs of the individual business. Consequently, to define an accounting system suitable for all businesses is simply impossible. What can be presented to students is a general description such as the following.

An *accounting system* may be defined as the method a business uses not only to process its data through the accounting cycle, but also to protect its cash and other assets from waste, fraud, and theft. This method includes forms, equipment, and procedures to process the accounting data and to provide the information needed by the business, the internal control measures necessary to safeguard valuable assets, and the people who perform these activities.

It is essential to observe that the above expanded version of an accounting system contains a number of necessary components. The forms include more than journals and ledgers; the equipment includes more than is used in a manual system; and the accounting system itself involves more job titles than accountants and accounting clerks. These and other components are explained in the following review of accounting fundamentals.

ACCOUNTING FUNDAMENTALS

1. Forms of an accounting system are the documents on which data are captured. Examples of forms are source documents (such as invoices and check stubs) on which original data about transactions are recorded, journals, and ledger accounts. Reports, such as income statements and balance sheets, are also frequently prepared on forms.
2. Many types of equipment are used in modern accounting systems. The equipment used may consist of devices and machines such as pens, file cabinets, adding machines, cash registers, one-write boards, and computers.
3. A procedure is a series of operations or steps that must be performed to complete a task. For example, the procedure for proving petty cash consists of all the steps that are followed in completing the petty cash book, counting the money in the petty cash fund, and comparing the amount on hand with the balance of petty cash recorded in the petty cash book.
4. Every accounting system must contain adequate internal control measures to ensure that assets belonging to the business are received when ordered, protected while in the custody of the business, and used only for business purposes.
5. Internal controls are not designed primarily to detect errors, but rather to reduce the opportunity for errors or dishonesty to occur.
6. A fundamental internal control principle for safeguarding assets is to separate the function of handling the asset from the function of recording the asset, and to cross-check one against the other according to planned routines.
7. The most important components of an accounting system are the people who make the system work. An accounting system can function efficiently only if the people who are involved in it perform their duties carefully and accurately.
8. Accounting systems vary, depending on the size of the business, the nature of its operations, and the need it has for particular information. No one accounting system is appropriate for every business. The forms, procedures, internal control measures, and equipment that are used should be tailored to the needs of the business.
9. Within an accounting system are a number of *subsystems,* which are methods of processing specific kinds of data and safeguarding assets for use in the main system. The number and types of subsystems a business uses depends mainly on the nature of its operations.

The last accounting fundamental poses an interesting question for the beginning teacher. How many subsystems should be included in a course of study aimed at introductory accounting students? In recent publications, authors have helped provide the answer by offering the study of the five major subsystems that have been designed to meet the varying needs of many businesses. These subsystems (often simply called *systems*) are for cash receipts, cash payments, purchases of merchandise for resale, sale of merchandise, and regular payroll. Suggested teaching methods will now be offered for two of these subsystems: a method for controlling petty cash and a method for controlling the regular payroll. Because the laws for treating payroll deductions and tax returns in Canada are different from those in the United States, separate procedures are discussed for each country. However, you should read both payroll sections, since several procedures apply to both countries.

Teaching a Subsystem for Controlling Petty Cash Expenditures

In this methods text, mention has been made several times of the importance of introducing a new concept in accounting through a spiral development. When the concept of a subsystem is being considered, teachers have learned that students respond well to an early study of the systems and procedures for controlling petty cash expenditures.

Teaching Steps

The following teaching steps may be considered in the development of the topic.

Review the Basic Internal Control Principles for Cash. Two important internal control measures should be reviewed before introducing the need for controlling petty cash expenditures. These are the daily deposit of all cash receipts intact in the business bank account and the issuance of a check for each cash payment.

Introduce the Need for a Petty Cash Subsystem. After emphasizing the two fundamental internal control principles for cash, discuss the impracticality of issuing checks for several small payments. From the discussion, students should conclude that the time and cost involved in verifying, approving, issuing, and recording checks for the payment of minor expenditures—such as postage due on incoming mail or a small freight bill on incoming goods—justify a separate method of controlling these petty items. The students are now ready to respond to a separate subsystem for treating such petty cash expenditures.

In presenting the need for a separate subsystem, some teachers use the role-playing technique. One student acts as the person delivering mail with the added responsibility of requesting postage due in the amount of 15 cents. A second student is assigned the role of preparing a check for the postage due and searching out two other students who are given the responsibility of cosigning all checks issued by the firm. Finally, another student is assigned the task of recording the transaction from the check stub to the journal. After the incident is acted out, the teacher discusses the time and cost involved in processing the check for 15 cents. From this role-playing, students easily conclude that a less costly system is needed to control petty cash expenditures.

Present an Overview of the Petty Cash Subsystem. Many teachers favor the technique of presenting a total view of the subsystem before the details of each section are studied. One modern method of analyzing the chief features of any subsystem is through a systems flowchart. As you will recall from Chapter 4, a systems flowchart provides a graphic presentation of the flow of data through an accounting system. A systems flowchart for a petty cash subsystem similar to the one illustrated in Figure 16.1 may be presented.

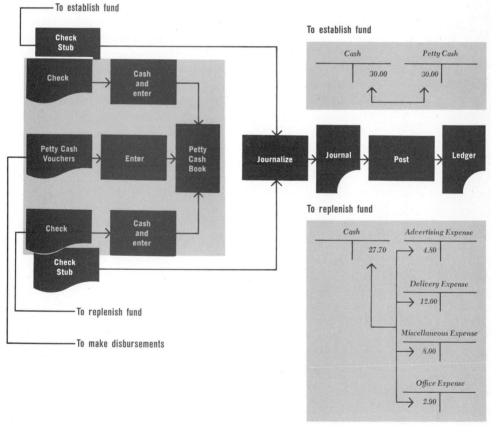

Figure 16.1

Although the systems flowchart can be presented on the chalkboard, many teachers prefer to use the overhead projector to show the three separate stages of the petty cash subsystem. Separate overlays or masks will ensure that the three stages of the systems flowchart are presented in their logical sequence: (1) the flow of information to establish the fund, (2) the flow to make disbursements, and (3) the flow to replenish the fund.

Some teachers argue that the introduction of such a systems flowchart should be delayed until the individual aspects of the subsystem are treated. Other teachers, however, argue in favor of presenting the total view both at the beginning and at the end when, in summary, the individual steps are reemphasized. Regardless of the timing, teachers agree that the use of a systems flowchart for presenting a petty cash subsystem offers the following advantages:

1. The three separate stages of the subsystem can easily be interpreted.
2. The internal control principle of dividing the responsibility can easily be demonstrated. The person assigned the responsibility of handling the cash (the petty cashier) is separated from the person assigned the accounting function of recording the cash transaction. To emphasize this point, some teachers show a separate color for those activities related only to the petty cashier's responsibilities.
3. The accounting analysis of establishing and replenishing the fund are clearly distinguished. In particular, the point can be made that the Petty Cash account does not change once the fund is established. .
4. And finally, the systems flowchart can demonstrate clearly how the fund is controlled through an earlier principle of issuing checks for all cash payments. In this case, however, checks are issued only to establish (or to increase) and replenish the fund.

Teach the Details of the Subsystem. After an overview of the subsystem, present the details of each individual part of the subsystem. For example, a discussion can occur about exactly how a check is prepared to establish a petty cash fund for $30. Avoid the pitfall of supporting the answer that the check would be made payable to the order of Cash or Petty Cash. As you may know, such an order invites a blank endorsement; consequently, the finder of such a check, if it becomes lost, can endorse the negotiable instrument without question. A better control of cash could be shown by demonstrating on a blank form the name of the petty cashier as the payee, so that proof is obtained of the payee's endorsement.

Other Teaching Points

Several other details must be taught in conjunction with the first stage of establishing the fund. Explain that the amount of the petty cash fund is determined by management, and that this amount is some constant round number. As previously suggested, another important detail is that the check is issued to one individual employee—the petty cashier—who is appointed sole custodian of the fund. As the systems flowchart shows, the petty cashier cashes the check, obtains the amount in money currency, and enters the amount of the fund in the Petty Cash Book. Of course, it should be explained that the money currency must be kept in a locked petty cash box or drawer.

The Petty Cash Book

The use of a Petty Cash Book in a subsystem for petty cash often invites a heated methods controversy. Some teachers argue in favor of presenting the Petty Cash Book as an important part of the subsystem. Other teachers, however, argue just as strongly that a book is not required; what is more important are the vouchers to account for each expenditure of petty cash. From actual business practice, it would appear that both views are correct; therefore, the best solution may be to acknowledge both practices.

When a Petty Cash Book is presented as part of the subsystem, it is important to use an illustration to demonstrate that the Book becomes a convenient record of entries only for the use of the petty cashier. Make sure students understand that the Petty Cash Book is not the accounting journal. This point can easily be clarified by directing their attention to the systems flowchart, which suggests that the person who handles the asset—the petty cashier—must not be the same person who makes the accounting entry to establish the fund; consequently, a second person—the accounting clerk—will record the accounting entry in the journal.

A final teaching point is essential in conjunction with the establishment of the fund. As the systems flowchart shows, the effect of recording the accounting entry to establish the fund is to create a current asset called Petty Cash; the balance of this account generally never changes. It should be explained, however, that two changes may occur: (1) where the total of the fund must be increased at some future time, a second check is issued to record the extra amount and (2) where the fund must be closed, the amount is deposited in the business bank account, and the accounting records show a reversing entry to debit Cash and credit Petty Cash.

Making Petty Cash Disbursements

In presenting the details of the second part of the subsystem, it is important to emphasize again that individual cash expenditures do not go through the accounting records. As the flowchart clearly shows, petty cash vouchers must be issued for all disbursements, and a record of these vouchers is made in the Petty Cash Book.

At this point, present an example of a petty cash voucher similar to the one illustrated in Figure 16.2.

The importance of internal control over these vouchers should be explained as the illustration is analyzed. Notice in the example that the voucher is prenumbered and that two signatures appear. One signature identifies the person who received the petty cash; therefore, the petty cash voucher is in fact a petty cash receipt. The other signature identifies the person who approved the disbursement of the petty cash. Since the voucher

No. 1   Amount $...1.$\frac{50}{100}$...............

PETTY CASH VOUCHER

Date ..Jan. 3, 19.—..........

Paid to...Weekly Press...............................

For...Advertisement in January 10 issue...

Charge to .....Advertising Expense.....................

OFFICE SERVICE CENTER
Approved by   Received by

..Roy Bell..............   ..John Larsen...............

Figure 16.2

is prenumbered and contains two signatures, it naturally follows that the voucher becomes the most important control document in the subsystem. The students must learn the internal control principle that, at any time, the total of petty cash payments approved on the vouchers and the remaining cash in the petty cash box must equal the established amount of the fund; consequently, as each payment is made an approved voucher must be placed in the petty cash box or drawer. In effect, the petty cashier is required to substitute the receipted and approved voucher for the cash disbursed. As the name suggests, the document "vouches" (gives evidence) for the petty cash disbursement.

When a Petty Cash Book forms part of the subsystem, explain and demonstrate how each voucher is recorded. It is important to emphasize that all voucher numbers must be accounted for; consequently, all spoiled vouchers must be kept on file.

Replenishing the Petty Cash Fund

The details of the final stage of this subsystem are often overlooked by some teachers. Students forget such important details as providing a proof of petty cash prior to the replenishment; summarizing the expenditures on a Petty Cash Requisition; and totaling, balancing, and ruling off the Petty Cash Book for the petty cash period. In addition students must be reminded that the Petty Cash account is not affected by the transaction to replenish the fund. Once again, a good technique to effect a better understanding of the correct journal entry is to return to the systems flowchart. From the flowchart, students should conclude that the Cash account must be affected since a check has been issued to replenish the fund. And, finally, students must be shown how to record the balance of the petty cash and the replenishment in order to begin the next petty cash period. A complete illustration as shown in Figure 16.3 may be used to offer this important explanation.

PETTY CASH BOOK — Page 1

Petty Cash Fund: Received	Petty Cash Fund: Paid Out	Date	Explanation	Voucher No.	Adv. Expense	Delivery Expense	Misc. Expense	Other Items: Account	Other Items: Amount
30 00		19— Jan. 2	Establish fund, Check 26	—					
	1 50	3	Ad in Weekly Press	1	1 50				
	1 35	4	Adding machine tapes	2				Office Expense	1 35
	3 75	5	Merchants Express	3		3 75			
	8 00	7	Window washing	4			8 00		
	1 55	8	Envelopes	5				Office Expense	1 55
	3 55	9	Merchants Express	6		3 55			
	3 30	12	Ad in Weekly Press	7	3 30				
	4 70	15	Valley Messengers	8		4 70			
30 00	27 70		Totals	—	4 80	12 00	8 00		2 90
	2 30	15	Cash on hand	—					
30 00	30 00								
2 30		Jan. 15	Cash on hand	—					
27 70		15	Replenish fund, Check 31	—					

Figure 16.3

Provide a Review of the Subsystem

After several reinforcement problems have been given to the students on the individual aspects of the subsystem, successful teachers agree that a review of the three stages must be given. One effective way to provide this review is to use the systems flowchart illustrated earlier. As part of this final review, you can introduce the term *Imprest System.* Briefly, this concept is easily understood when an analysis of the Petty Cash account is reviewed. Correctly analyzed, the Petty Cash account is a current asset. On a balance sheet, this current asset would appear immediately after Cash because the petty cash fund is a fixed amount of cash that can be redeposited at any time in the bank account. Since this fixed sum has been loaned or set aside from the regular cash in the bank, accountants have called this system of lending money the Imprest System of Petty Cash. From a cash control viewpoint, it is important to emphasize that this imprest system is controlled both by a check payment to create the fund and a check payment to replenish the fund.

Teaching Income Taxes and Payroll Records in the United States

The study of income taxes and payroll generally holds greater interest for most students than any other topic in accounting. Many class members are already working and filing tax returns, and the others will soon be doing so. In presenting these topics, teachers usually follow this sequence: (1) preparation of the individual income tax return, (2) preparation of the payroll, and (3) preparation of payroll taxes.

Preparing Individual Income Tax Returns

Intelligent citizenship requires an understanding of the basic concepts of income taxes, and there is no better opportunity in the high school for providing this understanding than that presented in accounting classes. Introduce the tax unit late in the first semester or early in the second semester. At this time, newspapers carry informational articles intended to aid the taxpayer, employees usually have received copies of their W-2 forms, and there is still sufficient time to cover the topic before the returns have to be filed.

One of the best sources of material on the federal income tax is the *Teacher's Kit on Teaching Federal Income Taxes,* distributed free of charge by the Internal Revenue Service and available from the local District Director of Internal Revenue. The kit consists of the following material:

1. Teacher's handbook.
2. Instructions for preparing Form 1040.
3. Transparency masters of Form 1040.
4. Students' handbooks.

The material in the kit follows the case-problem approach. This approach can be used to great effect to focus students' attention on fundamental questions, thus avoiding time-consuming involvement in their personal tax problems. (There is always the temptation to digress from the discussion to answer individual questions; however, only those teachers thoroughly familiar with income tax regulations should undertake passing judgment on personal tax problems.) Display a transparency of Form 1040—prepared from the master supplied in the kit—on the overhead projector. Distribute the students' handbooks, and fill in the entries on the projected form as students complete the forms at their desks. Follow this with a series of problems that relate to a specific part of the return—medical expenses, allowable deductions, use of tax tables, and so on.

STATE AND LOCAL INCOME TAXES. In those areas where state or local taxes are also levied on individuals, the treatment of federal income tax reporting should be followed by a similar discussion of state and local tax forms. In many instances, instructional materials are available from the state and local agencies; in other cases, instructional material will have to be created. In either event, the presentation should be a similar but briefer version of the one given for federal taxes.

SOCIAL SECURITY TAXES. Many teachers briefly survey social security taxes in conjunction with their development of income tax reporting. A teaching kit similar to the one on income taxes is available from the Social Security Administration or from local social security offices. The kit, entitled *Teaching Aids on Social Security,* contains the following:

1. Charts explaining how social security operates.
2. Problem sheets for student use.
3. Pamphlets on old-age and survivors insurance.
4. Forms used to establish and maintain records.

Local newspapers, radio and television broadcasts, and magazines are helpful sources of information on both social security and income taxes.

Preparing the Payroll

In developing a presentation on preparing the payroll, teachers generally agree on this sequence of topics: (1) introducing the need for a payroll subsystem, (2) timekeeping and computing earnings, (3) deductions from gross earnings, and (4) recording the payroll.

INTRODUCING THE NEED FOR A PAYROLL SUBSYSTEM. Students more clearly understand the need for a payroll subsystem when these points are made:

1. In profit-seeking enterprises, employees are hired to generate or support revenue-making activities. Management pays its employees an agreed salary or wage for a certain pay period. Therefore, a company's payroll will result in large cash payments on a regular basis.
2. Every employer is required by law to withhold from wages and salaries amounts for their employees' federal income taxes, social security taxes, state and local taxes where applicable, and unemployment or disability taxes where applicable. These deductions also result in a regular outflow of cash to the various governments.
3. Federal and some state laws require that employers maintain records for all salaries and wages paid to their employees, as well as for all deductions made from employees' pay.
4. Federal and state laws also require employers to provide employees with a summary of their annual salaries and wages on a statement, Form W-2, which is used when submitting individual tax returns.

By reacting to these four points and others that may be made in the discussion, students should conclude that an efficient payroll accounting subsystem must be organized not only to control the various payroll payments, but also to maintain adequate payroll records as required by law. Now introduce the idea that an efficient payroll subsystem would include procedures for timekeeping and computing gross earnings; calculating deductions from gross earnings; recording the payroll; maintaining payroll records; and disbursing payments to employees, governments, and other agencies.

TIMEKEEPING AND COMPUTING EARNINGS. Several important points should be made when discussing timekeeping and computing gross earnings. These can be summarized as follows:

1. Begin the study of payroll accounting by familiarizing students with the law that requires all employees to have a social security number before employers can process the payroll for them. Also discuss Form W-2 and the employer's responsibility for its completion.
2. Discuss the various salary or wage plans that will be used to determine an employee's gross earnings. Among these plans are the hourly-rate plan, the salary plan, the commission plan, the salary-commission plan, and the piece-rate plan.
3. Briefly discuss the factors that affect the employee's hours of work and wages. These factors include the agreement between the employer and the employee, state and federal labor department regulations, and union regulations where applicable.

After these points have been treated, proceed to demonstrate the computation of gross earnings for hourly-rated employees, for salaried employees, and for other employees. Although this demonstration will be performed manually, remember to stress the fact that under a computer method of processing the payroll, the various calculations would be performed by the program stored in the computer.

DEDUCTIONS FROM GROSS EARNINGS. Many students have difficulty correctly interpreting each payroll deduction. The following suggestions may help overcome some of these problems.

Explain and assign an order of priority to each type or class of authorized deduction. Generally the order of priority is (*a*) deductions required by law, (*b*) deductions required by collective bargaining agreements, and (*c*) voluntary deductions authorized by the employee.

Obtain current federal, state, and local tax tables, and demonstrate how the tables are used to compute deductions. Similarly, use current social security tables to compute FICA taxes, copies of collective bargaining agreements to compute union deductions, and examples of voluntary employee contributions such as those made to the Red Cross and the United Way to compute voluntary deductions.

Once the various compulsory and voluntary deductions have been explained, have students calculate several examples of employee's net pay.

RECORDING THE PAYROLL. At this stage, students are ready to learn about the payroll records required by law and how to make the necessary journal entries to record the payroll. In general, this involves three steps: (1) preparing a payroll summary called *payroll register,* (2) preparing a summary of the details of each employee's earnings in an employee's individual earnings record, and (3) journalizing and posting the payroll so that the general ledger accounts affected by the payroll can be updated.

Teaching the Payroll Register. Perhaps the best way to present the concept of a payroll register is by analyzing one displayed on the chalkboard or overhead projector. In the analysis, point out the following:

1. In some accounting systems, a payroll register is prepared for each different payroll plan. Thus a separate hourly payroll register may be prepared to summarize payroll information for hourly-rated workers; and a separate salary payroll register may be used for salaried employees.
2. The design and format of payroll registers vary from company to company and with the method of processing the payroll. For example, a payroll register prepared manually is different from one prepared by computer.
3. All payroll registers, however, contain at least the names and identification numbers of the employees, details of the employees' gross earnings and deductions, and the calculation of the employees' net pay.

After the payroll register has been analyzed, demonstrate how the payroll is proved, emphasizing the control measure involved in proving the payroll register before payment is made to employees and the journal entries are made.

Teaching the Employee's Individual Earnings Record. After the payroll register is prepared and proved, details of each employee's earnings are posted to the employee's individual earnings record. Emphasize the following points:

1. The record provides for each employee a full year's summary of pay periods, gross earnings, deductions, and net pay.
2. It serves as a basis for preparing Form W-2.
3. It is used by the employer to determine when an employee has reached the point of maximum contributions to FICA.
4. The Earnings, Deductions, and Net Pay columns are in the same order as they appear on the payroll register. In some designs, an additional column is provided for accumulated earnings.

Journalizing and Posting the Payroll. When the totals of the payroll register have been proved, the payroll data is ready to be recorded and posted to appropriate general ledger accounts. In some systems, the totals of each individual payroll register are posted directly to the general ledger. In this case, the payroll register becomes the journal, and it may be called a *payroll journal.* In other accounting systems, the totals of each payroll register are usually summarized in the form of a compound entry and recorded in the general journal. When recording, most teachers favor the use of two entries: the entry to record the dollar results of the payroll register and the entry to record the employer's additional expense resulting from each payroll.

Show the students that an analysis of the payroll register reveals that: (*a*) the total of gross earnings will be debited to an appropriate expense account such as Salaries Expense; (*b*) a liability account must be credited for each of the payroll deductions, because the amounts withheld do not belong to the employer; and (c) the total net pay must be credited to an appropriate liability account such as Salaries Payable. After the students have analyzed the payroll register totals, a compound journal such as the following may be demonstrated:

Salaries Expense	1,134.00	
Employee Income Taxes Payable		134.60
FICA Taxes Payable		66.34
Group Insurance Payable		18.00
Union Dues Payable		10.00
Salaries Payable		905.06
April 28 payroll.		

When demonstrating how to record the employer's additional payroll expense, review the employer's legal obligations to contribute to social security and to federal and state unemployment programs. An account called Payroll Taxes Expense is used to record the total debit of the various additional payroll expenses, and separate liability accounts are used to record the credits that must be eventually paid out. Show that the appropriate compound journal entry appears as follows:

Payroll Taxes Expense	102.63	
FICA Taxes Payable		66.34
Federal Unemployment Taxes Payable		5.67
State Unemployment Taxes Payable		30.62
Employer's taxes on April 28 payroll.		

Preparing Payroll Tax Returns

Federal and state governments have set up time schedules for all employers to report and pay payroll taxes. Demonstrate and explain each of the following forms used to forward these taxes:

1. Federal Tax Deposit (Form 501)
2. Employer's Quarterly Federal Tax Return (Form 941)
3. Transmittal of Income and Tax Statements (Form W-3)
4. Employer's Annual Federal Unemployment Tax Return (Form 940)

Where appropriate, also discuss state and local forms that must be completed by the employer.

Teaching Income Taxes and Payroll Records in Canada

While many of the accounting concepts are similar in Canada and the United States, the laws for treating payroll deductions and income tax returns are quite different; consequently, this special section is intended to highlight the Canadian treatment of teaching the important aspects of payroll procedures and income tax reporting.

In developing the topics for presenting a subsystem for controlling a payroll, Canadian teachers generally agree on this sequence: (1) introducing the need for a payroll subsystem, (2) timekeeping and computing earnings, (3) deductions from gross earnings, (4) recording the payroll, and (5) controlling payroll payments. Since many of the aspects for understanding the individual income tax are treated in the topics for payroll accounting, many teachers agree that a project on preparing an individual income tax return would logically follow the teaching of the subsystem for payroll.

Introducing the Need for a Payroll Subsystem

Teachers will find little difficulty in presenting the need for a payroll subsystem when these points are communicated to a beginning accounting class:

1. In profit-seeking enterprises, employees are hired to generate or support revenue-making activities. In the end, management rewards its employees by paying them an agreed salary or wage for a certain pay period. It is evident, therefore, that a company's payroll will result in large cash payments on a regular basis.
2. Every business that employs persons under a contract of service is required by Canadian law to deduct from wages and salaries premiums for unemployment insurance, contributions to the Canada Pension Plan, withholdings for individual income tax, and, in most provinces, the premium for the Provincial Health Insurance Plan. These payroll deductions will result in a regular outflow of cash to the government or governments.
3. By law and by provincial statutes, employers are required to maintain records for all salaries and wages paid to their employees, as well as for all deductions that are made from their employees' pay.
4. By law, employers are required to provide all employees with a summary of their annual remuneration paid and annual deductions on a tax slip called *T-4* for use in submitting an individual tax return.

By reacting to these four points and others that may be offered in the discussion, students should conclude that an efficient payroll accounting subsystem must be organized not only to control the various payroll payments, but also to maintain adequate payroll records as required by law. Introduce the idea that an efficient payroll subsystem would include procedures for timekeeping and computing gross earnings; calculating deductions from gross earnings; recording the payroll; maintaining payroll records; and disbursing the various cash payments to employees, governments, and other agencies. Before each of these activities is treated, it is worth mentioning that in a small business, these payroll functions are usually performed by one person—an accounting clerk. In larger firms, however, management will organize a separate payroll department or office to ensure that a proper division of responsibility occurs among the various payroll functions. Hence, a separate timekeeping function may be organized to be responsible for keeping all time records; a payroll accounting section may be organized to compute and prepare the payroll and maintain all payroll records; and a separate paymaster's function may be created to disburse the payroll.

TEACHING TIMEKEEPING AND COMPUTING EARNINGS. Several important aspects should be considered in lesson plans for the effective teaching of timekeeping and computing earnings. These can be summarized as follows.

It is useful and interesting to students to begin their study of payroll accounting with a basic view of hiring procedures for any profit-seeking enterprise. Here, you may present the function of a personnel department, distinguish between a contract *of* service and a contract *for* service, indicate the responsibility of the employee to acquire a social insurance number, and stress that the employer is responsible for having the new employee complete a tax form called *TD1* (an authorization form to deduct the correct rate of income tax). Also emphasize that all employees are required by Canadian law to have a social insurance number before an employer can process any payroll for them.

Another important topic here is to discuss the common salary or wage plans that will determine the gross earnings of the employee. Through class discussion, students can contribute their personal experience by offering the hourly-rate plan, the salary plan, the commission plan, the piece-rate plan, and combinations such as salary-commission plans.

A third important aspect is to discuss the factors that affect the employee's hours of work and wages. Three important factors should be identified: the contract of employment, the basic agreement between employer and union (where applicable), and the influence of government legislation. This last point is often overlooked by many teachers. Briefly, teachers should point out that, under the British North America Act (Canada's constitution), the power to enact labor legislation is largely the prerogative of the provinces. Consequently, laws exist in all provinces establishing maximum hours of work and minimum wages. In addition, the Canadian government has enacted similar legislation for employees hired to work for the national government. Since the details of the legislation vary with each province, contact the nearest department of labor to obtain the latest information on maximum hours and minimum wages.

Another important aspect is to acknowledge the reason for timekeeping. Briefly, an employer is required by law to keep a complete record of hours worked by each employee. In many firms, a separate timekeeper or timekeeping department is given the responsibility of preparing daily records of time worked by each employee. Of course, the type of record will vary with the type of employee wage plan. Two types may be offered to beginning accounting students: the familiar time card (often known as the *clock card*) for hourly-rated employees, and the attendance record for salaried personnel.

An important internal measure to control daily time records should be discussed with the class. In general, all employees paid under the hourly rate plan will be required to punch in and out on clock cards. To control the hours punched in and out on these cards, an accounting subsystem for payroll usually requires an independent record of this time. In most cases, the person in charge of the hourly-rated employees—the foreman—will be required to complete a daily report of time form. The foreman is required to show on this form the number of hours that each employee has worked, based upon personal observation of the employees at their jobs. When the foreman's report has been completed, a copy must be submitted to the payroll department, where it will be checked against the clock card records.

A similar internal check of the time worked by salaried employees will be required of heads of the various operating departments. For example, the sales manager may be required to sign the attendance time record kept for salaried personnel before the record is submitted for payroll processing. Where a piece-work basis of pay is in operation, the departmental report must show all details for remunerating employees on this payroll plan. Of course, such a piece-rate report must also be signed by a responsible department head before the form is forwarded to the payroll department.

Once the earlier points have been treated, demonstrate the computation of gross earnings for hourly rated employees, for salaried employees, and for other employees. Although this demonstration is usually done manually, it is important to acknowledge the fact that under a computer method of processing the payroll, the various calculations to arrive at the total gross earnings of each employee would be performed by the program stored within the computer.

TEACHING DEDUCTIONS FROM GROSS EARNINGS. Experienced teachers have reported that the area of teaching deductions from gross earnings provides the greatest student learning difficulty. Although the concept of take-home pay is easily understood, students will encounter difficulties in the correct interpretation of each payroll deduction. The following suggestions for several topics may help to overcome some of these difficulties.

Priority of Deductions. Construct a chart showing a priority schedule of payroll deductions. For large industrial plants, accountants usually assign an order of priority to each type or class of authorized deduction that may be made from an employee's pay. Such a plan would include three priorities: (1) those deductions required by law, (2) those deductions required by collective bargaining agreements, and (3) those voluntary deductions authorized by the employee. Once the chart has been constructed, it can be used to teach the payroll deductions in the order listed in the priority schedule.

Unemployment Insurance. For the employee's contribution to unemployment insurance, obtain the latest information from the Unemployment Insurance Premium Tables, which are supplied by The Department of

National Revenue—Taxation. These tables are available each January from the nearest district taxation office. And for the subsequent accounting treatment of these contributions, it is important to teach that the employer, by law, must also contribute a premium to be calculated at 1.4 times the employee's premium.

Canada Pension Plan. For payroll deduction to the Canada Pension Plan (in Quebec, the Quebec Pension Plan), consult the latest tables, which are included in the booklet containing the tables for unemployment insurance contributions. Like the unemployment insurance contribution tables, the contribution tables for the Canada Pension Plan are revised each calendar year. And do not forget to mention that by law the employer is required to make a contribution *equal* to the contribution deducted from the employee. This fact will have an effect on the future journal entry to record the complete payroll.

Deduction for Company Pension Plan. Although a company pension plan may be shown in a priority chart under the voluntary class of deductions, it should be treated immediately after the Canada Pension Plan deduction so that students will understand how the amount of income tax withheld is calculated. Briefly, most company pension plans are registered pension plans under the Canadian Income Tax Act. When company pension plans are registered, they have the same effect on the employer as the Canada Pension Plan. Like contributions to the Canada Pension Plan, contributions to a registered company pension plan must be made by both employee and employer. The employer's share is an equal one and will be identified as an additional payroll expense when the subsequent journal entry is examined.

Federal and Provincial Income Tax Deductions. Many teachers will agree that the most difficult deduction to present is the withholding amount for federal and provincial income taxes. First, there is the problem of identifying the fact that an amount for income tax must be withheld not only for the federal government, but also for the provincial government. Second, there is the problem of interpreting the correct "Net Claim Code" on the employee's TD1 tax deduction form. Third, there is the problem of emphasizing that, by law, the contributions to unemployment insurance, Canada Pension Plan, and company registered pension plan are tax deductible. This fact simply means that these contributions must be subtracted from the employee's gross earnings *before* the income tax tables for withholding may be used. And finally, there is the problem of acquiring the latest tax deduction tables. Since tax tables vary from province to province, it is important to obtain the latest tables for your province from the nearest office of the Department of National Revenue—Taxation. A separate booklet of income tax tables is available for the asking each new calendar year.

Deduction for the Provincial Health Insurance Plan. At the time of writing, most Canadian provinces have legislated compulsory deductions to cover the payment of the premium for their respective provincial health insurance plan. Since the plan and the premium to be deducted will vary with each province, acquire the latest information from the nearest provincial office of the Department of Health and Welfare.

Garnishments and Government Demands on Employee's Earnings. Students have heard of the term *garnisheeing an employee's wages,* but they are generally uninformed of the way this court order works. Briefly, a garnishment is an order from the Small Claims Court in support of a creditor's claim to recover money owing. This court order is directed to the debtor's employer, who must retain a portion of the employee's wages each payday and surrender the withheld sum to the Court. When a government demand is introduced, students are quite surprised to learn that the Department of National Revenue may issue an order in writing known as a *tax demand,* which orders the employer to deduct a lump sum or designated payments in settlement of the employee's outstanding income tax arrears. In addition, demands from the Unemployment Insurance Commission may be made for withheld payments to recover an overpayment of unemployment insurance benefits.

Union Initiation Fees and Union Dues. For this area of payroll deductions, students can contribute some general information and perhaps even explain the basic concepts involved. Add to the students' knowledge by acquiring a copy of a basic agreement from a local firm or a local union representative and then reviewing some of the articles that will affect payroll accounting. In addition, explain that the employer is required to have a written authorization from the employee before making deductions for union initiation fees and regular union dues. The reason for this written authorization is to recognize the fact that deductions for union dues are not covered by law. However, as part of the basic agreement between the union and employer, all employees covered by the agreement are usually required, as a condition of employment, to sign an authorized statement for deduction of their union dues.

Voluntary Deductions. Students should be able to offer examples of employee voluntary deductions for such items as safety shoes, group life insurance, Canada Savings Bonds, donations to community services, and savings in a credit union.

Computation of Net Pay. Once the various compulsory and voluntary deductions have been treated, have students calculate several examples of the employee's net pay.

TEACHING THE RECORDING OF THE PAYROLL. At this stage in the development of payroll accounting, students are ready to learn about the payroll records required by law and how to make the necessary journal entries to record the payroll. In general, a complete recording of every payroll identifies at least three areas of study: (1) preparing a payroll summary known as the payroll register, (2) preparing a summary of the details of each employee's earnings in an employee's individual earnings record, and (3) journalizing and posting the payroll so that the general ledger accounts affected by the payroll can be updated.

Teaching the Payroll Register. Many teachers will agree that the ideal method of presenting the concept of a payroll register is through the analysis of an illustration reproduced on the chalkboard or on the overhead projector. Since the calculations of gross earnings and the various deductions have been previously examined, students should have little difficulty with the correct analysis of the various columns in a payroll register. Add to the students' knowledge by providing the following points:

1. In some accounting systems, a payroll register is prepared for each different payroll plan. Thus, a separate hourly payroll register may be prepared to summarize the payroll for hourly-rated employees, and a separate salary payroll register may be used to summarize a particular pay period for salaried employees.

2. The actual design and format of payroll registers will vary from one business to another and with the method of processing the payroll. For example, the preparation of the register by hand will require a forms design quite different from that of a payroll register prepared by a computer method.

3. Regardless of how the payroll register is prepared, every payroll register will contain at least the names and identification numbers of the employees, the details of the employees' gross earnings, the details of the employees' payroll deductions, and the calculation of the employees' net pay.

After the payroll register has been viewed and analyzed, take care to show how the payroll is proved. The proof of any payroll register is done by adding and subtracting the appropriate totals across the register. Although the register proof is acknowledged automatically with the use of computers, many teachers demonstrate how the proof may be done on an adding machine tape. In demonstrating the proof, emphasize the control measure that all payroll registers must be proved before payment is made to employees and before journal entries are made to record the dollar results of each payroll.

Teaching the Employee's Individual Earnings Record. After a payroll register is prepared and proved, the details of each employee's earnings should be posted to the employee's individual earnings record. Demonstrate this procedure by posting payroll data from the register to one employee's earnings record. From the illustration, emphasize the following points.

1. The individual earnings record provides for each employee in one record a full year's summary of pay periods, gross earnings, deductions, and net pay.

2. The record serves as a basis for preparing important tax slips so that the employee can complete an income tax return.

3. It helps the employer to tell when the employee's earnings have reached the maximum points of contributions to unemployment insurance and the Canada Pension Plan.

4. In actual practice, the form varies directly with the method of processing the record.

5. The individual earnings record for a given pay period must agree with the payroll register for the same period and with the employee's subsequent payroll statement issued on paying the employee.

6. The Earnings, Deductions, and Net Pay sections are in the same order as they appear on the payroll register. This order is maintained so that the amounts can be efficiently posted to the employee's individual earnings record. Under some methods of processing the payroll, this order is important because the payroll register and individual employee's earnings record are prepared in one writing.

7. In many forms, an additional column is usually shown in the earnings record that does not appear on the payroll register. This column is for accumulated earnings and provides a current total of the gross earnings, so that the payroll clerk can easily notice when an employee has earned the maximum amount for the Canada Pension Plan and for the year-end reporting of gross earnings. In some accounting systems, the Accumulated Earnings column may also be known as *Year-to-Date Earnings.*

Journalizing and Posting the Payroll. When the totals of the payroll register have been proved, the payroll data is ready to be recorded and posted to appropriate general ledger accounts. As stated in Chapter 8, the totals of each individual payroll register are posted directly to the general ledger in some accounting systems. In this case, the payroll register becomes the journal, and it may now be called a *payroll journal.* For many other accounting systems, the totals of each payroll register are usually summarized in the form of a compound entry and recorded in the general journal. To teach this important area, most teachers favor the use of the general journal to present two distinct classes of entries: the entry to record the dollar results of the payroll register and the entry to record the employer's additional expenses resulting from each payroll.

Before the general journal entry is shown, relate the totals of the payroll register as follows. First, the total of gross earnings is debited to an appropriate expense account such as Wages or Salaries Expense. Second, for each of the payroll deductions, an appropriate liability account is credited because the amounts withheld do not belong to the employer; they must be paid to the national government, provincial government, or insurance agency as the case may be. (It is helpful to remind students that the employer acts as the collecting agency for these parties. Until these amounts are paid, they must be treated as current liabilities on the books of the employer.) And, finally, the total of the Net Pay column is credited to an appropriate liability account such as Wages or Salaries Payable. After the students have analyzed the payroll register totals, a compound general journal entry may be demonstrated as in Figure 16.4.

Before recording the employer's additional payroll expenses, review the

Wages Expense	1,291.30	
Unemployment Insurance Payable		18.49
CPP Contributions Payable		20.92
Company Pension Plan Payable		64.56
Income Tax Deductions Payable		139.30
OHIP Payable		17.91
Group Insurance Payable		24.00
Wages Payable		1,006.12
To record the payroll of hourly-rated employees for the week ended June 30.		

Figure 16.4

legal obligations of the employer to contribute to the payroll. Students must remember that the employer is obliged to contribute 1.4 times the employee's share of unemployment insurance, an equal dollar amount to the employee's Canada Pension Plan, and an equal dollar amount to a company registered pension plan. These amounts contributed by the employer represent additional expenses resulting from the payroll and must be journalized and posted to appropriate general ledger accounts. In practice, an account called *Payroll Taxes Expense* is commonly used to record the total debit of the various employer's additional payroll expenses. Of course, separate liability accounts would be used to record the credits that must eventually be paid on behalf of unemployment insurance, the Canada Pension Plan, and the company registered pension plan. A second compound entry in the general journal would be demonstrated as follows:

Payroll Taxes Expense	111.36	
Unemployment Insurance Payable		25.88
CPP Contributions Payable		20.92
Company Pension Plan Payable		64.56
To record the employer's payroll taxes resulting from the hourly-rated payroll of the week ended June 30.		

TEACHING PAYROLL DISBURSEMENTS. The final topic in the development of a payroll accounting subsystem is the disbursement of the various current liabilities that have been recorded in appropriate general ledger accounts. Of course, these various liabilities must be discharged by a series of individual cash payments. One logical order to present these cash payments is as follows: (1) paying the employees; (2) paying the Unemployment Insurance premiums, Canada Pension Plan contributions, and employees' withholdings for income taxes; and (3) paying other amounts owing.

Paying the Employees. Students should have little difficulty in providing the basic analysis of discharging the liability Salaries or Wages Payable through a cash payment. Present a discussion of paying the employees in cash (money currency), by check, and by bank transfer. In addition, present the concept of using a special payroll bank account to clear issued payroll checks.

Return of U.I., C.P.P., and Income Taxes. This disbursement may cause some difficulty. This is the method prescribed by the national government. Briefly, under federal law, the amount of income tax withheld from employees' earnings, together with the employees' and employer's contributions to the Canada Pension Plan and the employees' and employer's Unemployment Insurance premiums, must be remitted on a special form called *Form PD7AR,* "Tax Deduction—Canada Pension Plan—Unemployment Insurance Remittance Return." A certified check or money order, payable to the Receiver General of Canada, must be mailed to the Taxation Data Centre, Ottawa, by the 15th day of the month following that in which payrolls are recorded. The cash payment must be analyzed in the form of a double entry as follows.

Unemployment Insurance Payable	116.94	
CPP Contributions Payable	113.36	
Income Tax Deductions Payable	449.25	
Cash		679.55
To record check issued to the		
Receiver General of Canada		
per Form PD7AR.		

After the remittance has been received, the Taxation Data Centre returns a receipt of payment and an additional blank remittance form to process the next month's returns.

Payment of Other Current Liabilities. The remaining current liabilities created by the recording of the payroll should cause few student difficulties. Examples would be the issuing of separate checks to pay the contributions to the company pension plan, the premium for the provincial health insurance plan, and premiums for other liabilities such as Group Insurance Payable and Union Dues Payable.

Teaching Materials

Canadian teachers are fortunate to have access to *Teaching Taxes,* a teacher's education kit written and published by the Information Services Branch, Revenue Canada, Taxation, 875 Heron Road, Ottawa, Canada K1A OL8. Briefly, the kit provides the latest income tax information and is available on request from the Information Services Branch. The kit covers seven teaching areas:

1. Teaching Taxes Questionnaire.
2. Introduction to Canadian Federal Income Tax.
3. The Personal Income Tax System with illustrations.
4. Individual Income Tax Return with illustrations and exercises.

309

5. Filing Your Tax Return (The Self-Employed) with illustrations and exercises.
6. The Source Deduction Function of the Employer with illustrations.
7. Income Tax Questions and Answers.

One of the features of the kit is the inclusion of transparency masters from which teachers can make overhead transparencies of the various tax slips and sections of the individual tax return.

Problems, Questions, and Projects

1. Is it possible to present a concise definition of an accounting system that would be suitable for every business? Explain your answer.

2. A teaching definition of an accounting system has been suggested in this chapter. What component of this definition is essential to the success of the accounting system? Explain your answer.

3. Name in sequence the subsystems you would include in a course of study aimed at beginning accounting students. Give reasons for your selection. Also explain why you would begin with the first subsystem named on your list.

4. As stated in the definition, an important component of every accounting system consists of the internal control measures necessary to safeguard assets. Make a list of the internal control measures that are essential for the teaching of the subsystems for (a) cash receipts, (b) cash payments, (c) purchases of merchandise for resale, (d) the sale of merchandise, and (e) the regular payroll.

5. Write the performance goals that you would use in relation to the teaching of the subsystem for controlling petty cash expenditures.

6. Discuss how you would introduce the need for a separate petty cash subsystem.

7. Prepare an overhead transparency of the systems flowchart for the petty cash subsystem illustrated in this unit. Organize your layout so that the three stages of the system are presented in their respective order. Also show by different colors the internal control principle of separating the function of handling the asset from the function of recording the asset.

8. One teacher argues in favor of the systems flowchart by praising its use as an overview of the subsystem before the procedures are studied in detail. Another teacher also agrees with the use of the systems flowchart, but insists that its use be restricted until after the final detail of information has been studied. What is your view on the correct timing in presenting a systems flowchart?

9. One teacher instructs students to make a check payable to the order of "Petty Cash." Do you agree with this procedure? Explain why or why not.

10. Would you include the use of a petty cash book in your teaching of the subsystem for petty cash? Explain your answer.

11. Why is a petty cash subsystem often called an *imprest system?*

12. Prepare a simple basic case problem to use when first introducing personal income taxes.

13. Prepare a basic problem for use as an assignment for a payroll problem based on eight employees' timecards and the appropriate deductions for each worker. Sketch the payroll register that would be needed to record your problem data.

14. Prepare a lesson plan for teaching personal income taxes or the payroll register.

15. List the various types of deductions that you feel should be covered in a first-year accounting course in the topic dealing with personal income taxes.

Case Problems

1. One teacher argues against the use of systems flowcharts in accounting instruction for the following reasons:
   a. The flow of data often proves to be too confusing for the students.
   b. The flowchart is of little help in understanding systems work in accounting.
   c. The symbols in the systems flowchart are too difficult to learn.
   d. Students do not have templates for drawing the symbols.
   e. No subsequent use can be made of the flowchart once it is presented.
   f. Flowcharting belongs in the study of data processing, not accounting.

Do you agree or disagree with each of the arguments presented? Give reasons for your answer.

2. An experienced teacher has expressed his feelings that his students have too much difficulty in understanding systems, procedures, and forms. They have enough trouble learning about the journals, ledgers, and adjustments. Therefore, he has told his department chairperson that, until he gets better students in his class, he wants to teach only the steps of the accounting cycle, starting with journalizing. Do you agree or disagree with this teacher's reasoning? Give reasons for your answer.

CHAPTER 17

Integrating Data Processing
With Accounting Applications

In Chapter 1, five important points were made concerning the relationship of accounting with data processing. These points are worth repeating.

1. Data processing, when applied to accounting, relates to the *how*—how transactions are recorded, how classified, and how summarized. Thus, data processing represents the method of processing financial information.

2. In practice, there is no single method of processing all accounting data. Evidence exists to prove that accounting data may be processed by manual, mechanical, or electronic (computer) methods.

3. In practice, there is a decided trend toward the utilization of the computer method to process accounting data.

4. In practice, accounting is regarded as a functional responsibility; that is, accounting is responsible for the traditional functions such as payroll, accounts receivable, accounts payable, and the general ledger.

5. Those working in the accounting function must have an exposure to data processing methods in order to create accounting source data, to control the input of this data, and to interpret the output of the processed data.

Few teachers will disagree with the statement that a knowledge of data processing methods is very much a part of the study of modern accounting. In recent years, teachers and authors of accounting texts have attempted to integrate data processing with accounting instruction. Evidence in the field, however, shows little consensus on how this integration should occur. It is appropriate in this chapter, therefore, to offer suggestions on how data processing can be integrated with accounting.

Introduce the Concept of the Data Processing Cycle

The data processing cycle involves four steps: (1) *origination* of data, (2) *input* of data, (3) *manipulation* of data, and (4) *output* of information.

The origination of data involves collecting the data that must be processed; as in the accounting cycle, the data must be obtained from source documents. Thus, in data processing and in accounting, emphasis must be placed on the study of business forms, which provide the data to be processed.

The collected data to be processed is called *input*. Before any data can be processed, it must be entered into the system. In the traditional accounting system, data is entered by recording it in a journal. In other systems, data is entered on punched cards, punched tape, or magnetic tape. The relationship is the same—the data is entered in the system. Traditionally, however, only the manual method of performing these operations was taught. Today, the other data processing methods must be integrated with the study of accounting in order that students comprehend the relationship between the theory of accounting and the processing of accounting data.

The information that results from the processing is called the *output* of the system. In accounting, output includes statements and reports, such as the balance sheet, income statement, schedule of accounts receivable, schedule of accounts payable, schedule of cost of goods sold, statement of owner's equity, and postclosing trial balance.

The relationship between the accounting cycle and the data processing cycle can be developed throughout the course. The data processing cycle can also be related to other procedures. For example, the trial balance can be prepared as shown in Figure 17.1.

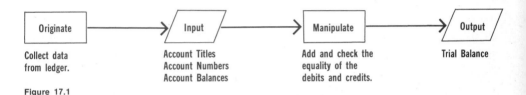

Originate	Input	Manipulate	Output
Collect data from ledger.	Account Titles Account Numbers Account Balances	Add and check the equality of the debits and credits.	Trial Balance

Figure 17.1

The four steps in the data processing cycle can also be used to process business data in order to obtain business information. Consider, for example, that the owner of a record store is trying to decide whether or not to increase the salary of one of the clerks. To help in arriving at a decision, the owner wants to know the total amount of sales the clerk made last week. The total amount of sales can be taught by following the steps shown in Figure 17.2.

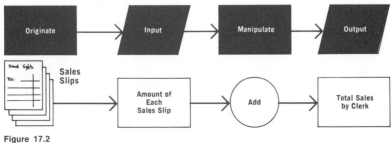

Figure 17.2

Teach the Accounting Before the Data Processing Method

Should accounting be taught before, after, or concurrently with data processing? This important question is often debated by teachers and curriculum planners. Notice that the issue does not question the validity of taking an introductory course in computer science before accounting. The real issue is to question whether any data processing device—pegboards, mechanical posting machines, or electronic computer—should be treated before the actual accounting information to be processed is taught. In our opinion, overwhelming evidence, supported at different educational levels, suggests that at least one accounting cycle of instruction be covered before a specific data processing method is introduced. Consider, for example, these extracts from several texts to support this view:

- "In this CompuGuide the problems have been written to supplement the first part of an introductory accounting text. The accounting cycle, inventory, interest, investment, and fixed assets accounting are among the financial problems of which the student must be aware as he applies his knowledge of accounting to the computerized world." (Wilbur F. Pillsbury, *Computer Augmented Accounting,* South-Western Publishing Co., Cincinnati.)

- "This book proceeds from the simple to the more complex applications including write-it-once accounting systems, punched-card accounting systems, and electronic data processing. Accounting principles should be taken concurrently or as a prerequisite." (Clarence B. Randall and Sally Weimer Burgly, *Systems and Procedures for Business Data Processing,* South-Western Publishing Co., Cincinnati.)

- "In the introductory course, this *Accounting Case* should be used after the study of the accounting cycle, special journals (including voucher register), subsidiary ledgers, and the perpetual inventory method." (Arthur W. Holmes et al., *Accounting Cases With Computer Adaptability,* Richard D. Irwin, Inc., Chicago.)

- "This book discusses the role of computers in the accounting process and the contribution of computer technology to the development of effective management-information systems. No previous background in computers is assumed, but a course in the fundamentals of accounting is presupposed." (David H. Li, *Accounting/Computers/Management Information Systems,* McGraw-Hill Book Co., New York.)

Teach the Concept of an Accounting Application

Some teachers prepare their students for the integration of data processing with accounting by introducing the idea of an accounting application during the study of the various accounting subsystems. In general, an accounting application may be described as the processing (manipulating) of a set of related input media to create (produce) a set of useful output media. Observe that the word *set* suggests more than one input medium and more than one output medium. Consider, for example, the technique of introducing the concept of a payroll accounting application for hourly-rated employees.

First, present the main components of a payroll subsystem in the traditional manner; that is, teach each topic separately but through a logical development. This method suggests that students study topics such as the computation of gross earnings, deductions from gross earnings, payroll records and procedures, and payroll tax returns without regard for how these areas are processed.

Next, introduce the idea that, under most data processing methods, it is possible to process the payroll register, the individual employee's earnings record, and the employee's pay check with attached pay statement all at the same time. In the language of accounting, the processing of such accounting data is acknowledged as an accounting application for payroll or, simply, a payroll application.

And finally, demonstrate how the payroll application is viewed by the steps learned earlier for the data processing cycle. Such a demonstration may be placed on the chalkboard or on an overhead transparency in a format similar to Figure 17.3.

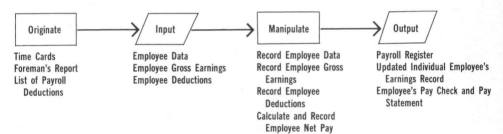

Figure 17.3 Data processing cycle for a payroll application.

Observe that the application does not single out any one particular data processing method. In fact, the payroll application is stated in such broad terms that it can be processed under any data processing method.

Some teachers will argue for the introduction of the application concept only at the time the formal study of data processing methods is introduced. At this time, it is common to acknowledge the application as a data processing application rather than an accounting application. Regardless of the terms used and the timing of such applications, the concept may be developed for other important accounting areas. In a first-year course, teachers will support applications for not only payroll, but also for accounts receivable, accounts payable, and for the general ledger.

315

Introduce Data Processing Methods Through a Spiral Development

When no previous introduction to data processing has occurred and, especially, when data processing methods are to be integrated with accounting applications, experienced teachers favor a spiral development to introduce four distinct methods of processing accounting data. Moving from the simple to the complex and from the known to the unknown, many teachers will first present manual data processing, then mechanical data processing and punched-card data processing, and finally, electronic data processing.

Manual Data Processing

This method has been the only one emphasized in the traditional accounting course. Recently, however, teachers have supported the introduction of business forms and manual devices that have been developed to improve the speed and accuracy of processing data.

Business forms play an important role in any accounting system. Forms are used to record data, to communicate data, and to store data. The forms should be designed to meet the specific needs of a business. Emphasize that the main function of business forms is to speed up work and reduce the possibility of error. Also ensure that accounting students learn the proper use of business forms and the way forms registers are used for internal control.

PEGBOARDS. In the traditional manual data processing method, a large amount of copying is required. In order to avoid copying, a pegboard (one-write board) is often used in small or medium-sized businesses. This commonly used device records accounting data simultaneously on several forms, as shown in Figure 17.4. Pegboards may be used to process accounting applications for payroll, accounts receivable, and accounts payable. In addition, manufacturers of pegboards have designed forms and special pegboards called *strip accounting* to process applications in manufacturing accounting and the general ledger. In the main, teachers have acquainted students with the pegboard form of data processing by presenting accounting applications for accounts receivable, accounts payable, and the payroll.

TABLES. Since manual computations are frequently made in manual data processing, tables should be introduced to teach the student how to read and use them—a technique that will assist students in performing manual operations. In addition, the use of school calculators and student-owned pocket calculators should be encouraged in order to make these computations.

EDGE-NOTCHED CARDS. In the presentation of manual data processing, do not overlook *edge-notched cards*. Briefly, edge-notched cards are convenient devices to use when sorting is required. They can be introduced as another way of processing, for example, installment sales. Through the study of an

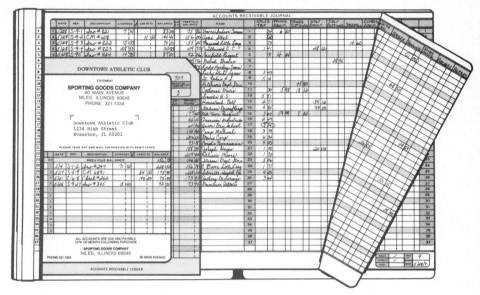

Figure 17.4 Processing accounts receivable on a pegboard.

entire application for accounts receivable, students can learn that edge-notched cards may be used for summarizing, as well as for recording and sorting. For example, monthly reports can be prepared by needle-sorting the cards, as shown in Figure 17.5, and by using an adding machine. Examples of such reports include a sales report by product, a sales report by sales personnel, and an aging report of accounts receivable.

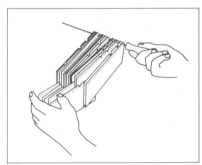

McBee Systems

Figure 17.5 Needle sorting of edge-notched cards.

A final point is worth considering when teaching manual data processing. In presenting the manual processing of accounts receivable and accounts payable, acknowledge the fact that many small firms take short cuts in journalizing and posting. As you will recall, suggestions for teaching

317

the journalizing of batch totals, for direct posting from source documents, for journalless accounting, and for ledgerless accounting were offered in Chapter 9.

Mechanical Data Processing

This method uses mechanical equipment to improve speed and accuracy. Some machines used are calculators, adding machines, cash registers, and accounting machines.

When using imprinting devices and automatic typewriters, students encounter the terms *constant data* and *variable data*. These terms, used in many areas of processing, should become familiar to them.

Accounting involves the arithmetical processes of addition, subtraction, multiplication, and division. The accounting student should not be required to perform all computations manually but should be given the opportunity to use adding machines or calculators for problem-solving exercises.

The cash register is a device commonly used in accounting systems. Accounting students should become acquainted not so much with the actual operation of the cash register as with the part the register plays in collecting data for accounting records. Cash proofs and detailed audit strips should be a part of any business student's vocabulary. Problems should be provided that permit the student to discover what role cash proofs and audit strips play in accounting work.

Accounting machines are now commonly used in small offices. These mechanical devices speed up and increase the accuracy of posting. Again, students should not only become acquainted with these devices but also learn how they apply the one-write technique to the processing of accounts receivable, accounts payable, and payroll.

Punched-Card Data Processing

In this method, equipment is used to perform the various operations by using data punched into cards. *What* a machine does is the important point, not *how*. The introduction to punched-card equipment, therefore, should be based on what a punched-card machine can do to speed up accounting work.

The application of punched-card data processing to accounting problems can be illustrated in several ways. The method for updating accounts receivable can be presented by describing the machines used and the form of the cards used to carry the data. Other examples can be procedures for sales and inventory control. By using a few punched cards, you can illustrate the movement of data through the machines.

In presenting an overview of data processing methods, some teachers have eliminated punched-card data processing for two chief reasons:

There is a decided trend in the direction of computers to process accounting data. Teachers point to the fact that many unit-record machines have been replaced by computer installations.

The features of the punched card and the unit-record principle can easily be introduced in the study of a computer system when input and output media and input and output devices are presented.

On the other hand, some teachers support the teaching of a complete topic on punched-card data processing for these reasons:

1. The punched card is still a popular input medium in the processing of accounting data.
2. The unit-record principle is best understood when studied under the punched-card method of data processing.
3. Punched card machines are still in evidence in spite of a decided trend toward the computerization of accounting applications.
4. The study of punched-card data processing supports the spiral development technique of presenting data processing methods.
5. The study of punched-card data processing leads easily to the presentation of an area often overlooked—the study of common language media such as punched tape and edge-punched cards.

The solution to the above controversy would be for teachers to make a continuing study of data processing trends in their business communities as well as to follow trends in current writings.

Electronic Data Processing

In the language of data processing methods, electronic data processing is computer data processing. Some teachers will argue that, in addition to manual methods, the only other method that should be integrated with the study of accounting applications is the use of the computer.

While all teachers agree that an exposure to the computer must be included in the presentation of data processing methods, not all agree on what should be included in this exposure. Two points of view are usually argued. Some teachers support the presentation of computer concepts only; that is, the concepts of how a computer functions are presented without the students' actually writing computer programs. Other teachers argue that, in addition to the presentation of computer concepts, students must be trained to write a program in one of the high-level computer languages such as FORTRAN or COBOL.

As stated earlier, the skill to write a successful program, especially in a high-level computer language, is best acquired in a separate computer course. In short, there is just not enough time in an introductory or subsequent accounting course to teach the skill of computer programming. However, there is time in one accounting course to present enough of an exposure so that students can understand how the common accounting applications are processed through a computer method. The following teaching suggestions are offered to guide this exposure. **319**

PRESENT THE ADVANTAGES OF ELECTRONIC DATA PROCESSING. If a spiral development of manual, mechanical, and punched-card data processing has been presented previously, the students' interest can be captured by discussing several distinct advantages of the computer over the other methods. Such a presentation need not be technical and should include speed, communication, storage, program, branching and looping, and the representation of data. After a discussion of these advantages, students should easily conclude that the most superior method of data processing is the computer method.

TEACH THE COMPONENTS OF A COMPUTER SYSTEM. A computer system consists of three essential pieces of equipment: an input device, a central processor, and an output device. Before a study is made of each of these pieces of equipment, it is important to emphasize the main principle of computer data processing. In simple terms, once the data and instructions have been entered into the computer system, the equipment processes the data through the input, manipulation, and output steps of the data processing cycle without human intervention. The four steps of the data processing cycle may be related to the computer method as follows. First, the origination step involves collecting the data. This step usually does not directly involve the computer. In the second or input step, the data to be processed is entered into the computer through an input device. The third step, manipulation, is performed by a central processor. This part of the computer system is made up of three units:

1. The storage unit (memory) receives and stores the program, the input data, and the results of partially processed data.
2. The arithmetic/logic unit performs computations according to the program. It can also compare data and make a decision as to the next procedure to be performed.
3. The control unit interprets the instructions of the program and directs and coordinates all units.

The fourth and final step—the output step—is performed by an output device, which reports the information obtained from the data that has been processed.

PRESENT A FLOWCHART OF A COMPUTER SYSTEM. Once students have learned the main components of a computer system, they are ready to learn how a computer functions, without becoming involved with "hardware" or "software" explanations. One way to simplify the explanation of how a computer functions is through the presentation of a flowchart showing the flow of data and instructions through a computer system. A flowchart, such as Figure 17.6, may be presented on the chalkboard or overhead.

From the illustration, students must conclude that every computer system involves two flows, the flow of data and the flow of instructions. Of course, any simple example may be used to help students distinguish between the data and the instructions. Once students have a grasp of the main components and the flow of data and instructions in a computer

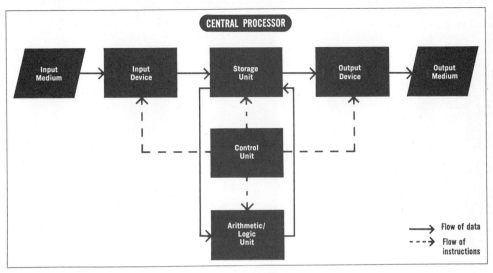

Figure 17.6

system, they are ready to learn more about the "hardware" and "software" aspects of electronic data processing.

PRESENT A SIMPLIFIED VERSION OF THE HARDWARE ASPECTS. The hardware or equipment aspects of the computer system are best presented in relation to the three main components presented earlier.

Input Devices. Emphasize the fact that many different devices are used to provide input data to computers. One effective way to present the various input devices is to illustrate both the input device and its related input medium. For example, the familiar punched-card reader may be illustrated on an overhead or on slides together with the related input medium, the punched card. Other input devices that should be illustrated and discussed are the punched-tape reader, the magnetic-tape unit, the magnetic character reader, the optical scanner, the console typewriter, and such devices as telecommunication devices, keyboard terminals, transaction recorders, magnetic-disk units, and magnetic-card units.

The Central Processor. The heart of any computer system is the central processor, commonly called the Central Processing Unit (CPU). Illustrations may be presented to show that the three units of the CPU (storage unit, arithmetic/logic unit, control unit) may be housed in one cabinet, or they may be separate pieces of equipment connected by a cable. Each unit should be presented to offer a simplified understanding of its main function.

Output Devices. As the word suggests, the output of a computer is the result of processing the input. Students must conclude that a computer system may have several output devices, so that the information may be produced in a form that people can read or in a machine language that can be retained for future processing. Since an output medium is characteristic

321

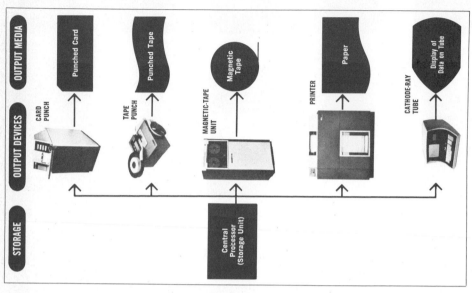

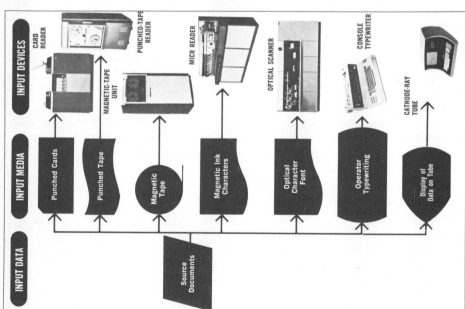

Figure 17.7

of every output device, present illustrations and a discussion of both the output device and its related medium. For example, one common output device is the printer, which has as its related output medium the continuous paper forms to produce the hard copy of the output. Other common output devices that should be presented are the console typewriter, the card punch, the cathode-ray tube display, the magnetic-tape unit, and the punched-tape unit.

One teacher presents a chart, such as the one in Figure 17.7, at the end of the hardware discussion. The chart summarizes the relationships between the various input media and input devices, and between the various output devices and output media.

Another teacher uses the same format but assigns students the responsibility of presenting a bulletin-board display. In the display, students are asked to collect pictures of various input and output devices, the central processor, and actual samples of various input and output media.

PRESENT A SIMPLIFIED VERSION OF THE SOFTWARE ASPECTS. In the earlier presentation of how a computer functions, it was emphasized that the computer operates because a series of detailed instructions have been placed within the central processor. At this stage of developing computer concepts, the students are ready to learn more about these detailed instructions. In the language of electronic data processing, the writing of these detailed instructions is called *programming* the computer or, more technically, developing the software for the computer system. In order to expose students to programming concepts without involving them in the actual writing of programs in a high-level computer language, follow these steps.

1. Introduce the term *program* to relate to the series of detailed instructions that tells the computer in a step-by-step sequence exactly what to do and when to do it.
2. Emphasize that a separate program must be prepared for each processing job. Students will react quickly to the idea that a separate program would be prepared for each accounting application to be processed through the computer.
3. Acknowledge the position of programmer and the six basic activities commonly associated with programming: analyzing the problem, planning the program, coding the instructions, compiling the program, testing the program, and documenting the program.
4. Develop each of the six basic activities of a programmer.

Steps in Programming. The first step in programming a particular application presents no teaching problem. Students readily accept the principle that before the operations necessary to complete the job can be planned, the programmer must define the problem. This definition involves determining where the input data can be obtained and what must be done to it to provide the output required.

323

The second activity, planning the program, does offer a teaching consideration because students generally find it difficult to think through the step-by-step sequence of operations required to solve the problem. Since the steps to be followed are often difficult to put into words, teachers agree that the best approach is to train students to use the technique of the programmer, that is, to outline the specific operations in a program, or procedure, flowchart. The interest and confidence of students can be gained by reviewing the problem to be solved before a flowchart is attempted. For example, first review a payroll procedure for the printing of a payroll check for hourly-rated employees; then demonstrate and explain a program flowchart through an illustration such as the one shown in Figure 17.8.

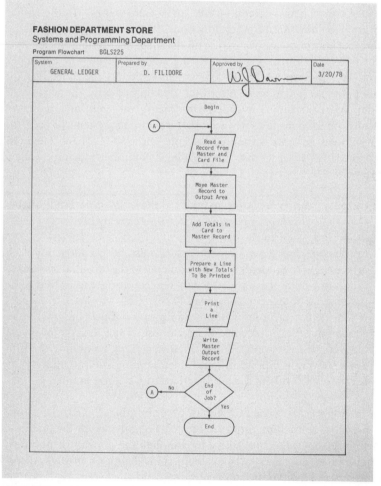

Figure 17.8

Teachers agree that the third activity, coding the instructions, generates the greatest student-learning problem. The question here is to decide whether accounting students in an accounting course can be trained to write the actual machine instructions in a machine language and/or a high-level language. In general, the trend is to present a conceptual view of coding and leave the actual skill training to other courses. A good foundation for future learning can be established, however, by distinguishing between a machine language and a high-level language such as FORTRAN, COBOL, or BASIC. Present short examples to show how the codes differ between a machine language and a non-machine language. In addition, illustrate a coding sheet to show the students what a programmer actually does to carry out this important activity.

The next activity, compiling the program, can be kept quite basic by explaining that each line of the coded program must be recorded on some input medium, such as punched cards, punched tape, or magnetic tape. In the presentation of this activity, care must be taken to distinguish the source program, the compiler program, and the object program. Some teachers prepare actual illustrations to show the difference among the three.

Testing the program offers little difficulty for student learning. Students react quickly to the term *debugging* when it is related to the process of locating and correcting errors in a program. Of course, the *why* of this activity must be emphasized; otherwise, students usually fail to recall this important procedure.

The final activity, documenting the program, is best understood when students learn why all the documents used to prepare the program must be filed in a manual for future reference. Emphasize that copies of the operating instructions and the object program are also filed so that they can be used again in the future.

DESCRIBE ACCOUNTING APPLICATIONS OF ELECTRONIC DATA PROCESSING. In order to illustrate how accounting data can be processed in a computer system, describe at least one accounting application. Some teachers, in presenting a spiral development of data processing methods, will describe the same accounting application to offer a comparison between the computer and the other methods. For example, an accounts receivable application can be used to show that the computer will not only update accounts receivable more efficiently, but also do more than the other methods. One teacher offers this comparison. Under the manual pegboard method the processing of the sales journal, the customer's account, and the customer's statement is possible. On the other hand, under stored programs, the computer can produce the customer's bill of sale (or customer's statement), update the accounts receivable file, produce a sales register (journal), update the inventory file, and produce the costing entry for the cost of the goods sold. Other accounting applications could also be offered to prove that computer data processing is a superior method of processing accounting information.

A Final Consideration

In presenting an integration of accounting with data processing, some teachers have unfortunately organized their instruction so that a greater amount of time is taken up with the hardware and software aspects of computers than with a well-balanced program of instruction in accounting. What these teachers have failed to understand is simply the fact that the most rapid area of change today is in the hardware and software fields of electronic data processing. This is not to suggest that the accounting teacher eliminate the teaching of some integration of accounting with computer data processing. In fact, the accounting teacher must be aware of changes not only in data processing methods, but in accounting practice as well. Today, accounting theorists are offering the practitioner the opportunity to introduce methods of presenting inflation accounting models and current-value accounting models to join the traditional method of reporting accounting data on a historical cost basis. It is the responsibility of accounting teachers, therefore, to introduce concepts related to these new accounting models just as soon as they are supported by the accounting profession, governments, and business.

Problems, Questions, and Projects

1. An experienced teacher introduces the application of the data processing cycle first through a simple problem. Consider this example: the report card of Jill Mann shows a first semester grade of 90 and a second semester grade of 80. The problem is to find the student's final grade based on the average of the two semester grades.

Show the flowchart of the data processing cycle; then, immediately below each symbol, show a translation of each step to solve the problem.

2. Assume that you were going to teach the steps of the accounting cycle in relation to the four steps of the data processing cycle. Prepare a transparency master showing this relationship.

3. On separate sheets of paper, prepare transparency masters to present the data processing cycle for the following accounting applications:

   a. accounts receivable
   b. accounts payable
   c. the general ledger

4. Would you introduce the concept of the accounting application before, during, or after the formal study of data processing methods? Give reasons for your answer.

5. Assume that you are planning a course of study integrating data processing with accounting applications. What data processing method or methods would you teach in this course? Give reasons for your answer.

6. Suppose that you had the use of only six pegboards for an accounting class of thirty-six students. Explain how you would make effective use of these pegboards to teach your students the manual processing of accounting applications.

7. The unit-record principle is an important component of a punched-card data processing system. How would you explain this principle to beginning students? Use an example in your explanation.

8. Do you believe that accounting teachers should teach their students to write computer programs in FORTRAN or COBOL as part of a first or second course in accounting? Give reasons for your answer.

9. Prepare a transparency master of the flowchart of a computer system similar to the one illustrated in Figure 17.6 of this chapter. You may wish to prepare additional masters that can be used as overlays to show separately the flow of data and the flow of instructions.

10. Distinguish between the hardware and software aspects of a computer system.

11. Even if equipment is available, teachers have found that it is difficult to illustrate the movement of data through a computer. Through an appropriate computer problem, however, and by demonstrating work similar to the work performed by a programmer, the teacher can resolve this difficulty. Present a simple problem and illustrate how this problem is solved through the activities of a programmer.

12. Give an example to explain the difference between a machine language and a programming (mnemonic) language.

13. In some computer systems, an input device may also be used as an output device. Give two examples to explain this statement.

14. Prepare performance goals for the four main data processing methods presented in this chapter. Assume that you are preparing these objectives for use in an accounting course in which students have had no previous data processing exposure.

Case Problems

1. Joan Hill, an experienced accounting teacher of ten years, has just successfully completed a high-level programming course in FORTRAN. With her experience and newly acquired skill in computing, Mrs. Hill is anxious to experiment with a totally integrated approach to the study of computing and accounting. Her school board has supported her request to experiment by offering her use of the board's IBM 1130 Computing System to process student programs. She summarizes her approach to the course of instruction as follows:

    a. For the first half of the course, students will be introduced to computer concepts and FORTRAN programming.

    b. During the computer concepts portion of the course, students will write programs using a machine language called HYPO (hypothetic machine language). No accounting problems will be used; only very elementary math problems such as subtracting one number from another, multiplying two factors, and dividing one number by another will be solved. Since no card punches are available, Mrs.

Hill plans to have the students code their programs on specially designed 80-column mark-sensed cards.

c. For student reinforcement of FORTRAN, again, no accounting problems will be used since students would have no prior exposure to accounting. To overcome the lack of card punch machines, Mrs. Hill plans to use a specially designed mark-sensed 80-column card. These cards would be processed at the board of education on the IBM 1130 system.

d. At the end of the first semester, students will complete an examination based on topics covered in the first half of the course.

e. For the second half of the course, students would be introduced to these accounting applications in this order: payroll; accounts receivable; accounts payable; and the general ledger. Mrs. Hill will present accounting concepts for the application, and then provide reinforcement of the accounting application by requiring the students to solve problems in FORTRAN.

f. At the end of the second semester, students will complete an examination on writing a computer program in FORTRAN to process one of the accounting applications studied in the course.

Mrs. Hill asks you to express your opinions on her proposed approach. Discuss what you like about her experiment. Do you think that the experiment will be successful? Explain.

2. An experienced teacher requests permission of the department chairman to offer a one-semester course called *Applied Accounting.* In presenting the request, the teacher offers the following information:

a. The proposed course would be offered for one semester and would require a prerequisite of two semesters of introductory accounting (one complete course in accounting).

b. Four accounting applications would be treated in this order: accounts receivable, accounts payable; payroll; and the general ledger.

c. Each application will contain essentially the same format. For example, the accounts receivable application will include first, an overview of the sales system; second, a review, or the formal study as the case may be, of different methods of processing sales and accounts receivable. Here, the teacher proposes to cover manual methods (to include the traditional journal/ledger system, the journalless system, the ledgerless/journalless system, and the one-write system), mechanical methods (the posting machine only); and the electronic data processing method (including both large and mini-computer systems). The teacher believes that the punched card accounting method is very much obsolete and, therefore, it would be excluded. And, finally, the actual accounts receivable application problem would be related to a specific firm such as a furniture and appliance store. This application would include a set of sales and related transactions for a one-month period. Source documents would be essential in the application, which would take the students to the end of the trial balance stage, that is, to the stage of reconciling the accounts receivable ledger with the control account of the general ledger.

d. A similar format would be used for presenting accounts payable except for one addition: the need to present the use of a vouchers payable system to control accounts payable would be emphasized.

e. For the payroll application, essentially the same format would be used except that both an hourly-rated payroll register and a salaries payroll register would be used.

f. For the general ledger application, students would first review the general ledger system; then study the three data processing methods of updating the general ledger and preparing a monthly set of financial statements; and, finally, solve a general ledger application problem that is related to the other three accounting applications.

g. Since only twelve pegboards and three accounting machines would be available, the teacher states that students would process all accounting applications by manual and mechanical methods only. However, all students would be required to present a written report explaining the details of processing each application through a computer system.

h. Each application would lend itself to a division of responsibility so that the work of one student could be checked against the work of another. For example, four groups of students could be working simultaneously: one group on each of the four applications. At the end of one month's transactions, the general accounting clerk would check the balance of Accounts Receivable Control with the total of Accounts Receivable supplied by a different person, the Accounts Receivable clerk. To give another example, under the mechanical method of data processing, one clerk in accounts receivable can batch the daily invoices, run off a prelist of the batch on an adding machine tape, and then supply the batch for posting to the accounting machine operator, a different clerk. At the end of the daily posting run, the total of the posting proof sheet would be checked with the total of the prelist for an agreement. The teacher states that there are numerous other possibilities to accomplish the objective of introducing the principle of internal control within each accounting application.

i. At different intervals, students would be rotated to allow everyone to experience all facets of each application.

What is your evaluation of this teacher's proposal?

Index